VIRTUAL REALITY
S Y S T E M S

ACM SIGGRAPH Books Series

This book is published as part of the SIGGRAPH Books Series with ACM Press Books, a collaborative effort among ACM SIGGRAPH, ACM Press, and Addison-Wesley Publishing Company. The SIGGRAPH Books Series publishes books on theory, practice, applications, and imaging in computer graphics and interactive techniques, some developed from courses, papers, or panels presented at the annual ACM SIGGRAPH conference.

Editor

Steve Cunningham, California State University, Stanislaus

Editorial Board

Mike Bailey, San Diego Supercomputer Center

Judith R. Brown, The University of Iowa

Wayne Carlson, ACCAD, The Ohio State University

George S. Carson, GSC Associates

Ed Catmull, Pixar

Tom DeFanti, University of Illinois, Chicago

Richard L. Phillips, Los Alamos National Laboratory

Andries van Dam, Brown University

ACM Membership Information

Founded in 1947, ACM is the oldest and largest educational scientific society in the information technology field. Through its high-quality publications and services, ACM is a major force in advancing the skills and knowledge of IT professionals throughout the world. From a dedicated group of 78, ACM is now 85,000 strong, with 34 special interest groups, including SIGGRAPH, and more than 60 chapters and student chapters.

For more than 25 years, SIGGRAPH and its conferences have provided the world's forum for the interchange of information on computer graphics and interactive techniques. SIGGRAPH members come from many disciplines and include researchers, hardware and software systems designers, algorithm and applications developers, visualization scientists, educators, technology developers for interactive visual communications, animators and special-effects artists, graphic designers, and fine artists.

For further information about ACM and ACM SIGGRAPH, contact:

ACM Member Services
1515 Broadway, 17th floor
New York, NY 10036–5701
Phone: 1–212–626–0500
Fax: 1–212–944–1318
E-mail: ACMHELP@ACM.org

ACM European Service Center
Avenue Marcel Thiry 204
1200 Brussels, Belgium
Phone: 32–2–774–9602
Fax: 32–2–774–9690
E-mail: ACM_Europe@ACM.org

VIRTUAL REALITY
SYSTEMS

JOHN VINCE

Bournemouth University

ACM Press Books

SIGGRAPH Series

ADDISON-WESLEY

HARLOW, ENGLAND • READING, MASSACHUSETTS • MENLO PARK, CALIFORNIA • NEW YORK
DON MILLS, ONTARIO • AMSTERDAM • BONN • SYDNEY • SINGAPORE
TOKYO • MADRID • SAN JUAN • MEXICO CITY • SEOUL • TAIPEI

Pearson Education Limited
Edinburgh Gate
Harlow
Essex CM20 2JE
England

and Associated Companies throughout the world

Visit us on the World Wide Web at:
http://www.pearsoneduc.com

Cover designed by Designers & Partners of Oxford incorporating
images created by Evangelina M. S. Sousa
Typeset by Colset Private Limited, Singapore.

Printed in Singapore (KKP)

First printed 1995

ISBN 0-201-87687-6

10 9 8 7 6 5 4 3
04 03 02 01 00

British Library Cataloguing in Publication Data
A catalogue record for this book is available from the British Library.

Library of Congress Cataloging in Publication Data
Vince, John (John A.)

    Virtual reality systems / John Vince.
      p. cm.
    Includes index
    ISBN 0-201-87687-6
    1. Human-computer interaction.   2. Virtual reality. I. Title.
QA76.9.H85V53 1995
006–DC20   95-2741
                                  CIP

This book is affectionately dedicated to Annie, Samantha, Anthony, and my dog Ben. I virtually disappeared from their lives for over a year, but now VR together again!

Foreword

Although much has been claimed of virtual reality, it is often difficult to differentiate fact from fiction. This book successfully outlines the core technolgies which underline the principle of virtual reality and the way it is being applied today, as well as the promise that it holds for the future.

There has been a wealth of media coverage which both leads us and can mislead us into imagining that virtual reality is the answer to every problem. However, virtual reality is really just a new way of interfacing to computers. Virtual reality provides a true three dimensional interface to a range of computer applications.

The underlying technologies and principles have evolved over the last 25 years. Ivan Sutherland first wrote about a computer generated illusion: 'The screen is a window through which one sees a virtual world. The challenge is to make that world look real, act real, sound real, feel real.' It has taken over 20 years for computer graphics and display technologies to become a cost-effective means of creating virtual realities, and there is still a long way to go before virtual reality becomes cost effective for all computer users.

The essence of a virtual reality is immersion. This is the ability to *immerse* the computer user in a computer generated experience, as an active participant, as opposed to a passive viewer. This book provides the basic taxonomy which helps us define the elements of a virtual reality, and it explains the basic technologies used to create this *immersive* and *interactive* experience. It explains the human physiology, and psychology so vital in achieving this experience. It brings the reader quickly up to date on the state of the art in hardware and software technologies now applied in creating virtual reality.

All new developments in the human computer interface have had a significant gestation period, during which the various ways that the new interface can be applied are investigated and validated. This process of validation is common for all high technology products, and follows fairly classical market development trends. What is interesting about virtual reality is that, as a fundamentally new way of working with computers, its impact will be very widespread. But in order to assimilate this technology into the wide range of potential application areas, a great deal of work remains to be done. Within each potential application area, software developers, hardware developers, and end users have to spend considerable resources, building prototype systems, and validating and refining these systems before virtual reality will see widespread use. It is the extent of this investment which will result in the rapid evolution of the market.

The first generation of truly immersive virtual reality applications is appearing in high unit-cost industries such as aerospace, automotive, and construction, where the high cost of the virtual reality system and the software development can be easily justified in terms of design, maintenance, or operational savings. But as the cost of the underlying technology falls, even widespread consumer applications will become practical. The availability of home virtual reality consoles, which will provide virtual shopping, adventure games, competitive sports, education and so on, is now only a few years away.

What enthuses me about virtual reality is that the experience remains as compelling today as it was several years ago when I first became involved in this technology. There is something magical about putting on a head mounted display, and suddenly being transported from the real world with all its every-day problems, into this virtual world, with its own quite different problems. Whatever the task, it is that sense that you are there, but not actually there, which never fails to captivate.

This book provides an excellent introduction to the current state of the art in virtual reality and helps to set the foundations for a common taxonomy of virtual reality technologies and applications. The text will be an excellent reference for students and experts alike.

Charles Grimsdale
Managing Director, Division Ltd
April 1995

Preface

This book has presented some interesting challenges. The first was to complete it by the agreed contract date; the second was to get it printed before the contents became out of date, and the third was to write it without the aid of a VR system! Towards the end, there was a strong temptation to include just one more case study, include another write-up on a new light-weight HMD – but time was running out, and I decided to call a halt.

I wrote the book for a number of reasons. The main one was to extend my own understanding of the subject. For even though I have been associated with computer graphics and flight simulation for more years than I care to remember, virtual reality was another new exciting domain to discover. I was eager to learn the tricks that were used for collision detection, object picking, head tracking, teleporting and tactile feedback. To discover this information involved considerable reading, program writing, evaluating hundreds of equations, attending VR conferences, talking to experts, trying immersive demonstrations and some simple hard thinking.

I know that I have been unable to address every aspect of VR, and I am convinced that this is impossible. Things are moving so fast with VR systems and their applications, a live running commentary is the only way to report on the subject's development. Nevertheless, hopefully, I have managed to distil the data I have gathered into a form that will be useful to the inquisitive reader.

Chapter 1 provides an introduction to VR and virtual environments, and explains the nature of VR technology, how it functions, and its application.

Chapter 2 retraces relevant technological developments over the past 200 years, and attempts to illustrate the connectivity between one idea and another. VR has not suddenly appeared – it is just another piece of a jigsaw puzzle we call 'progress'.

As I thought that some readers would be coming to VR without any formal knowledge of computer graphics, I used Chapter 3 to provide an overview of the subject. It covers everything from Cartesian coordinates to shading algorithms, and should provide a sufficient foundation for the topics discussed in later chapters.

Virtual environments are central to VR, and Chapter 4 introduces readers to modelling elements such as space curves, polygons, surface patches and CSG. It only provides a cursory description to these structures, as there are many excellent texts that cover this subject area in greater depth.

Chapter 5 describes the role of geometric transformations in positioning objects within a VE. Particular emphasis has been given to transformation notation, and how concatenated transforms are developed for object picking, flying and scaling VEs. The chapter ends with a mathematical analysis of collision detection.

Chapter 6 provides an outline of a generic VR system in terms of the individual system elements and how they interact with one another. It also investigates the various system configurations and how they work in practice.

Chapter 7 explores some of the mathematical techniques used for animating features of a VE. A number of worked examples should help the reader appreciate the advantages of parametric techniques, especially when applied to translations, rotations, inbetweening and object deformation.

Hopefully, readers will find Chapter 8 useful, as it examines the problems of simulating dynamic physical systems such as falling objects, rotating wheels, elastic collisions, projectiles, pendulums, springs and flight dynamics.

Although I make no claim to being an expert on human factors, I thought that I should include a brief chapter on the subject. Consequently, Chapter 9 reviews the mechanisms of sight, sound, touch and equilibrium, which should help readers understand the technological problems of interfacing humans to virtual worlds.

Because VR hardware is evolving so rapidly, I was very conscious of the dangers of including too many references to specific products. Many of them will only have a short commercial life; nevertheless, it was essential to include a cross-section of systems and peripherals currently available. Hopefully, the systems described in Chapter 10 will provide a snapshot of what is currently available, and future trends.

To describe the role of VR software, I thought that I should take a close look at a real system. It was difficult to decide which one to select, and in the end, I decided to investigate three popular software products from Sense8, Superscape and Division. No doubt their technical specifications will change with time, but the overviews I have given in Chapter 11 will still serve a useful purpose.

Chapter 12 reviews current and potential applications for virtual reality. In particular, it looks at a range of applications in engineering, entertainment, science and training.

Finally, Chapter 13 concludes the book with a look towards the future.

I do hope that the following thirteen chapters will provide you with a better understanding of the nature of virtual reality systems. You will find none of the 'hype' that is still perpetuated by some authors, but I hope that you will detect a sense of enthusiasm behind my words, as I believe that virtual environments will play a significant role in all aspects of future human endeavour.

Acknowledgements

Acknowledging people's help in preparing a book is always dangerous, as it is so easy to forget someone who made a valuable contribution. Hopefully, I will not forget anyone – if I do, I apologise now!

To begin with I would like to thank Charles Grimsdale for the advice he gave in preparing the book's outline, and for reading and commenting upon most of the chapters. Charles' experience in the world of VR was invaluable, and I am so pleased that he managed to find the time to write the Foreword, especially while looking after the day-to-day management of Division Ltd.

Ian Andrew, at Superscape Ltd, gave me some excellent demonstrations of his VR system that clarified many of the features associated with modelling virtual worlds. Ian also found the time to comment upon an early version of the manuscript, for which I am grateful.

I would like to acknowledge the help I received from Stephen Ghee at Division who always answered the phone when I tackled him about some software problem. A big thank you to Pierre duPont, who supplied valuable technical case-study information and illustrations for the book.

Bob Stone has been fantastic with his enthusiastic support with technical material, demonstrations and background data. Not far from Bob, at the University of Hull, Rob Macredie, Nick Avis and Derek Wills read some early chapters and helped clarify some fuzzy writing.

David Burder, a world authority on 3D, lent me his ear many times on the phone to discuss points on stereoscopic matters. Thank you David for your help.

I openly acknowledge the technical support I had from VR research papers from around the world. Without this basic research, nothing would ever happen. In particular, I am grateful to have come across the paper on transformations by Warren Robinett and Richard Holloway – without it, Chapter 5 would have been difficult! Similarly, Chapter 8 would be missing a valuable section without Mark Brown's help on aircraft dynamics.

I even imposed upon my neighbour, Ron Woodham, to read several draft chapters. His critical eye was most useful.

It is impossible to write any book without cases of manuals, technical brochures and transparencies. Therefore I gratefully acknowledge the assistance of: Adaptive Optics Associates, Ascension Technology, ATMA Rendering Systems, BioControl Systems, Colt VR, Crystal River Engineering, Division, EXOS, Fakespace, General Reality, GMS, IBM, INA, Info Disp, InSys, Liquid Image, Logitech, n-Vision, Polhemus, Reflection Technology, Sense8, Shooting Star Technology, Silicon Graphics, Spaceball Technologies, StrayLight, Superscape, Thomson Training & Simulation, Virtuality Group and Virtual Research. I also thank the assistance of Chris Longhurst, Ian Whyte, Mel Slater, Paul Rea, Rae Earnshaw and Steve Webb. I must thank my copy-editor, Lynne Balfe, for transforming my manuscript into a readable document.

In spite of the help of all these people, especially the professional assistance of Simon Plumtree, Nicky Jaeger, Lesley Raper, Sheila Chatten and Stephen Bishop at Addison-Wesley, if there are any mistakes, the blame rests with me!

John Vince
April 1995

Contents

Trademark notice

3D Studio™, and CDK™ and AutoCAD™ are trademarks of Autodesk, Inc.

Acoustetron™, Alphatron™, Beachtron™ and Convolvotron™ are trademarks of Crystal River Engineering, Inc.

ADL-1™ is a trademark of Shooting Star Technology.

Advanced MouseStick™ is a trademark of Gravis, Inc.

Alias™ is a trademark of Alias, Inc.

BioMuse™ is a trademark of BioControl Systems, Inc.

Bonk™, Cozmik-Debris™, CyberTron™, StrayLight™ and Wing-Nuts™ are trademarks of StrayLight Corporation.

BOOM™, BOOM2C™ and BOOM3C™ are trademarks of Fakespace, Inc.

Computervision™ is a trademark of Computervision, Inc.

CyberEye™ is a trademark of General Reality Company.

CrystalEyes™ is a trademark of StereoGraphics Corporation.

CyberGlove™ is a trademark of Virtual Technologies.

DataGlove™ is a trademark of VPL Research, Inc.

Datavisor™ is a trademark of n-Vision, Inc.

DEC™ is a trademark of Digital Equipment Corporation.

Denali™ is a trademark of Kubota Pacific Computer, Inc.

Dextrous HandMaster™, Force ArmMaster™, Force Feedback Master™, PowerStick™, SAFiRE™ and TouchMaster™ are trademarks of EXOS, Inc.

dVISE™, dVS™, ProVision 100™ and VCToolkit™ are trademarks of Division, Ltd.

FaceTrax™ and Multi-Trax™ are trademarks of Adaptive Optics Associates.

Fastrak™ and Isotrak™ are trademarks of Polhemus, Inc.

The Bird™ and Flock of Birds™ are trademarks of Ascension Technology Corporation.

Geometry Ball Jr.™ is a trademark of CIS Graphics, Inc.

GL™, IRIS™, IRIX™, Onyx™, RealityEngine™, SGI™ and Silicon Graphics™ are trademarks of Silicon Graphics, Inc.

Gold 1000™ is a trademark of Ad Lib, Inc.

IBM™, RISC System™ and IBM PC™ are trademarks of International Business Machines Corporation.

InSys™ is a trademark of Intelligent Systems Solutions, Ltd.

Jack™ is a trademark of University of Pennsylvania.

Logitech™, Ligitech 3D Mouse™ and Logitech Head Tracker™ are trademarks of Logitech, Inc.

Microsoft™, MS-DOS™, Windows™ and Windows NT™ are trademarks of Microsoft Corporation.

MRG2™ is a trademark of Liquid Image, Inc.

Multigen™ is a trademark of Multigen, Inc.

Music Quest MIDI™ is a trademark of Music Quest, Inc.

Pancake Window™, Wide-Eye™, Agile-Eye™, Strike-Eye™, Sim-Eye™ and VIM™ are trademarks of Kaiser Electro-Optics, Inc.

Pentium™ and Touchstone Delta™ are trademarks of Intel Corporation.

Private Eye™ is a trademark of Reflection Technology, Inc.

Pro/Engineer™ is a trademark of Parametric Technology.

Quantel™, Harry™ and Paintbox™ are trademarks of Quantel, Ltd.

Real Light™ is a trademark of ATMA Rendering Systems.

SCL™, Superscape™, Virtual Reality Toolkit™ and VRT™ are trademarks of Superscape, Ltd.

Sense8™ and WorldToolKit™ are trademarks of Sense8 Corporation.

Sound Blaster™ is a trademark of Creative Labs, Inc.

SPACE™ is a trademark of Thomson Training and Simulation, Ltd.

Spaceball 2003™ is a trademark of Spaceball Technologies, Inc.

Space Mouse™ is a trademark of Gesellschaft für 3-D Systeme mbH.

Sun™, SPARC™, SPARC2™, SPARC10™ and SPARC20 are trademarks of Sun Microsystems, Inc.

UNIX™ is a trademark of AT&T Bell Laboratories.

VActor Experession™ is a trademark of SimGraphics, Inc.

VEGAS™ is a trademark of Colt VR, Ltd.

Virtual Boxing™, Virtuality™, Visette 2™, Vocalizer™, V-PC™, X-treme Strike™ and Zone Hunter™ are trademarks of Virtuality Group plc.

VR4™ is a trademark of Virtual Research.

Wavefront™ is a trademark of Wavefront Technologies, Inc.

1

Virtual Reality and Virtual Environments

1.0 Introduction

Although computers have been in existence in one form or another for over 50 years, it is only during the last decade that the general public could consider them as another household gadget. Personal computers are now used at home for organizing accounts, desktop publishing, letter writing, student homework and games. For many, this has been a major revolution, but whether we know it or not, we are in the midst of another revolution – one that is destined to transform the way we work and the way we communicate with other human beings.

Science fiction writers have already been exploring the role of computers in a future world, and have described a synthetic 3D universe that is as believable as the real physical universe. Such 'Virtual Reality' (VR) systems create a 'cyberspace' where it is possible to interact with anything and anyone on a virtual level. In these bizarre worlds, conventional laws of space and time need not hold – anything can be simulated, so long as it can be programmed.

The key technologies behind such imaginative writing are real-time computer graphics, colour displays and simulation software. Computer graphics provides the basis for creating the synthetic images, while a Head-Mounted Display (HMD) supplies the user's eyes with a stereoscopic view of a computer-generated world. Complex software creates the Virtual Environment (VE), which could be anything from 3D objects to abstract databases. As well as providing visual images of the virtual world, such systems can also create acoustic images that accurately simulate the sounds within a virtual environment. One could imagine other devices that provide tactile (touch) and haptic (force) images to complete the sense of illusion. Add a touch of creative writing, and exciting scenarios unfold with convincing credibility.

In the late 1980s, embryonic VR systems became commercially available, and on a wave of media hype one was led to believe that the future had already arrived. However, this was not the case. The worldwide publicity VR systems attracted caught everyone's attention and imagination, and almost overnight the word 'virtual' found its way into everyday parlance.

In the past few years, VR has matured considerably. New hardware platforms and software environments have appeared, supported by a young, dynamic, professional workforce. The industry is now well established and is leading us towards a truly exciting future.

Now that the potential of VR systems has been appreciated, research organizations around the world have embarked upon projects to perfect the primary technologies and to investigate the complex issues of human factors, the human–computer interface and real-time hardware. Simultaneous with these developments, the term 'virtual reality' has been quietly ignored by some, in preference for the term 'Virtual Environment (VE) systems'. The latter avoids any possible implication that there is any ambition to remodel the universe! No doubt, some applications will revolve around constructing very lifelike scenes, but the substitution of the word 'environment' for 'reality' provides the scope to encompass application areas where realism is not paramount. However, in the entertainment industry the term 'virtual reality' is well established, and it would be foolish to substitute another name – especially now that almost every child knows what VR means!

Irrespective of whether we refer to such systems as virtual reality or virtual environment systems, let us continue to explore them from the standpoint of their key technologies. For the sake of simplicity, both terms will be used throughout this book.

1.1 Computer graphics

During the digital computer's relatively short existence it has been successfully applied to problem areas such as invoicing, stock control, weather forecasting, payroll, desktop publishing, banking and insurance – which all impact upon our daily lives in one way or another. These are natural applications for a machine that was developed to process raw numeric data. But apart from these mundane, yet essential, uses for computers, their most exciting applications have been in the areas of design and graphics. Nowadays, architects, artists, interior designers, engineers, product designers, graphic designers and animators are all major users of computers.

The domain of computer graphics is now well established and developed to such a sophistication that the majority of text and imagery we come across in books, newspapers, television, films and magazines has been processed by a computer at some stage. Computer graphics techniques can be used to store

3D objects as geometric descriptions, which can then be converted into an image by specifying information such as the object's colour, position and orientation in space, and from what location it is to be viewed. A practical example is found in architectural design where detailed geometric descriptions are input to a CAD system, which can then render perspective views of the scene. The benefits of such techniques are manifold, which is why CAD is so vital to automotive design, civil engineering, 3D animation and molecular modelling.

The success of CAD has been greatly influenced by low-cost graphic workstations that can support the real-time interactive manipulation of large graphic databases. It has also depended upon the evolution of effective software tools for preparing this data, together with graphics hardware such as digitizers, scanners, plotters and display screens. Developments in multi-processor architectures and networked systems have also dramatically reduced the time needed to execute programs, often making it possible to solve problems in minutes, where previously it had taken hours.

1.2 Real-time computer graphics

Computer graphics has a history extending back to the 1960s, and has evolved through various types of technology such as graph plotters (which are still in use), vector display systems, storage tube displays and raster-based screens, which still remain the most popular method for displaying images. Raster technology has been central to the development of television, and the wealth of knowledge associated with this subject is so extensive that it has had a profound influence upon the graphical application of computers. And whether this application is in the processing of images, or in the generation of synthetic images from 3D databases, speed is of the essence.

Early users of computer graphics systems had to tolerate delays of minutes or hours to render a single image, but with the advent of faster processors, multiprocessor systems, pipeline architectures, maths co-processors and ASIC technology, complex images can now be created in tens of milliseconds.

Although 'bottlenecks' still remain in computer graphics systems, particularly in the rendering of very large databases, there are workstations capable of displaying detailed, high-resolution, coloured images with update rates of 20 Hz or more, which has opened up new and exciting modes of interacting with computers. Indeed, even personal and micro computers provide an adequate graphics performance to support real-time flight simulator programs.

Now that computer graphics systems are able to react within our own time frame, new human–computer interfaces become possible, which is the whole rationale for VR. VR systems encompass computer graphics applications where users are able to interact with computers in totally new ways. But before examining these modes, it will be useful to explore the role of VEs in the world of flight simulation.

1.3   Flight simulation

A flight simulator is a training system where pilots can acquire flying skills without involving a real aeroplane or airports. Simulators are used by professional pilots to practise flying strategies under emergency or hazardous conditions, or to train on new aircraft types. Plate 1 shows a modern full-flight simulator.

Simulating the complex behaviour of an aircraft requires accurate modelling and the integration of several real-time systems that include instrumentation, flight dynamics, navigation, weather, hydraulics, engines and graphics. These systems involve a mixture of real and simulated features. For example, the simulator cockpit is a lightweight replica of that in a specific craft such as a Boeing 767-400 or an Airbus 340. Each instrument is electrically driven by real-time computers that generate output signals based upon a software model describing its behaviour. Hydraulic rams are used to subject the entire simulator to g-forces based upon the linear and rotational acceleration parameters computed by the flight dynamics model, and real-time Image Generators (IGs) simulate the images seen from a real cockpit.

Real-time IGs have been used in flight simulators since the 1980s. Prior to this, rigid scale models were constructed depicting an airport and its immediate surrounding environment. With the aid of a small video camera, views of this model were displayed upon monitors fixed to the windows of the simulator cockpit. When the pilot manoeuvred the simulator into a take-off mode, the equations describing the plane's dynamics were evaluated to determine its new position in space. This data was then used to move the video camera to a new position, and by repeating this process at a rate of approximately 30 Hz, the pilot experienced the visual sensation of flying.

There were many disadvantages associated with scale models: to begin with, they were large (50 m²) and required substantial levels of illumination; their size and manufacturing cost made it impractical to have a separate model for every international airport in the world – therefore, a single generic model was a practical solution. But apart from these restrictions, it was impossible to simulate different weather conditions such as rain, snow and fog, which have a major influence on the safety conditions during landing and taking-off. However, with computer graphics techniques it was possible to replace the physical scale model with a geometric description, which, although it resolved many of the above restrictions, introduced a new set of problems.

Moving the 3D model from the physical domain into the virtual domain immediately resolved the problems of storage and illumination. However, these virtual models still required building, and even with today's efficient modelling tools and powerful workstations, several hundred hours are needed to model a large international airport.

When this geometric database is loaded into an IG, it is possible to view the virtual model from any position in space, but when the IG is interfaced to the real-time computer system simulating the plane's flight dynamics, the simulator's position and heading parameters can be used to control the perceived flight path within the VE.

Perhaps one of the greatest benefits of this virtual approach to model building is the control one has over the rendered synthetic image. For instance, by modifying a software parameter, a 3D model can be rendered with an illumination level simulating any time of the day. Furthermore, other computer graphics techniques can be used to simulate different degrees of haze, fog, cloud cover, rain, snow and lightning strikes. The technique of texture mapping enables photographs of real-world scenes to be integrated with the real-time images. Aerial and satellite photographs can also be used to provide extremely high levels of realism that convince pilots that they are flying over this terrain when, in reality, they are only three or four metres above the ground in the safety of a simulator.

1.4   Virtual environments

In the following chapters we will discover that VE systems have many potential areas of application. For the moment though, it will be useful to continue with the flight simulator example where a computer is used to create a perspective view of a 3D virtual world, and the view of this world is determined by the orientation of the simulated aircraft. VE systems extend this methodology in two important areas: the first concerns user immersion, and the second relates to the degree of interaction the user has with the virtual environment.

1.4.1   Visual feedback and immersion

The sensation of being immersed within a VE is greatly influenced by the user's integration with the synthetic images. In the case of a flight simulator, the pilot and co-pilot sit inside a replica cockpit and gaze through the windows into a 200° panoramic mirror reflecting the computer-generated graphics. This creates a realistic sensation of being in a real plane flying over some 3D landscape; however, the crew are not allowed to leave the cockpit and explore this virtual world.

Some VR systems, on the other hand, provide each user with a personal view of the virtual environment using an HMD which visually isolates them from the real world. The user can acquire a positive sense of being immersed in the VE, which is further enhanced when touch and sound are introduced. Figure 1.1 shows a typical VR HMD. What is important in both approaches is that the user experiences a 'first-person' view of the VE, which opens up totally new interaction modalities.

Although a flight simulator's panoramic display system does not contain

Figure 1.1   Captivated by an immersive VR system. (Courtesy Liquid Image Corporation)

stereoscopic information, the fact that the image is collimated, and one's peripheral vision is stimulated, creates a very strong sense of being immersed in a 3D world. An HMD, on the other hand, can provide the left and right eyes with two separate images that include parallax differences, which, given the right conditions, produce a realistic stereoscopic sensation.

Immersion is further enhanced by allowing the user's head movements to control the gaze direction of the synthetic images; this provides the brain with motion parallax information to complement other visual cues. Naturally, this requires tracking the user's head in real time, and if the user's head movements are not synchronized with the images, the result can be disturbing.

Therefore, any display system that provides the user with a realistic, 'first-person' view of the virtual world, and is directly controlled by the user, is critical in creating the sensation of immersion or presence.

1.4.2 Interaction

When visually immersed within a VE there is a natural inquisitive temptation to reach out and touch virtual objects. Obviously this is impossible, as there is nothing to touch. The user's sense of immersion can be greatly enhanced by including part of a 'virtual body', such as a hand, in the VE. This requires that the computer database describing the VE is extended to incorporate a simple 3D hand, normally consisting of a palm, thumb and four fingers. Each of these elements can move to mimic normal hand and finger movements. The user now sees in the HMD a 3D virtual hand as part of the stereoscopic scene. If the user also wears an interactive glove, or a similar device, any movements their own hand makes can be tracked and used to control the status of the virtual hand. The user has now been coupled to the VE in a way that allows some high-level interaction to occur.

Imagine the following scenario. You are equipped with an HMD to which an IG is sending real-time stereoscopic images. As you move your head the computer responds with appropriate new views of an imaginary room which contains a table and chair. Your hand is fitted with an interactive glove to monitor your finger movements and hand position in space, which in turn control the movement of the virtual hand. If you now stretch out your real hand towards the virtual chair you will see the virtual hand move in sympathy. While you are making these exploratory movements, the status between your virtual hand and the VE can be investigated. For example, the system could be monitoring whether the virtual hand is touching any of the objects in the environment. If a 'touch' condition arises, the system can be programmed to respond in a variety of ways. First, the chair could be moved as though it had been pushed, and further hand movements could move the chair in different directions. Second, the chair could become attached to the virtual hand as though it had been picked up, and however you moved your hand, the chair would move about with it. Third, the colour of the chair could alter in response to the touch condition. One could invent many other possible reactions to this situation. For the moment, though, the important thing to appreciate is the ability to interact with virtual objects.

Although HMDs and interactive gloves have become two important features of VR, it would be unrealistic to expect all future VR systems to follow this configuration. To begin with, some applications may not require the user to be visually isolated from the real world. An architect, for example, might not want to wear any form of headgear for long periods of time while exploring a virtual building. Perhaps a boom-mounted display system will be sufficient to provide the level of interaction needed for this mode of work. Desktop VR systems will also continue to provide an intermediate solution where virtual environments can be constructed and visualized without an immersive experience. On the other hand, users of VR game systems will enjoy the excitement of being immersed within imaginary interactive worlds, away from the distractions of the real world.

1.4.3 Tactile feedback

An obvious extension to the modes of interaction just mentioned would be to allow the user to touch and feel virtual objects – to a certain extent, this is already possible. However, providing the level of tactile feedback we experience in the real world is currently impossible, and may remain so, unless a technology evolves that provides direct communication with the brain. In the meantime, if we want to provide some simple form of touch stimulus, tactile gloves are available that activate small pads along the fingers to simulate a 'touching' sensation. Thus when a collision is detected between the user's virtual hand and a virtual object, the glove is activated to simulate the touch condition. The user, however, will not be suddenly aware of the object's mass, as there is no mechanism for engaging the user's arm muscles.

If it is necessary to transmit forces from the virtual domain, then we need to involve some hardware that the user can grasp, or can be fitted to the user, perhaps in the form of an external skeleton. For example, force feedback is used on the flight controls in a flight simulator so that the pilot experiences the real physical forces that are encountered in real planes. But if we wanted to simulate the physical mass of an object, then articulated manipulators could be used to create such forces. These systems do exist, and are being used to provide force feedback in molecular modelling systems.

It can be appreciated that for certain applications, tactile and force feedback will play a very important role in VE systems, and we will explore the technology further in Chapter 10.

1.4.4 Acoustic feedback

Most computer users are familiar with working on hardware that makes hardly any noise at all. Perhaps the only sound users are really conscious of is the action of the keyboard while typing. During recent years, however, acoustic prompts have become a useful feature in interactive systems. They remind us that we are attempting to perform something beyond the capabilities of the system, such as writing to an unformatted disc, or that a menu has been selected without acknowledging some request. The source of this sound is incidental – the fact that it is synchronized with some erroneous action is sufficient to warn us of our mistake.

In a VR system, sound becomes a natural feature to complement the interactive visual and tactile domains. For example, one could imagine the simulation of a wide range of sound effects such as collision noises, scraping noises, the sounds of natural phenomena such as thunder, waves breaking on a beach and water being poured. When immersed within a 3D virtual world it would seem only natural that when two virtual objects collided that the associated sound appeared to come from the same location. Current generation hardware is already capable of supplying binaural signals that model the attenuation of pressure waves entering the user's ear canals, and thus simulate the way our ears influence perceived sounds in the real world. These provide valuable audio cues for the brain to localize the source of sounds.

Binaural audio also opens up a wide range of new applications for VR systems in the acoustic and visual design of interiors, for it is already possible to simulate how multiple sound sources are influenced by reflective objects. Furthermore, technology is available to support stationary and moving sound sources, non-uniform emitters and Doppler effects, all of which can be experienced by a user independent of their head orientation.

1.5 Virtually here

Computer systems had to undergo considerable evolutionary changes before their current popularity could be enjoyed. No longer do they require special environmental conditions; most systems will function in normal offices, and are so user friendly that very little tuition is required.

Although VR systems are, by their very nature, exciting and futuristic, that is not a valid reason why they should be used by industry or commerce. They, like any other technological aid, must prove their worth. We must demonstrate that through their use, a task is easier, quicker or less tiring; or the end product is cheaper, more efficient, more reliable, and so on. It just so happens that we are already discovering that in some cases VR provides the only solution to a problem! Like computers, VR technology will undergo considerable development, which will give rise to a range of products and systems to meet the specific needs of different users.

1.6 What is required?

Basically, VR systems exploit a mode of interaction that becomes possible with immersive real-time computer graphics systems. Therefore, one of the primary requirements of any computer intended for a VR application is that it is able to update images at high speed. Ideally, this should be no slower than conventional video frame refresh rates which are 25 Hz for PAL and 30 Hz for NTSC. To achieve this image update rate calls for specialist IGs as used in flight simulators, which, currently, are relatively expensive and could not be realistically integrated into a general-purpose VR system. Other alternatives are found in graphics workstations and dedicated multiprocessor imaging systems. Their update rates vary from 10 to 60 Hz, and provide a cost-effective solution that is satisfactory for many applications. Personal computers also provide a cost-effective platform for desktop VR systems. A single Pentium processor, with 8 Mb RAM, is a typical configuration for software products such as Superscape's VRT, or Sense8's WorldToolKit.

1.6.1 Virtual databases

Before any image can be displayed, a 3D database is required describing the VE. If this consists of only a room containing a table and chair, their geometric description is a trivial exercise. However, no matter how small or large the VE is, software is needed for its preparation and someone has to build it to the required level of detail. In flight simulation, building a library of databases representing the major international airports is no trivial matter. Experienced modellers are required, capable of working with interactive workstations to develop accurate geometric descriptions of runways, control towers, terminal buildings, planes, motorways, hotels, houses, bridges, rivers, seascapes, mountains and clouds.

Other VE applications will involve totally different types of data: for example, an architect might be interested in interacting with a building's interior, perhaps with a view to exploring different lighting scenarios. On the other hand, an aerospace engineer might want to process a database describing a 3D gas turbine engine. Both of these applications raise a serious issue associated with display technology – complexity.

1.6.2 Real-time image generation

If an IG is updating an image at a rate of 50 Hz then less than 20 ms is available to compute each image. Naturally, the size of the 3D database will have a major influence on whether this update rate is possible or not. In reality, the controlling factor is how much of the database is in the field of view of the VR user. For instance, in an architectural application, if the user was so close to a wall that it was the only object in view, there would be no difficulty in updating the image in real time. But if the user's field of view incorporated a detailed atrium with spiral staircases, walkways, windows, offices, shadows and reflections, it might be difficult to render the scene in 20 s, let alone 20 ms!

The time taken to render an image has always been a major issue in the world of computer graphics, especially with animated sequences. Computer animators have become accustomed to waiting 5, 10 or 20 minutes to render a single frame of an animated sequence. Furthermore, when each second requires 25 frames, they may wait hours or days to generate an animated sequence that lasts for only a few seconds. There are two main reasons for such long rendering times: the first is due to the large databases they process – often measured in hundreds of thousands of surface elements; the second concerns the level of realism they want to introduce, such as photographic textures decorating the virtual objects, the incorporation of shadows, environmental reflections and anti-aliasing. The price paid for such attention to detail is the time needed to execute the display algorithms.

Fortunately, the processing performance of computers is advancing in leaps and bounds, which will address the problem of rendering scenes of large databases in real time. Such systems exist today, but they are so expensive that they find their way into only military or special research projects. Nevertheless, low-cost real-time IGs are appearing, and in time will be capable of satisfying the needs of cost-effective VR systems.

Although the image update rate is a vital parameter for any VR system, system latency cannot be ignored. Graphics engines are often based upon a pipeline architecture where image generation is divided into four sequential stages. The first stage is where the graphic database is transformed into the viewer's current frame of reference. Objects are clipped against the boundaries of the viewer's field of view, and back-facing polygons rejected. The second stage subjects the visible polygons to a perspective projection. The third stage produces the rendered image, and the fourth stage displays the image. If a fixed time slice is given to each stage, such as 20 ms, there will be a delay of at least 60 ms before the image associated with the current viewpoint is displayed. This pipeline latency can be reduced by increasing the update rate, but then there is less time for each stage of processing. No matter what happens in the future concerning hardware speed, latency will always exist. All that we need to ensure is that it remains at a tolerable level, and does not interfere with real-time activities.

1.6.3 Database interaction

Image generation is only one feature of a VR system. Interaction with the database also requires special attention. For example, detecting when the virtual hand interferes with features of the database can also place a heavy demand upon processing performance. This mode of collision detection requires that the volume taken up by the hand must be tested against equivalent volumes associated with the virtual objects. The time spent in testing for potential collisions reduces by organizing the database hierarchically, and whenever parts of the environment move, this hierarchy must be recomputed.

If the database is subject to a high level of interaction, then problems arise if the virtual objects must behave like their physical, real-world counterparts. For example, if a virtual chair is placed on a virtual table, it should not fall through the table's top. In the real world this occurs naturally because of the atomic forces that prevent one solid object penetrating another. However, in the virtual world of computer graphics, where objects are represented by collections of numbers, anything is possible if it can be programmed correctly. This, however, is easier said than done, and introduces the extremely complex world of physical simulation.

1.6.4 Physical simulation

Developing the issue of interaction further, consider what might happen if only two legs of the chair are touching the table top. In real life, the chair would pivot about the two legs in contact with the table, and fall under the influence of gravity towards the floor. During the accelerated fall, the chair may even have collisions with the table. Eventually, part of the chair will strike

Figure 1.2   A workstation-based VR system. (Courtesy Superscape, Ltd.)

the floor, and after a sequence of complex bounces it will arrive at some stable position. Although this level of realism is attractive, it requires significant levels of computing power to simulate the dynamics.

Another situation where collision detection and the simulation of dynamic behaviour could be important is in the application of VR in space simulation exercises. Here, a gravity-free or low-gravity environment must be created where an astronaut can rehearse scenarios such as undertaking external mechanical repairs to a spacecraft, or performing docking manoeuvres with other craft. Simulating such behaviour requires special mathematical techniques, which in turn could demand substantial computational processing performance and introduce unwanted latency.

1.6.5   Non-immersive VR systems

VR systems can be divided into three groups: immersive, non-immersive and hybrid. Immersive systems, as we have just seen, replace our view of the real world with computer-generated images that react to the position and orientation of the user's head. A non-immersive system, on the other hand, leaves the user visually aware of the real world but able to observe the virtual world through some display device such as a graphics workstation, as shown in Figure 1.2. The user navigates the virtual environment using a device such as a Space Mouse, as shown in Figure 1.3. This device enables the user to translate and rotate the viewpoint using six degrees of freedom.

Figure 1.3 The Space Mouse provides the user with six degrees of freedom – three are used to translate along an axis, and three rotate about an axis. (Courtesy Gesellschaft für 3-D Systeme mbH).

In recent years there has been some discussion as to whether the latter-configuration is strictly a VR system – and in some quarters the dispute continues. However, in spite of these arguments, workstation-based systems have generally been classed as 'through-the-window' VR systems. Such systems have evolved naturally and appeared simply because computers have become increasingly faster. This does not create any real problems if we just accept that real-time graphics is at the heart of all VR systems. We simply acknowledge that it is possible to view this virtual world through the window of a conventional screen (non-immersive), or through an HMD (immersive), or some other wide field of view 'first-person' device.

1.6.6 Hybrid VR systems

A hybrid VR system permits the user to view the real world with virtual images superimposed over this view – such systems are also known as 'augmented reality' systems. A practical example is found in the HMDs used by fighter pilots, which allow the pilot to view their outside world simultaneously with overlaid synthetic graphics. The extra graphics can overlay topographic data upon the pilot's view of the outside terrain, perhaps highlighting targets, boundaries or tactical landmarks. The effectiveness of these augmented reality systems obviously relies heavily upon the accurate 3D tracking of the user and their gaze direction.

This hybrid approach to the interaction with VEs gives rise to some interesting future scenarios. For instance, one can envisage service engineers working with HMDs that superimpose 3D graphics over their view of a machine undergoing a service. These graphics could identify the location of important parts, or even remind the engineer how to dismantle and reassemble various components.

Another scenario which promises similar benefits is in medicine. In this field, doctors and surgeons are already used to using image data derived from 3D scanners; however, such data is traditionally displayed upon a video screen. Imagine the medical benefits if a surgeon could see the patient through a lightweight HMD which integrated 3D graphic data derived from other sources. Perhaps the data, as in the case of ultrasound scanners, is also being captured in real time, thus providing the medical practitioner with pseudo X-ray vision.

1.6.7 The CAVE

At SIGGRAPH 92, the Electronic Visualization Laboratory at the University of Illinois at Chicago demonstrated the CAVE (Cave Automatic Virtual Environment), which has since become a major attraction at SIGGRAPH exhibitions.

A CAVE enables one or more persons to experience the sensation of being completely surrounded by high-resolution, 3D video and audio. It is a room formed from three rear-projection screens for walls (3 metres by 2.75 metres) and a down-projection screen for the floor. High-resolution (1280×512) video projectors display computer-generated, stereo images at a field rate of 120 Hz, while computer-controlled amplifiers relay sampled sound through a network of speakers.

Inside a CAVE, a user wears a pair of stereo shutter glasses to select the left and right images – the end result is an overwhelming sensation of immersion within a virtual environment. A Silicon Graphics Onyx with three Reality-Engines is the source of the images, and the viewpoint is determined by tracking equipment worn on the user's head and hand. The room is large enough to permit other viewers to share the same experience.

As mentioned earlier, flight stimulators use a similar display system, the only subtle difference is that the image is collimated to a distance where stereo is unimportant.

CAVEs have proved to be very useful in exploring visualizations of precomputed datasets; a user can do everything that can be achieved with a workstation, but with the obvious advantages of full immersion. When extra processing power is available for integrating simulation software, the user can interactively explore new scenarios, and experience a real-time visual response.

Typical applications for a CAVE have included: interactive molecular modelling, scientific visualization, sound simulation, architecture, weather simulations and medical modelling.

1.7 The benefits of virtual reality

1.7.1 The virtual domain

The virtual domain is not new, and if being pedantic about the term, it could be argued that dreaming is a virtual domain, where we explore imaginary or threatening scenarios without suffering the consequences. The virtual domain created by a computer is much more flexible. To begin with, unlike dreams, we have total control of the subject. Moreover, software enables a process to be halted at any time, and restarted at a later date. The virtual domain of computers offers reliability, speed, ease of access, compactness and security, and is easily transmitted to other computers located in distant parts of the world.

This virtual domain takes on a special significance when it is used for holding geometric descriptions of real-world objects. CAD systems have explored this feature for many years, yet it is only recently, with the advent of fast workstations, that a new interpretation has been placed upon these images. The ability to manipulate a CAD model in real time reinforces the idea of handling a virtual object – it is as though it actually had some form of existence. It can be viewed from any direction; integrated with other objects into an assembly; the surface properties can be changed; it can be weighed; and it can even be stressed until it breaks. These are truly amazing techniques, yet today we take them all for granted.

1.7.2 Virtual reality

Virtual reality takes us one step closer to virtual objects by making us a part of the virtual domain. Whether through the use of panoramic displays, HMDs or boom displays, the sensation of immersion reinforces our belief that the virtual domain is real.

We know from experience that when viewing a 3D scene on a computer display, the image is fixed to the screen. No matter how we move our heads, the image remains unaltered, apart from an overall adjustment of perspective. However, if the head is tracked in three-space, and used to control the viewpoint of the displayed scene, something intriguing occurs. The image is no longer frozen to the screen; we are looking into a volume of space behind it, like a fish tank. The virtual domain now takes on a different reality.

The next logical stage is to extend the size of the images to provide a wide field of view – we then become immersed in the virtual domain, which is no longer a small volume of space, but a true virtual environment. It is this dramatic change from being on the outside looking in, to actually *being there*, that makes VR so compelling. Just as a photograph can never capture the experience of actually being somewhere, a 2D screen can never approach the sense of presence associated with immersive displays.

1.7.3   The benefits

Nature has demonstrated through evolutionary forces that those species able to control and adapt to a changing environment have a distinct advantage over other life forms. During our own survival, we have acquired special skills to explore the world through sight, sound and touch. Therefore, it seems obvious that there are distinct advantages in giving the virtual domain the same number of spatial dimensions found in the real world, and, if possible, making us a part of this domain.

Stereoscopic vision enables us to assess the size of a distant object quickly; we can be looking at the stars at one moment, and, one second later, be examining the surface detail of our skin. We can almost instantly determine the speed of another object, and decide whether its trajectory endangers our life. We build mechanisms as delicate as a watch, electrical circuits that are visible only with a microscope, and design complex systems such as a space satellite. We are embedded in three-space, and we understand this space intimately.

We do not need to invent reasons for the existence of VR systems. They are a natural development for the tools we use to control our environment. And as so many design procedures are already computerized, immersive VR systems will simply enhance existing human–computer interfaces. Instead of manipulating an image of a virtual mechanical component, we will design the component as if it existed. Instead of trying to imagine what it would be like to stand inside an imaginary atrium, an architect can actually discover first-hand.

Virtual reality will be used to model and explore familiar environments associated with kitchens, planes, offices, studios, ships, submarines, cars and hospitals. It will also be used to explore unfamiliar environments found in molecules, atoms, galaxies, viruses, bacteria and crystals. However, we also employ spatial models to understand abstract problems found in mathematics, economics, simulation, artificial life and networks.

There will be few barriers to VR technology. In fact, VR will create totally new ways for manipulating and visualizing all types of computer data. If X-ray data is available for a patient, then augmented reality can be used to integrate the virtual domain with the real domain. If pilots can learn to fly a new plane using a flight simulator, then surgeons can learn new surgical skills using a medical simulator.

In order to appreciate the hidden potential of VR systems we will explore in greater depth some of the relevant subject areas and how integrated systems function. We will then study how the technology is currently being applied, and also explore how the technology could evolve and be used in a wide variety of applications.

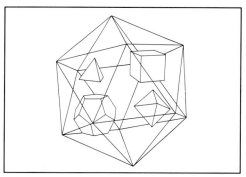

Left eye view

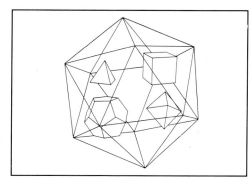

Right eye view

Green image

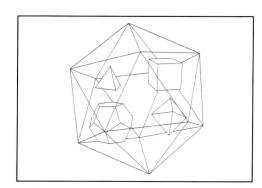

Red image

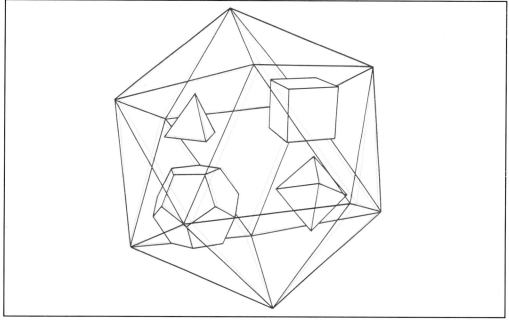

Stereographic image. © Arthur N. Girling

Above: The statue of Liberty. © David Burder

Opposite: Two stereographic computer-generated images by Kenneth Snelson. © Kenneth Snelson

Over page: Manhattan, by helicopter. © David Burder

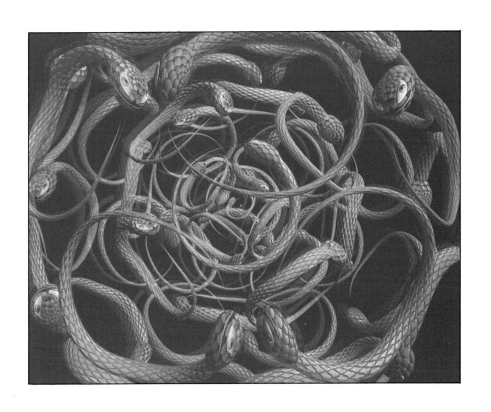

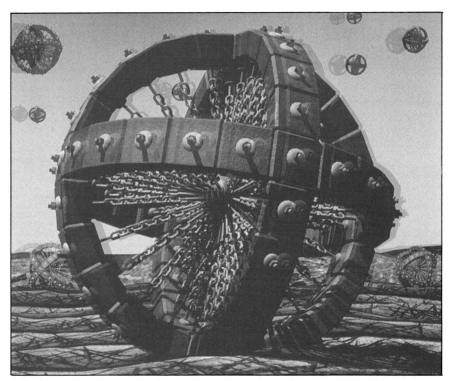

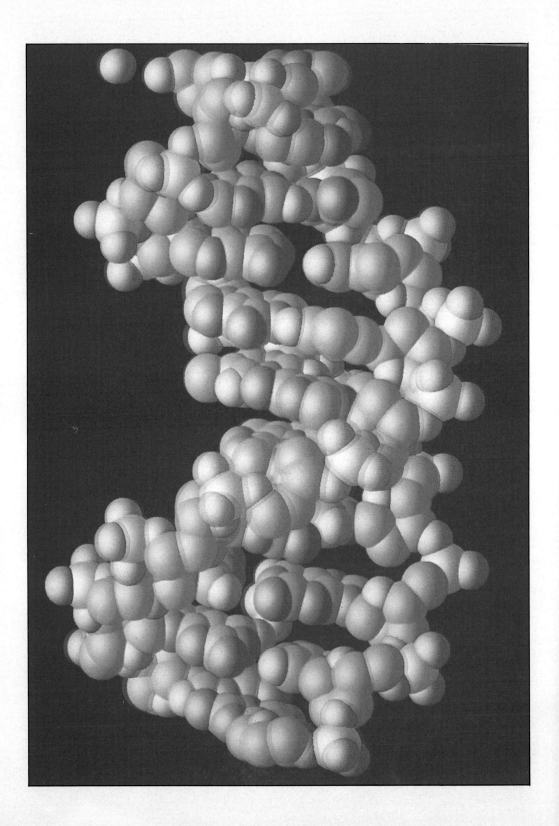

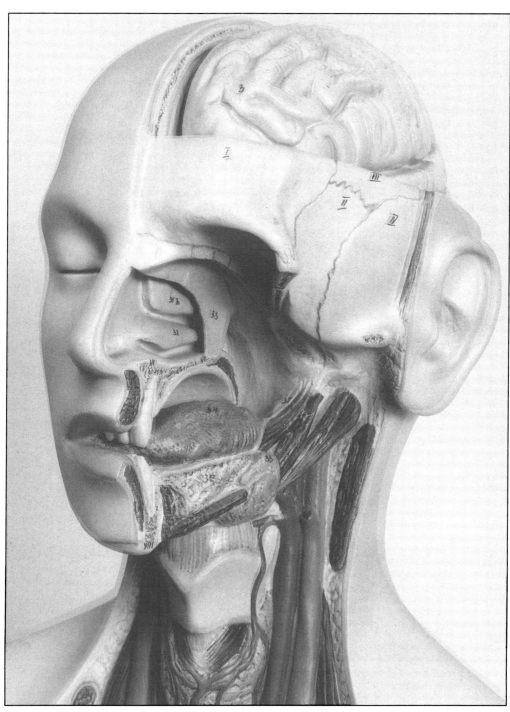

Above: A cut away human head. © David Burder

Opposite: A computer-generated DNA molecule.
© David Burder

Single Image Auto Stereograph. David Burder

2

The Historical Development of VR

2.0 Introduction

Like most technologies, VR did not suddenly appear. It emerged in the public domain after a considerable period of research and development in industrial, military and academic laboratories. The emergence of VR was closely related to the maturity of other technologies such as real-time computer systems, computer graphics, displays, fibre optics and 3D tracking. Then, at some critical moment, when each technology could provide its own individual input, a crude working system appeared.

It is not unusual for these embryonic systems to be of no practical use to anyone apart from their inventors, but they do establish the idea and are a vital stage of creative design. They also provide a base from which to extrapolate the concept into the future, and by keeping an open mind, a variety of paths the technology can follow may be predicted. Predicting the future with any precision, however, is fraught with problems, no matter how qualified and familiar with technology one is. History reminds us that there is a time and place for everything to happen, and, irrespective of how useful, exciting and revolutionary a product appears to be, it will not succeed unless the right conditions exist.

Successful invention is above all about timing; where a product meets a specific need, such as spectacles. It is also about marketing; where a product is produced that people did not know they needed, such as an electric toothbrush. Successful invention also concerns money, time, energy, efficiency, speed, convenience and social attitudes, which collectively give inventors some scope.

VR systems were not developed to meet a specific need; they were developed because they were possible. Now that several years have elapsed since their public debut, we are in a position to review their potential. The development and fine-tuning of these systems continues, but in the meantime applications are emerging that confirm that we are dealing with a powerful and creative way of interacting with computer-based systems.

Looking back over the historical development of modern technology, it is interesting to see how one idea spawns another. Very rarely is there a dramatic break in this flow. VR obviously depended upon the existence of the computer, not to mention the associated field of computer graphics. The latter relies heavily upon television technology, and both the technology of television and computers would not exist without electricity. So it is interesting to trace back in time, to see how each major technological breakthrough brought us one step towards today's VR systems.

2.1   Scientific landmarks

Being able to count and calculate is vital to every aspect of our daily lives – whether it be in the computation of price discounts, or keeping track of our age. The tools and techniques we use today have evolved over thousands of years, but it was during the seventeenth and eighteenth centuries that calculating machines started to become widely used.

The nineteenth century started with Jacquard using punched cards to control a weaving loom, and finished with Hollerith using punched cards in an electric tabulating machine for the 890 USA census. Before the century had finished, the Tabulating Machine Company was founded, which eventually became IBM.

The nineteenth century was alive with invention and discovery, and great minds such as Faraday, Babbage, Maxwell and Edison established the foundations of today's technology.

1777 Charles Earl Stanhope invented the first logic machine.

1800 J. M. Jacquard used punched cards to control a weaving loom.

1821 Michael Faraday discovered the principle of the electric motor.

1823 Charles Babbage developed the difference engine.

1824 Peter Roget described the persistence of vision.

1832 Charles Wheatstone invented the stereoscope.

1833 Charles Babbage proposed the analytical engine.

1854 George Boole published his method for solving problems in logic.

1860 Lord Kelvin used the ball and disk integrator for analogue computing.

1873 James Clerk Maxwell published his 'Treatise on Electricity and Magnetism'.

1883 Thomas Edison discovered the thermionic effect.

1888 Heinrich Hertz discovered radio waves.

1889 Léon Bollée built a direct multiplication machine.

1890 Herman Hollerith designed an electric tabulating system for the USA census.

1896 Herman Hollerith formed the Tabulating Machine Company – today's IBM.

At the turn of the twentieth century, atomic physics was advancing in leaps and bounds, and Einstein's theory of relativity revolutionized the classical mechanistic interpretation of the universe. Baird invented television. Relay technology paved the way for automatic calculators, and the logical minds of Russell, Whitehead, Turing and Shannon opened the way for finite-state machines.

1910 Bertrand Russell and Albert North Whitehead published *Principia Mathematica*, which described the methods of symbolic logic.

1924 John Logie Baird produced television objects in outline.

1926 John Logie Baird demonstrated the television of moving objects.

1936 Alan Turing showed that certain algorithms could not be solved.

Konrad Zuse built a relay calculator.

1937 Claude Shannon described an 'Electric Adder to Base Two' in his master's thesis at MIT.

George Stibitz built an electric adder to the base two at Bell Laboratories.

Howard Aiken proposed the need for a new kind of computing machine.

1938 Thomas Watson (president of IBM) implemented Aiken's idea for a new type of computing machine at Harvard University.

1940 Link Aviation developed the first flight trainer.

1943 The US Army began planning the ENIAC computer.

British Post Office engineers operated their Colossus computer to decode Germany's Enigma codes.

Almost halfway through the century computers became a reality. They were large, delicate and unreliable, and no one could have predicted that one day we would be using digital calculators in a watch!

1944 The Harvard Computation Laboratory completed their automatic, general-purpose, digital computer.

Gordon Brown at MIT was asked to build a simulator for multi-engined aircraft.

1945 Konrad Zuse developed a simple programming language 'plan calculus'.

John von Neumann began work on a fully automatic, digital, all-purpose computing machine.

1946 J. Presper Eckert and John W. Mauchly designed ENIAC at the Moore School.

MIT's Project Whirlwind was used for real-time air traffic control and aircraft simulation.

George Stibitz completed the first Model V relay calculator.

1947 Adele Goldstine and John von Neumann developed flow diagrams for describing programs.

J. Presper Eckert and John Mauchly's company built UNIVAC – the first computer designed for commercial use.

1948 Adele Goldstine and John von Neumann developed a program to interpret other programs.

William Shockley *et al.* invented the transistor at Bell Telephone Laboratories.

F. C. Williams used CRTs as memory delay lines and created patterns of dots.

1949 Maurice Wilkes built the EDSAC computer at Cambridge University.

F. C. Williams and T. Kilburn built the MADM computer at Manchester University.

1950 The Whirlwind computer at MIT used a CRT for output.

1955 John von Neumann described 'self-reproducing automata'.

By the mid-1950s digital computers were appearing at a number of universities in the United States and the United Kingdom. The technology of electronics was still based upon thermionic valves, but this was soon to change with the advent of integrated circuits.

Morton Heilig's arcade experience exploited film technology to provide customers with an imaginary journey through Manhattan traffic. The user experienced a 3D view of the journey with vibrating handlebars and seat. Even the wind velocity varied as the user's speed changed in the traffic. To clinch the effect of immersion, the aromas of car fumes and passing pizza parlours were released at key points in the experience. Whether Heilig realized it or not, he had created passive 'virtual' experiences which were to be made interactive with the help of computers. Within a further five years, computer graphics appeared and revealed another area of research and invention.

1956 Morton Heilig invented the Sensorama.

US Patent 3,059,519 – inventor: Stanton, CRT-based binocular 'headgear'.

1957 M. L. Heilig patented a pair of head-mounted goggles fitted with two colour TV units.

1958 The first monolithic integrated circuit was demonstrated.

1960 The Boeing Corporation coined the term 'computer graphics'.

1961 Integrated circuits were used in commercial computers.

1962 W. Uttal, assigned to IBM, patented a glove for teaching touch typing.

Ivan Sutherland is often referred to as the 'father' of computer graphics. Not because he invented it, but because of his insight into its potential. His doctoral thesis on SKETCHPAD revealed how computers could be used for interactive graphics. Further projects combined the use of computer graphics with head-mounted displays. Although the term 'virtual reality' was still to be coined, the technology was beginning to take shape.

1963 Ivan Sutherland submitted his doctoral thesis 'SKETCHPAD: A man–machine graphical communication system'.

1965 Ivan Sutherland published *The Ultimate Display*.

1966 Tom Furness began work on display systems for pilots.

1968 Ivan Sutherland published *A Head-mounted Three Dimensional Display*.

In the 1970s raster graphics progressed rapidly through the research of Gouraud and Phong. Many others contributed to related topics such as modelling, data structures and hidden-surface removal.

1971 Redifon Ltd (UK) began manufacturing flight simulators with computer graphics displays.

Henri Gouraud submitted his doctoral thesis 'Computer display of curved surfaces'.

1973 Bui-Tuong Phong submitted his doctoral thesis 'Illumination for computer generated images'.

1976 P. J. Kilpatrick published his doctoral thesis 'The use of a kinematic supplement in an interactive graphics system'.

1977 Dan Sandin and Richard Sayre invented a bend-sensing glove.

1979 F. H. Raab *et al.* described the Polhemus tracking system.

Eric Howlett (LEEP Systems, Inc.) designed the Large Expanse Enhanced Perspective (LEEP) Optics.

By the 1980s VR was ready to be recognized as a viable technology. Computers were small, inexpensive and fast; researchers in computer graphics were producing some stunning images. It just needed a few more years to develop some related peripherals such as gloves and better displays, and VR would be recognized.

1980 Andy Lippman developed an interactive video disk to drive around Aspen.

1981 Tom Furness developed the 'virtual cockpit'.

G. J. Grimes, assigned to Bell Telephone Laboratories, patented a data entry glove.

1982 Thomas Zimmerman patented a data input glove based upon optical sensors, such that internal refraction could be correlated with finger flexion and extension.

1983 Mark Callahan built a see-through HMD at MIT.

Myron Krueger published *Artificial Reality*.

1984 William Gibson wrote about 'cyberspace' in *Neuromancer*.

Mike McGreevy and Jim Humphries developed VIVED (Virtual Visual Environment Display) system for future astronauts at NASA.

1985 VPL Research, Inc. was founded.

Mike McGreevy and Jim Humphries built an HMD from monochrome LCD pocket television displays.

1987 Jonathan Waldern formed W Industries.

Tom Zimmerman *et al.* developed an interactive glove.

1989 Jaron Lanier, CEO of VPL, coined the term 'virtual reality'.

VPL Research and Autodesk introduced commercial head-mounted displays.

Robert Stone formed the Virtual Reality & Human Factors Group at ARRL.

Eric Howlett built the LEEPvideo System I HMD.

VPL Research, Inc. began selling the EyePhone that used LCD displays and LEEP optics.

Autodesk, Inc. demonstrated their PC-based VR CAD system, Cyberspace, at SIGGRAPH'89.

Robert Stone and Jim Hennequin co-invented the Teletact I Glove.

Reflection Technologies produced the Private Eye.

Divison was founded.

The 1990s began with the founding of Sense8; W Industries selling commercial VR systems for interactive games; and Division announcing a general-purpose VR system for research and development.

1990 Fred Brooks et al. developed the force feedback GROPE system at UNC at Chapel Hill.

J. R. Hennequin and R. Stone, assigned to ARRL, patented a tactile feedback glove.

Sense8 Corporation founded by Pat Gelband.

ARRL ordered Division's first VR system.

1991 W Industries sold their first Virtuality system.

Richard Holmes, assigned to W Industries, patented a tactile feedback glove.

Division sold their first VR system.

1992 T. G. Zimmerman, assigned to VPL Research, patented a glove using optical sensors.

Division demonstrated a multi-user VR system.

Thomas DeFanti *et al*. demonstrated the CAVE system at SIGGRAPH.

1993 SGI announced the RealityEngine.

1994 InSys and the Manchester Royal Infirmary launched Europe's first VR R&D Centre for minimally invasive therapy.

The Virtual Reality Society was formed.

Division released Pixel-Planes 5 & 6 developed at the University of North Carolina at Chapel Hill.

A surgeon at Johns Hopkins Hospital removed a gall bladder with the aid of an HMD.

Virtuality announced their Series 2000 system.

Kaiser Electro-Optics, Inc. were awarded a two-year contract by ARPA, to develop a wide field of view HMD.

DTI and SERC funded a £2.5m 'Virtuosi' project for remotely accessed virtual workplaces.

IBM and Virtuality announced the V-SPACE system.

Division demonstrated an integrated multi-platform VR system at I-ITSEC, Orlando.

As we move towards the twenty-first century, the pace of technological development continues to increase. Even though we have a clear knowledge of our history, it is still difficult to forecast with any precision just what will be around in 10 years' time. All that we can say with some confidence is that computers will become smaller, faster and cheaper. Programs will become more sophisticated and 'intelligent'. Computers will find their way into more and more aspects of our lives and, hopefully, VR will play an important role in the human–computer interface. However, what no one knows at the moment is whether digital computers are the only way forward. Could another revolutionary technology emerge that forces us to replace everything we have designed over the past century? Who knows, but we will return to this question in Chapter 13.

3

3D Computer Graphics

3.0 Introduction

3D computer graphics is a large and complex subject and is supported by many excellent books. However, to provide a reasonable level of continuity, this chapter covers specific computer graphics topics that are directly relevant to VR systems. Those readers wishing to gain a deeper technical insight into this subject should refer to the recommended references.

The following techniques will form the basis for modelling VEs, creating stereoscopic views and rendering images. These individual topics are extremely large and it will be impossible to cover them all to any significant depth; nevertheless, they will be described to a level of detail sufficient to support the concepts associated with VR systems.

3.1 The virtual world space

In order to render coloured images of a virtual world we require some geometric basis or set of rules upon which to base our computations. The Cartesian system employs a set of 3D axes, where each axis is orthogonal to the other two. Figure 3.1 illustrates such a scheme where a right-handed set of axes is used to locate uniquely any point P with Cartesian coordinates (x,y,z). Although a left-handed system would work equally well, a right-handed system is frequently employed in computer graphics applications. The right-hand system requires that when using one's right hand, the outstretched thumb, first and middle fingers align with the x-, y- and z-axes respectively.

Various modelling schemes are used to construct VEs and some are described in Chapter 4. The majority of these modelling strategies construct

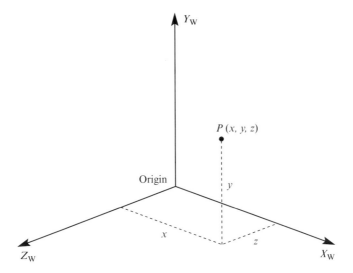

Figure 3.1 A Cartesian set of axes is used to locate uniquely a point in the virtual world. The point *P* has coordinates (*x*,*y*,*z*) which are the axial offsets from the origin. Note that this axial system is right-handed, as the thumb, first finger and middle finger can be aligned with the *x*-, *y*-, and *z*-axes respectively.

models from a mixture of planar polygons, surface patches or implicit surfaces, all of which employ a Cartesian coordinate description. If we assume the existence of a virtual world constructed from Cartesian coordinates, the next stage is to consider how it can be viewed from any arbitrary position in space. In computer graphics and computer animation the idea of a *viewer* or *camera* is used to describe this imaginary observer. But as VR systems involve real-time interaction between the user and the VE, perhaps it is relevant to rename this as the *Virtual Observer* (VO).

3.2 Positioning the virtual observer

The VO always has a specific location within the VE and will gaze along some line of sight. Furthermore, the VO has two eyes which, ideally, receive two different views of the environment to create a 3D stereoscopic image. To achieve these two perspective views, a standard computer graphics procedure is used to recompute the VE's coordinate geometry relative to the VO's frame of reference. The procedure used depends upon the method employed to define the VO's frame of reference within the VE, which may involve the use of direction cosines, *XYZ* fixed angles, *XYZ* Euler angles or quaternions. We will examine how each of these techniques could be implemented.

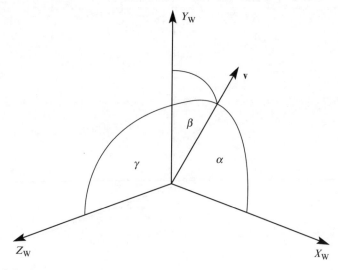

Figure 3.2 The unit vector **v** can be defined by three angles α, β and γ. As their cosines are equal to the components of the unit vector, they are called direction cosines.

3.2.1 Direction cosines

A unit 3D vector has three axial components which are also equal to the cosines of the angles formed between the vector and the three axes. These angles are known as direction cosines and can be computed by taking the dot product of the vector and the axial unit vectors. Figure 3.2 shows these angles.

These direction cosines enable any point $P(x,y,z)$ in one frame of reference to be transformed into $P'(x',y',z')$ in another frame of reference as follows:

$$\begin{bmatrix} x' \\ y' \\ z' \end{bmatrix} = \begin{bmatrix} r_{11} & r_{12} & r_{13} \\ r_{21} & r_{22} & r_{23} \\ r_{31} & r_{32} & r_{33} \end{bmatrix} \begin{bmatrix} x \\ y \\ z \end{bmatrix} \tag{3.1}$$

where:

r_{11}, r_{12} and r_{13} are the direction cosines of the secondary x-axis
r_{21}, r_{22} and r_{23} are the direction cosines of the secondary y-axis
r_{31}, r_{32} and r_{33} are the direction cosines of the secondary z-axis

To illustrate this operation, consider the situation shown in Figure 3.3(a) that shows the two axial systems mutually aligned. Evaluating the direction cosines results in the following matrix transformation:

$$\begin{bmatrix} x' \\ y' \\ z' \end{bmatrix} = \begin{bmatrix} 1 & 0 & 0 \\ 0 & 1 & 0 \\ 0 & 0 & 1 \end{bmatrix} \begin{bmatrix} x \\ y \\ z \end{bmatrix} \tag{3.2}$$

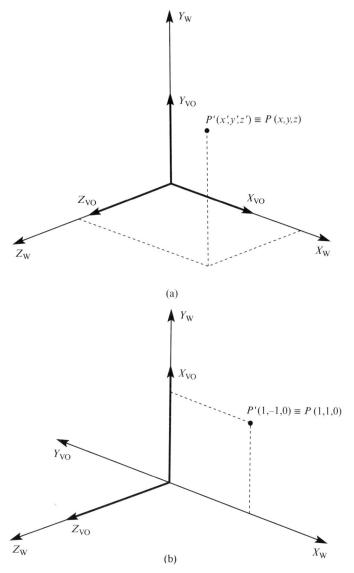

Figure 3.3 (a) As the two axial systems are coincident, any point $P' \equiv P$.
(b) The orientation of the VO's axial system with the virtual world is such that the
point $P(1,1,0)$ in the VE $\equiv P'(1,-1,0)$ for the VO.

which obviously implies that $(x',y',z') = (x,y,z)$. In Figure 3.3(b) the matrix
operation becomes:

$$\begin{bmatrix} x' \\ y' \\ z' \end{bmatrix} = \begin{bmatrix} 0 & 1 & 0 \\ -1 & 0 & 0 \\ 0 & 0 & 1 \end{bmatrix} \begin{bmatrix} x \\ y \\ z \end{bmatrix} \qquad \textbf{(3.3)}$$

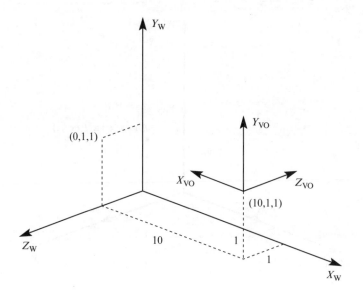

Figure 3.4 This illustrates how the VO's frame of reference is located within the virtual world. The point $(0,1,1)$ in the world is equivalent to the point $(10,0,0)$ for the VO.

and substituting the coordinates $(1,1,0)$ for (x,y,z) produces values of $(1,-1,0)$ for (x',y',z') in the new frame of reference, which can be confirmed visually.

If the VO is offset by (t_x,t_y,t_z), the transformation relating points in the VE to the VO's frame of reference can be expressed as a compound operation consisting of a translation back to the origin, followed by a change of axial systems. This can be represented by:

$$
\begin{bmatrix} x' \\ y' \\ z' \\ 1 \end{bmatrix} = \begin{bmatrix} r_{11} & r_{12} & r_{13} & 0 \\ r_{21} & r_{22} & r_{23} & 0 \\ r_{31} & r_{32} & r_{33} & 0 \\ 0 & 0 & 0 & 1 \end{bmatrix} \begin{bmatrix} 1 & 0 & 0 & -t_x \\ 0 & 1 & 0 & -t_y \\ 0 & 0 & 1 & -t_z \\ 0 & 0 & 0 & 1 \end{bmatrix} \begin{bmatrix} x \\ y \\ z \\ 1 \end{bmatrix}
\tag{3.4}
$$

(Note that the matrices are expressed in homogeneous coordinates.)

To illustrate this process, consider the configuration shown in Figure 3.4. The values of t_x, t_y and t_z are $(10,1,1)$, and the direction cosines are as shown in the following matrix operation:

$$
\begin{bmatrix} x' \\ y' \\ z' \\ 1 \end{bmatrix} = \begin{bmatrix} -1 & 0 & 0 & 0 \\ 0 & 1 & 0 & 0 \\ 0 & 0 & -1 & 0 \\ 0 & 0 & 0 & 1 \end{bmatrix} \begin{bmatrix} 1 & 0 & 0 & -10 \\ 0 & 1 & 0 & -1 \\ 0 & 0 & 1 & -1 \\ 0 & 0 & 0 & 1 \end{bmatrix} \begin{bmatrix} x \\ y \\ z \\ 1 \end{bmatrix}
\tag{3.5}
$$

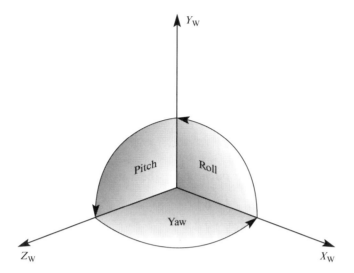

Figure 3.5 In a right-handed axial system the yaw, roll and pitch angles have positive angles of rotation as shown.

which concatenates to:

$$
\begin{bmatrix} x' \\ y' \\ z' \\ 1 \end{bmatrix} = \begin{bmatrix} -1 & 0 & 0 & 10 \\ 0 & 1 & 0 & -1 \\ 0 & 0 & -1 & 1 \\ 0 & 0 & 0 & 1 \end{bmatrix} \begin{bmatrix} x \\ y \\ z \\ 1 \end{bmatrix}
$$

(3.6)

Substituting the coordinates $(0,0,0)$ for (x,y,z) in (3.6) produces $(10,-1,1)$ for (x',y',z'), which can be confirmed from Figure 3.4. Similarly, substituting the coordinates $(0,1,1)$ for (x,y,z) produces $(10,0,0)$ for (x',y',z) which is also correct.

3.2.2 *XYZ* fixed angles

Another approach for specifying orientation involves the use of three separate rotations about a fixed frame of reference – these angles are frequently referred to as yaw, pitch and roll. Great care should be taken with these angles when referring to other books and technical papers. Sometimes a left-handed system of axes is used rather than a right-handed set, and the vertical axis may be the y-axis or the z-axis. The matrices representing the rotations can consequently vary greatly. In this book, all Cartesian coordinate systems are right-handed, and the vertical axis is *always* the y-axis.

The roll, pitch and yaw angles can be defined as follows: *roll* is the angle of rotation about the z-axis; *pitch* is the angle of rotation about the x-axis; *yaw* is the angle of rotation about the y-axis. Figure 3.5 illustrates these rotations and also shows the sign convention. The homogeneous matrices representing these rotations are as follows:

- Rotate through an angle *roll* about the *z*-axis:

$$
\begin{bmatrix}
\cos roll & -\sin roll & 0 & 0 \\
\sin roll & \cos roll & 0 & 0 \\
0 & 0 & 1 & 0 \\
0 & 0 & 0 & 1
\end{bmatrix}
\tag{3.7}
$$

- Rotate through an angle *pitch* about the *x*-axis:

$$
\begin{bmatrix}
1 & 0 & 0 & 0 \\
0 & \cos pitch & -\sin pitch & 0 \\
0 & \sin pitch & \cos pitch & 0 \\
0 & 0 & 0 & 1
\end{bmatrix}
\tag{3.8}
$$

- Rotate through an angle *yaw* about the *y*-axis:

$$
\begin{bmatrix}
\cos yaw & 0 & \sin yaw & 0 \\
0 & 1 & 0 & 0 \\
-\sin yaw & 0 & \cos yaw & 0 \\
0 & 0 & 0 & 1
\end{bmatrix}
\tag{3.9}
$$

One popular sequence for applying these rotations is: roll, pitch then yaw. Therefore, if the VO is located within the VE using these angles, the coordinate transformation relating vertices in the VE relative to the VO can be derived from the inverse operations. These effectively rotate through angles: *−roll*, *−pitch* and *−yaw* and are the transpose of the above matrices, that is:

- Rotate through an angle *−roll* about the *z*-axis:

$$
\begin{bmatrix}
\cos roll & \sin roll & 0 & 0 \\
-\sin roll & \cos roll & 0 & 0 \\
0 & 0 & 1 & 0 \\
0 & 0 & 0 & 1
\end{bmatrix}
\tag{3.10}
$$

- Rotate through an angle *−pitch* about the *x*-axis:

$$
\begin{bmatrix}
1 & 0 & 0 & 0 \\
0 & \cos pitch & \sin pitch & 0 \\
0 & -\sin pitch & \cos pitch & 0 \\
0 & 0 & 0 & 1
\end{bmatrix}
\tag{3.11}
$$

- Rotate through an angle *−yaw* about the *y*-axis:

$$\begin{bmatrix} \cos yaw & 0 & -\sin yaw & 0 \\ 0 & 1 & 0 & 0 \\ \sin yaw & 0 & \cos yaw & 0 \\ 0 & 0 & 0 & 1 \end{bmatrix} \quad (3.12)$$

As described above, the VO will normally be translated from the origin by (t_x, t_y, t_z). This will mean that the coordinate transform from the VE to the VO must be evaluated as follows:

$$\begin{bmatrix} x' \\ y' \\ z' \\ 1 \end{bmatrix} = [-roll]\,[-pitch]\,[-yaw]\,[-translate] \begin{bmatrix} x \\ y \\ z \\ 1 \end{bmatrix} \quad (3.13)$$

which can be represented by a single homogeneous matrix:

$$\begin{bmatrix} x' \\ y' \\ z' \\ 1 \end{bmatrix} = \begin{bmatrix} T_{11} & T_{12} & T_{13} & T_{14} \\ T_{21} & T_{22} & T_{23} & T_{24} \\ T_{31} & T_{32} & T_{33} & T_{34} \\ T_{41} & T_{42} & T_{43} & T_{44} \end{bmatrix} \begin{bmatrix} x \\ y \\ z \\ 1 \end{bmatrix} \quad (3.14)$$

where:

$$\begin{aligned}
T_{11} &= \cos yaw \cos roll + \sin yaw \sin pitch \sin roll \\
T_{12} &= \cos pitch \sin roll \\
T_{13} &= -\sin yaw \cos roll + \cos yaw \sin pitch \sin roll \\
T_{14} &= -(t_x T_{11} + t_y T_{12} + t_z T_{13}) \\
T_{21} &= -\cos yaw \sin roll + \sin yaw \sin pitch \cos roll \\
T_{22} &= \cos pitch \cos roll \\
T_{23} &= \sin yaw \sin roll + \cos yaw \sin pitch \cos roll \\
T_{24} &= -(t_x T_{21} + t_y T_{22} + t_z T_{23}) \\
T_{31} &= \sin yaw \cos pitch \\
T_{32} &= -\sin pitch \\
T_{33} &= \cos yaw \cos pitch \\
T_{34} &= -(t_x T_{31} + t_y T_{32} + t_z T_{32}) \\
T_{41} &= 0 \\
T_{42} &= 0 \\
T_{43} &= 0 \\
T_{44} &= 1
\end{aligned} \quad (3.15)$$

This, too, can be verified by a simple example. For instance, consider the situation shown in Figure 3.4, where the following conditions prevail:

$$\begin{aligned}
roll &= 0° \\
pitch &= 0° \\
yaw &= -180°
\end{aligned} \quad (3.16)$$

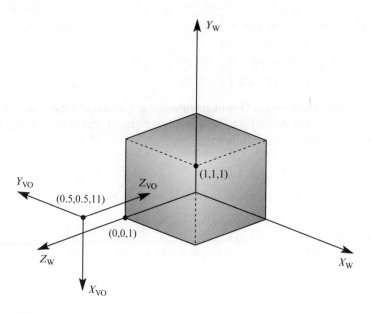

Figure 3.6   The VO has been subjected to a roll of 90°, a pitch of 180°, followed by a translation of (0.5,0.5,11). Consequently, the point (1,1,1) in the world is equivalent to (−0.5, −0.5,10) for the VO, and the point (0,0,1) in the world is equivalent to (0.5,0.5,10) for the VO.

$$t_x = 10$$
$$t_y = 1$$
$$t_z = 1$$

The transformation is:

$$
\begin{bmatrix} x' \\ y' \\ z' \\ 1 \end{bmatrix} = \begin{bmatrix} -1 & 0 & 0 & 10 \\ 0 & 1 & 0 & -1 \\ 0 & 0 & -1 & 1 \\ 0 & 0 & 0 & 1 \end{bmatrix} \begin{bmatrix} x \\ y \\ z \\ 1 \end{bmatrix}
$$

(3.17)

which is identical to (3.6) used for direction cosines. Another example is shown in Figure 3.6 where the following conditions exist:

$$roll = 90°$$
$$pitch = 180°$$
$$yaw = 0°$$
$$t_x = 0.5$$
$$t_y = 0.5$$
$$t_z = 11$$

(3.18)

then:

$$
\begin{bmatrix} x' \\ y' \\ z' \\ 1 \end{bmatrix} = \begin{bmatrix} 0 & -1 & 0 & 0.5 \\ -1 & 0 & 0 & 0.5 \\ 0 & 0 & -1 & 11 \\ 0 & 0 & 0 & 1 \end{bmatrix} \begin{bmatrix} x \\ y \\ z \\ 1 \end{bmatrix}
\tag{3.19}
$$

Substituting the coordinates $(1,1,1)$ for (x,y,z) in (3.19) produces the coordinates $(-0.5,-0.5,10)$ for the point (x',y',z'). Similarly, substituting the coordinates $(0,0,1)$ for (x,y,z) produces $(0.5,0.5,10)$ for (x',y',z'), which can be visually verified using Figure 3.6.

3.2.3 *XYZ* Euler angles

XYZ fixed angles are relative to a fixed frame of reference, whereas *XYZ* Euler angles are relative to the local rotating frame of reference. To illustrate this subtle difference, let us consider an example where a second frame of reference is first subjected to a pitch rotation and then a yaw rotation relative to the rotating frame of reference. Figure 3.7(a) shows two frames of reference mutually aligned. Figure 3.7(b) shows the orientation of the VO's frame after it is subjected to a pitch rotation of 90° about X'. Figure 3.7(c) shows the new orientation after the VO's frame is subjected to a yaw rotation of 90° about Y'. The new orientation of the VO's frame could have been achieved using *XYZ* fixed angles by first performing a yaw rotation of 90°, followed by a pitch rotation of 90°.

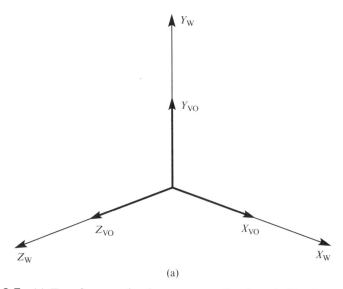

(a)

Figure 3.7 (a) Two frames of reference mutually aligned. (b) The VO's frame rotated through a 90° angle of pitch about X_{VO}. (c) The VO's frame rotated through a 90° angle of yaw about Y_{VO}.

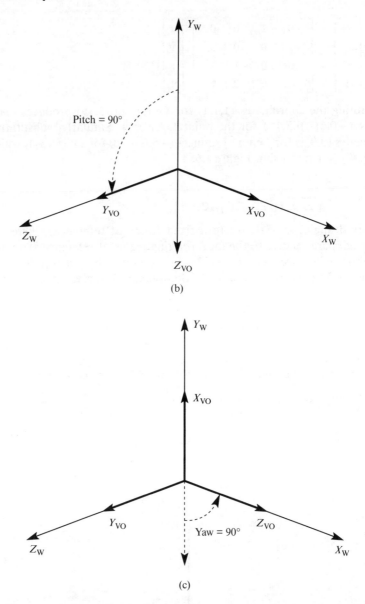

Figure 3.7 (continued)

Consider another example shown in Figure 3.8(a) where the two frames of reference are initially mutually aligned. Figure 3.8(b) shows the orientation of the VO's frame after it is subjected to a roll rotation of 90° about Z_{VO}. Figure 3.8(c) shows the orientation of the VO's frame after it is subjected to a yaw rotation of 90° about Y_{VO}. However, the new orientation of the VO's frame could have been accomplished using XYZ fixed angles by first performing a yaw rotation of 90°, followed by a roll rotation of 90°.

From these two simple examples, it can be seen that a compound rotation formed by successive roll, pitch and yaw rotations about a fixed frame of reference is equivalent to a compound angle formed by reversing the sequence of roll, pitch and yaw about the rotating frame of reference. This can be shown to hold for any compound combination of angles.

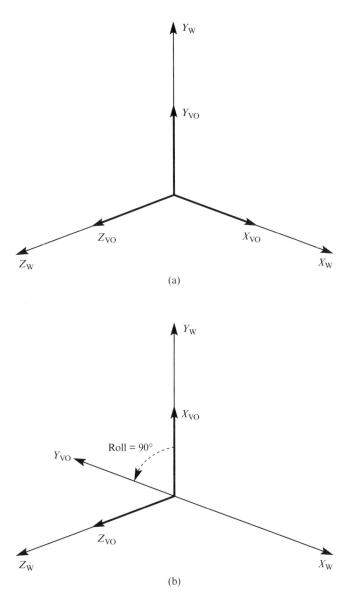

(a)

(b)

Figure 3.8   (a) The two frame of reference are mutually aligned. (d) The VO's frame is rotated through a 90° angle of roll about Z_{VO}. (c) The VO's frame is rotated through a 90° angle of yaw about Y_{VO}.

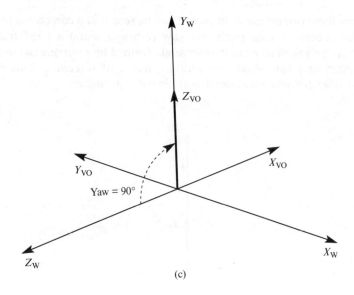

Figure 3.8 (continued)

Without developing the matrices for roll, pitch, yaw and translate again, we can state that if a VO is located in the VE using *XYZ* Euler angles, then any point (x,y,z) in the VE is equivalent to (x',y',z') for the VO given the following:

$$\begin{bmatrix} x' \\ y' \\ z' \\ 1 \end{bmatrix} = [-yaw][-pitch][-roll][-translate] \begin{bmatrix} x \\ y \\ z \\ 1 \end{bmatrix} \qquad (3.20)$$

(Note that the only difference between this operation and that used for *XYZ* fixed angles is that the roll, pitch and yaw matrices have been reversed.)

This, too, can be represented by the single homogeneous matrix operation:

$$\begin{bmatrix} x' \\ y' \\ z' \\ 1 \end{bmatrix} = \begin{bmatrix} T_{11} & T_{12} & T_{13} & T_{14} \\ T_{21} & T_{22} & T_{23} & T_{24} \\ T_{31} & T_{32} & T_{33} & T_{34} \\ T_{41} & T_{42} & T_{43} & T_{44} \end{bmatrix} \begin{bmatrix} x \\ y \\ z \\ 1 \end{bmatrix} \qquad (3.21)$$

where:

$T_{11} = \cos yaw \cos roll - \sin yaw \sin pitch \sin roll$
$T_{12} = \cos yaw \sin roll + \sin yaw \sin pitch \cos roll$
$T_{13} = -\sin yaw \cos pitch$
$T_{14} = -(t_x T_{11} + t_y T_{12} + t_z T_{13})$
$T_{21} = -\cos pitch \sin roll$

$T_{22} = \cos pitch \cos roll$

$T_{23} = \sin pitch$

$T_{24} = -(t_x T_{21} + t_y T_{22} + t_z T_{23})$

$T_{31} = \sin yaw \cos roll + \cos yaw \sin pitch \sin roll$

$T_{32} = \sin yaw \sin roll - \cos yaw \sin pitch \cos roll$ (3.22)

$T_{33} = \cos yaw \cos pitch$

$T_{34} = -(t_x T_{31} + t_y T_{32} + t_z T_{33})$

$T_{41} = 0$

$T_{42} = 0$

$T_{43} = 0$

$T_{44} = 1$

This matrix operation is now tested with two examples.

Example 3.1

If a VO is oriented in the VE using XYZ Euler angles in the sequence roll, pitch, yaw and translate with the following values:

$roll = 0°$

$pitch = 90°$

$yaw = 90°$ (3.23)

$t_x = 0$

$t_y = 0$

$t_z = 0$

substituting these conditions in (3.22) produces:

$$\begin{bmatrix} x' \\ y' \\ z' \\ 1 \end{bmatrix} = \begin{bmatrix} 0 & 1 & 0 & 0 \\ 0 & 0 & 1 & 0 \\ 1 & 0 & 0 & 0 \\ 0 & 0 & 0 & 1 \end{bmatrix} \begin{bmatrix} x \\ y \\ z \\ 1 \end{bmatrix}$$ (3.24)

Substituting the coordinates $(1,1,0)$ for (x,y,z) in (3.24) produces $(1,0,1)$ for (x',y',z') for the VO, which can be confirmed from Figure 3.9.

Example 3.2

If a VO is orientated in a VE using XYZ Euler angles in the sequence roll, pitch, yaw and translate with the following values:

$roll = 180°$

$pitch = 90°$

$yaw = 90°$ (3.25)

$t_x = 2$

$t_y = 2$

$t_z = 0$

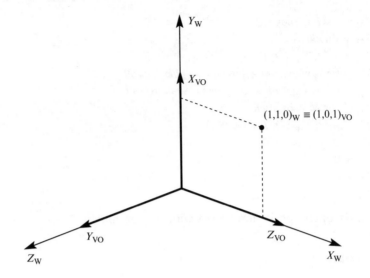

Figure 3.9   If the VO has been subjected to *roll* = 0°, *pitch* = 90° and *yaw* = 90°, using *XYZ* Euler angles, then the VO's frame of reference is as shown. Consequently, a point (1,1,0) in the virtual world is (1,0,1) for the VO's frame of reference.

Substituting these conditions in (3.22) produces:

$$\begin{bmatrix} x' \\ y' \\ z' \\ 1 \end{bmatrix} = \begin{bmatrix} 0 & -1 & 0 & 2 \\ 0 & 0 & 1 & 0 \\ -1 & 0 & 0 & 2 \\ 0 & 0 & 0 & 1 \end{bmatrix} \begin{bmatrix} x \\ y \\ z \\ 1 \end{bmatrix} \tag{3.26}$$

Substituting the coordinates (1,1,0) for (*x*,*y*,*z*) in (3.26) produces (1,0,1) for (*x'*,*y'*,*z'*) for the VO, which can be confirmed from Figure 3.10.

3.2.4   Quaternions

Quaternions provide a useful mechanism for describing rotations about some arbitrary axis, and were developed by Sir William Rowan Hamilton in the mid nineteenth century. Originally, he was looking for a way to rotate a 3D vector by multiplying it by another. However, it took 15 years of toil before he stumbled upon the idea of using a 4D notation – hence the name 'quaternion' (Hamilton, 1969).

A quaternion can also be used to describe the orientation of the VO relative to the VE's frame of reference. In order to develop the equation that performs this transformation we will have to understand the action of quaternions in the context of rotations.

A quaternion **q** is a quadruple of real numbers and can be defined as:

$$\mathbf{q} = [s, \mathbf{v}] \tag{3.27}$$

where s is a scalar and $\mathbf{v}$ is a 3D vector. If we express the vector $\mathbf{v}$ in terms of its components, we have:

$$\mathbf{q} = [s + x\mathbf{i} + y\mathbf{j} + z\mathbf{k}] \tag{3.28}$$

where s, x, y and z are real numbers.

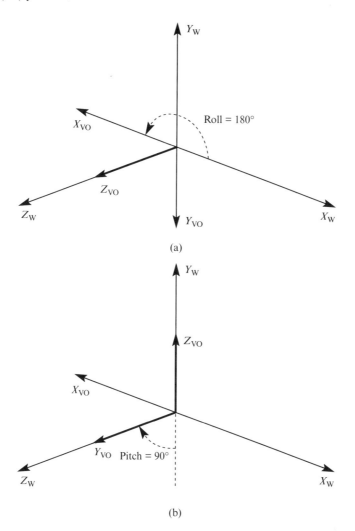

(a)

(b)

Figure 3.10 (a) The frame of reference is first subjected to a roll of 180°. (b) The frame of reference is then subjected to a pitch of 90° relative to the last orientation. (c) The frame of reference is then subjected to a yaw relative to the last orientation. (d) The frame of reference is then subjected to a translation of (2,2,0) relative to the world's coordinate system.

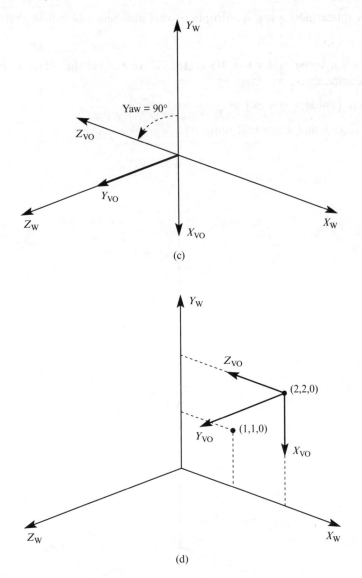

Figure 3.10 (continued)

Two quaternions are equal if, and only if, their corresponding terms are equal. Furthermore, as with normal vectors, they can be added and subtracted as follows:

$$\mathbf{q}_1 \pm \mathbf{q}_2 = \left[(s_1 \pm s_2) + (x_1 \pm x_2)\mathbf{i} + (y_1 \pm y_2)\mathbf{j} + (z_1 \pm z_2)\mathbf{k} \right] \qquad \textbf{(3.29)}$$

The following rules must be used when multiplying quaternions:

$$i^2 = j^2 = k^2 = -1$$

$$ij = k \qquad jk = i \qquad ki = j \tag{3.30}$$

$$ji = -k \qquad kj = -i \qquad ik = -j$$

Therefore, given two quaternions q_1 and q_2:

$$q_1 = [s_1, v_1] = [s_1 + x_1 i + y_1 j + z_1 k] \tag{3.31}$$

$$q_2 = [s_2, v_2] = [s_2 + x_2 i + y_2 j + z_2 k] \tag{3.32}$$

the product $q_1 q_2$ is given by:

$$q_1 q_2 = [(s_1 s_2 - x_1 x_2 - y_1 y_2 - z_1 z_2) + (s_1 x_2 + s_2 x_1 + y_1 z_2 - y_2 z_1)i$$
$$+ (s_1 y_2 + s_2 y_1 + z_1 x_2 - z_2 x_1)j + (s_1 z_2 + s_2 z_1 + x_1 y_2 - x_2 y_1)k] \tag{3.33}$$

(3.33) can be rewritten using the dot and cross product notation:

$$q_1 q_2 = [(s_1 s_2 - v_1 \cdot v_2), s_1 v_2 + s_2 v_1 + v_1 \times v_2] \tag{3.34}$$

As the cross-product operation is noncommutative, quaternion multiplication is also noncommutative.

For any quaternion q:

$$q = [s + xi + yj + zk] \tag{3.35}$$

its inverse q^{-1} is given by:

$$q^{-1} = \frac{[s - xi - yj - zk]}{|q|^2} \tag{3.36}$$

where $|q|$ is the magnitude or modulus of q and is given by:

$$|q| = \sqrt{s^2 + x^2 + y^2 + z^2} \tag{3.37}$$

Furthermore, it can be shown that:

$$qq^{-1} = q^{-1}q = [1 + 0i + 0j + 0k] = 1 \tag{3.38}$$

Any position vector can be represented as a quaternion with a zero scalar term. For example, a point $P(x,y,z)$ is represented in quaternion form by:

$$P = [0 + xi + yj + zk] \tag{3.39}$$

This form is used for rotating individual vertices about an axis.

Returning to the original application for quaternions, that is, to rotate vectors, let us consider how this is achieved. It can be shown that a position vector u can be rotated about an axis by some angle using the following operation:

$$u' = quq^{-1} \tag{3.40}$$

where the axis and angle of rotation are encoded within the unit quaternion q, whose modulus is 1, and u' is the rotated vector. For example, say we needed to rotate a vector through an angle θ about an axis defined by u. The quaternion for achieving this is given by:

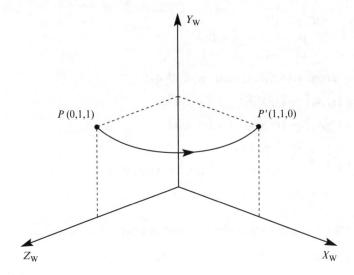

Figure 3.11 Rotating $P(0,1,1)$ through a yaw angle of 90° transforms it into $P'(1,1,0)$.

$$\mathbf{q} = [\cos \theta/2, \; \sin \theta/2 \, \mathbf{u}] \tag{3.41}$$

where $\mathbf{u}$ is a unit vector.

A simple application of this notation is found in roll, pitch and yaw rotations. For instance, a roll rotation about the z-axis is given by the quaternion:

$$\mathbf{q}_{roll} = [\cos \theta/2, \; \sin \theta/2 [0,0,1]] \tag{3.42}$$

while a pitch rotation about the x-axis is given by:

$$\mathbf{q}_{pitch} = [\cos \theta/2, \; \sin \theta/2 [1,0,0]] \tag{3.43}$$

and a yaw rotation about the y-axis is given by:

$$\mathbf{q}_{yaw} = [\cos \theta/2, \; \sin \theta/2 [0,1,0]] \tag{3.44}$$

where θ is the angle of rotation.

Let us apply these quaternions in an example to verify their action. Consider the point $P(0,1,1)$ which is to be rotated about the vertical y-axis by 90°, as shown in Figure 3.11. From this figure we can see that the rotated point P' has the coordinates $(1,1,0)$.

As the point P can be represented by a position vector $\mathbf{P}$, it can be rotated by evaluating the quaternion $\mathbf{P}'$:

$$\mathbf{P}' = \mathbf{q}\mathbf{P}\mathbf{q}^{-1} \tag{3.45}$$

where the vector component of $\mathbf{P}'$ will store the rotated coordinates.

The quaternion $\mathbf{q}$ is given by:

$$\mathbf{q} = [\cos 90°/2, \; \sin 90°/2 [0,1,0]] \tag{3.46}$$
$$= [\cos 45°, \; [0, \sin 45°, 0]] \tag{3.47}$$

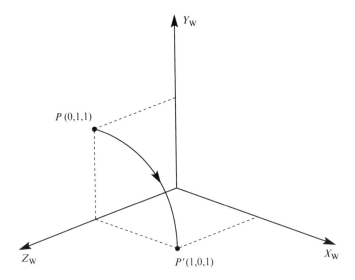

Figure 3.12   Rotating $P(0,1,1)$ through a roll angle of $-90°$ transforms it into $P'(1,0,1)$.

and the inverse quaternion $\mathbf{q}^{-1}$ is given by:

$$\mathbf{q}^{-1} = \frac{[\cos 90°/2, \ - \sin 90°/2 [0,1,0]]}{|\mathbf{q}|^2} \tag{3.48}$$

As unit quaternions are being used, the denominator of (3.48) can be ignored as it equals unity. Therefore, this simplifies to:

$$\mathbf{q}^{-1} = [\cos 45°, \ [0,-\sin 45°,0]] \tag{3.49}$$

If we evaluate $\mathbf{q}\mathbf{P}\mathbf{q}^{-1}$ in two stages, we have:

- Stage 1

$$\mathbf{q}\mathbf{P} = [\cos 45°, \ [0,\sin 45°,0]] \, [0,[0,1,1]] \tag{3.50}$$
$$= [-\sin 45°, \ [\sin 45°, \cos 45°, \cos 45°]] \tag{3.51}$$

- Stage 2

$$\mathbf{q}\mathbf{P}\mathbf{q}^{-1} = [-\sin 45°, \ [\sin 45°, \cos 45°, \cos 45°]] \, [\cos 45°, \ [0,-\sin 45°,0]] \tag{3.52}$$
$$= [0,[\sin 90°, \ 1, \ \cos 90°]] \tag{3.53}$$
$$\mathbf{P}' = [0,[1,1,0]] \tag{3.54}$$

and the vector component of $\mathbf{P}'$ confirms that P is indeed rotated to $(1,1,0)$.

We will evaluate one more example before continuing. Consider a roll rotation about the x-axis as illustrated in Figure 3.12. The original point has coordinates $(0,1,1)$ and is to be rolled through an angle of $-90°$. From the figure we see that this should finish at $(1,0,1)$.

This time the quaternion $\mathbf{q}$ is defined by:

$$\mathbf{q} = [\cos -90°/2, \sin -90°/2[0,0,1]] \tag{3.55}$$

and the point to be rotated in quaternion form is $\mathbf{P} = [0,[0,1,1]]$. Evaluating this in two stages we have:

- Stage 1

$$\begin{aligned}\mathbf{qP} &= [\cos -90°/2, [0,0,\sin -90°/2]] [0,[0,1,1]] \tag{3.56}\\ &= [-\sin -45°, [-\sin -45°, \cos -45°, \cos -45°]] \tag{3.57}\end{aligned}$$

- Stage 2

$$\begin{aligned}\mathbf{Pq}^{-1} &= [-\sin -45°, [-\sin -45°, \cos -45°, \cos -45°]]\\ &\quad [\cos -45°, [0,0,-\sin -45°]] \tag{3.58}\\ &= [0,[-\sin -90°, \cos -90°, 1]] \tag{3.59}\\ \mathbf{P'} &= [0,[1,0,1]] \tag{3.60}\end{aligned}$$

Once more, the vector component of $\mathbf{P'}$ confirms that P is rotated to $(1,0,1)$.

If we define three quaternions to represent the rotations of roll, pitch and yaw, then by multiplying them together we can arrive at a single quaternion representing the compound rotation. For example, if the individual quaternions are defined as:

$$\begin{aligned}\mathbf{q}_{\text{roll}} &= [\cos roll/2, \sin roll/2[0,0,1]] \tag{3.61}\\ \mathbf{q}_{\text{pitch}} &= [\cos pitch/2, \sin pitch/2[1,0,0]] \tag{3.62}\\ \mathbf{q}_{\text{yaw}} &= [\cos yaw/2, \sin yaw/2[0,1,0]] \tag{3.63}\end{aligned}$$

then they can be represented by a single quaternion $\mathbf{q}$:

$$\mathbf{q} = \mathbf{q}_{\text{yaw}}\mathbf{q}_{\text{pitch}}\mathbf{q}_{\text{roll}} = [s + x\mathbf{i} + y\mathbf{j} + z\mathbf{k}] \tag{3.64}$$

where:

$$\begin{aligned}s &= \cos yaw/2 \cos pitch/2 \cos roll/2 + \sin yaw/2 \sin pitch/2 \sin roll/2\\ x &= \cos yaw/2 \sin pitch/2 \cos roll/2 + \sin yaw/2 \cos pitch/2 \sin roll/2\\ y &= \sin yaw/2 \cos pitch/2 \cos roll/2 - \cos yaw/2 \sin pitch/2 \sin roll/2\\ z &= \cos yaw/2 \cos pitch/2 \sin roll/2 - \sin yaw/2 \sin pitch/2 \cos roll/2\end{aligned} \tag{3.65}$$

This, too, can be examined for correctness by evaluating an example. For instance, given the following conditions let us derive a single quaternion $\mathbf{q}$ to represent the compound rotation:

$$roll = 90° \qquad pitch = 180° \qquad yaw = 0° \tag{3.66}$$

Therefore the values of s, x, y and z are:

$$s = 0 \qquad x = \cos 45° \qquad y = -\sin 45° \qquad z = 0 \tag{3.67}$$

and the quaternion $\mathbf{q}$ is:

$$\mathbf{q} = [0,[\cos 45°, -\sin 45°, 0]] \tag{3.68}$$

If the point $P(1,1,1)$ is subjected to this rotation, the rotated point is given by:

$$\mathbf{P'} = \mathbf{qPq}^{-1} \tag{3.69}$$

Evaluating $\mathbf{qPq}^{-1}$ in two stages:

- Stage 1

$$\mathbf{qP} = [0, [\cos 45°, -\sin 45°, 0]] [0, [1,1,1]] \tag{3.70}$$
$$= [0, [-\sin 45°, -\cos 45°, \sin 45° + \cos 45°]] \tag{3.71}$$

- Stage 2

$$\mathbf{qPq}^{-1} = [0, [-\sin 45°, -\cos 45°, \sin 45° + \cos 45°]]$$
$$[0, [-\cos 45°, \sin 45°, 0]] \tag{3.72}$$
$$\mathbf{P'} = 0, [-1, -1, -1]] \tag{3.73}$$

Therefore, the coordinates of the rotated point are $(-1, -1, -1)$ which can be confirmed by the diagrams in Figure 3.13. Notice that this compound quaternion is equivalent to XYZ fixed angles. If XYZ Euler angles were required, the quaternion sequence would have to be reversed as follows:

$$\mathbf{q} = \mathbf{q}_{\text{roll}} \mathbf{q}_{\text{pitch}} \mathbf{q}_{\text{yaw}} \tag{3.74}$$

A quaternion can also be represented as a matrix. For example, given the quaternion $[s + x\mathbf{i} + y\mathbf{j} + z\mathbf{k}]$ then the equivalent matrix is given by:

$$\begin{bmatrix} M_{11} & M_{12} & M_{13} \\ M_{21} & M_{22} & M_{23} \\ M_{31} & M_{32} & M_{33} \end{bmatrix} \tag{3.75}$$

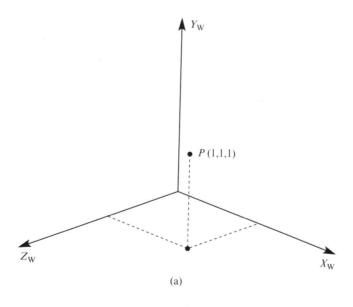

(a)

Figure 3.13 (a) Original position of $P(1,1,1)$. (b) Position of P after a 90° roll. (c) Position of P after a 90° roll followed by a 90° pitch.

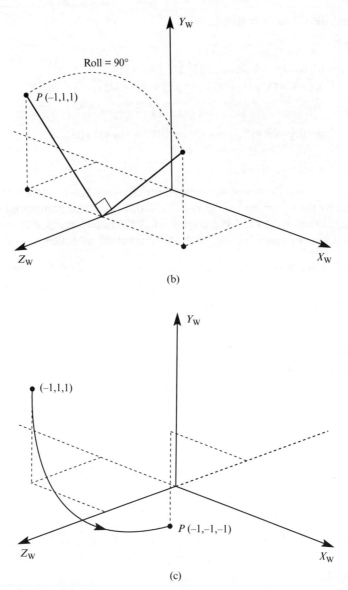

Figure 3.13 (continued)

where:

$$M_{11} = 1 - 2(y^2 + z^2)$$
$$M_{12} = 2(xy - sz)$$
$$M_{13} = 2(xz + sy)$$
$$M_{21} = 2(xy + sz)$$
$$M_{22} = 1 - 2(x^2 + z^2) \qquad \qquad \text{(3.76)}$$

$$M_{23} = 2(yz - sx)$$
$$M_{31} = 2(xz - sy)$$
$$M_{32} = 2(yz + sx)$$
$$M_{33} = 1 - 2(x^2 + y^2)$$

Substituting the values of s, x, y and z from (3.67), we have:

$$s = 0 \qquad x = \cos 45° \qquad y = -\sin 45° \qquad z = 0 \qquad\qquad (3.77)$$

Therefore, the matrix transformation is:

$$\begin{bmatrix} x' \\ y' \\ z' \end{bmatrix} = \begin{bmatrix} 0 & -1 & 0 \\ -1 & 0 & 0 \\ 0 & 0 & -1 \end{bmatrix} \begin{bmatrix} x \\ y \\ z \end{bmatrix} \qquad\qquad (3.78)$$

If we substitute $(1,1,1)$ for (x,y,z) in (3.78), the rotated point becomes $(-1,-1,-1)$, which is correct.

We have seen that a quaternion has an equivalent matrix, which when applied to a vertex, rotates it about an axis. If the orientation of the VO is in the form of a unit quaternion, the transpose of the same matrix is equivalent to rotating the frame of reference in the opposite direction. For example, if the VO is oriented with a yaw rotation of 180°, that is, looking along the negative z-axis, the orientation quaternion is $[0,[0,1,0]]$. The transpose of (3.75) is:

$$\begin{bmatrix} -1 & 0 & 0 \\ 0 & 1 & 0 \\ 0 & 0 & -1 \end{bmatrix} \qquad\qquad (3.79)$$

Any vertex (x,y,z) in the VE has coordinates (x',y',z') in the VO's frame of reference defined by:

$$\begin{bmatrix} x' \\ y' \\ z' \end{bmatrix} = \begin{bmatrix} -1 & 0 & 0 \\ 0 & 1 & 0 \\ 0 & 0 & -1 \end{bmatrix} \begin{bmatrix} x \\ y \\ z \end{bmatrix} \qquad\qquad (3.80)$$

If the vertex (x,y,z) is $(1,1,1)$, (x',y',z') becomes $(-1,1,-1)$. However, it is unlikely that the VO will be in this position, as it will normally be translated from the VE's origin. Consequently, a translation matrix will have to be introduced as used in (3.4), (3.13) and (3.20).

3.3 The perspective projection

In the last section we examined various ways of orientating the VO within the VE, and each technique provided a mechanism for developing a matrix to

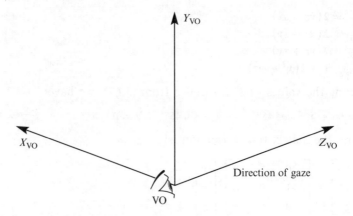

Figure 3.14   The virtual observer (VO) is located at the origin of its local frame of reference and is gazing along the positive z-axis.

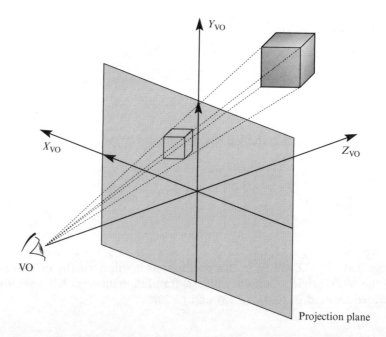

Figure 3.15   A standard computer graphics technique for creating a perspective projection is to trace lines from points on an object back to the observer, VO. A perspective image can be constructed from the points on a projection plane intersecting the lines.

change the coordinate values of points in the VE's frame of reference to the VO's frame of reference. After this operation, the virtual objects and the VO (who is effectively located at the origin of this local frame of reference, and is gazing along the positive z-axis) share a common space. This is shown in Figure 3.14.

Figure 3.15 develops this configuration further by introducing a projection plane located at the XY plane. Leonardo da Vinci also used this concept to describe the action of the perspective projection. The plane is used to capture a perspective projection of objects located within the VO's field of view. Figure 3.15 shows that a box located beyond the projection plane can be drawn in perspective upon the same plane by tracing lines from points on the object back to the VO. For any given line, its intersection point with the projection plane identifies the corresponding position of the point in a perspective projection. This process is applied to the eight vertices of the box, and by joining together relevant projected vertices with straight lines, a *wire frame* view can be captured upon the projection plane. It does not matter whether the object is behind or in front of the projection plane.

The geometry of this projection is very simple and is illustrated in Figure 3.16. Part (a) shows the plan elevation, and using the geometry of similar triangles one can see that:

$$\frac{x_p}{d} = \frac{x}{z + d} \tag{3.81}$$

therefore:

$$x_p = \frac{xd}{z + d} \tag{3.82}$$

Similarly, Figure 3.16(b) shows a side elevation where:

$$\frac{y_p}{d} = \frac{y}{z + d} \tag{3.83}$$

therefore:

$$y_p = \frac{yd}{z + d} \tag{3.84}$$

Consequently, by subjecting every vertex of an object to these transformations a perspective projection of the object can be obtained.

The action of d is one of scaling; by increasing its value, the size of the perspective image increases, and vice versa. The degree of perspective captured in the projection does not change; this depends upon the relative distance between the object and the VO. Therefore, within a virtual world the numerical values of the coordinate data are not important, as the size of the perspective image can be compensated for by a suitable value of d or by controlling the field of view.

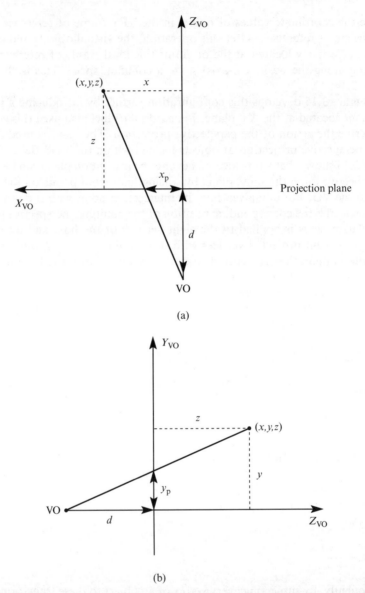

Figure 3.16 (a) A plan elevation of the geometry depicted in Figure 3.15. (b) A side elevation. The values of x_p and y_p are derived using the geometry of similar triangles.

3.3.1 Control of perspective

Whether the model data is interpreted as some massive architectural scene or as a desktop object is determined by the relative numerical value of the z-coordinates. For example, when a set of xy-coordinates are individually

Table 3.1 The field of view of a lens and its related focal length.

Focal length (mm)	Field of view
20	94°
28	75°
35	63°
50	46°
85	28.5°
135	18°
200	12°
300	8.25°

divided by relatively large z-values, the numerical results are consistently small, and little perspective is detected in the resulting image. But when the same set of xy-coordinates are individually divided by relatively small z-values, the values are much larger and have a wider numerical distribution, and the corresponding image contains dramatic perspective characteristics. This provides the opportunity of creating bizarre 3D views of VEs where perspective is outlandishly exaggerated. This would probably give rise to loss of equilibrium in a VR system and should be used with care.

3.3.2 Field of view

Owners of cameras will know that the camera's Field Of View (FOV) is controlled by the focal length of the lens. A short focal length lens, say 28 mm, provides a wide-angle view that can be useful for interiors, while a telephoto lens, say 135 mm, can be used for portraits and distant scenes. Table 3.1 lists a range of lens focal lengths and fields of view.

We also need to control the FOV captured during the perspective projection, as this should match the FOV of the final display system. For instance, imagine a car simulator based upon VR technology; it might employ three projection screens to display the forward, left and right views for the driver. The forward view could have a FOV of 60°, whereas the side views only 40°. Therefore, if the images were to appear natural to the driver, the FOV of the images should match the FOV of the projection system. The forward view of the virtual driver must capture a 60° FOV, while the side views capture only 40°. The same technique is also used in flight simulator displays and HMDs.

The FOV of the perspective image can be controlled by fixing limits for the x- and y-coordinates visible to the VO. Points inside these ranges are visible, and points outside are invisible. The visible scene is then mapped onto the final display medium. We will return to this process in Section 3.6.

3.4 Human vision

The nature of human vision is complex, and although there is a large body of knowledge describing the action of the retina and signal propagation along the optic nerve and its arrival in the visual cortex, the very nature of *seeing* still remains a mystery. Nevertheless, in spite of these gaps in our knowledge, there is sufficient understanding of the basic mechanisms associated with the action of vision to exploit various visual processes. For example, we know that objects in the outside world are projected onto the eye's retina (the photosensitive surface at the back of the eye) upside-down, and horizontally transposed. This does not seem to concern the brain as it is able to convert the images into a form that matches other mappings of the world obtained from the senses of sound, smell and touch.

3.4.1 Monocular depth cues

The estimation of depth was, and still is, vital to our survival. In earlier times of human development, the need to gauge the distance of a dangerous animal accurately was obviously very important, but it is just as relevant today when attempting to navigate a busy highway. However, it is not essential to have two eyes for estimating depth, for monocular depth cues arise in *motion parallax* and *perspective*.

Motion parallax cues
Motion parallax cues arise when there is relative motion between the observer and some environment. For instance, when looking at a cluster of objects with one eye, any slight head movement exposes depth features that remain hidden when stationary. Motion parallax is a very powerful depth cue and is exploited by flight simulator panoramic display systems. Such systems reflect into the simulator's cockpit a collimated image of a virtual airport derived from a spherical back-projection screen. When stationary, the user tends to obtain depth information from perspective features, however, when the simulated aircraft moves relative to the virtual world, the user experiences an overwhelming sensation of three-dimensional depth. Furthermore, as these display systems can totally encompass the visual field (some mirrors have a horizontal FOV of 200°), peripheral vision becomes stimulated and complements the pseudo-3D effect to create an impressive sensation of being totally immersed within a virtual world.

Perspective depth cues
When we are visually familiar with something, such as the shape of a car, a house or another person, it is possible to estimate accurately their depth through the size of the image projected upon the eye's retina. Such changes in image size are known as perspective depth cues. When we see, for example,

the shape of a person who appears to be only 5 cm high when measured at arm's length, the first supposition made by the brain is that this is not a miniature person, but a person of normal height standing about 20 metres away. Obviously, the brain can be easily fooled by staging contrived illusions that incorporate false perspective cues.

3.4.2 Binocular depth cues

Although we are totally accustomed to viewing the world through two eyes, we can still extract depth information with one eye. However, two eyes do provide us with two extra cues, one of which is very important. Binocular vision enables us to measure depth using *eye convergence* and *stereoscopic vision*. Of the two, stereoscopic vision is the more useful.

Eye convergence
Eye convergence is a measure of the angle between the eyes' optical axes when fixating upon some point. For example, when our eyes are relaxed and gazing towards some distant car on the horizon, the convergence angle is near zero. However, if the car is travelling towards us, the shape of the eyes' lenses alter to accommodate the changing distance of the object. Simultaneously, the eye muscles pull the eyes inwards in an attempt to keep the centre of visual interest positioned over the two sensitive foveae. However, there is a physical limit to the angle of eye convergence one can tolerate, and objects placed too close to the eyes appear double, and also cause eye strain.

Stereopsis and stereoscopic vision
Stereopsis describes the process of obtaining two distinct views of an object when viewed with two eyes, and stereoscopic vision describes the three-dimensional sensation of depth associated when seeing with two eyes. This is the effect we want to exploit in an HMD to create the sensation of being immersed within a VE and enhance the sensation of presence.

Corresponding points and binocular disparity
The action of the human visual system is described further in Chapter 9, where it is shown that *corresponding points* on the two retinas can explain the action of 3D stereoscopic vision. Briefly, it appears that pairs of corresponding points on the two retinas are effectively directed towards the same point in space. Consequently, when we fixate upon a point on an object, eye convergence allows us to align the eyes such that points on the object are seen at corresponding points on the two retinas. A consequence of this alignment of images is that the object does not appear three-dimensional. Those points on the object that do not have corresponding points are perceived as overlapping double images. The disparity between the two images is used by the brain to measure depth and is called *binocular disparity*.

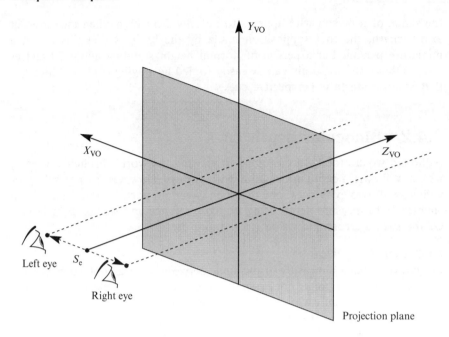

Figure 3.17 The left and right eyes are separated by a distance of S_e. In this example the eyes are gazing along lines of sight parallel with the z-axis.

3.4.3 Stereoscopic viewing

The *raison d'être* of VR systems is to interface the user to the computer-generated images as closely as possible, especially with the 3D benefits of stereoscopic vision. To achieve this, two distinct views of the VE must be derived with some degree of horizontal parallax. When these images are finally viewed by the user, a realistic stereoscopic sensation is perceived.

Stereoscopic vision helps us estimate depth, and works up to distances of approximately 30 metres – beyond this, the disparity between the images captured by the left and right eyes is insignificant. Signals that drive the left and right eyes to position the foveae over an area of interest also help the brain to locate objects in the external world.

If this degree of sophistication is to be simulated within a VR system, a mechanism is needed to track the orientation of the user's eyes, as well as the head. For the moment though, we will ignore this extended mode of visual interaction and continue with the assumption that the user is gazing at a distant horizon. The user has two parallel lines of sight aligned with the z-axis. Figure 3.17 illustrates these two lines of sight, with an interocular distance (the distance between the two pupils) of S_e, which is approximately 6.5 cm.

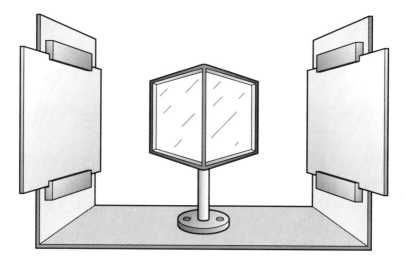

Figure 3.18 An original stereoscope.

3.4.4 The stereoscope

Stereoscopic photography was first described in 1832 by the English physicist Charles Wheatstone, who invented the stereoscope. This is a device for creating a three-dimensional image from two separate flat photographs. The photographs must contain parallax information that arises when positioning a camera at two viewpoints separated by approximately 6.5 cm. It was left to Sir David Brewster, in Scotland, to perfect the instrument, and today it is often called 'Brewster's Stereoscope'. Figure 3.18 shows an original. Readers are invited to don the red and green glasses supplied with this book and view the images in the stereographic plate section. (See Section 3.15.)

3.5 Stereo perspective projection

In Section 3.3 we covered the underlying geometry associated with deriving a perspective projection of 3D objects. This same technique can now be extended to obtain left and right stereo views of the object, which can be realized as follows.

In Figure 3.19(a) we see a pair of eyes gazing towards a box. To obtain the view from the left eye we position this eye at the origin, shift the box by a corresponding amount to the right (Figure 3.19b), and perform the projective analysis. To obtain the view from the right eye we position this eye at the origin, shift the original box by a corresponding distance to the left (Figure 3.19c), and perform a similar analysis.

Figure 3.20(a) shows a plan view of the VO's frame of reference with

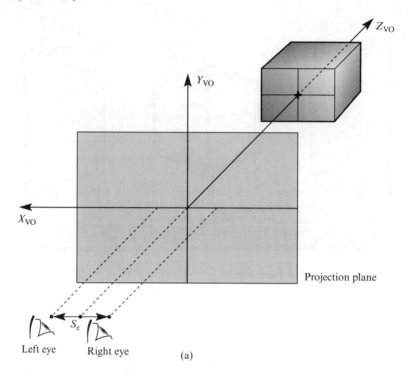

(a)

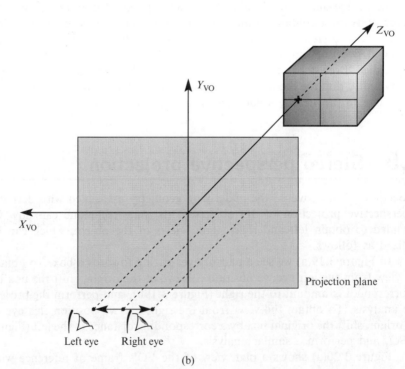

(b)

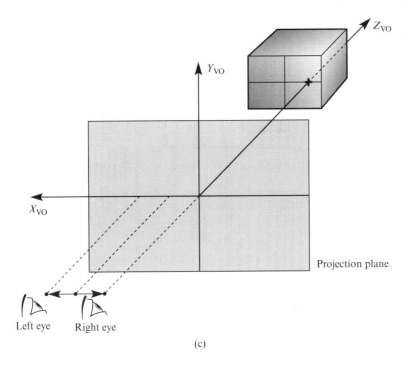

(c)

Figure 3.19 (a) The left and right eyes of the VO are gazing towards the box. (b) To compute the perspective projection of the box such that the left eye is gazing along the z-axis, the box's x-coordinates are translated by $-S_e/2$. (c) To compute the perspective projection of the box such that the right eye is gazing along the z-axis, the box's x-coordinates are translated by $S_e/2$.

the left eye positioned at the origin. The viewing plane is located d from the origin and the interocular distance is S_e. Any point on the object $P(x,y,z)$ must now be translated $-S_e/2$, and it can be observed that:

$$\frac{x_{pl}}{d} = \frac{x - \dfrac{S_e}{2}}{z + d} \tag{3.85}$$

therefore:

$$x_{pl} = \frac{d\left(x - \dfrac{S_e}{2}\right)}{z + d} \tag{3.86}$$

Similarly, Figure 3.20(b) shows a side elevation of the VO's frame of reference where it can be seen that:

$$\frac{y_{pl}}{d} = \frac{y}{z + d} \tag{3.87}$$

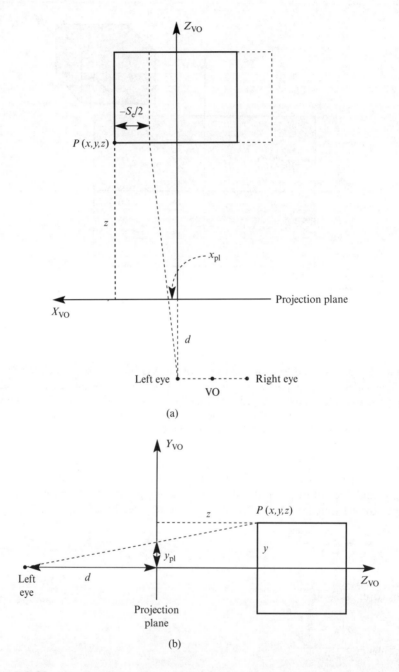

Figure 3.20 (a) A plan elevation of the geometry relating the VO's left eye, the projection plane and the box. (b) A side elevation of the geometry relating the VO's left eye, the projection plane and the box.

therefore:

$$y_{pl} = \frac{dy}{z + d} \qquad (3.88)$$

Thus the line joining $P(x,y,z)$ with the eye intersects the viewing plane at $(x_{pl}, y_{pl}, 0)$. Similarly, for the right eye, x_{pr} and y_{pr} are given by:

$$x_{pr} = \frac{d\left(x + \dfrac{S_e}{2}\right)}{z + d} \qquad (3.89)$$

$$y_{pr} = \frac{dy}{z + d} \qquad (3.90)$$

We can observe the effect of these relationships with an example. For instance, consider the case of an observer with an interocular distance of 6.5 cm looking towards a cube with 10 cm sides. The cube's centre intersects the z-axis as shown in Figure 3.21 and the nearest side of the cube is 40 cm from the observer. Substituting these values into the perspective projection formulae we obtain values for x_{pl}, y_{pl}, x_{pr} and y_{pr} as shown in Table 3.2. The distance of the projection plane d is 20 cm.

If these images are viewed using a stereoscope, it might be difficult to fuse a complete 3D image. A confused image can arise consisting of a central portion where a narrow 3D box appears, with spurious lines left and right. There is a natural reason for this that stems from the way we observe objects in the real world. For instance, with the above example, where we are looking at a 10 cm cube from a distance of 60 cm. In order to see the cube in focus, and as a single fused image, we must focus and allow both eyes to fixate upon the cube by adjusting their convergence angle – then we obtain a natural 3D view of the cube.

However, our computer model does not include any convergence angle. It assumes that the two eyes are gazing at infinity, and if we try looking at our cube – by fixating upon some point in the distance – we, too, will see two overlapping views. Ideally, the geometric model used for computing the stereo pair requires to know the fixating point, then it can rotate the virtual eyes and their respective projection planes to mimic convergence.

A compromise is to keep the above geometric model with parallel lines of sight, and to simulate convergence by causing the images to overlap in the HMD. To achieve this, the display may employ diverging or converging optics, which will be discussed in Chapter 10. This also implies that the perceived 3D view of the VE will not possess the same level of stereoscopic realism we associate with real-world images. Furthermore, the term 'immersion' must be interpreted rather loosely, as it does not mean that the virtual images derived from HMDs can ever replace the sensation of seeing as we know it.

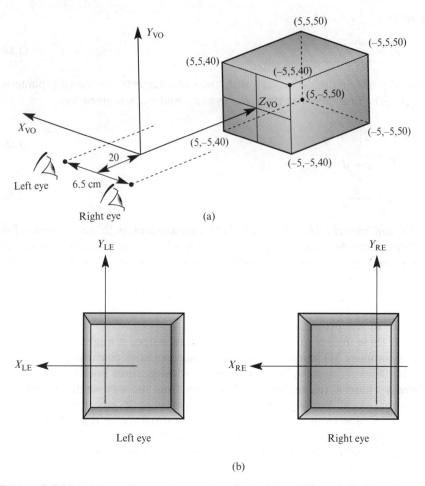

(a)

(b)

Figure 3.21 (a) The position of the VO's eyes relative to the box. (b) The approximate views seen by the left and right eyes. Note that the axes are for the left and right eyes.

Table 3.2 The first three columns show the coordinates of a cube's vertices. The next two columns identify the perspective projected points for the left eye. The last two columns identify the perspective projected points for the right eye. The two images are shown in Figure 3.21.

x	y	z	x_{pl}	y_{pl}	x_{pr}	y_{pr}
5	5	40	0.58	1.67	2.75	1.67
5	−5	40	0.58	−1.67	2.75	−1.67
−5	5	40	−2.75	1.67	−0.58	1.67
−5	−5	40	−2.75	−1.67	−0.58	−1.67
5	5	50	0.5	1.43	2.36	1.43
5	−5	50	0.5	−1.43	2.36	−1.43
−5	5	50	−2.36	1.43	−0.5	1.43
−5	−5	50	−2.36	−1.43	−0.5	−1.43

3.6 3D clipping

As described earlier, a perspective projection of an object is captured on a projection plane by tracing straight lines from any point on the object to the observer. The line's intersection with the plane identifies the projected point. Obviously, this procedure is valid only for objects within the observer's field of view, therefore any objects behind, above, below, to the left or to the right of the observer must be discarded. Unfortunately, there will be many occasions when part of an object is visible and the rest is invisible, which implies that every object must be trimmed or *clipped* against some visible viewing envelope or volume. Moreover, this 3D clipping must be applied separately for the left and right eyes.

3D clipping algorithms are a fundamental feature of computer graphics systems, and are implemented in hardware in many graphics workstations. Consequently, they will be described here only at a superficial level.

Figure 3.22(a) illustrates the viewing volumes for the left and right eyes. Their pyramid shape is dictated by the rectangular shape of display screens. Figure 3.22(b) shows a single viewing volume for one eye, and identifies the projection plane and two boundary planes called the *near* and *far clipping planes*. These delimiting planes are also known as the *hither* and *yon planes* respectively. The same diagram also confirms that the viewing volume is a truncated pyramid, which is why it is also called the *viewing frustum*.

The action of a 3D clipping algorithm is to establish, as efficiently as possible, whether an object requires clipping or not, and various strategies have been developed to speed this process. For example, if every object has an associated rectangular bounding box that completely contains the object, and if every vertex of this box is visible, then the object must be completely visible. Similarly, if every vertex of the bounding box is invisible, so, too, is the associated object. In the other cases the object must be investigated for possible clipping.

3.6.1 Clipping algorithms

Two popular methods are the Cohen–Sutherland and Cyrus–Beck clipping algorithms. The Cohen–Sutherland approach employs a 6-bit code to describe whether the end of a line is visible or not. Performing a logical AND on the codes for two end points determines whether the line is visible, invisible or partially visible. In the last case, the line is repeatedly subdivided and the visibility test applied until the entire line has been processed.

The Cyrus–Beck algorithm clips lines against a 3D convex polyhedron using a parametric definition of a 3D line. The line's parameter is then used to determine where the line potentially intersects with any of the viewing frustum's six boundary planes. The above algorithms are described in great detail in various computer graphics texts. (Foley *et al.*, 1990; Rogers, 1985; Watt, 1993).

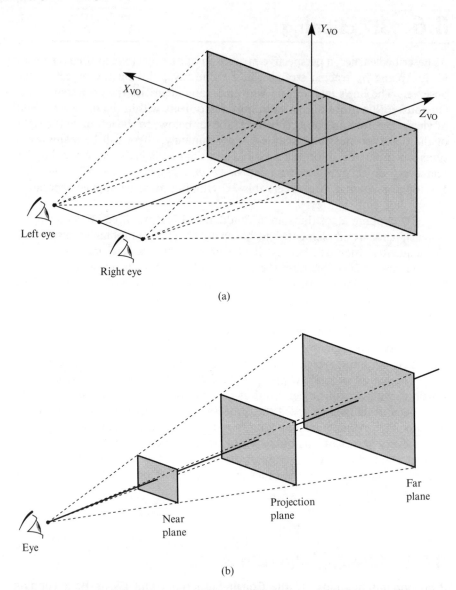

Figure 3.22 (a) The two viewing volumes associated with the left and right eyes.
(b) A single viewing frustum with the near, projection and far planes.

3.6.2 Back-face removal

As clipping is a relatively computationally expensive process, any way of
reducing the number of polygons to be clipped must be investigated, and *back-
face removal* is one such technique. Using the relative orientation of the

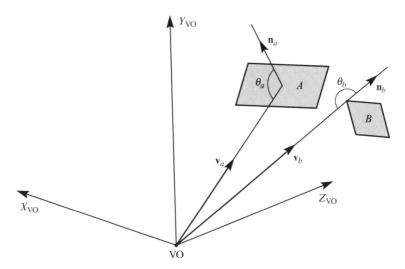

Figure 3.23 Surface A is visible to the VO as θ_a is less than 90°, whereas surface B is invisible as θ_b is greater than 90°.

polygon with the observer, polygons are divided into two classes: visible and invisible. For example, consider the situation shown in Figure 3.23, where we see two polygons labelled A and B, which are visible from only one side. Polygon A has a surface normal $\mathbf{n}_a$ with which the view vector $\mathbf{v}_a$ subtends an angle θ_a. If this angle is less than 90° the polygon is potentially visible, otherwise it is invisible, as shown with polygon B. The angle θ_a is related to the dot product of two vectors, which in this case is derived as follows:

$$\cos \theta_a = \frac{\mathbf{n}_a \cdot \mathbf{v}_a}{|\mathbf{n}_a|\,|\mathbf{v}_a|} \qquad (3.91)$$

If $\cos \theta_a$ is positive, then the surface is visible, otherwise it is invisible.

This test for visibility must be applied for both the VO's eyes, as it is possible that a surface is visible to one eye, and invisible to the other. It also implies that should the VO wander inside a virtual object constructed from a single skin of polygons, the object's inside would be invisible as all the surface normals are pointing away from the VO. As the back-face removal strategy removes these polygons, the VE user will effectively see through the object. If this effect is not required, the interiors of objects will require modelling, or the condition must be detected by the system and communicated to the user in some suitable manner. Figure 3.24 shows a model of an aeroplane in its wireframe description, back faces removed and hidden lines removed.

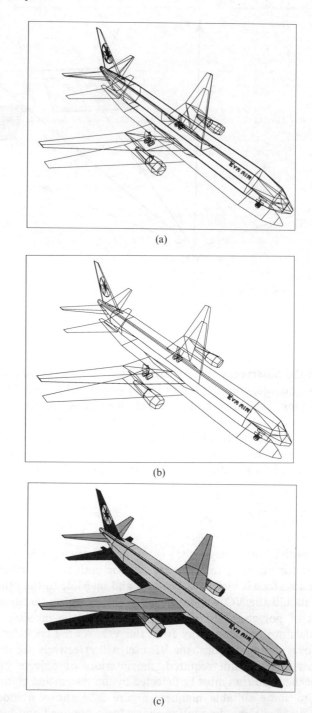

(a)

(b)

(c)

Figure 3.24 Three views of a plane: (a) wire-frame; (b) back faces removed; (c) flat shaded. (Courtesy Thomson Training and Simulation, Ltd.)

3.7 Colour theory

The sensory domains of touch, smell, sound, equilibrium and vision rely upon highly sophisticated systems for converting signals from the external world into sensations that we describe with a rich vocabulary of words. Such sensations have only a subjective existence which means that in order to analyse them we need to understand the action of various human physiological processes. In the case of sight, we need to know the action of the eye, the optic nerve and its connection to the brain. But apart from these personal mechanisms, we must also have a model of the stimuli that invoke a visual sensation.

We now accept that light is nothing more than a small 'visible' band of electromagnetic radiation with wavelengths ranging from approximately 400 nm to 700 nm. Slightly longer wavelengths are sensed as heat, and very long wavelengths are used for radar and radio communications. Slightly shorter wavelengths, such as ultra-violet rays, cause sunburn, while much shorter rays are X-rays and gamma-rays.

If we alter the wavelength of a light source, starting at 400 nm and finishing at 700 nm, we experience a range of colour sensations that comprise the visible colour spectrum. This consists of a continuous blend of hues such as violet, blue, green, yellow and red. However, the eye's retina, which captures the image via an internal lens, does not contain one type of cell that reacts to different wavelengths. It contains two types of receptors, rods and cones, which provide us with sensitive night-time vision and day-time colour vision respectively.

Rod light-receptors are sensitive to low levels of illumination and create images composed of different shades of grey. During the process of converting the incident light energy into an electrical signal, a light-sensitive pigment rhodopsin or visual purple decomposes into other chemicals. As rhodopsin contains the protein scotopsin, rod vision is also known as *scotopic vision*. Cones, on the other hand, operate in daylight, and their sensitivity to wavelength is the mechanism by which we experience the sensation of colour. It is also known as *photopic vision* because the protein photopsin is used in the electrochemical process.

The central region of the retina is called the fovea and is tightly packed with receptors, with a definite bias towards cones. Towards the retina's periphery, rods dominate which accounts for the eye's high sensitivity in these areas. The fovea's ability to give rise to a rich range of colour sensations is based upon three types of cone light-receptors that are sensitive to three significant overlapping portions of the spectrum. The sensitivity curves for these cones are shown in Figure 3.25, where the 'blue' cones peak at approximately 445 nm, the 'green' cones at 535 nm, and the 'red' cones at 570 nm. The sampling action of the cone light-receptors over different portions of the spectrum provides the brain with signals that are eventually experienced as various colour hues.

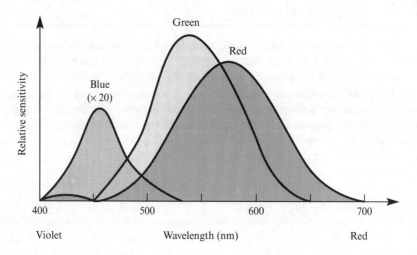

Figure 3.25 These curves show the relative sensitivity of the cone receptors in the human eye. Note that the blue response is scaled by a factor of 20.

Thomas Young and H. von Helmholtz conducted many experiments to discover the action of the eye, and demonstrated that by mixing three primary colour light sources, a wide gamut of colours are seen. An interesting discovery in these experiments was that the choice of primary colours could vary considerably without having a significant effect on the perceived colour. This was accounted for by the broad bands of wavelengths covered by the cones. Although this simple model for colour vision does not account for all the phenomena associated with colour sensations, it is one that can be implemented within computer graphics programs for creating useful images.

3.7.1 Colour spaces

A colour space is a domain where specific colours can be defined in terms of useful parameters. For example, the Young–Helmholtz model proposes that a colour consists of three additive primary components: red, green and blue. Figure 3.26 shows a spatial interpretation of this model where each axis measures the amount of red, green and blue. The diagram clearly locates familiar colours, such as yellow, cyan and magenta, and also reminds us that white light consists of equal amounts of red, green and blue light. Remember, however, that the green cone receptors are more sensitive than the red cones, and that the blue cone receptors are the weakest of the three. Consequently, 'equal amounts of red, green and blue light', means the amount of light emitted by a display pixel.

In this RGB colour space it is difficult to determine intuitively the components for salmon pink, or a desaturated yellow-orange. Nevertheless,

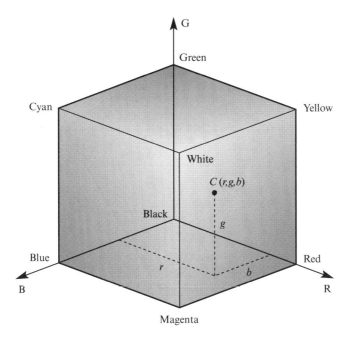

Figure 3.26 The RGB colour cube shows how any colour C can be defined in terms of three additive primary colour components r, g and b.

it supports the concept of creating images from levels of red, green and blue, which are then viewed upon some suitable tricolour screen.

Another colour space that plays a useful role at the human–computer interface is based upon the parameters of hue, saturation and value. In the HSV colour space: hue identifies the underlying colour; saturation controls the level of white light desaturating the colour; and value is a measure of the colour's darkness or lightness. Figure 3.27 shows a spatial interpretation of this space that is organized as a hexcone as derived from a diagonal projection through the RGB colour space.

In the HSV colour space a colour has hue, saturation and value. Hue is described by an angular rotation about the value axis; saturation is controlled by the orthogonal distance from the value axis, and value is a measurement along the value axis. When working with this model, one can select levels of hue, saturation and value which can then be modified to converge upon some desired colour. Many interactive interfaces will provide the user with the HSV and the RGB colour spaces, which provide the best of both worlds.

These two colour spaces may appear to be totally independent of one another, but they are closely related, and algorithms exist for converting between the two systems (Foley *et al.*, 1990; Glassner, 1990; Rogers, 1985).

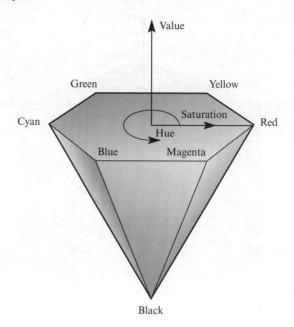

Figure 3.27 The HSV colour space describes colours using the parameters hue, saturation and value, where: hue identifies the underlying colour; saturation, the level of white light; and value, the colour's darkness or lightness.

3.7.2 Colour-based algorithms

The ability to create a full-colour image from the three additive primaries, red, green and blue, is central to the technologies of television and computer graphics. Moreover, this strategy permeates the algorithms used for rendering coloured views of a VE. Such algorithms compute three colour separations for an image, which, when projected or displayed, create a coloured image. The number of bits allocated to each primary colour controls the final number of colours displayed. When 8 bits are available for each primary, this provides an individual intensity range of 256, which ultimately results in approximately 16.8 ($256 \times 256 \times 256$) million potential colour values.

A VE can be constructed from objects assigned colours using three primary colour reflection coefficients, and light sources emitting three levels of primary colours. With the aid of various reflection models it is possible to compute the three reflected light components that eventually establish the primary intensities for a pixel. These models and algorithms are described in greater detail in Section 3.10.

3.8   Simple 3D modelling

This section takes a cursory glance at simple 3D modelling so that the following sections within this chapter can be described in the context of a complete system. Chapter 4 describes a variety of modelling techniques relevant to VE systems.

We have already covered the matrix techniques for manipulating Cartesian coordinates, but so far we have not examined how such coordinates are organized to represent some coherent object. There are many ways of constructing virtual objects, and the choice of a particular system depends very much upon realism, functionality, real-time performance, accuracy and modelling tools. These issues are discussed in Chapter 4, so for the purpose of this exercise we will only consider some of the geometric issues relevant to shading and illumination.

3.8.1   Geometric considerations

Euler's rule

Euler's rule states that for a polyhedron without holes, the number of edges is always the sum of the faces and vertices minus two:

$$\text{Edges} = \text{faces} + \text{vertices} - 2 \tag{3.92}$$

In the case of a cube, there are 12 edges, 6 faces and 8 vertices, which obviously satisfies this rule. Similarly, a four-sided pyramid has 8 edges, 5 faces and 5 vertices, which also maintains this relationship. One simple method of modelling a cube is to store the 3D coordinates of each vertex in tabular form, together with another table that identifies the 12 edges and their associated vertices. A cube is illustrated in Figure 3.28 together with its associated data tables. The *vertex table* stores the coordinates for the eight vertices, while the *edge table* identifies the 12 edges in terms of the vertex numbers in the vertex table.

If we wish to display this object, it can be shown only as 12 separate edges. It will be impossible to create a shaded view of the object as there is no information available to describe the formation of individual faces. However, this requirement is satisfied by defining the model with a vertex table and a face table – such an arrangement is shown in Figure 3.29. For example, face number 4 is identified by the vertex sequence: 5, 8, 2 and 1, and face number 6 is identified by the vertices: 1, 4, 6 and 5. Note that all of the vertex sequences have been specified taking a clockwise journey around the boundary, as viewed from the outside of the cube. Such an arrangement is often very important to rendering programs that have to compute surface normal vectors. The clockwise sense in itself is not important, as an anticlockwise sequence would work just as well, but a consistent approach to face definition is normally required.

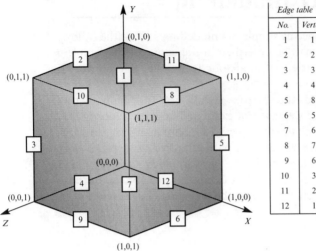

Edge table		
No.	Vertex	Vertex
1	1	2
2	2	3
3	3	4
4	4	1
5	8	5
6	5	6
7	6	7
8	7	8
9	6	4
10	3	7
11	2	8
12	1	5

Vertex table			
No.	x	y	z
1	0	0	0
2	0	1	0
3	0	1	1
4	0	0	1
5	1	0	0
6	1	0	1
7	1	1	1
8	1	1	0

Figure 3.28 The unit cube can be stored as a table of vertices and edges as shown in the tables.

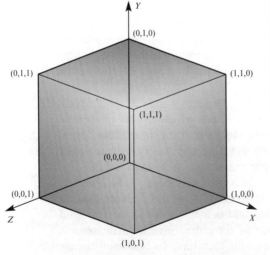

Face table				
No.	Vertices			
1	1	2	3	4
2	4	3	7	6
3	6	7	8	5
4	5	8	2	1
5	2	8	7	3
6	1	4	6	5

Vertex table			
No.	x	y	z
1	0	0	0
2	0	1	0
3	0	1	1
4	0	0	1
5	1	0	0
6	1	0	1
7	1	1	1
8	1	1	0

Figure 3.29 The last four columns of the face table identify the entries in the vertex table that belong to a specific surface.

Surface normals

To illustrate this point further, let us use the arrangement shown in Figure 3.29 to derive surface normal vectors for each face; these can be computed using the cross product of two edges. The first face contains vertices 1, 2, 3 and 4. Therefore, if we form two vectors v_1 and v_2 from the first three vertices, we have v_1 directed from vertex 1 to vertex 2, and v_2 directed from vertex 2 to vertex 3. This is shown in Figure 3.30(a). The vectors v_1 and v_2 can now be computed by subtracting the respective coordinate values:

$$v_1 = [(0-0),(1-0),(0-0)] = [0,1,0] \tag{3.93}$$
$$v_2 = [(0-0),(1-1),(1-0)] = [0,0,1] \tag{3.94}$$

and the cross product $v_1 \times v_2$ produces [1,0,0], which is a unit vector directed along the positive x-axis. This is a valid surface normal, but it is pointing to the inside of the object. A simple strategy to ensure that this normal points to the half-space defining the outside of the object is to reverse v_1 or v_2. If we reverse v_2 and perform the cross product again we have:

$$v_2 = [(0-0),(1-1),(0-1)] = [0,0,-1] \tag{3.95}$$

and the cross product $v_1 \times v_2$ produces [-1,0,0] which is now directed along the negative x-axis. If we now apply this process to the first three vertices of every face, we arrive at the normal unit vectors as shown in Figure 3.30(b).

We can now see that if polygon faces are defined in an arbitrary sequence, it will give rise to spurious surface normals that are required for lighting calculations. This could result in surfaces not being rendered, or even in shading the inside of a surface instead of its outside! Modelling software must be sensitive to such issues, especially in situations when models are imported from other systems.

Surface planarity

Another geometric consideration concerns the surface planarity of polygons forming the boundary of an object, for if a polygon is defined as a chain of arbitrary edges, it will be very easy to construct twisted surfaces. Although these surfaces do not create any problems in their storage, they cause problems when they are rendered, and also when geometric calculations are performed upon them. For example, the twisted polygon shown in Figure 3.31 provides neither a mechanism for computing a unique surface normal, nor any useful description of the surface. As this level of geometric analysis is required in rendering polygons, a twisted polygon would give rise to unpredictable graphical interpretations. Moreover, collision detection between objects and 'touch' conditions experienced by the VO would also be subject to errors because of the inconsistent model definition.

If nonplanar surfaces are an essential feature of the VE the data can be

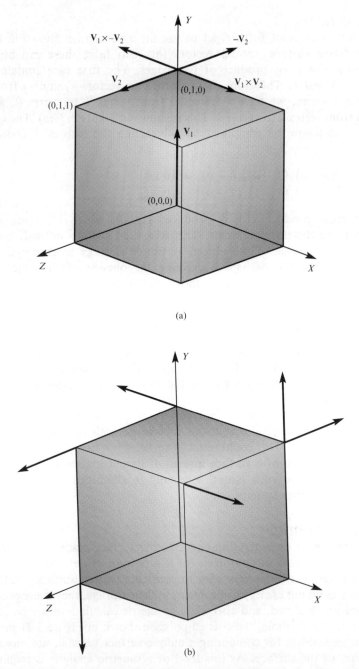

(a)

(b)

Figure 3.30   (a) The cross product of the vectors v_1 and v_2 creates a third vector pointing along the edge of the box. If one of the vectors is reversed, the third vector behaves as a surface normal. (b) These six surface normals have been derived by computing the cross product of the two vectors formed from the first two edges in a face. One vector has been reversed.

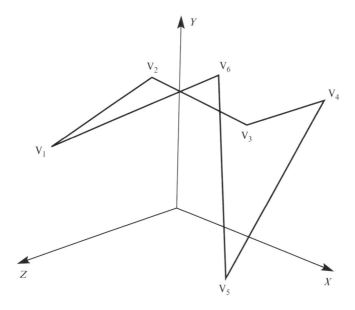

Figure 3.31 A twisted polygon formed from a chain of nonplanar vertices.

converted into a mesh of triangles – which are always planar. However, such *triangulation* techniques are capable of computing many solutions to the problem, and have to be guided by a strategy, such as keeping the triangles equilateral, as far as possible.

The simplicity of a triangle is also another point in its favour – not only is it planar, but its consistent three sides also simplify the design of data files and data structures. Furthermore, it is easily rendered, especially by hardware, and lends itself to geometric analysis.

3.8.2 Modelling tools

It was mentioned earlier that an airport environment for a flight simulator could take six months to build. The reason for this is that the final database may contain several hundred thousand surface elements and light points, together with colour, texture and transparency characteristics. Building such a database from a mixture of maps, photographs and technical drawings requires great skill. Not only must the models be accurate, but they must not exceed the rendering capacity of the real-time image generator. Currently, there is no way that a flight simulator database could include a mountain range built with a fractal definition, as such a scheme would create an unacceptably high number of polygons. Consequently, if the mountains are to appear three-dimensional, they must be created carefully with just a few dozen surfaces.

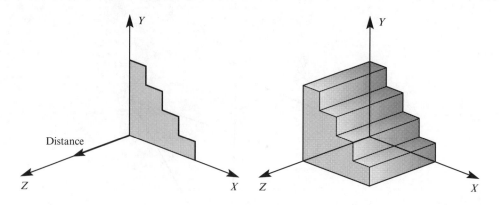

Figure 3.32   The flight of steps on the right-hand side was created by extending the cross section shown on the left-hand side.

Any ridges formed by a pair of triangles can be hidden with the judicious use of texture mapping.

Modellers who create these databases work with high-speed graphics workstations using software tools for model construction. For example, a model could be developed in 3D with the aid of side, front and plan elevations. When working in any of these views, the system automatically *knows* how to address the internal data structure and could even warn the modeller when geometric integrity was being compromised.

Extruding

One useful modelling tool enables an entire polygonal boundary representation to be created from a cross-section and a swept distance. Such an approach is illustrated in Figure 3.32, which shows how a flight of steps is developed from a simple cross-section. Obviously, the same program is capable of building a wide range of extruded models. The technique can be further enhanced by performing the extrusion in several steps, and at each step the cross-section is rotated and/or scaled.

Swept surfaces

The turning action of a lathe can be simulated to create swept surfaces. Figure 3.33 shows the same cross-section used in Figure 3.32, but this time it is rotated to develop a swept surface. The smaller the step angle, the smoother the surface, which increases the polygon count.

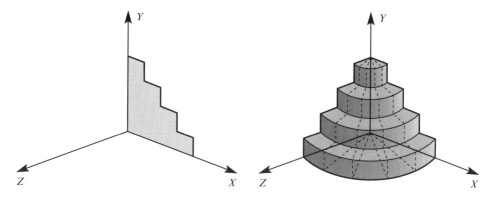

Figure 3.33   If the contour on the left-hand side is rotated in small steps, a swept surface can be formed as shown on the right-hand side.

3.9   Illumination models

The last section gave a cursory introduction to the construction of simple 3D models so that we could examine how a virtual world could be illuminated and rendered. Basically, two approaches are available to create a coloured view of a 3D scene. The first, which is not very flexible, simply assigns a fixed colour to every surface of an object. No matter how the object is viewed, its colours remain constant. The second approach attempts to simulate the interaction of light sources with coloured surfaces, which is the technique now used in most computer graphics systems.

3.9.1   Point light sources

The simplest light source to model is a point light source, as it requires only a position in space and intensity. By definition, it radiates light energy equally in all directions. The intensity of the light is generally specified in terms of the three additive primary colour components, red, green and blue, which, you will recall, are mixed in different proportions to define a required colour. There is nothing to prevent this colour and intensity being specified using the HSV colour space, for this approach enables the colour to be controlled independently of its intensity. However, whichever technique is used, the light source eventually requires a location in space (L_x, L_y, L_z) and a luminous value $(I_{red}, I_{green}, I_{blue})$.

Calculating the level of light incident on a surface is a function of the angle between the surface normal and an incident ray. If we ignore the fall-off in intensity associated with the normal propagation of light, the incident light flux is given by:

$$I_i = I_p \cos \theta \tag{3.96}$$

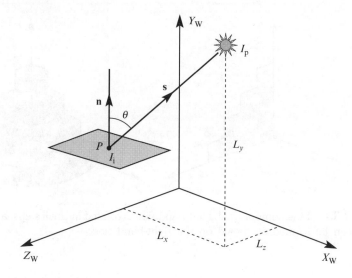

Figure 3.34   The intensity of the incident light I_i at P is proportional to $\cos \theta$.

where I_p is the intensity of the point light source, and θ is the angle subtended by the incident ray and the surface normal. This is shown in Figure 3.34. For example, given the following conditions: $P(p_x, p_y, p_z)$ is a point on a surface, $[n_1, n_2, n_3]^T$ is the surface normal $\mathbf{n}$, (L_x, L_y, L_z) is the location of the point light source and I_p is the light source intensity, then the vector $\mathbf{s}$, directed to the light source is given by:

$$\mathbf{s} = \begin{bmatrix} s_1 \\ s_2 \\ s_3 \end{bmatrix} = \begin{bmatrix} L_x - p_x \\ L_y - p_y \\ L_z - p_z \end{bmatrix} \tag{3.97}$$

and the angle θ between the two vectors $\mathbf{s}$ and $\mathbf{n}$ is found by evaluating the dot product $\mathbf{s} \cdot \mathbf{n}$:

$$\mathbf{s} \cdot \mathbf{n} = |\mathbf{s}||\mathbf{n}| \cos \theta \tag{3.98}$$

where $|\mathbf{s}|$ and $|\mathbf{n}|$ are the magnitudes of $\mathbf{s}$ and $\mathbf{n}$ respectively. Consequently, the surface intensity I_i can be computed by:

$$I_i = \frac{I_p(s_1 n_1 + s_2 n_2 + s_3 n_3)}{|\mathbf{s}||\mathbf{n}|} \tag{3.99}$$

3.9.2   Directional light source

Directional light sources are assumed to be located so far away that all of the incident light rays are parallel. This means that if we ignore the fall-off in intensity during the light's journey, the intensity of the light

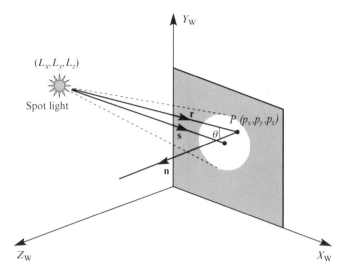

Figure 3.35 The point P is illuminated if the angle between the ray vector **r** and direction vector **s** does not exceed the half-angle of the spot light.

incident upon a surface is a function of the cosine of the angle formed with the surface normal and the original light source intensity.

3.9.3 Spot light source

A spot light source, as the name suggests, mimics the illumination characteristics of a directed beam of light with its associated spot angle. Typically it will have intensity, position, direction and angle of illumination. For example, in Figure 3.35 a point $P(p_x, p_y, p_z)$ is illuminated if the angle between the ray vector **r** and the direction vector **s** does not exceed the half-angle of the spot light. The intensity at this point can also be a function of the incident angle, or be modulated by some function controlling the intensity across the spot.

3.9.4 Ambient light

Unless we allow for light to be reflected from one surface to another, there is a very good chance that some surfaces will not receive any illumination at all. Consequently, when these surfaces are rendered, they will appear black and unnatural. In anticipation of this happening, illumination schemes allow the existence of some level of background light level called the *ambient light*. This is incorporated as a constant within the lighting calculations, and is set to some convenient value; typically it accounts for 20–25% of the total illumination.

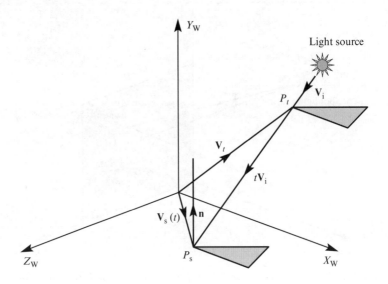

Figure 3.36 The shadow triangle on the ground plane is computed by projecting lines through the vertices of the illuminated triangle.

3.9.5 Shadows

Shadow generation is still regarded as a luxury in stop-frame computer animation, simply because of the computational overhead. Therefore, it will be some time before we find realistic shadows in real-time image generation. Some false shadows, however, can be introduced into certain scenes as shadow polygons that are built into the database. In some cases they travel over a surface in unison with the movements of objects, but they do not change their shape with any changes in surface geometry. This form of visual deception has been a vital feature of video games and flight simulators, where they provide a useful visual cue for locating the relative position of an object to the ground plane.

There are several approaches to shadow generation, including shadow volumes (Crow, 1977), shadow z-buffer (Williams, 1978), shadow polygons (Appel, 1968), radiosity (Goral *et al.*, 1984), ray tracing (Whitted, 1980) and light volumes (Max, 1986). Although very realistic images can be produced using these algorithms, they are still difficult to implement in real time. If, however, we are willing to compromise realism for real-time working, then shadows can be introduced by restricting them to the ground plane and vertical walls.

Anticipating that the final equations will be simplified, let us develop a general solution for a shadow projected onto the ground plane. Figure 3.36 shows a scenario where a triangle is facing the source of illumination defined by the unit vector $\mathbf{V}_i$. For a parallel light source, $\mathbf{V}_i$ will be constant for each vertex on the triangle. For a point light source, $\mathbf{V}_i$ must be computed for each vertex.

If P_t is a vertex on the triangle and P_s is the equivalent shadow vertex, the position vector $\mathbf{V}_s(t)$ for P_s is given by:

$$\mathbf{V}_s(t) = \mathbf{V}_t + t\mathbf{V}_i \qquad \text{where } t > 0 \tag{3.100}$$

If the unit surface normal vector $\mathbf{n} = [A,B,C]^T$ the shadow plane equation is:

$$Ax_s + By_s + Cz_s = 0 \tag{3.101}$$

Therefore:

$$A(x_t + tx_i) + B(y_t + ty_i) + C(z_t + tz_i) = 0 \tag{3.102}$$

Solving for t:

$$t = \frac{Ax_t + By_t + Cz_t}{Ax_i + By_i + Cz_i} = -\frac{\mathbf{n} \cdot \mathbf{V}_t}{\mathbf{n} \cdot \mathbf{V}_i} \tag{3.103}$$

For the ground plane $\mathbf{n} = [0,1,0]^T$, therefore t simplifies to:

$$t = \frac{y_t}{y_i} \tag{3.104}$$

Therefore:

$$\mathbf{V}_s = \mathbf{V}_t - \frac{y_t}{y_i}\mathbf{V}_i \tag{3.105}$$

This equation reminds us that a shadow will not be cast if $\mathbf{n} \cdot \mathbf{V}_i < 0$. It also confirms that when the light source is parallel and overhead, $y_i = -1$ and $t = y_t$.

Any triangle facing the source of illumination will create a shadow triangle that can be rendered with a suitable colour.

To create shadows on vertical walls, the associated surface normal is modified in the above equations. For example, to compute shadows on the YZ-plane, the surface normal $\mathbf{n} = [1,0,0]^T$ which redefines t as:

$$t = \frac{x_t}{x_i} \tag{3.106}$$

The major drawback with this technique is that it reduces the number of objects that can be rendered in any frame. However, the extra cues might make it worth while. Recent 3D video games have demonstrated that real-time shadows are possible if we make the above restrictions.

3.9.6 Transparency

Transparency is an important attribute that needs to be incorporated within our models, otherwise it will be impossible to simulate the effects of glass and other transparent media. Normally it is implemented by associating a transparency coefficient with a polygon or surface patch that varies between zero and one. The renderer uses this parameter to compute the transmitted light level of illuminated surfaces behind the transparent surface. Apart from enabling glass to be modelled, variable transparency is used by IGs to fade one model description out and another in. This avoids the sudden removal of one model description and the substitution of another.

3.9.7   Increasing realism

There is always room for adding extra realism into synthetic image generation; however, when working in a real-time domain the few milliseconds that are available to render an image restrict such luxuries. Nevertheless, it is worth mentioning them, as one day they will become feasible.

Multiple light sources

So far we have considered the existence of only one light source. There is, however, nothing to stop the VE being illuminated by dozens of different light sources, that is, if we have the computing power to evaluate the calculations in real time. But including several light sources introduces the problem of light-balancing, which prevents some surfaces from being over illuminated, and others remaining in shadow. Furthermore, as light sources may be interactively moved within the VE, the more light sources there are, the greater the chance that unbalanced lighting will result.

Intensity fall-off with distance

When we observe outdoor scenes illuminated by the sun, or indoor environments illuminated by internal light sources and via windows, we are considering very complex illumination models. Such scenarios involve multiple diffuse reflections, specular reflections, colour bleeding, multiple shadowing and frequency absorption. Consequently, we must not be surprised that some physical laws require slight modification when implemented within a VE. One such law concerns the fall-off in intensity with distance; where the intensity of light radiation falls off as a function of the inverse square of the propagation distance. However, simple tests have shown that good results can be obtained by dividing the light source intensity by $(d + k)$, where d is the distance of the VO from the illuminated surface, and k is some system-defined constant.

An alternative approach involves a decay function based upon empirical observation and is defined as:

$$F(d) = R^d \tag{3.107}$$

where d is the distance from the light source to the surface, and R is a decay parameter. For example, if at 2 units from a light source the intensity is attenuated by 0.5, then R needs to be set accordingly. R is computed as follows:

$$R = atten^{(1/d)} \tag{3.108}$$

This ensures that when $d = 2$, and $atten = 0.5$, then $R = 0.707$; therefore,

$F(2) = 0.5$. When $d = 3$, $F(3) = 0.353$. Thus specific levels of attenuation can be associated with any light source to create a desired effect.

Negative light

Although the above virtual light sources are used to accumulate light levels incident upon a surface, there is nothing to prevent reversing the sign of some of the individual intensities. This effectively creates a 'shadow source', as the affected area has light subtracted away from it.

X-ray sources

X-rays can be used in the real world to penetrate the surface of objects and reveal the contents of their interiors. Similarly, the action of an X-ray source can be simulated by using a spot light source that effectively allows the user to see through objects. This can be implemented by first identifying those surfaces intersected by the 'X-ray' source, and then altering their transparency attribute. The degree of transparency can be controlled by the intensity of the source. Performing this in real time is no mean task, and requires high-performance image generators.

3.10 Reflection models

Now that we have a variety of ways of illuminating the VE, we need similar models for describing the reflective behaviour of this imaginary light. Considerable research effort has gone into developing these models, some even take into account the microfacets associated with different surfaces, and their orientation (Cook and Torrance, 1982; Glassner, 1989; Rogers, 1985; Torrance and Sparrow, 1967). Unfortunately, such schemes are beyond the scope of this text.

Taking a simplistic approach to light reflection, we can express the behaviour of light with diffuse and specular reflection. Light reflected by a diffuse surface is radiated equally in all directions and is therefore independent of the observer's position, while light reflected by a polished surface creates a specular highlight for certain viewpoints.

3.10.1 Diffuse reflection

Rough surfaces such as carpets, textiles and some papers exhibit diffuse reflection properties, but their internal structure can also give rise to surface gloss effects. Simulating such effects requires a knowledge of how light is influenced by the directional characteristics of materials in order that a distribution function can be derived. However, to compute the underlying diffuse component, all that we need to know is the reflection coefficient of the surface, K_d, the intensity of the light source I_i, and the cosine of the angle subtended by the incident light and the surface normal. This arrangement is shown in

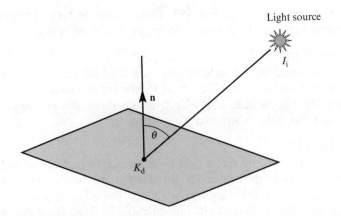

Figure 3.37   This action of diffuse relfection is a function of the light source intensity I_i, $\cos \theta$ and the reflection coefficient of the surface K_d.

Figure 3.37. The diffuse term I_d for one light source is expressed as:

$$I_d = I_i K_d \cos \theta \tag{3.109}$$

The $\cos \theta$ term is found by computing the dot product of the surface normal and the light ray vector. In general, there will be three such expressions associated with the red, green and blue components of the light model.

3.10.2   Specular reflection

Smooth or polished surfaces can be simulated by combining a diffuse reflection with a specular highlight. This extra spot of light represents the reflection of the light source into the observer's field of view, and is a powerful visual cue for distinguishing between matte and polished surfaces. The size of the highlight can be used to describe a range of surfaces from satin-type effects to polished lacquered finishes.

As the visibility of the highlight depends upon the relative position of the observer to a surface, this geometry must be incorporated within our calculations, and is shown in Figure 3.38. Here we see that when an incident ray represented by **L** is reflected, the angle of reflection equals the angle of incidence θ. However, if the observer is displaced by an angle ϕ, the intensity of the specular highlight will be attenuated accordingly. A useful subterfuge is to modulate the intensity by a $\cos^g \phi$ term, where g is a gloss parameter. The complete expression is:

$$I_s = I_i K_s \cos^g \phi \tag{3.110}$$

where I_i is the light source intensity, K_s is a colour-independent specular coefficient, ϕ is the error angle, and g is the gloss parameter.

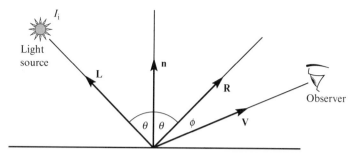

Figure 3.38 Specular reflections are based upon this geometry where ϕ represents the angle the observer is offset from the reflected ray **R**.

3.10.3 The complete reflection expression

This simple reflection model has three elements, ambient, diffuse and specular, for each of which there will be a red, green and blue component. For one light source this can be summarized as:

$$I = I_{ambient} + \left[I_{diffuse} + I_{specular} \right] \tag{3.111}$$

$$I = I_a K_a + \left[I_i K_d \left(\mathbf{L} \cdot \mathbf{n} \right) + I_i K_s \cos^g \phi \right] \tag{3.112}$$

where the term in brackets has to be computed for every light source.

3.11 Shading algorithms

Now that we have established how to construct simple 3D models from polygons, and how to view them from an arbitrary location in the VE, we can consider how the perspective projection of an object can be rendered using the illumination models outlined earlier. The renderer must form a coloured pixel-based image from the geometric database of the VE using the illumination models, which may sound a trivial exercise, but is quite complex.

Commercial computer animation systems have very sophisticated renderers to create the images that eventually form an animated sequence. Such systems do not work in real time. Typically, rendering times vary between several seconds to fractions of hours, which means that an animated sequence could require many hours of computer time. The reasons for these long rendering times are the large databases which have to be manipulated, the complex model descriptions and the level of realism in the image.

A large database may include several thousand objects, each of which contains dozens of triangles. Not all of these elements may be visible, but the renderer may still have to access them all to identify those that are seen. The geometric descriptions may not be explicit, but perhaps are computed by some procedure. They may even be derived from some parametric surface patch description that is being modified at each frame of the animation. Consequently, for each frame, the patches may be converted into a mesh of triangles that are then rendered. Such computer processing makes real-time operation difficult on current workstations.

The pixel nature of the final image also creates problems if attempting to display very small features or straight edges. Certain small features may be smaller than the spatial resolution of a pixel and will result in some form of visual approximation. An object containing straight edges will also cause problems when it is converted into a pixel description, and will result in jagged pixel edges. Such sampling artefacts are described as *aliasing*. However, they can be minimized by implementing various anti-aliasing algorithms, which are generally computationally expensive. Some modern image generators do implement anti-aliasing strategies in hardware and can therefore work in real time.

The renderer must be capable of creating an accurate image, free from holes or other blemishes, no matter what configuration of objects it is given. This is asking a lot of any program, and even the very best commercial systems must be expected to 'crash' under some conditions.

In a VR system, where the user is interactively modifying the graphic database, there are some excellent opportunities to destroy its geometric integrity. For instance, an object could be pushed inside another, which may not be expected by the renderer. A light source could be moved such that it coincides with a vertex of an object, which could cause havoc in lighting calculations as it creates null vectors. Consequently, the system software supporting the VE must ensure that the user cannot introduce inconsistencies into the database that could eventually 'surprise' the renderer.

In spite of all the problems associated with rendering, it is possible to create some truly amazing realistic scenes. For the moment, however, such levels of realism are the realm of stop-frame animation and are not found on VR systems. Therefore, we will continue this section and explore the rendering process from the standpoint of real-time VR systems.

3.11.1 The frame store

In order to simplify the description of these shading algorithms, we will assume the existence of a memory device called a frame store that will store the image for display purposes. Normally, this store is double-buffered, which allows the display of one frame while another is being rendered. The spatial resolution of the frame store will match that of the display device, and we will further assume that each additive primary colour is encoded to a resolution of 8 bits. In practice, this will vary from system to system.

3.11.2 Mapping to the display device

The perspective projection creates a planar coordinate description of the scene formed upon the projection plane. This can be expressed as fractional values

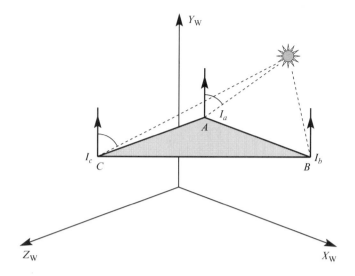

Figure 3.39 Gouraud shading computes the light intensities at the vertices A, B and C and then linearly interpolates them across the surface.

of the screen space, which enables the projection to be mapped to different resolution displays. For instance, let the perspective domain be bounded by the rectangular limits $(0,0)$ to $(1,1)$, and the screen space domain be bounded by pixel addresses ranging from $(0,0)$ to $(colmax, rowmax)$. A point (x_{persp}, y_{persp}) is mapped into (x_{pixel}, y_{pixel}) as follows:

$$x_{pixel} = colmax\ x_{persp} \tag{3.113}$$
$$y_{pixel} = rowmax\ y_{persp} \tag{3.114}$$

This assumes that the aspect ratio of the projection matches that of the display device. If this were not so, the image would appear distorted.

The position of the VO's line of sight is expected to be located at the centre of the display, however this is not always the case. Some HMDs do not have their optical centres aligned with the centre pixel, which means that a single eye may see more to the right than it does to the left. This, unfortunately, can give rise to distortion at the peripheral portions of the image.

3.11.3 Gouraud shading

Flat shading

Gouraud shading (Gouraud, 1971) interpolates light intensities across a polygon using key values taken at its vertices. For example, Figure 3.39 shows three vertices $A(x_a, y_a)$, $B(x_b, y_b)$ and $C(x_c, y_c)$, which have intensities of I_a, I_b and I_c respectively.

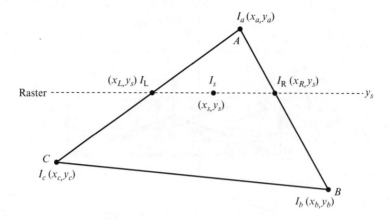

Figure 3.40   Gouraud shading shades a polygon by linearly interpolating light intensities from key points on the surface.

The intensity I_s at a point (x_s, y_s) on the raster y_s is given by the expression:

$$I_s = \frac{I_L(x_R - x_s) + I_R(x_s - x_L)}{x_R - x_L} \tag{3.115}$$

Figure 3.40 shows this diagrammatically. This linear interpolation process is performed for the red, green and blue colour components.

Smooth shading

The above algorithm creates a faceted view of an object. However, if the normals used in the original illumination calculations are replaced by *averaged normals*, then a smooth shading effect results. The nature of these average normals can be understood with reference to Figure 3.41. It can be seen that the three surface normals associated with their respective surfaces can be averaged into a single normal that can be used for the lighting calculation. Any edge separating two polygons will now have two average normals associated with it. This will control the colour intensities along the edge, with the result that the edge pixels become common to both polygons. If the orientation of these polygons is not too great, the eye will have difficulty in locating the join. Unfortunately, the eye possesses image-enhancing characteristics that accentuate spatial changes in intensity and give rise to a banding effect called *Mach bands*.

3.11.4   Phong shading

To compute specular reflections we require access to a surface normal at the point of incidence, which requires substantial computation if undertaken in the 3D object space. Phong's approach (Phong, 1973) developed Gouraud's

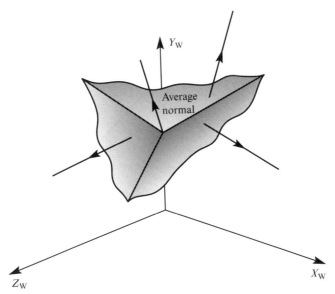

Figure 3.41 The three separate surface normals can be replaced by an average normal at the common vertex; this can then be used for smooth shading.

linear interpolation algorithm by interpolating surface normals rather than light intensities.

From Figure 3.42 we can see that the triangle ABC has three average normals $\mathbf{n}_a$, $\mathbf{n}_b$ and $\mathbf{n}_c$. If these are now linearly interpolated in image space, we can compute a surface normal for any pixel associated with the surface. This is shown in Figure 3.43, where for any raster y_s we can derive a left-hand normal $\mathbf{n}_L$, and a right-hand normal $\mathbf{n}_R$. These can be interpolated to derive a normal $\mathbf{n}_s$ for a pixel (x_s, y_s). The normals $\mathbf{n}_L$ and $\mathbf{n}_R$ are given by:

$$\mathbf{n}_L = \frac{\mathbf{n}_a(y_s - y_c) + \mathbf{n}_c(y_a - y_s)}{y_a - y_c} \tag{3.116}$$

$$\mathbf{n}_R = \frac{\mathbf{n}_a(y_s - y_b) + \mathbf{n}_b(y_a - y_s)}{y_a - y_b} \tag{3.117}$$

which can then be used to create $\mathbf{n}_s$:

$$\mathbf{n}_s = \frac{n_L(x_R - x_s) + n_R(x_s - x_L)}{x_R - x_L} \tag{3.118}$$

The pseudo-surface normal $\mathbf{n}_s$ can now be used in the specular lighting calculations, and will create a smooth-shaded object with any associated highlights.

Although Gouraud- and Phong-shaded scenes are acceptable for most applications, modern computer animation renderers are far more sophisticated. However, there is no real pressure to create these images in real time,

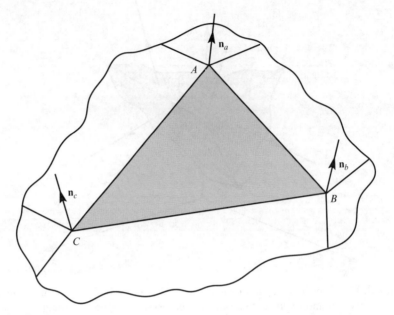

Figure 3.42 n_a, n_b and n_c are the average surface normals for the vertices A, B and C. These are linearly interpolated in image space to derive a normal for any pixel.

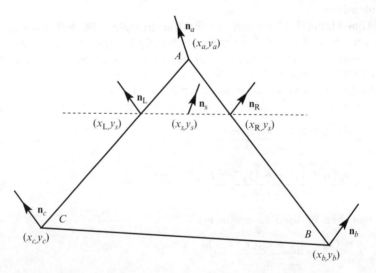

Figure 3.43   Phong shading computes a pseudo-surface normal for every pixel. This is linearly interpolated from n_L and n_R, which, in turn, are linearly interpolated from n_a to n_c, and n_a to n_b respectively.

whereas VR systems have to employ techniques that produce images of a reasonable quality in a time frame measured in milliseconds, rather than seconds or minutes.

3.12   Radiosity

Radiosity is a global illumination model that attempts to simulate the multiple diffuse reflections that occur between surfaces. Such situations arise naturally in any office or room containing furniture. It is interesting to examine the soft shadow effects that accompany objects such as a telephone resting on a desk, or a chair placed near a wall. Even coloured objects can influence the colour of other objects placed nearby. Recreating all of these effects that are a natural feature of the real world seems to be an insurmountable task. Nevertheless, radiosity provides a mechanism by which a VE can be rendered with similar levels of realism.

In order to compute these subtle changes in illumination across a surface, the surface is reduced to a mesh of small patches. Light intensities are then computed for each patch which are interpolated to create very realistic scenes. Extra realism is achieved by reducing the patch size which also requires more computation time.

Radiosity is a measure of the energy leaving a surface, and can be expressed as the sum of the emitted energy and the reflected energy. Therefore, we must discover how every patch interacts with every other patch in the environment. This leads to a set of simultaneous equations that summarize the energy interchanges using form factors that represent the fractional energy leaving one patch and arriving at another. A solution to this family of equations is effected using the Gauss–Seidel method (Watt, 1993), which yields radiosity values for each patch. From these radiosity values it is possible to Gouraud-shade surfaces which now contain realistic areas of light and shadow.

One important feature of this approach is that because the light is diffuse, the rendered scene is independent of the observer. This enables a VE to be processed off-line to compute the radiosities, and then rendered in real time. Naturally, if objects are moved to new positions in the VE, new radiosities have to be computed.

3.12.1   Progressive refinement

During the evolution of radiosity as a computer graphics technique, it has been known for some scenes to take in excess of one week to compute! One can easily imagine environments constructed from several thousand polygons, which in turn could generate 100K patches or more. Solving such large sets of equations is far from a trivial exercise. However, even though this numerical approach is not a natural choice for a VR system, the work of

Cohen *et al.* (1988) has provided an alternative approach based upon a 'progressive image refinement'.

The progressive refinement technique works towards a final image in a number of iterations, and as each iteration can be evaluated in a short period of time, it can be implemented in a VR system. There is nothing to prevent the VO from exploring the VE as this takes place, so long as the quality of the images is sufficient for them to undertake their work, and the process is not distracting.

Readers who are interested in acquiring a greater knowledge of this topic are highly recommended to read Alan and Mark Watt's description (Watt and Watt, 1992).

3.13 Hidden-surface removal

The renderer's task is quite complex, as it has to compute the light levels in a scene and also ensure that objects are correctly ordered within the VO's field of view. This last feature may seem to be a simple task, as the VE database has an accurate 3D description of the geometry. However, numerical accuracy within computers can give rise to annoying problems in computer graphics. For example, when close to, it is easy to distinguish between two surfaces separated by a small distance. However, at large distances, their relative z-coordinates become very similar, and in some situations can be masked by numerical rounding errors. One way to overcome this phenomenon is to assign priority levels to surfaces, such that the renderer always knows that one surface is in front of another. This occurs in flight simulation with runway markings. In reality, the paint is physically touching the tarmac, and the only sure way to simulate this sharing of a surface is with priority numbers.

Over the last 25 years or so, a number of algorithms have been developed for removing lines from a line-based image. Similarly, hidden-surface removal techniques have been developed that take into account the partial intersection of objects and transparent objects. Not all of these techniques are relevant to VR systems, although there is every reason to expect that with increased processor performance, and more efficient algorithms, they will find their way into the real-time domain. Consequently, we will investigate only three algorithms that are currently employed in VR systems.

3.13.1 The painter's algorithm

The painter's algorithm sorts surfaces within the VO's field of view in depth sequence. Once this list is established, it renders the surfaces starting with the most distant and finishing with the nearest. This ensures that the nearest objects mask more distant ones, but the nature of the algorithm prevents the correct rendering of interpenetrating objects, and also the implementation of anti-aliasing.

Some overlapping objects can give rise to situations where for one part of the scene object *A* is in front of object *B*, and for another part the opposite is true. This, however, can be resolved by dividing the offending object in two to resolve the conflict.

3.13.2 Scan-line algorithm

As the name suggests, the scan-line algorithm renders an image on a line-by-line basis, normally starting with the topmost raster and working down to the bottom of the image. For any line, the algorithm examines the list of objects intersected and, using depth data, proceeds to render the individual portions of the object. The incremental nature of the algorithm provides an ideal opportunity for implementing transparency effects, interpenetrating objects and anti-aliasing.

Real-time processing

An interesting aspect of this algorithm is that its performance can be increased by introducing multiple processors. For example, one processor can be used to partition the screen into four horizontal zones such that the rendering load is distributed equally in these zones. Four further processors, each having their own copy of the renderer and the database, can render their portion of the image. Although it might be considered impractical to involve too many processors in this task, it does provide a cost-effective strategy for achieving real-time image generation in a VR system.

3.13.3 The z-buffer algorithm

Sorting is a feature of the painter's and scan-line algorithms. The first sorts objects into *z*-depth sequence, while the latter sorts objects into their vertical position on the screen, and then sorts object spans across the raster. The z-buffer algorithm dispenses with sorting by introducing a depth buffer that always maintains the *z*-depth for the nearest surface rendered into a pixel. Some workstations incorporate this buffer in hardware, which greatly speeds up the rendering process, but if there are insufficient bits for each memory word, then the depth resolution of objects is limited.

Before rendering begins, the depth buffer is primed with a value equal to the depth of the far clipping plane; this ensures that anything beyond this plane is not rendered. Polygons are then rendered in an arbitrary sequence. When the first visible polygon is rendered, the depth of the polygon is computed at every pixel affected. As these depths will be smaller than the initial value, they will be used to overwrite the depth buffer. The frame store is then loaded with corresponding colour intensities. As subsequent polygons are rendered, their depths are compared with those currently held, and if they are nearer than these, then they too will overwrite the depth buffer.

If the pixel depths are found to be greater than the current values, this implies that the points on the polygon are more distant than the previously held points, and therefore invisible. Consequently, these pixels will not be updated and that part of the surface will remain hidden. Continuing in this manner, the z-buffer algorithm can accept polygons in any sequence and handle the intersections of objects at a pixel level.

As there is no natural mechanism for retaining the opacity levels of surfaces, the basic z-buffer algorithm cannot support transparency. Furthermore, anti-aliasing the image is restricted as there is no facility to retain a list of those polygons that impact upon a pixel.

3.14 Realism

In recent years, researchers all over the world have demonstrated that computer graphics techniques are capable of incredible levels of realism. Many of the computer animation sequences that have been created on a stop-frame basis have been a stimulus for developing VR systems. It requires very little persuasion to see the amazing potential of interacting with photo-realistic 3D scenes. Unfortunately, many of these animation sequences require many days or weeks to prepare, for each frame requires 5, 10 or 15 minutes to render on a relatively powerful workstation. Because so much time is available for each frame, the renderer can incorporate many features for improving image quality. Very often, such techniques are beyond the realm of any real-time system, where only 20 ms may be available to render an image. Nevertheless, with increased processor performance, specialist ASICS, and the trend towards multiprocessor systems, real-time image quality is improving in leaps and bounds. Effects that are currently in the domain of the non-real-time world will eventually be a standard feature of VR systems.

Image realism can be increased on two fronts: first, the image content can be improved by incorporating real-world textures, atmospheric effects, shadows and complex surface forms; second, the displayed image can be kept free of any artefacts introduced by the rendering process.

3.14.1 Texture mapping

Texture mapping enables synthetic or real-world images to be incorporated into a computer-generated image. For instance, a VR system could provide a facility to explore a museum housing paintings by well-known artists. To introduce these images into the VE, the paintings (or photographs of the paintings) are scanned into a digital format and held within the IG as texture maps. Perhaps the internal resolution of these maps might be 512×512 texels, 24 bits deep, which means that each painting requires 0.75 Mbytes of texture memory.

The texture mapping algorithm must now ensure that when various

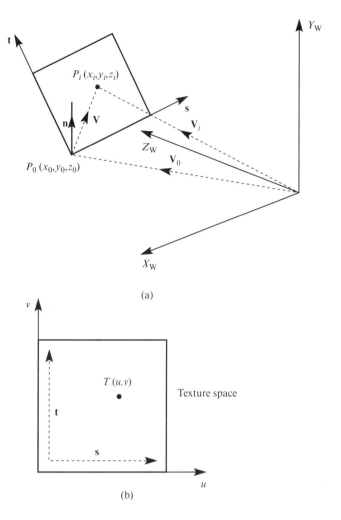

Figure 3.44   An arbitary-polygon where any point $P_i(x_i,y_i,z_i)$ (part a) corresponds with the point $T(u,v)$ on the texture map (part b).

paintings are potentially visible to a VO moving through the museum, polygons that identify the location of the painting are replaced by the texture map. The mapping process must adjust the size of the image to reflect the viewer's distance, and introduce the correct level of perspective. Although the painting's changing size is a trivial computation, calculating the correct perspective is a compute-intensive operation.

To appreciate the level of work involved we will develop some of the geometry behind texture mapping. Figure 3.44 shows a polygon located in an arbitrary position, and a texture map T addressed by parameters u and v, which vary from 0 to 1. If the following conditions exist:

n is a unit vector normal to the polygon

s is a unit vector orthogonal to **n**

$P_0(x_0,y_0,z_0)$ is a reference point on the polygon mapped to $T(0,0)$

$P_i(x_i,y_i,z_i)$ is a point to be mapped to $T(u,v)$

k is a scaling term for the texture map

then:

$$\mathbf{V}_i = \mathbf{V}_0 + \mathbf{V} \tag{3.119}$$

where:

$$\mathbf{V} = \begin{bmatrix} x_i - x_0 \\ y_i - y_0 \\ z_i - z_0 \end{bmatrix} \tag{3.120}$$

Then:

$$\mathbf{V} \cdot \mathbf{s} = |\mathbf{V}||\mathbf{s}| \cos \theta \tag{3.121}$$

but as:

$$\cos \theta = \frac{ku}{|\mathbf{V}|} \qquad \text{and} \qquad |\mathbf{s}| = 1 \tag{3.122}$$

then:

$$\mathbf{V} \cdot \mathbf{s} = uk \tag{3.123}$$

therefore:

$$u = \frac{\mathbf{V} \cdot \mathbf{s}}{k} \qquad v = \frac{\mathbf{V} \cdot \mathbf{t}}{k} \tag{3.124}$$

where the vector **t** is given by the cross product of **n** and **s**, and is equal to:

$$\mathbf{t} = \begin{bmatrix} n_2 s_3 - n_3 s_2 \\ n_3 s_1 - n_1 s_3 \\ n_1 s_2 - n_2 s_1 \end{bmatrix} \tag{3.125}$$

The above technique applies only for the mapping of a single point on the polygon into the texture map.

It is highly likely that the boundary of a pixel mapped back onto the polygon is irregular and covers several texture elements. When this occurs, the relevant texels must be averaged to fix the final pixel intensity. This can be avoided if the single texture map is replaced by a stack of texture maps of different resolutions, and the mapping algorithm automatically selects the map resolution that minimizes the computation (Williams, 1983).

As with all computer graphics algorithms, there are short cuts that can save time and bring a useful effect into the real-time domain. In the case of texturing, the texture map can be mapped direct to the image space and distorted to give the impression of perspective. This can be acceptable when the polygons are small, but for large polygons the eye and brain quickly notice that the perspective is simulated.

Flight simulator IGs employ specialist hardware to map texture over the database correctly. This greatly enhances the realism of the scene and provides speed and height cues which are so vital for low-level flying, landing and take-off scenarios.

3.14.2 Aliasing

The pixel nature of computer images requires that any displayed image must appear as a regular matrix of coloured light points. If the picture contains around 500K pixels or more, the discreteness can be difficult for the eye to detect. However, some images can cause annoying visual artefacts, especially those that contain high-contrast edges that become near vertical or near horizontal. Under these conditions, edges lose their sharpness and acquire a jagged sawtooth pattern. Similarly, textured materials containing fine regular detail can also give rise to moiré patterns that swirl as the textures move. This is a common problem with television screens that have only 625 lines (UK) or 512 lines (USA). This form of image degradation is known as aliasing.

3.14.3 Anti-aliasing

Anti-aliasing algorithms attempt to prevent the occurrence of these artefacts by various strategies. A simple, though not foolproof, technique is to render the image to twice the resolution and then compute a standard resolution image by averaging pixel values. A more analytical approach is to compute the impact each surface element has on a pixel, and to accumulate the final pixel value with the aid of weighting functions. This results in edges losing their jaggedness but introduces a certain image 'softness' in the process, which is much more acceptable. Although one can imagine the level of computation anti-aliasing introduces, it is still possible to perform it in real time.

3.14.4 Bump mapping

Bump mapping was developed by James Blinn (1978) and increases realism by modulating the surface normal during lighting calculations. The modulation is normally derived from a high-contrast photograph of a textured surface, which imposes a similar 'bumpy' effect to the rendered surface. The 'bump map' is introduced into the IG either from a video source or from the output from a paint program, or is even computed using a procedure. During the rendering stage, the intensity levels are used to disturb the surface normal when computing specular highlights. This results in a surface that appears to be covered in a mottled texture to create areas of light and shadow. Some IGs can perform this in real time and use it for creating realistic sea surfaces reflecting the sun.

3.14.5 Environment mapping

Objects such as silver cutlery and chrome-plated articles reflect their immediate surroundings and distort them depending upon their surface topology. Such effects can be simulated by environment mapping, which is a standard feature of stop-frame computer animation. For example, a highly polished sphere placed inside a room would show different reflections of the room's interior depending upon its position and the location of the VO. Rather than analyse this geometry with a simulated room, environment mapping enables the room's floor, ceiling and four walls to be stored as six texture maps, which can then be mapped back onto the sphere.

Although this form of texture mapping would apply only to specific objects, it can be appreciated that introducing realism into real-time imagery causes processing problems, especially when attempting to employ them all simultaneously.

3.15 Stereographic images

Included with the book are a pair of 'red and green' glasses that can be used to view the stereographic images in the plate section. The first page of this section shows how a stereogram is created: two separate images are created for the left and right eye; the left is printed in green ink, and the right image in red ink; the stereogram is then formed by overlaying the two images with a suitable horizontal overlap.

The computer-generated examples employ the geometry described earlier, and the views of Manhattan and the Statue of Liberty were taken from a moving helicopter, which accounts for the accentuated stereoscopic effect. A head-mounted display system can also provide this level of image depth, but two separate image generators must provide the left- and right-hand views of a scene.

4

Geometric Modelling

4.0 Introduction

When we build anything in the real world, whether it is a wall, bookcase or a greenhouse, we use real materials and a variety of fixings such as nails, screws, rivets and glue. We may work to a detailed plan, or make it to measure as we go along. The structure may be supported externally, or it may incorporate internal elements that provide extra rigidity. We may have to fit hinges for hanging doors, magnetic catches to hold them back, sliders to ease the movement of drawers, stays to support lids, and attach various fixtures such as knobs, handles and locks.

In the virtual world of 3D computer graphics there are no building regulations. There is no gravitational field tugging at objects, and as there are no materials, we can ignore the problems of strength, sharp edges, rigidity, and so on. Nevertheless, to create a virtual object we still require to know an object's dimensions. From this basic geometry we can describe individual elements separately, and assemble them to form the required object. The final numerical description encodes the object's shape and form, and if this data remains constant, the object's geometric integrity is safe.

Representing objects numerically provides us with incredible flexibility. However, this numerical world is devoid of any natural physical attributes that we take for granted in the real world. For example, when we push against a drawer, it stops when it comes against the limit of its travel. A door will only swing so far before its rotation is restricted by its frame, another object, or by the action of its hinges. A trolley on wheels will bump up and down as it is moved across a carpeted room, and any contents will shake and rattle. Such phenomena do not occur naturally in the virtual world. Numbers do not rattle, nor do they swing or slide. But if that is what we want, we can design procedures that simulate such behaviour.

Modelling, then, is not just concerned with shape; it may require the description of how linked elements are connected, or the constraints controlling the degree of travel, or the permitted angle of rotation. Such parameters can then be investigated by procedures used to subject the model to various forms of dynamic behaviour. For example, CAD systems are frequently used to investigate whether a mechanism will interfere with other surfaces when placed in different configurations. For instance, a winding mechanism on a car door must not jam during the window's travel. Similarly, a car's front wheel must not touch body panels when it is rotated, and this must be for any load condition that might change the wheel's orientation. The database storing the computer model must be capable of maintaining this wide range of geometric and attribute data. It must also be able to accept adjustments that might occur within a real-time interactive environment.

In Chapter 3 the only modelling element considered was a planar polygon, and we know from our experience of the real world that it is not one of Nature's favourite features. In fact, it is difficult to think of a naturally occurring perfectly flat surface, apart from that found on a small area of liquid, or in the faceted structures of crystals. Although we construct walls, ceilings and shelves with flat surfaces, curved surfaces are vital to an object's functionality and individual aesthetic. Therefore, if we are to build virtual environments that simulate real-world scenes, it would be useful to model both planar and curved surfaces. This, however, takes us into the capabilities of real-time systems, and what restrictions they may impose upon the way our models are defined.

Computer graphics researchers have developed a wealth of modelling systems that include polygons, surface patches, fractals, particle systems, voxels and constructive solid geometry. These are all standard features of non-real-time systems. However, when we move into the real-time domain, the system's image update rate imposes severe limitations on how the VE is modelled.

Further complications arise if we want to interact with the models. For example, an object may consist of an assembly of discrete parts that can be moved individually. However, when the assembly is assigned a new position, the individual elements must all move together, which introduces the concept of groups. Consequently, the modelling of such objects requires the introduction of hierarchies where single entities can be formed into more complex structures. Fortunately, this can be implemented through suitable data structures.

Another important feature that influences modelling stems from the display system's real-time operating capacity. One common strategy for minimizing the number of polygons comprising any image frame is to allow the display channel to reject models or model features that take it towards an overload condition. Just exactly how this is achieved varies from system to system. Nevertheless, VEs may have to be modelled at several different levels of detail so that the system can automatically select the most suitable description that permits an adequate update rate.

Finally, we can anticipate all types of other problems that complicate the modelling process when a model is animated. For example, if a virtual elastic ball is required to bounce like its real-world counterpart, its shape must adjust to the geometry of any surface it strikes. Computing this in real time is non-trivial, therefore it may have to be simulated by precomputing the anticipated changes in geometry in advance and retrieving them when required.

This brief introduction shows how 3D modelling goes beyond the geometric description of objects, and warns us of a convoluted maze of techniques that permit dynamic interaction in a real-time mode. Let us now consider these individual issues in greater depth, starting with some numerical tools to aid model building.

4.1 From 2D to 3D

The Cartesian approach for fixing points in space employs orthogonal coordinates relative to an arbitrarily defined origin. When used as an abstract mathematical system they can be associated with spaces of any number of dimensions. But when used for describing geometric features of the physical world, only spaces up to three dimensions are readily understood and visualized. Moving from an *n*-dimensional space to an $(n + 1)$-dimensional space simply involves the introduction of an extra value fixing the datum in the extra dimension. Moving from an *n*-dimensional space to an $(n - 1)$-dimensional space involves a projection, such as the perspective projection previously described.

Any 2D data set is easily converted into a 3D structure by introducing a third parameter, which would normally become the *z*-coordinate. Figure 4.1

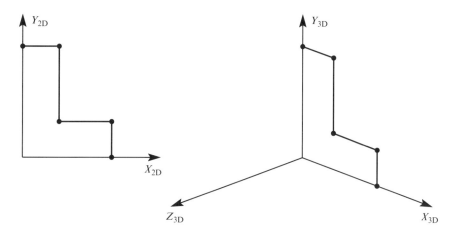

Figure 4.1 The 2D shape is converted into a 3D lamina by assigning every vertex a zero *z*-coordinate.

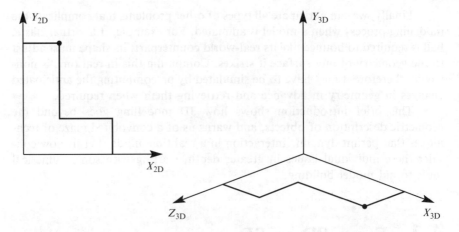

Figure 4.2 In this example, the 2D shape is converted into a 3D lamina by applying the following assignments: $x_{3D} = y_{2D}$, $y_{3D} = 0.0$, $z_{3D} = x_{2D}$.

shows how the simple 2D L-shape becomes three-dimensional by associating every vertex with a zero z-coordinate. The final orientation of the lamina can be further controlled by manipulating the coordinate from 2D to 3D. For example, a 3D vertex (x_{3D}, y_{3D}, z_{3D}) can be created from a 2D vertex (x_{2D}, y_{2D}) by setting the z-coordinate to some suitable value. The following assignment produces the orientation shown in Figure 4.2:

$$x_{3D} = y_{2D}$$
$$y_{3D} = 0 \qquad\qquad (4.1)$$
$$z_{3D} = x_{2D}$$

Notice how an infinite range of orientations becomes possible by mixing different assignment combinations with sign changes, and replacing the zero term with other numerical values. This simple subterfuge provides a useful way of introducing 2D shapes into a 3D VE.

4.1.1 Extrusions

Modern manufacturing processes include die casting, plastic moulding, lathe turning and extruding. Such techniques have evolved over time and it is very easy to recognize these processes in everyday objects. For example: aluminium door handles are cast in a die; plastic cups are moulded in a press; wooden stair spindles are turned on a lathe, and double-glazed window frames are extruded. As many of these artefacts have found their way into the domain of computer graphics, similar modelling schemes have been developed for their virtual construction.

The extrusion process involves a die through which material is forced.

This results in long strips of material having the same cross-sectional shape of the die. This is a simple process to simulate in software. All that is required is the shape of the cross-section, and the length of extrusion. Figure 3.32 shows how a flight of steps is constructed from a simple 2D shape.

As the vertex sequence in the original shape can be defined in a clockwise or anticlockwise order, this will influence the vertex order of the extruded 3D polygons. For example, if the extrusion procedure expects the original die shape to be anticlockwise, as viewed from the positive z-axis, it might construct a 3D object from anticlockwise polygons as viewed from the object's outside. On the other hand, if the vertices were clockwise, the same procedure would construct the 3D object from clockwise polygons. In the latter case, there is a very good chance that the renderer will render the inside of the object, rather than the outside, as its surface normals are pointing inwards!

The basic idea of extruding can be developed by rotating the die shape by a small angle at discrete stages. For example, Figure 4.3(a) shows the original die shape together with its axis of rotation. If there is zero rotation during the first extrusion we create the 3D object shown in Figure 4.3(b). However, if the reference die shape is rotated through a small angle and used to extrude a second portion of the object, the twisted object in Figure 4.3(c) emerges. If this rotation is continued, a long twisted rectangular extrusion is formed.

Another development of this process is to scale the die shape about the axis of rotation at each stage of extrusion. This results in a tapered, twisted form. One drawback of the technique is that it results in twisted polygons, which do not render consistently. This, however, is resolved by dividing them into triangles.

4.1.2 Swept surfaces

The sweeping or turning operation was mentioned very briefly in Section 3.8.2 and is used to model objects that could be turned on a lathe. Again, the sequence of the master 2D shape can be critical when using a particular software procedure. If reversed, it results in rendering the object's inside, rather than its outside. Here are variations to the basic technique such as off-setting the 2D contour from the axis of rotation. Figure 4.4(a) shows a polygon off-set from the y-axis. If the sweeping procedure rotates the polygon in small angles to develop the swept surface, the result is a torus, as shown in Figure 4.4(b). The master shape could be rotating, or even scaled during the sweeping process, and as long as it returns to its original form, a continuous surface results.

4.1.3 Arbitrary polygonal objects

Although extrusions and swept surfaces are useful 3D forms, arbitrary polygonal objects require special modelling tools. Objects such as planes,

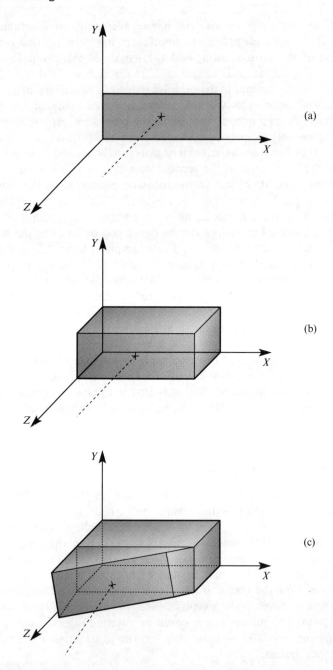

Figure 4.3   (a) The original die shape is shown together with its axis of rotation. (b) The shape is extruded a short distance. (c) The die shape is rotated before a second extrusion.

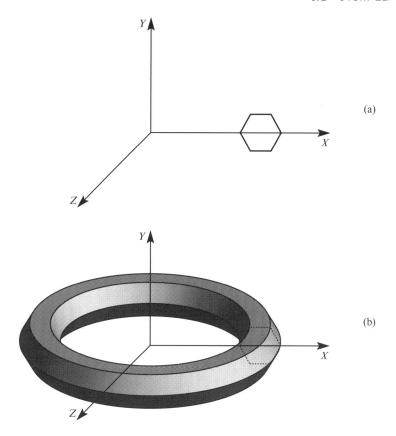

Figure 4.4   The two stages of modelling a torus. (a) A polygon is offset from the *y*-axis. (b) The polygon is rotated to form the surface of a torus.

faces, fish and hands from polygons can be modelled using interactive tech-niques or even using physical models.

Various commercial modelling systems are available that enable a 3D irregular model to be built interactively. One CAD approach develops a 3D surface from dimensions associated with the six orthographic elevations. Another approach allows the modeller to interact freely in real time with the developing model geometry, with the model being viewed from any direction. Extra triangles or polygons are then added individually using explicit dimen-sions, or with implicit measurements taken from the model. For example, it would be possible automatically to divide a space into a number of identical segments. Figure 4.5 shows how a model of a plane is constructed over several stages.

3D digitizers
When a physical model actually exists, a 3D digitizer can be used to capture the surface geometry. Such devices are able to work within a volume of space

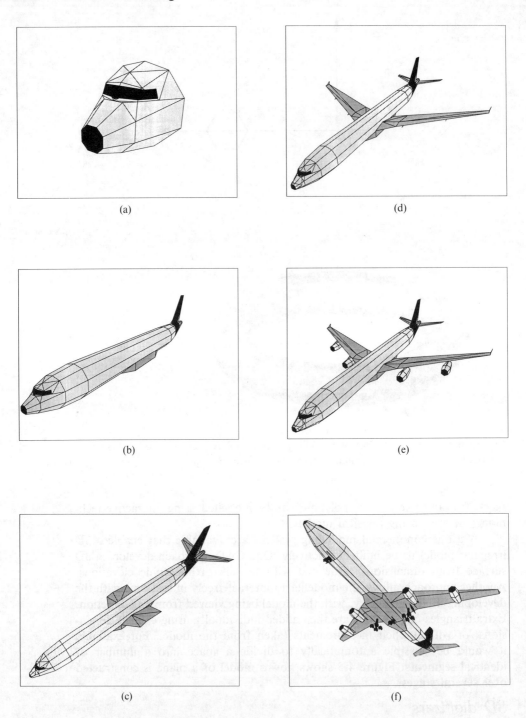

(a)

(d)

(b)

(e)

(c)

(f)

Figure 4.5   These show how a model of an aircraft is developed over six stages. Note that in this modelling system, the vertical axis is the z-axis.

approximately $1 \, m^3$. The model is first prepared by drawing a mesh of triangles or polygons over the surface. Their size is adjusted to capture the variable level of detail of the model's surface. Each vertex of the mesh is then digitized using the digitizer's probe, which measures the 3D coordinates. Simultaneously, the host computer records the vertices in the digitized sequence. Unfortunately, this approach establishes the coordinates only of the mesh vertices. Further information is required to connect the vertices into triangles or polygons. This can either be input manually, or the model can be digitized originally in a polygon sequence. With the latter approach, the duplicated vertices have to be recognized by the digitizing software to ensure that the final mesh is free from holes or other artefacts.

A scanning laser digitizer can capture the surface geometry of an object in several seconds. The process involves placing the object on a rotating table and, in one rotation, a vertical scanning laser probes the surface at discrete points. For each point, a 3D position is recorded. The resulting data can then be filtered to provide the required geometric granularity and then converted into triangles. As the digitizing process involves the reflected light from the laser, objects with undercuts cannot be used. However, systems exist capable of integrating the data obtained from a scanning laser digitizer with a linear laser digitizer, which is capable of digitizing concave regions.

4.2 3D space curves

3D contours are often required in VEs to serve a variety of purposes. For instance, it may be impossible to compute in real time the complex path of some object. Therefore, if this can be performed off-line, the trajectory can be introduced as a 3D contour by way of a data file, and the object moved along it at discrete time steps. It may also be necessary to input 3D curves that form static features of a model such as hanging cables, which have a catenary basis. Similarly, in the case of molecular modelling, perhaps helical contours may be required for modelling protein structures. Whatever the application, such data input is a trivial exercise, and will not be explored further.

4.2.1 Parametric space curves

If a 3D contour has a parametric description and can be evaluated in real time, we simply compute, as efficiently as possible, the three functions generating the x-, y- and z-coordinates. For example, the flight path of a projectile could be described using a time parameter t, as follows:

$$y = vt \sin \theta - \tfrac{1}{2} gt^2$$
$$z = vt \cos \theta \qquad\qquad (4.2)$$
$$x = wt$$

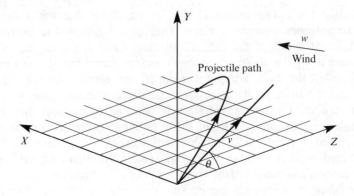

Figure 4.6 The trajectory of the projectile can be evaluated by computing the individual x-, y- and z-coordinates using parametric expressions.

where:

> v is the initial speed of the projectile
>
> θ is the vertical angle of projection relative to the z-axis
>
> t is a parameter for time
>
> w is the wind speed in the x-direction

Figure 4.6 illustrates this arrangement.

By evaluating x, y and z in real time, for different values of the parameter t, an object can be animated along this trajectory. The same technique can be applied to create a wide variety of similar space curves.

4.2.2 Bézier space curves

A Bézier space curve is derived from a sequence of control points that determine the curve's geometry. When three control points are used, a quadratic curve is formed between the first and last points, while the middle control point influences the overall shape. When four control points are used, a cubic curve is formed between the first and last points, while the two middle points provide the shape-forming features. Any Bézier curve $C(u)$ of degree n can be defined using $n + 1$ control points $p_i(i = 0,1,2,\ldots,n)$ and is given by:

$$C(u) = \sum_{i=0}^{n} p_i B_{i,n}(u) \tag{4.3}$$

where $B_{i,n}(u)$ is a blending function, using the terms of a Bernstein polynomial, and ultimately determines the influence the control points have on the curve's shape. The parameter u is evaluated over the range $0 \leqslant u \leqslant 1$. The blending function $B_{i,n}(u)$ is defined as:

$$B_{i,n}(u) = {}^nC_i u^i (1 - u)^{n - i} \tag{4.4}$$

Table 4.1 The first column shows the status of the controlling parameter u. The next three columns show the changing values of the Bézier basis functions, and the last three columns show the coordinate values of the Bézier curve.

u	$B_{0,2}(u)$	$B_{1,2}(u)$	$B_{2,2}(u)$	$C_x(u)$	$C_y(u)$	$C_z(u)$
0.0	1.00	0.00	0.00	1.00	1.00	0.00
0.1	0.81	0.18	0.01	0.81	1.17	0.19
0.2	0.64	0.32	0.04	0.64	1.28	0.36
0.3	0.49	0.42	0.09	0.49	1.33	0.51
0.4	0.36	0.48	0.16	0.36	1.32	0.64
0.5	0.25	0.50	0.25	0.25	1.25	0.75
0.6	0.16	0.48	0.36	0.16	1.12	0.84
0.7	0.09	0.42	0.49	0.09	0.93	0.91
0.8	0.04	0.32	0.64	0.04	0.68	0.96
0.9	0.01	0.18	0.81	0.01	0.37	0.99
1.0	0.00	0.00	1.00	0.00	0.00	1.00

where ^nC_i is the binomial coefficient, and is given by:

$$^nC_i = \frac{n!}{i!(n-i)!} \tag{4.5}$$

For example, a curve of degree two (a quadratic) produces the following blending function values:

$$\begin{aligned}
B_{0,2}(u) &= (1-u)^2 \\
B_{1,2}(u) &= 2u(1-u) \\
B_{2,2}(u) &= u^2
\end{aligned} \tag{4.6}$$

while a curve of degree three (a cubic) produces the following blending function values:

$$\begin{aligned}
B_{0,3}(u) &= (1-u)^3 \\
B_{1,3}(u) &= 3u(1-u)^2 \\
B_{2,3}(u) &= 3u^2(1-u) \\
B_{3,3}(u) &= u^3
\end{aligned} \tag{4.7}$$

In the quadratic case the Bézier curve $C(u)$ is given by:

$$C(u) = p_0(1-u)^2 + p_1 2u(1-u) + p_2 u^2 \tag{4.8}$$

and in the cubic case $C(u)$ is given by:

$$C(u) = p_0(1-u)^3 + p_1 3u(1-u)^2 + p_2 3u^2(1-u) + p_3 u^3 \tag{4.9}$$

As an example, let us evaluate a quadratic Bézier curve formed by the control points $p_0(1,1,0)$, $p_2(0,2,1)$ and $p_2(0,0,1)$. Table 4.1 summarizes the values of the basis functions for various values of u, and the accumulated coordinate components that form the Bézier curve. Figure 4.7 illustrates this curve.

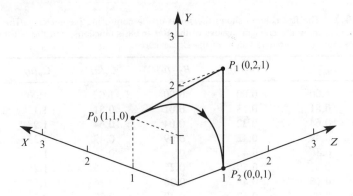

Figure 4.7   The quadratic Bézier curve formed from the values listed in Table 4.1.

One can also specify a Bézier curve using matrix notation, and the quadratic and cubic forms are given by:

$$C(u) = \begin{bmatrix} u^2 & u & 1 \end{bmatrix} \begin{bmatrix} 1 & -2 & 1 \\ -2 & 2 & 0 \\ 1 & 0 & 0 \end{bmatrix} \begin{bmatrix} p_0 \\ p_1 \\ p_2 \end{bmatrix} \tag{4.10}$$

$$C(u) = \begin{bmatrix} u^3 & u^2 & u & 1 \end{bmatrix} \begin{bmatrix} -1 & 3 & -3 & 1 \\ 3 & -6 & 3 & 0 \\ -3 & 3 & 0 & 0 \\ 1 & 0 & 0 & 0 \end{bmatrix} \begin{bmatrix} p_0 \\ p_1 \\ p_2 \\ p_3 \end{bmatrix} \tag{4.11}$$

One obvious limitation with Bézier curves is that, even in the cubic form, four control points are insufficient to define a complex convoluted path. However, this can be overcome by using a piecewise approach, which entails forming the final curve from a sequence of smaller curve segments. The nature of Bézier curves is such that their derivatives at the start and end points are equal to the slopes connecting these points to their neighbouring control point. Thus slope continuity can be preserved over any number of segments by matching the starting slope of one segment with the trailing slope of the previous segment. This is illustrated in Figure 4.8.

4.2.3   B-spline space curves

B-spline curves provide a useful alternative approach to curve definition and, like Bézier curves, have a parametric as well as a matrix definition. However, whereas Bézier curves always pass through their first and last control points, B-spline curves must be forced to do so.

A B-spline curve $C(u)$ can be derived from four control points $p_i(i = 0,1,2,3)$ as follows:

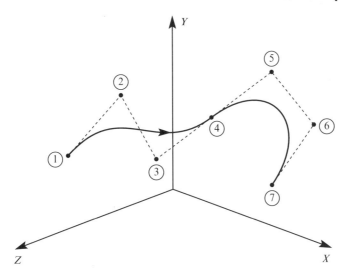

Figure 4.8 Long Bézier curves are formed by joining together several simple segments. In this example, the first segment formed by points 1, 2, 3 and 4 forms a continuous curve with the second segment formed by the points 4, 5, 6 and 7. Slope continuity is maintained by ensuring that the slope of the line segment between points 3 and 4 equals the slope of the line segment between points 4 and 5.

$$C(u) = \frac{1}{6} [u^3 \ u^2 \ u \ 1] \begin{bmatrix} -1 & 3 & -3 & 1 \\ 3 & -6 & 3 & 0 \\ -3 & 0 & 3 & 0 \\ 1 & 4 & 1 & 0 \end{bmatrix} \begin{bmatrix} p_0 \\ p_1 \\ p_2 \\ p_3 \end{bmatrix} \tag{4.12}$$

where $0 \leqslant u \leqslant 1$. If a curve is computed using four control points, it would create only a small segment of a cubic B-spline. However, if six control points are used, $p_i(i = 0,1,2,\ldots,5)$, a continuous curve is formed by computing three curve segments using points $p_i(i = 0,1,2,3)$, $(i = 1,2,3,4)$ and $(i = 2,3,4,5)$. This can be illustrated by considering just five control points to form a 2D B-spline, $(0,1)$, $(1,2)$, $(3,2)$, $(3,1)$ and $(2,0)$, as shown in Figure 4.9. By applying the above matrix operation to the first four control points, and then to the last four, a B-spline curve results. These results are given in Table 4.2 and shown graphically in Figure 4.9.

The curve could have started at p_0 and finished at p_4 by repeating the first and last point three times as follows: $p_0, p_0, p_0, p_1, p_2, p_3, p_4, p_4$ and p_4, which would require six curve segments.

4.2.4 Catmull-Rom spline space curves

Spline curves can be classified into two categories: those that pass through their control points, and those that do not. The former class of curves is called

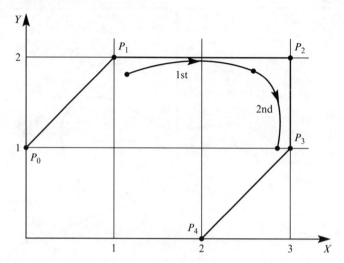

Figure 4.9 From the five control points it is possible to construct two segments of a B-spline curve with first- and second-order slope continuity.

Table 4.2 The x- and y-coordinates of a 2D B-spline curve formed from two segments. The first column shows the value of the parameter u, while the following two pairs of columns list the individual coordinates for the two curve segments.

	First segment		Second segment	
u	x	y	x	y
0.0	1.17	1.83	2.67	1.83
0.1	1.32	1.88	2.76	1.78
0.2	1.48	1.91	2.83	1.71
0.3	1.65	1.94	2.88	1.64
0.4	1.81	1.95	2.92	1.56
0.5	1.98	1.96	2.94	1.48
0.6	2.14	1.95	2.94	1.39
0.7	2.29	1.94	2.93	1.30
0.8	2.43	1.91	2.91	1.20
0.9	2.56	1.88	2.88	1.10
1.0	2.67	1.83	2.83	1.00

an interpolating spline, whilst the latter is called an approximating spline, such as a B-spline curve.

Catmull–Rom splines are interpolating splines and exploit parabolic blending to achieve their result, and can be defined as follows:

$$
C(u) = [u^3 \quad u^2 \quad u \quad 1] \begin{bmatrix} -0.5 & 1.5 & -1.5 & 0.5 \\ 1.0 & -2.5 & 2.0 & -0.5 \\ -0.5 & 0.0 & 0.5 & 0.0 \\ 0.0 & 1.0 & 0.0 & 0.0 \end{bmatrix} \begin{bmatrix} p_0 \\ p_1 \\ p_2 \\ p_3 \end{bmatrix} \tag{4.13}
$$

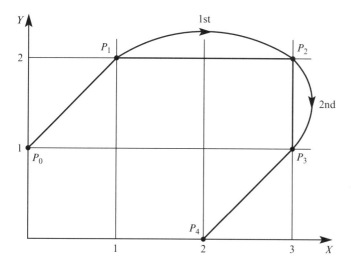

Figure 4.10 From the five control points it is possible to construct two segments of a Catmull-Rom spline that actually pass through the points.

Table 4.3 The x- and y coordinates of a 2D Catmull-Rom spline computed in two segments. The first column shows the value of the parameter u, while the following two pairs of columns list the individual coordinates for the two curve segments.

	First segment		Second segment	
u	x	y	x	y
0.0	1.00	2.00	3.00	2.00
0.1	1.17	2.05	3.09	1.94
0.2	1.37	2.08	3.14	1.86
0.3	1.59	2.11	3.18	1.77
0.4	1.82	2.12	3.19	1.67
0.5	2.06	2.13	3.19	1.56
0.6	2.30	2.12	3.17	1.45
0.7	2.52	2.11	3.14	1.33
0.8	2.71	2.08	3.10	1.22
0.9	2.88	2.05	3.05	1.10
1.0	3.00	2.00	3.00	1.00

where $0 \leqslant u \leqslant 1$, and $p_i(i = 0,1,2,3)$ are four control points.

If we compute a Catmull–Rom spline for the same control points used for the B-spline curve we obtain the values shown in Table 4.3, and the curve shown in Figure 4.10.

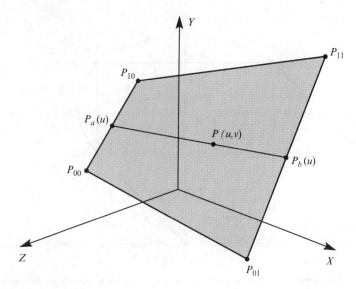

Figure 4.11   A surface defined by four points can be described geometrically using bilinear interpolation.

4.3   3D boundary representation

In Section 3.8 we briefly examined some of the issues relevant to modelling VEs and concluded that if polygons were used their planarity would be important to rendering and collision detection. We also noted that triangles were always planar and, nowadays, they provide a consistent surface element to render at a hardware level. In this section we will see how various schemes for describing 3D surface boundaries can be represented as meshes of triangles. Although this process may be only an approximation of the original surface, the errors are normally small and can be tolerated.

4.3.1   Bilinear surfaces

Imagine that it is required to develop a surface skin from four points P_{00}, P_{10}, P_{01} and P_{11} located in space as shown in Figure 4.11. One could think of many ways of performing this task, all resulting in different surfaces. One way, however, is to interpolate linearly the coordinate values of the points to create a bilinear surface. Any point on the surface can be accurately calculated using the following analysis.

Any point along the line $\{P_{00}, P_{10}\}$ is given by:

$$P_a(u) = (1 - u)P_{00} + uP_{10} \qquad \text{for } 0 \leqslant u \leqslant 1 \tag{4.14}$$

Similarly, any point on the line $\{P_{01}, P_{11}\}$ is given by:

$$P_b(u) = (1 - u)P_{01} + uP_{11} \tag{4.15}$$

If a line connects the points $P_a(u)$ and $P_b(u)$, then any point $P(u,v)$ on this line is given by:

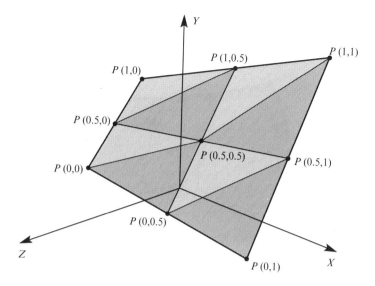

Figure 4.12 These points form a twisted surface that can be split into eight triangles using bilinear interpolation.

$$P(u,v) = (1 - v) P_a(u) + v P_b(u) \qquad \text{for } 0 \leqslant u, v \leqslant 1 \tag{4.16}$$

which has an expanded matrix form expressed as:

$$P(u,v) = [(1 - u) \quad u] \begin{bmatrix} P_{00} & P_{01} \\ P_{10} & P_{11} \end{bmatrix} \begin{bmatrix} (1 - v) \\ v \end{bmatrix} \tag{4.17}$$

and can also be expressed as:

$$P(u,v) = [u \quad 1] \begin{bmatrix} -1 & 1 \\ 1 & 0 \end{bmatrix} \begin{bmatrix} P_{00} & P_{01} \\ P_{10} & P_{11} \end{bmatrix} \begin{bmatrix} -1 & 1 \\ 1 & 0 \end{bmatrix} \begin{bmatrix} v \\ 1 \end{bmatrix} \tag{4.18}$$

Anticipating that this surface will be twisted, it can be converted into a triangular mesh by first computing a grid of points at regular intervals of u and v, and connecting them into triangles. Figure 4.12 shows how a surface can be divided into eight triangles by computing the points where u and v equal 0.5. Obviously, the smaller the triangles are, the smoother the surface becomes, but the IG load also increases.

4.3.2 Bézier surface patches

Bézier surface patches are an extension of Bézier curves, and although it is difficult to render them in real time, they are still a useful modelling tool. In practice, a model is built from Bézier patches that are then reduced to a mesh of triangles, which are easily rendered in real time.

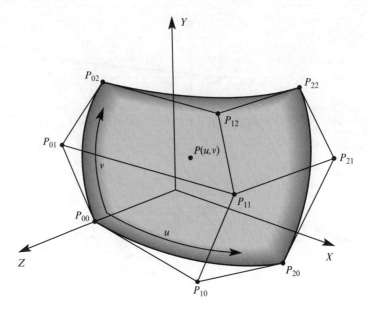

Figure 4.13 A quadratic Bézier patch requires nine points to describe its surface geometry. The four corner points actually touch the surface, but the other five control points act as attractors.

Quadratic Bézier surface patches

Like Bézier space curves, Bézier surface patches can be quadratic, cubic, quartic, and so on. In the quadratic form, four control points are used to define the patch corners, and five further points determine the surface geometry. Figure 4.13 shows an example where the corner points are: P_{00}, P_{02}, P_{20} and P_{22}. The remaining points push and pull the surface into shape.

A parameter u is used to address the surface in the direction P_{00} to P_{20}, and P_{02} to P_{22}, and a second parameter v is used to address the surface from P_{00} to P_{02}, and P_{20} to P_{22}. Therefore, any point $P(u,v)$ can be defined as follows:

$$P(u,v) = \begin{bmatrix} (1-u)^2 & 2u(1-u) & u^2 \end{bmatrix} \begin{bmatrix} P_{00} & P_{01} & P_{02} \\ P_{10} & P_{11} & P_{12} \\ P_{20} & P_{21} & P_{22} \end{bmatrix} \begin{bmatrix} (1-v)^2 \\ 2v(1-v) \\ v^2 \end{bmatrix} \quad \textbf{(4.19)}$$

which is also equivalent to:

$$P(u,v) = \begin{bmatrix} u^2 & u & 1 \end{bmatrix} \begin{bmatrix} 1 & -2 & 1 \\ -2 & 2 & 0 \\ 1 & 0 & 0 \end{bmatrix} \begin{bmatrix} P_{00} & P_{01} & P_{02} \\ P_{10} & P_{11} & P_{12} \\ P_{20} & P_{21} & P_{22} \end{bmatrix} \begin{bmatrix} 1 & -2 & 1 \\ -2 & 2 & 0 \\ 1 & 0 & 0 \end{bmatrix} \begin{bmatrix} v^2 \\ v \\ 1 \end{bmatrix}$$

$$\textbf{(4.20)}$$

For example, say we wanted to model the surface illustrated in Figure 4.14(a) where the four corners were located on the plane $Y = 0$, and one edge of the surface is raised slightly. Figure 4.14(b) shows the arrangement of control points where only points P_{11} and P_{21} are given any y value. If we make $P_{11} = (0.5,1.0,0.5)$ and $P_{21} = (1,0.5,0.5)$, this will lift the right-hand edge. If it is too much, or insufficient, the positions of P_{11} and P_{21} are adjusted accordingly.

Let us evaluate the above function (4.20) to discover the height of the raised edge. This will involve only the y terms.

$$P(1,0.5) = \begin{bmatrix} 1 & 1 & 1 \end{bmatrix} \begin{bmatrix} 1 & -2 & 1 \\ -2 & 2 & 0 \\ 1 & 0 & 0 \end{bmatrix} \begin{bmatrix} 0 & 0 & 0 \\ 0 & 1 & 0 \\ 0 & 0.5 & 0 \end{bmatrix} \begin{bmatrix} 1 & -2 & 1 \\ -2 & 2 & 0 \\ 1 & 0 & 0 \end{bmatrix} \begin{bmatrix} 0.25 \\ 0.5 \\ 1 \end{bmatrix} \quad \text{(4.21)}$$

which makes $P(1,0.5) = 0.25$. This is easily confirmed by the nature of Bézier surface patches which ensures that an edge's geometry is governed only by the control points on the edge – in this case P_{20}, P_{21} and P_{22}. Moreover, as the y values of P_{20} and P_{22} are zero, the mid-point must be half the y-coordinate of P_{21}, which is 0.25. The height of the surface under P_{11} is given by:

$$P(0.5,0.5) = \begin{bmatrix} 0.25 & 0.5 & 1 \end{bmatrix} \begin{bmatrix} 1 & -2 & 1 \\ -2 & 2 & 0 \\ 1 & 0 & 0 \end{bmatrix} \begin{bmatrix} 0 & 0 & 0 \\ 0 & 1 & 0 \\ 0 & 0.5 & 0 \end{bmatrix} \begin{bmatrix} 1 & -2 & 1 \\ -2 & 2 & 0 \\ 1 & 0 & 0 \end{bmatrix} \begin{bmatrix} 0.25 \\ 0.5 \\ 1 \end{bmatrix}$$

$$\text{(4.22)}$$

which equals 0.3125.

Multi-patch objects

It is unlikely that one patch will be sufficient to describe anything useful, so a mechanism is needed to construct multi-patch objects. Fortunately one exists, and it is similar to the approach used to construct piecewise Bézier space curves. To join two Bézier curves without revealing the join, slope continuity must be maintained across the boundary. This is achieved by matching the slope of the trailing control point span of the first curve to the leading control point span of the second curve, as was shown in Figure 4.8. Similarly, with Bézier surface patches, slope continuity across the boundary is maintained if:

(1) The control points at the boundary between the two patches are identical, and

(2) the polygons formed by the control points at the boundary edge are coplanar for both patches.

Figure 4.15 illustrates this configuration.

Cubic Bézier surface patches

A cubic Bézier surface patch description requires 16 control points. Four points locate the corners, and twelve control points are available to model the surface. Figure 4.16 shows an example. The patch touches points P_{00}, P_{03},

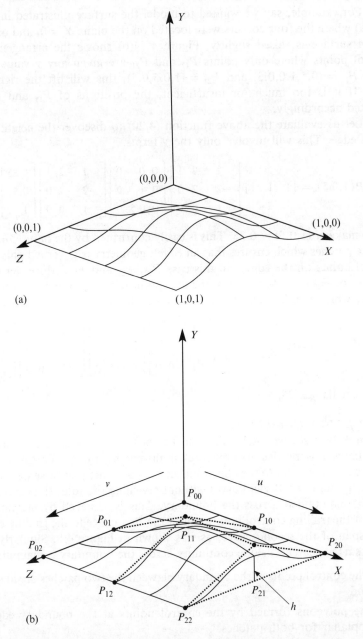

(a)

(b)

Figure 4.14 (a) A surface like this can be modelled by using control points. (b) This shows the position of the control points to lift the edge of the surface shown in part (a).

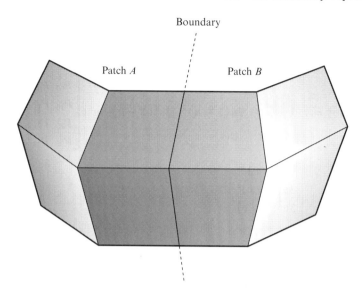

Figure 4.15 A continuous surface patch can be created from two patches *A* and *B* by preserving slope continuity of the polygons created by the control points sharing the boundary.

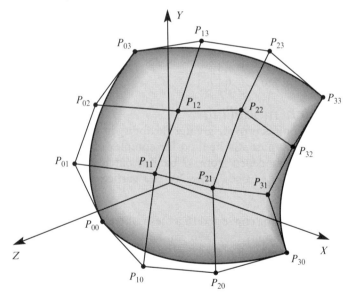

Figure 4.16 Sixteen control points are required to describe a cubic Bézier surface patch. The four corner points touch the patch, but the remaining twelve points control the surface geometry.

P_{30} and P_{33}, and is pushed and pulled by the influence of the remaining points.

Any point $P(u,v)$ on the patch is defined as follows:

$$P(u,v) = [(1-u)^3 \quad 3u(1-u)^2 \quad 3u^2(1-u) \quad u^3] \begin{bmatrix} P_{00} & P_{01} & P_{02} & P_{03} \\ P_{10} & P_{11} & P_{12} & P_{13} \\ P_{20} & P_{21} & P_{22} & P_{23} \\ P_{30} & P_{31} & P_{32} & P_{33} \end{bmatrix}$$

$$\begin{bmatrix} (1-v)^3 \\ 3v(1-v)^2 \\ 3v^2(1-v) \\ v^3 \end{bmatrix} \tag{4.23}$$

which can be rearranged as:

$$P(u,v) = [u^3 \quad u^2 \quad u \quad 1] \begin{bmatrix} -1 & 3 & -3 & 1 \\ 3 & -6 & 3 & 0 \\ -3 & 3 & 0 & 0 \\ 1 & 0 & 0 & 0 \end{bmatrix} \begin{bmatrix} P_{00} & P_{01} & P_{02} & P_{03} \\ P_{10} & P_{11} & P_{12} & P_{13} \\ P_{20} & P_{21} & P_{22} & P_{23} \\ P_{30} & P_{31} & P_{32} & P_{33} \end{bmatrix}$$

$$\begin{bmatrix} -1 & 3 & -3 & 1 \\ 3 & -6 & 3 & 0 \\ -3 & 3 & 0 & 0 \\ 1 & 0 & 0 & 0 \end{bmatrix} \begin{bmatrix} v^3 \\ v^2 \\ v \\ 1 \end{bmatrix} \tag{4.24}$$

Multiple patch modelling

The extra control points provide greater flexibility in modelling a single patch, but multiple patches must still be used for complex objects. For instance, the Utah teapot can be modelled from 32 bicubic patches (Watt, 1993). As each patch shares common vertices, only 306 3D vertices have to be defined.

Mesh conversion

The surface patch can be converted to a mesh of triangles by evaluating values of $P(u,v)$ at discrete points that then can be connected to form triangles. The simplest method of achieving this is to evaluate $P(u,v)$ at regular intervals of u and v, and then connect them accordingly. An ideal solution would adjust the triangle size according to the curvature of the surface.

4.4   Other modelling strategies

The modelling schemes outlined above provide us with sufficient techniques to build a wide variety of virtual environments; however, many more strategies exist which, unfortunately, are beyond the scope of this book. Nevertheless, it is worth mentioning some of them and providing some useful references.

4.4.1 B-spline surface patches

Modern CAD systems use B-splines that can accurately model a wide range of curves and surfaces. They are similar to Bézier curves and surfaces but do have distinct advantages. Perhaps the most important one concerns the influence of the control points. With the Bézier formulation a control point influences the entire surface patch, with the consequence that if a control point is moved for any reason it will upset the geometry for the entire patch, whereas control points on B-splines have only a local influence. Like other surface patches, B-splines are difficult to render in real time unless they are first converted to a mesh of polygons or triangles (Farin, 1988; Loop and De Rose, 1990; Piegl, 1991; Vince, 1992; Watt and Watt, 1992).

4.4.2 Coons bicubic surface patches

Another surface patch description was developed by Coons at MIT (Coons and Herzog, 1967). This develops a continuous rectangular surface patch using the tangents associated with each corner. Multiple patches can be formed by matching these tangents at the corner joins. A second feature involves a 'twist vector' that physically twists the surface at the corners to provide further adjustment. Like other parametric surface patches it has a simple matrix description (Vince, 1992).

4.4.3 Constructive solid geometry

Constructive Solid Geometry (CSG) employs a small group of geometric primitives to construct more complex structures. The original definition is based upon mathematical descriptions for the primitives, such as equations for a plane, sphere, cylinder, torus, or cone. For example, a rectangular box has six sides, therefore it can be modelled from the intersection of six half-spaces. However, if the box has a circular hole drilled through to its centre, then this can be described in CSG terms as a cylinder 'subtracted' from a box. The 'subtract' operation is a Boolean operation that describes how the geometry of the box and cylinder are to be combined. Other operations include 'union' and 'intersection'. Complex structures are developed as a binary tree data structure that can be rendered using a ray caster. As might be expected, this is too slow for a VR system, but the CSG definition can be converted into a polygonal description (Arbab, 1990; Foley, 1990).

4.4.4 Boolean set operations

CSG uses Boolean operations to build complex objects from a small set of geometric primitives, but the same operations can be used on polyhedral objects. Many modern CAD systems provide users with interactive tools to trim one surface against another, cut holes of any shape from a surface, or even cut an object in two using different cutting surfaces. Because of the time needed to undertake these logical operations, they can be considered only as an off-line modelling tool for VR systems. (Laidlaw *et al.*, 1986; Thibault and Naylor, 1987).

4.4.5 Voxels

Non-invasive scanning such as Computerized Axial Tomography (CAT), and Positron Emission Tomography (PET) construct internal views of the human body from data slices. Each slice could contain 512×512 voxels (volume elements), and there could be 512 such slices. Collectively they represent a numerical description of the organic material in this volume. Once this data is captured, it is possible to render views of this volume from any direction. A variety of visualization techniques enable specific types of material encoded in the voxels to be made transparent. This allows a surgeon access to internal areas to investigate specific features or abnormal growths. Special systems have been developed capable of manipulating and displaying this data in real time. Apart from this medical use for voxels, they have restricted application (Galyean, 1991).

4.4.6 Procedural modelling

Procedural modelling involves the action of a procedure to develop the final geometry of an object. For example, a dodecahedron is not a procedural model as it has a precise structure and can be formed only from 12 regular hexagons. A torus, however, is modelled procedurally as it has an infinite number of forms depending upon the major and minor radii and the size of the surface polygons.

Procedural modelling can also be used to simulate the changing geometry of a bouncing ball. For example, if a ball has been modelled from several Bézier patches, a procedure can store the relevant control points. If the procedure also stores the physical properties of the ball such as its mass and elasticity, these can be used to compute the ball's shape when it strikes a hard surface. With a knowledge of the ball's velocity, the procedure can modify certain control points, which in turn, will alter the geometry of the Bézier patches. When converted into a mesh of triangles the ball can be rendered and animated. It might not be physically correct, but it might be visually acceptable.

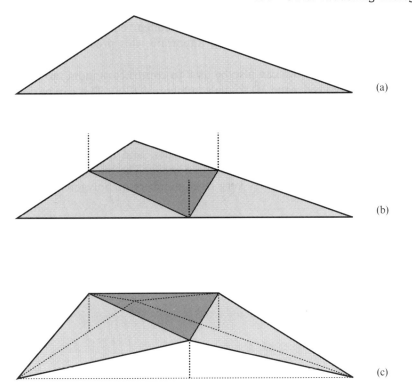

Figure 4.17   These three stages of subdivision show how a single triangle can be used to divide into four other triangles. After three more subdivisions there would be 256 triangles.

4.4.7 Fractals

Fractals were developed by Benoit Mandlebrot (Mandlebrot and van Ness, 1968) and describe data sets that exhibit self-similarity. In visual terms this can be understood by looking at certain types of trees or ferns. For instance, close to, a small twig on a branch looks like a large tree, that is, if one ignores its leaves. A branch, which is made from a collection of twigs, also looks like a tree from a certain distance. A tree, which is made from a trunk and a collection of branches, certainly looks like a tree at the right distance. Although this analysis is not precise, it is approximately true, and the term 'statistically self-similar' is used to describe such structures.

Self-similar structures can be used for modelling very complex objects without the need to store complex levels of detail. In the case of a tree one can start with a trunk and locations for possible branches. However, instead of modelling the branches, the original trunk is randomly scaled and oriented at the branch nodes. As each branch also contains the nodes for branches, the original trunk can be further scaled and oriented to form the twigs. This process can be continued until the final level of detail is too small to be seen. Looking closely at such a tree the hidden regularity of the structure is easily seen. But if this is not too important, this procedural technique is very powerful.

Fractal techniques can also be used to construct random terrain ranges. For example, consider the 3D triangle in Figure 4.17(a). This can be converted into four triangles by dividing the edges at their mid-points as shown in Figure 4.17(b). If these mid-points are displaced randomly up or down, the triangular mesh in Figure 4.17(c) emerges. Applying this technique to the new four triangles produces sixteen triangles, and if continued to further levels it creates a very realistic mountain range. The one drawback with this procedure is that it generates very large numbers of polygons very quickly.

5

Geometrical
Transformations

5.0 Introduction

It has already been mentioned that a VE is not just a collection of polygons. A VE is a hierarchical structure that determines what a user can or cannot do. This structure contains the fundamental geometric descriptions of the VE, together with other relevant attributes such as lighting, colour, texture and sound. It is highly likely that it will contain procedures capable of building objects, and other procedures that determine the size, orientation and position of different parts of articulated objects.

Take, for example, a scenario where a user is immersed in an environment displaying a box resting on a table. If the user reaches out and touches the box, there is no reason why the box should move. The system must be prepared in advance to indicate that the box is able to move, given the right conditions. Even with this type of preparation, what would happen if the box were pushed beyond the extent of the table's top? Probably nothing, unless this condition had been anticipated during the definition of the box. If the box has to fall, then the rate of acceleration must be specified, and if the box is supposed to bounce off the floor, then these dynamics must be described somewhere within the structure. This sounds like a lot of work – and it really is for large environments. Recall that a VE for a flight simulator requires several hundred hours to build! Such environments, however, are not typical of most VR applications, and we should not be too intimidated by this example.

To begin with, an interactive Graphical User Interface (GUI) may be used to assemble some of the objects for the database. A typical system provides the user with menu-driven tools to define the various objects and how these objects are assembled to form the VE. The system must enable the user to quit at any stage, file to disk the current database, and recover the work later. At any reasonable stage of development, it should be possible to investigate how the database behaves when used as an interactive VE. The system should also provide the user with debugging aids to track down faults. Such aids might include the display of surface normals, points, edges, light sources, collision boxes, bounding boxes and frames of reference. These could help identify faults in geometry, object attributes, modes of interaction and other conditions.

Some objects may be generated by procedures, which are executed at run time and evaluated every time a frame is displayed. Such procedures may be organized as a hierarchy and refer to other internal library procedures. However, no matter how the VE is represented, efficient mechanisms must exist to permit the real-time modification of the hierarchical structure. This might consist of moving individual vertices to new positions, moving an object to the current position of the VO's hand, or moving a light source to a different orientation.

Let us now examine the geometrical transformations used to organize a VE.

5.1   Frames of reference

To construct a VE we require a 3D Cartesian frame of reference within which objects and the VO are located. Objects are modelled relative to their own frame of reference, which will probably have extra axes about which certain elements rotate. The VO has its individual frame of reference that is used to capture the perspective projection of the VE. For consistency, these three frames of reference are declared as right-handed coordinate systems and are illustrated in Figure 5.1. Objects are first modelled within their Object Coordinate System (OCS) which can be visualized to be coincident with the World Coordinate System (WCS) representing the VE. In Figure 5.1 these two systems are separated for clarity. Various modelling transformations are then used to scale, rotate, shear and translate objects to locate them in the VE. Similarly, the VO's position is fixed using data from the 3D head tracking system.

5.2   Modelling transformations

The four transformations considered here – scale, reflection, rotate and translate – are normally applied in this sequence because it is simple to envisage the overall operation. The transformations are normally expressed as matrices that can be concatenated to a single transform matrix. When a view of the VE is rendered, this matrix is computed and applied to reveal the

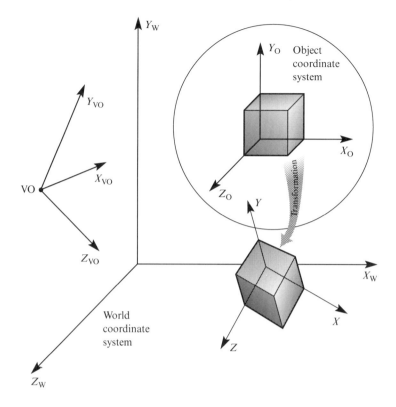

Figure 5.1 The relationship between the three frames of reference for the world, VO and object coordinate systems.

object's actual position in the VE. Otherwise, the object is held in the database in its original coordinate form together with its modelling transformations. This strategy is observed only as far as is possible, for if the coordinates of an object were continuously processed by thousands or millions of sequential transformations, errors would accumulate through the finite numerical precision of digital computers.

Although the transformations are generally evaluated in the sequence 'scale, reflection, rotate and translate', they will be explained in the logical sequence 'translate, scale, reflection and rotate'.

5.2.1 Translate

The translate transformation enables an object to be positioned anywhere within a VE simply by specifying three offset values that are associated with every 3D vertex of the object. The offsets are held within a matrix associated with an object, and only when the object is required for rendering, or some other task such as collision detection, is the matrix applied to reveal the

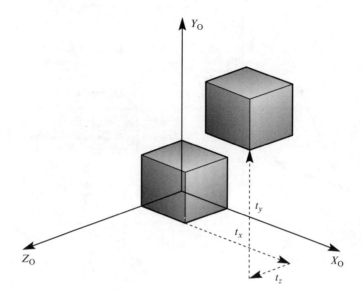

Figure 5.2   An object can be translated in space simply by adding three offsets, t_x, t_y and t_z to the x-, y- and z-coordinates.

object's true position. This idea is fundamental to all types of transformations, as it means that an object's position, scale or orientation can be controlled by updating matrix elements rather than by disturbing an object's coordinate values.

Because the translation transformation requires a value to be added to a vertex, the matrix representing this 3D action must be a 4×4 matrix to incorporate the translation terms. The homogeneous form accommodates this very elegantly.

Any vertex (x,y,z) can be located at (x',y',z') by adding t_x, t_y and t_z to x, y and z respectively:

$$x' = x + t_x$$
$$y' = y + t_y \qquad \text{(5.1)}$$
$$z' = z + t_z$$

which can be represented by the following homogeneous matrix operation:

$$
\begin{bmatrix} x' \\ y' \\ z' \\ 1 \end{bmatrix}
=
\begin{bmatrix} 1 & 0 & 0 & t_x \\ 0 & 1 & 0 & t_y \\ 0 & 0 & 1 & t_z \\ 0 & 0 & 0 & 1 \end{bmatrix}
\begin{bmatrix} x \\ y \\ z \\ 1 \end{bmatrix}
\qquad \text{(5.2)}
$$

An object can now be moved about a VE simply by modifying the translation offsets as shown in Figure 5.2. Furthermore, this transform can be concatenated with other matrices controlling the object's size and orientation.

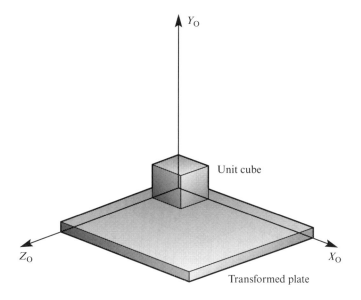

Figure 5.3   A unit cube can be transformed into a thin plate by using a scaling transform that scales the x-, y- and z-coordinates by different amounts.

5.2.2   Scale

The scaling transformation alters the size of an object by scaling all of its coordinates relative to the origin of the OCS. The matrix operation representing this action is:

$$\begin{bmatrix} x' \\ y' \\ z' \\ 1 \end{bmatrix} = \begin{bmatrix} S_x & 0 & 0 & 0 \\ 0 & S_y & 0 & 0 \\ 0 & 0 & S_z & 0 \\ 0 & 0 & 0 & 1 \end{bmatrix} \begin{bmatrix} x \\ y \\ z \\ 1 \end{bmatrix} \qquad (5.3)$$

where S_x, S_y and S_z are the individual scale factors for the x-, y- and z-coordinates respectively. Having individual scale factors means that an object can be scaled by different amounts in different directions to create a stretching or squashing effect. For example, a unit cube can be transformed into a thin plate 5 by 0.1 by 4 units as follows:

$$\begin{bmatrix} x' \\ y' \\ z' \\ 1 \end{bmatrix} = \begin{bmatrix} 5 & 0 & 0 & 0 \\ 0 & 0.1 & 0 & 0 \\ 0 & 0 & 4 & 0 \\ 0 & 0 & 0 & 1 \end{bmatrix} \begin{bmatrix} x \\ y \\ z \\ 1 \end{bmatrix} \qquad (5.4)$$

Figure 5.3 illustrates the effect of this transformation.

When objects offset from the origin are scaled, their offsets are also

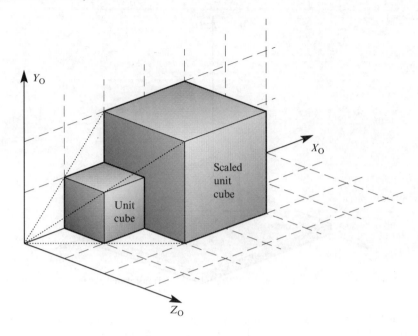

Figure 5.4   Because the unit cube is offset one unit in the *x*-direction, when it is scaled by a factor of two, the scaled cube is offset by two units.

scaled. This is because the scaling action is relative to the OCS's origin. To appreciate this effect, consider the situation shown in Figure 5.4 where a unit cube is offset along the *x*-axis by one unit and then scaled by a factor of two. The scaled cube is offset by two units. If this is not desired, and the cube's corner identified by (1,0,0) has to be coincident with the scaled version, then this can be effected as follows. First, the offset unit cube is translated such that the vertex undergoing zero scaling is placed at the origin; second, the scaling is performed; and third, the scaled cube is returned to its original position. In matrix terms, this is represented by:

$$
\begin{bmatrix} x' \\ y' \\ z' \\ 1 \end{bmatrix} = \begin{bmatrix} 1 & 0 & 0 & t_x \\ 0 & 1 & 0 & t_y \\ 0 & 0 & 1 & t_z \\ 0 & 0 & 0 & 1 \end{bmatrix} \begin{bmatrix} S_x & 0 & 0 & 0 \\ 0 & S_y & 0 & 0 \\ 0 & 0 & S_z & 0 \\ 0 & 0 & 0 & 1 \end{bmatrix} \begin{bmatrix} 1 & 0 & 0 & -t_x \\ 0 & 1 & 0 & -t_y \\ 0 & 0 & 1 & -t_z \\ 0 & 0 & 0 & 1 \end{bmatrix} \begin{bmatrix} x \\ y \\ z \\ 1 \end{bmatrix}
$$

(5.5)

which concatenates to:

$$
\begin{bmatrix} x' \\ y' \\ z' \\ 1 \end{bmatrix} = \begin{bmatrix} S_x & 0 & 0 & t_x(1 - S_x) \\ 0 & S_y & 0 & t_y(1 - S_y) \\ 0 & 0 & S_z & t_z(1 - S_z) \\ 0 & 0 & 0 & 1 \end{bmatrix} \begin{bmatrix} x \\ y \\ z \\ 1 \end{bmatrix}
$$

(5.6)

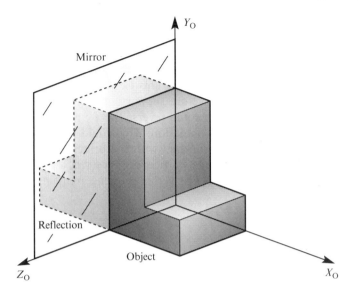

Figure 5.5 The object's reflection can be computed by reversing the sign of every x-coordinate.

For the above example the matrix would be:

$$
\begin{bmatrix} x' \\ y' \\ z' \\ 1 \end{bmatrix} = \begin{bmatrix} 2 & 0 & 0 & -1 \\ 0 & 2 & 0 & 0 \\ 0 & 0 & 2 & 0 \\ 0 & 0 & 0 & 1 \end{bmatrix} \begin{bmatrix} x \\ y \\ z \\ 1 \end{bmatrix}
\tag{5.7}
$$

5.2.3 Reflection

If we imagine a mirror positioned in one of the planes associated with the principal axes, a reflection of an object can be computed by reversing the sign of either the x-, y- or z-coordinates. For example, consider the situation illustrated in Figure 5.5 where a reflection is required about the YZ-plane. If we reverse the sign of every x-vertex, and leave the y- and z-coordinates untouched, the resultant object is a reflection of the original object. In matrix terms, this is expressed as follows:

$$
\begin{bmatrix} x' \\ y' \\ z' \\ 1 \end{bmatrix} = \begin{bmatrix} -1 & 0 & 0 & 0 \\ 0 & 1 & 0 & 0 \\ 0 & 0 & 1 & 0 \\ 0 & 0 & 0 & 1 \end{bmatrix} \begin{bmatrix} x \\ y \\ z \\ 1 \end{bmatrix}
\tag{5.8}
$$

Similarly, if the signs of the y-coordinates are reversed, a reflection occurs about the ZX-plane; and if the signs of the z-coordinates are reversed, a reflection occurs about the XY-plane.

A consequence of the reflection is that a polygon's vertex sequence is also reversed, which destroys any convention in use to maintain vertex sequences in a clockwise or anticlockwise sequence. This can be corrected by reversing the relevant entries in the data structure supporting the vertex entries.

It is probably evident that we could reverse the x-, y- and z-coordinates in one operation, or any other combination. This could place the reflection in any one of the eight octants associated with the principal axes. When an odd number of sign changes are made, vertices are reversed, and when an even number of sign changes are made, the vertex sequence remains unchanged.

5.2.4   Rotation

As described in Chapter 3, orientation can be specified in a variety of ways, and for completeness we will review the techniques in the context of modelling transformations.

Direction cosines

Direction cosines employ the cosines of angles formed between two frames of reference, and are useful only when there is immediate access to these angles. The matrix formulation is:

$$
\begin{bmatrix} x' \\ y' \\ z' \\ 1 \end{bmatrix} = \begin{bmatrix} r_{11} & r_{21} & r_{31} & 0 \\ r_{12} & r_{22} & r_{32} & 0 \\ r_{13} & r_{23} & r_{33} & 0 \\ 0 & 0 & 0 & 1 \end{bmatrix} \begin{bmatrix} x \\ y \\ z \\ 1 \end{bmatrix} \tag{5.9}
$$

where:

r_{11}, r_{12} and r_{13} are the direction cosines of the secondary x-axis
r_{21}, r_{22} and r_{23} are the direction cosines of the secondary y-axis
r_{31}, r_{32} and r_{33} are the direction cosines of the secondary z-axis

Note that this matrix is the transpose of that used to convert points in one frame of reference to another. This is because an object rotation is equivalent to rotating the frame of reference by an equal angle in the opposite direction.

As an example, say we needed to rotate the pyramid in Figure 5.6(a) through a pitch angle of 90° about the x-axis. To begin with, we imagine the position of the rotated frame of reference $[X_0' \; Y_0' \; Z_0']$ shown in Figure 5.6(b), and compute the direction cosines for this Cartesian system as follows:

$$
\begin{bmatrix} 1 & 0 & 0 & 0 \\ 0 & 0 & -1 & 0 \\ 0 & 1 & 0 & 0 \\ 0 & 0 & 0 & 1 \end{bmatrix} \tag{5.10}
$$

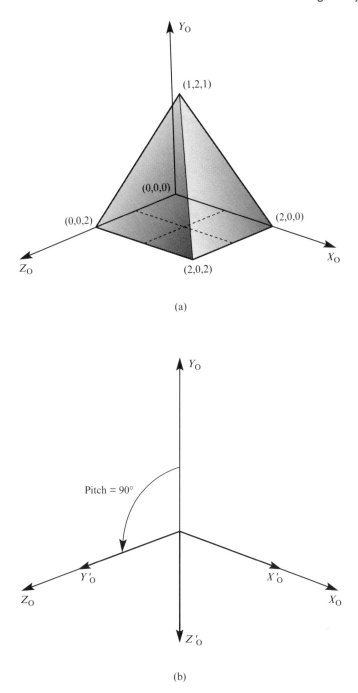

(a)

(b)

Figure 5.6 (a) The original position of the pyramid showing the coordinates of the vertices. (b) The orientation of the axes after a pitch of 90°. (c) The position of the pyramid after applying the matrix operation.

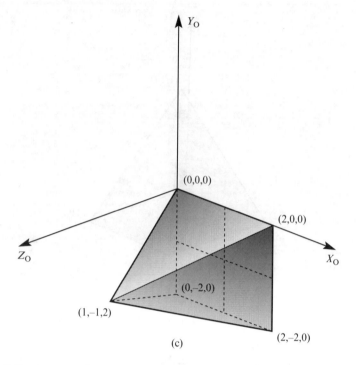

Figure 5.6   (continued)

If we substitute the coordinates of the pyramid in the following transformation we obtain the rotated pyramid shown in Figure 5.6(c):

$$\begin{bmatrix} x' \\ y' \\ z' \\ 1 \end{bmatrix} = \begin{bmatrix} 1 & 0 & 0 & 0 \\ 0 & 0 & -1 & 0 \\ 0 & 1 & 0 & 0 \\ 0 & 0 & 0 & 1 \end{bmatrix} \begin{bmatrix} x \\ y \\ z \\ 1 \end{bmatrix} \tag{5.11}$$

Compound rotations

A compound rotation can be accomplished by subjecting an object to a sequence of matrix operations. To illustrate this, consider the action of rolling the pyramid of Figure 5.6 90° about the z-axis, after performing the 90° pitch rotation. Figure 5.6(c) shows the position of the pyramid after the pitch rotation, and Figure 5.7(a) shows the position of the axes rotated through a roll angle of 90°. The matrix operation for this extra transformation is:

$$\begin{bmatrix} x' \\ y' \\ z' \\ 1 \end{bmatrix} = \begin{bmatrix} 0 & -1 & 0 & 0 \\ 1 & 0 & 0 & 0 \\ 0 & 0 & 1 & 0 \\ 0 & 0 & 0 & 1 \end{bmatrix} \begin{bmatrix} x \\ y \\ z \\ 1 \end{bmatrix} \tag{5.12}$$

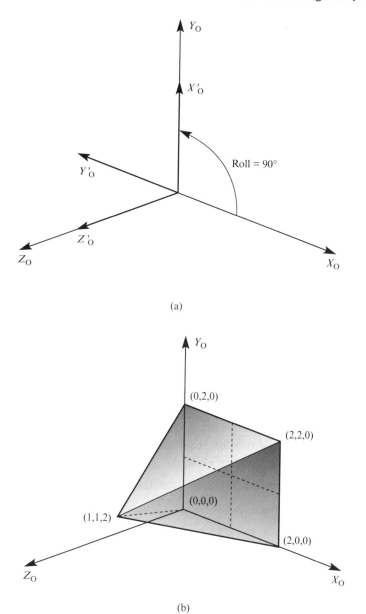

(a)

(b)

Figure 5.7 (a) The position of the axes after a 90° roll. (b) The final position of the pyramid after being subjected to a roll of 90°.

and if we apply it to the last orientation of the pyramid we obtain the position shown in Figure 5.7(b). The compound rotation could have been achieved by concatenating the two matrices as follows:

$$
\begin{bmatrix} x' \\ y' \\ z' \\ 1 \end{bmatrix} = \begin{bmatrix} 0 & -1 & 0 & 0 \\ 1 & 0 & 0 & 0 \\ 0 & 0 & 1 & 0 \\ 0 & 0 & 0 & 1 \end{bmatrix} \begin{bmatrix} 1 & 0 & 0 & 0 \\ 0 & 0 & -1 & 0 \\ 0 & 1 & 0 & 0 \\ 0 & 0 & 0 & 1 \end{bmatrix} \begin{bmatrix} x \\ y \\ z \\ 1 \end{bmatrix} \tag{5.13}
$$

which is equivalent to:

$$
\begin{bmatrix} x' \\ y' \\ z' \\ 1 \end{bmatrix} = \begin{bmatrix} 0 & 0 & 1 & 0 \\ 1 & 0 & 0 & 0 \\ 0 & 1 & 0 & 0 \\ 0 & 0 & 0 & 1 \end{bmatrix} \begin{bmatrix} x \\ y \\ z \\ 1 \end{bmatrix} \tag{5.14}
$$

If the original coordinates for the pyramid are substituted into this transformation it will be subjected to a pitch and roll rotation and finish up in the position shown in Figure 5.7(b). As the rotations are relative to the original frame of reference, they are equivalent to *XYZ* fixed angles.

XYZ fixed angles

XYZ fixed angles describe the angles of rotation applied to an object relative to its fixed frame of reference – namely, the OCS. By definition, the three angles of rotation are roll, pitch and yaw, where:

>   *roll* is the angle of rotation about the *z*-axis
>   *pitch* is the angle of rotation about the *x*-axis
>   *yaw* is the angle of rotation about the *y*-axis

The three matrices performing these transformations are:

$$
\begin{bmatrix} \cos roll & -\sin roll & 0 & 0 \\ \sin roll & \cos roll & 0 & 0 \\ 0 & 0 & 1 & 0 \\ 0 & 0 & 0 & 1 \end{bmatrix} \tag{5.15}
$$

$$
\begin{bmatrix} 1 & 0 & 0 & 0 \\ 0 & \cos pitch & -\sin pitch & 0 \\ 0 & \sin pitch & \cos pitch & 0 \\ 0 & 0 & 0 & 1 \end{bmatrix} \tag{5.16}
$$

$$
\begin{bmatrix} \cos yaw & 0 & \sin yaw & 0 \\ 0 & 1 & 0 & 0 \\ -\sin yaw & 0 & \cos yaw & 0 \\ 0 & 0 & 0 & 1 \end{bmatrix} \tag{5.17}
$$

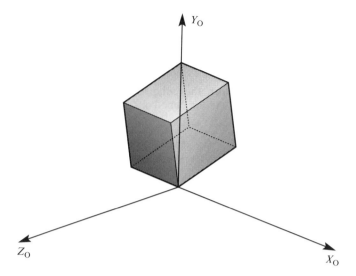

Figure 5.8 A cube oriented such that a diagonal is coincident with the y-axis.

and they can be combined together in any arbitrary sequence. However, as rotations are noncommutative, that is, the chosen sequence generally leads to a unique result, a consistent sequence of evaluation must be observed.

To illustrate their usage, consider the problem of rotating a cube such that one of its diagonals is coincident with the y-axis, as illustrated in Figure 5.8. If we begin with a cube positioned as shown in Figure 5.9(a), it can be rotated 45° about the y-axis (Figure 5.9b); it is then rolled 54.736° about the z-axis (Figure 5.9c). The matrix transformations to achieve this are:

$$
\begin{bmatrix}
\cos 54.736° & -\sin 54.736° & 0 & 0 \\
\sin 54.736° & \cos 54.736° & 0 & 0 \\
0 & 0 & 1 & 0 \\
0 & 0 & 0 & 1
\end{bmatrix}
\begin{bmatrix}
\cos 45° & 0 & \sin 45° & 0 \\
0 & 1 & 0 & 0 \\
-\sin 45° & 0 & \cos 45° & 0 \\
0 & 0 & 0 & 1
\end{bmatrix}
\tag{5.18}
$$

which concatenates to:

$$
\begin{bmatrix}
0.408 & 0.816 & 0.408 & 0.0 \\
0.577 & 0.577 & 0.577 & 0.0 \\
-0.707 & 0.0 & 0.707 & 0.0 \\
0.0 & 0.0 & 0.0 & 1.0
\end{bmatrix}
\tag{5.19}
$$

We can see from Figure 5.9 that the point $(1,1,1)$ is transformed to $(0.0,1.732,0.0)$, which results from applying the above matrix.

So far, all the rotations have been about one of the principal axes associated with the OCS, so let us now consider rotations about axes parallel to these reference axes. Consider the situation shown in Figure 5.10 where a cube has to be rotated about an axis that passes through the point $(x_r, 0, z_r)$, and is parallel to the y-axis. This can be performed if we first imagine the axis of rotation Y_r to be the y-axis of the rotational frame of reference. If we then compute the cube's coordinates relative to this frame of reference we can perform the rotation and then return the cube to its original frame. The entire sequence consists of: first, translate the cube $(-x_r, 0, -z_r)$; second, rotate it about the

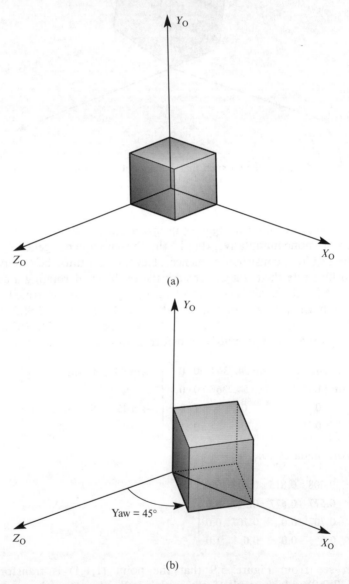

(a)

(b)

Figure 5.9 (a) The starting position of the cube. (b) The position of the cube after applying a yaw rotation of 45°. (c) The final position of the cube after applying a roll rotation of 54.736°.

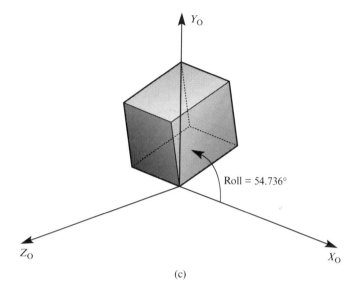

(c)

Figure 5.9 (continued)

y-axis; and third, translate it $(x_r,0,z_r)$. In matrix form this is:

$$
\begin{bmatrix} x' \\ y' \\ z' \\ 1 \end{bmatrix} = \begin{bmatrix} 1 & 0 & 0 & x_r \\ 0 & 1 & 0 & 0 \\ 0 & 0 & 1 & z_r \\ 0 & 0 & 0 & 1 \end{bmatrix} \begin{bmatrix} \cos\theta & 0 & \sin\theta & 0 \\ 0 & 1 & 0 & 0 \\ -\sin\theta & 0 & \cos\theta & 0 \\ 0 & 0 & 0 & 1 \end{bmatrix} \begin{bmatrix} 1 & 0 & 0 & -x_r \\ 0 & 1 & 0 & 0 \\ 0 & 0 & 1 & -z_r \\ 0 & 0 & 0 & 1 \end{bmatrix} \begin{bmatrix} x \\ y \\ z \\ 1 \end{bmatrix} \quad (5.20)
$$

which concatenates to:

$$
\begin{bmatrix} x' \\ y' \\ z' \\ 1 \end{bmatrix} = \begin{bmatrix} \cos\theta & 0 & \sin\theta & x_r(1-\cos\theta) - z_r\sin\theta \\ 0 & 1 & 0 & 0 \\ -\sin\theta & 0 & \cos\theta & z_r(1-\cos\theta) + x_r\sin\theta \\ 0 & 0 & 0 & 1 \end{bmatrix} \begin{bmatrix} x \\ y \\ z \\ 1 \end{bmatrix} \quad (5.21)
$$

where (x,y,z) is the vertex to be rotated, θ is the angle of rotation, and (x',y',z') is the rotated vertex.

Concatenated forms for the x- and z-axes are respectively:

$$
\begin{bmatrix} 1 & 0 & 0 & 0 \\ 0 & \cos\theta & -\sin\theta & y_r(1-\cos\theta) + z_r\sin\theta \\ 0 & \sin\theta & \cos\theta & z_r(1-\cos\theta) - y_r\sin\theta \\ 0 & 0 & 0 & 1 \end{bmatrix} \quad (5.22)
$$

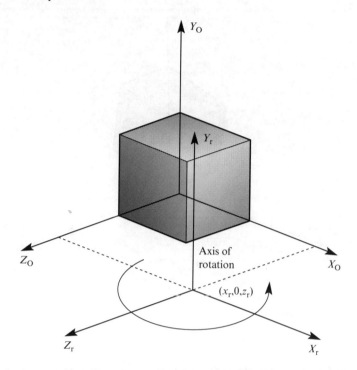

Figure 5.10   To rotate the cube about the axis of rotation, the cube is first translated $(-x_r, 0, -z_r)$, in effect to position the axis of rotation at the origin. The rotation is performed and the rotated cube translated $(x_r, 0, z_r)$ to compensate for the original translation.

$$
\begin{bmatrix}
\cos\theta & -\sin\theta & 0 & x_r(1-\cos\theta) + y_r\sin\theta \\
\sin\theta & \cos\theta & 0 & y_r(1-\cos\theta) - x_r\sin\theta \\
0 & 0 & 1 & 0 \\
0 & 0 & 0 & 1
\end{bmatrix}
\tag{5.23}
$$

XYZ Euler angles

XYZ Euler angles are the angles of rotation applied to an object relative to a frame of reference that moves with the object. In some respects, they are more convenient than *XYZ* fixed angles as it is easier to visualize the orientation of an object when subjected to a compound rotation.

If we specify a compound rotation using *XYZ* fixed angles of roll, pitch and yaw, the transform matrices are applied to the object in that sequence:

$$
\begin{bmatrix} x' \\ y' \\ z' \\ 1 \end{bmatrix} = [yaw]\,[pitch]\,[roll] \begin{bmatrix} x \\ y \\ z \\ 1 \end{bmatrix}
\tag{5.24}
$$

However, if *XYZ* Euler angles are used, the sequence is reversed as follows:

$$
\begin{bmatrix} x' \\ y' \\ z' \\ 1 \end{bmatrix} = [roll]\,[pitch]\,[yaw] \begin{bmatrix} x \\ y \\ z \\ 1 \end{bmatrix}
\tag{5.25}
$$

We will confirm this with an example.

Consider the scenario shown in Figure 5.11(a) where an object is located at the origin of the OCS. Two sets of axes have been drawn: one representing the absolute OCS, and another representing an imaginary set that travels with the object. If the object is first rolled about the z-axis through an angle of 90° it will end up as shown in Figure 5.11(b). Note the new position of the imaginary axes. The object is now subjected to a 90° pitch rotation about the travelling x-axis, which leaves the object positioned as shown in Figure 5.11(c). The last rotation consists of a 90° yaw rotation about the travelling y-axis, which leaves the object as shown in Figure 5.11(d). If the point *P* on the original object has coordinates (2,1,5), its final rotated position *P'* in the OCS is (−2,5,1). We can now compute the coordinates of *P'* by using the roll, pitch and yaw matrices.

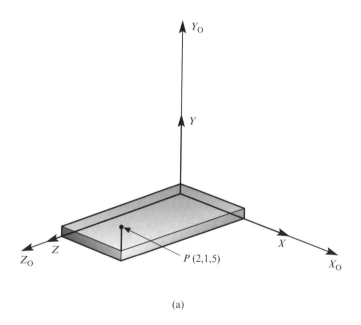

(a)

Figure 5.11 (a) The original object. (b) Applying a roll of 90° about the Z-axis. (c) Applying a pitch of 90° about the X-axis. (d) Applying a yaw of 90° about the Y-axis.

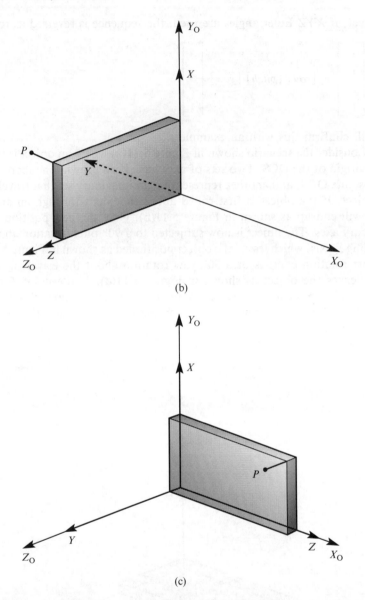

(b)

(c)

Figure 5.11 (continued)

The three matrices are as follows:

$$
\begin{array}{ccc}
\text{Roll} & \text{Pitch} & \text{Yaw} \\
\begin{bmatrix} 0 & -1 & 0 & 0 \\ 1 & 0 & 0 & 0 \\ 0 & 0 & 1 & 0 \\ 0 & 0 & 0 & 1 \end{bmatrix} &
\begin{bmatrix} 1 & 0 & 0 & 0 \\ 0 & 0 & -1 & 0 \\ 0 & 1 & 0 & 0 \\ 0 & 0 & 0 & 1 \end{bmatrix} &
\begin{bmatrix} 0 & 0 & 1 & 0 \\ 0 & 1 & 0 & 0 \\ -1 & 0 & 0 & 0 \\ 0 & 0 & 0 & 1 \end{bmatrix}
\end{array}
$$

(5.26)

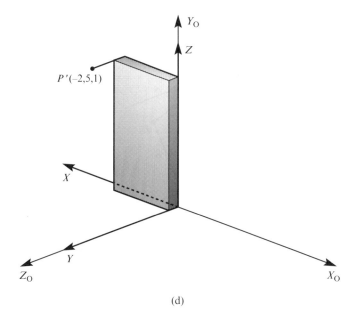

(d)

Figure 5.11   (continued)

which concatenate to:

$$\begin{bmatrix} -1 & 0 & 0 & 0 \\ 0 & 0 & 1 & 0 \\ 0 & 1 & 0 & 0 \\ 0 & 0 & 0 & 1 \end{bmatrix} \tag{5.27}$$

and if we subject the coordinates $(2,1,5)$ to this transformation, we obtain $(-2,5,1)$.

Rotations about an arbitrary axis

Rotations about an arbitrary axis are slightly more complex than those previously covered. To begin with, we will assume that the axis passes through the origin. Figure 5.12 shows a typical situation where a point P is rotated through an angle θ about an axis defined by a unit vector $\mathbf{A}$, to P'. Let H be a point on $\mathbf{A}$ such that $\mathbf{U}$ is orthogonal to $\mathbf{A}$, and let $\mathbf{V} = \mathbf{A} \times \mathbf{U}$.

From Figure 5.12 we observe that in the plane PHP':

$$\mathbf{U}' = \cos \theta \, \mathbf{U} + \sin \theta \, \mathbf{V} \tag{5.28}$$

As:

$$\mathbf{U} = \mathbf{P} - \mathbf{H} \tag{5.29}$$

then:

$$\mathbf{V} = \mathbf{A} \times (\mathbf{P} - \mathbf{H}) \tag{5.30}$$

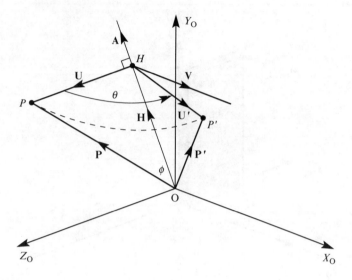

Figure 5.12   The geometry associated with rotating a point P through an angle θ to P' about an axis $\mathbf{A}$.

Therefore:

$$\mathbf{V} = \mathbf{A} \times \mathbf{P} - \mathbf{A} \times \mathbf{H} = \mathbf{A} \times \mathbf{P} \tag{5.31}$$

Similarly:

$$\mathbf{H} = |\mathbf{P}| \cos \phi \, \mathbf{A} \tag{5.32}$$

$$\mathbf{H} = \frac{|\mathbf{P}| (\mathbf{A} \cdot \mathbf{P}) \mathbf{A}}{|\mathbf{A}| |\mathbf{P}|} \tag{5.33}$$

$$\mathbf{H} = (\mathbf{A} \cdot \mathbf{P}) \mathbf{A} \tag{5.34}$$

Therefore:

$$\mathbf{P}' = \mathbf{H} + \mathbf{U}' \tag{5.35}$$

$$= (\mathbf{A} \cdot \mathbf{P}) \mathbf{A} + \cos \theta \, \mathbf{U} + \sin \theta \, \mathbf{V} \tag{5.36}$$

$$= (\mathbf{A} \cdot \mathbf{P}) \mathbf{A} + \cos \theta \, (\mathbf{P} - (\mathbf{A} \cdot \mathbf{P}) \mathbf{A}) + \sin \theta \, \mathbf{A} \times \mathbf{P} \tag{5.37}$$

$$= \cos \theta \, \mathbf{P} + (1 - \cos \theta) \mathbf{A} (\mathbf{A} \cdot \mathbf{P}) + \sin \theta \, \mathbf{A} \times \mathbf{P} \tag{5.38}$$

We can test this relationship with the example illustrated in Figure 5.13, where the point $P(0,1,0)$ is rotated through 90° to P' about the axis defined by the unit vector $\mathbf{A}$. By inspection, we can see that the rotated point P' has coordinates $(0.5, 0.5, 0.707)$. Using the above relationship we have:

$$\mathbf{A} = \begin{bmatrix} 0.707 \\ 0.707 \\ 0.0 \end{bmatrix} \qquad \mathbf{P} = \begin{bmatrix} 0.0 \\ 1.0 \\ 0.0 \end{bmatrix} \tag{5.39}$$

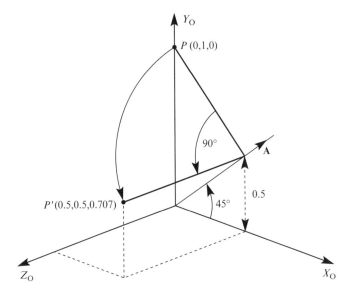

Figure 5.13 The point $P(0,1,0)$ is to be rotated $90°$ about the unit vector $A = [0.707,0.707,0.0]$. The rotated point P' has coordinates $(0.5, 0.5, 0.707)$.

$$\mathbf{P'} = \cos 90° \,\mathbf{P} + \left(1 - \cos 90°\right)\mathbf{A}\left(\mathbf{A}\cdot\mathbf{P}\right) + \sin 90°\,\mathbf{A}\times\mathbf{P} \tag{5.40}$$
$$= \mathbf{A}\left(\mathbf{A}\cdot\mathbf{P}\right) + \mathbf{A}\times\mathbf{P} \tag{5.41}$$

$$= \begin{bmatrix} 0.707 \\ 0.707 \\ 0.0 \end{bmatrix} \left(\begin{bmatrix} 0.707 \\ 0.707 \\ 0.0 \end{bmatrix} \cdot \begin{bmatrix} 0.0 \\ 1.0 \\ 0.0 \end{bmatrix} \right) + \begin{bmatrix} 0.707 \\ 0.707 \\ 0.0 \end{bmatrix} \times \begin{bmatrix} 0.0 \\ 1.0 \\ 0.0 \end{bmatrix} \tag{5.42}$$

$$= \begin{bmatrix} 0.707 \\ 0.707 \\ 0.0 \end{bmatrix} 0.707 + \begin{bmatrix} 0.0 \\ 0.0 \\ 0.707 \end{bmatrix} \tag{5.43}$$

$$= \begin{bmatrix} 0.5 \\ 0.5 \\ 0.707 \end{bmatrix} \tag{5.44}$$

The vector expression for computing $\mathbf{P'}$ can also be represented in matrix terms as:

$$\mathbf{P'} = \left[\cos\theta\,I + \left(1 - \cos\theta\right)AA^{\mathrm{T}} + \sin\theta\,J\right]\mathbf{P} \tag{5.45}$$

where:

$$I = \begin{bmatrix} 1 & 0 & 0 \\ 0 & 1 & 0 \\ 0 & 0 & 1 \end{bmatrix} \quad A = \begin{bmatrix} a_x \\ a_y \\ a_z \end{bmatrix} \quad J = \begin{bmatrix} 0 & -a_z & a_y \\ a_z & 0 & -a_x \\ -a_y & a_x & 0 \end{bmatrix} \tag{5.46}$$

A general rotation matrix

To conclude this digression on rotation transformations, we will examine one last matrix which can be used to generate *all* of the above rotation matrices. The matrix rotates points about an arbitrary axis passing through the origin. This includes x-, y- and z-axes.

$$\begin{bmatrix} ka_x^2 + c & ka_xa_y - sa_z & ka_xa_z + sa_y \\ ka_xa_y + sa_z & ka_y^2 + c & ka_ya_z - sa_x \\ ka_xa_z - sa_y & ka_ya_z + sa_x & ka_z^2 + c \end{bmatrix} \qquad (5.47)$$

where $[a_x, a_y, a_z]^T$ is the unit vector aligned with the axis; θ is the angle of rotation; $c = \cos\theta$, $s = \sin\theta$, and $k = (1 - \cos\theta)$. For example, consider a pitch rotation of $\theta = 90°$ about the x-axis. This makes:

$$[a_x, a_y, a_z]^T = [1,0,0]^T \qquad c = 0 \qquad s = 1 \qquad k = 1 \qquad (5.48)$$

The matrix operation becomes:

$$\begin{bmatrix} x' \\ y' \\ z' \end{bmatrix} = \begin{bmatrix} 1 & 0 & 0 \\ 0 & 0 & -1 \\ 0 & 1 & 0 \end{bmatrix} \begin{bmatrix} x \\ y \\ z \end{bmatrix} \qquad (5.49)$$

If the point $(1,1,0)$ is subjected to this pitch rotation, it finishes up at $(1,0,1)$, which is correct. By providing values for the matrix elements, points can be rotated about arbitrary axes.

There is an interesting link between the matrix (5.47) and the equivalent matrix for a quaternion (3.75). Given a quaternion **q**, such that:

$$\mathbf{q} = [s + x\mathbf{i} + y\mathbf{j} + z\mathbf{k}] \qquad (5.50)$$

Therefore:

$$\cos\theta/2 = s \qquad (5.51)$$

$$a_x = \frac{x}{\sin\theta/2} \qquad (5.52)$$

$$a_y = \frac{y}{\sin\theta/2} \qquad (5.53)$$

$$a_z = \frac{z}{\sin\theta/2} \qquad (5.54)$$

Substituting the values of a_x, a_y, a_z and $\cos\theta/2$ in (5.47) produces the matrix:

$$\begin{bmatrix} 1 - 2(y^2 + z^2) & 2(xy - sz) & 2(xz + sy) \\ 2(xy + sz) & 1 - 2(x^2 + z^2) & 2(yz - sx) \\ 2(xz - sy) & 2(yz + sx) & 1 - 2(x^2 + y^2) \end{bmatrix} \qquad (5.55)$$

which is how (3.76) was derived!

Plate 2 A radiosity scene. Produced by ATMA Rendering Systems srl, Milan, Italy, using Real Light.

Plate 3 A VIP using a very important display system. (Courtesy Fakespace, Inc.)

Plate 4 The V-PC VR system from Virtuality and IBM. (Courtesy Virtuality Ltd and IBM Ltd)

2

3

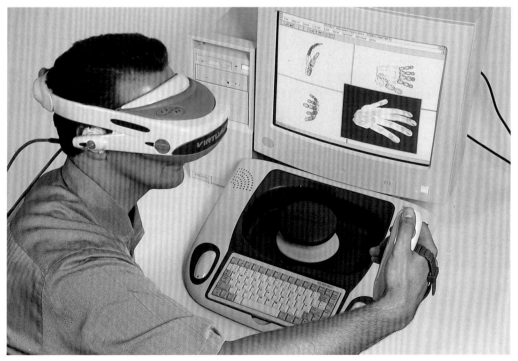

4

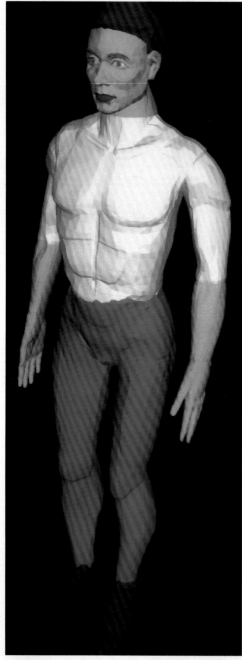

5

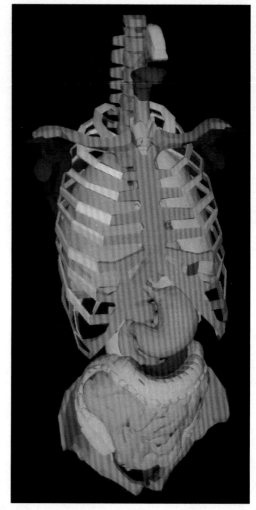

6

Plate 5 A human model from the *Jack* system. (Courtesy GMS Ltd and the University of Pennsylvania)

Plate 6 An interior view of a human model from the *Jack* system. (Courtesy GMS Ltd and the University of Pennsylvania)

Plate 7 A manipulator arm built for Hermes, the European Space Shuttle, using Sense8's WTK. (Courtesy Sense8 Corporation)

Plate 8 Two views of the Trent 800 aero engine. (Courtesy InSys Ltd and Rolls-Royce Ltd)

7

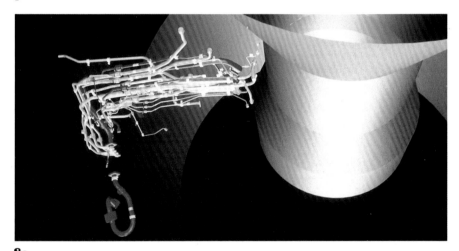

8a

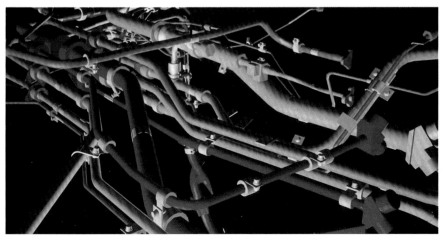

8b

Plate 9 Two interior views of the Trident nuclear submarine. (Courtesy InSys Ltd and Vickers Shipbuilding and Engineering Ltd)

Plate 10 A view of a virtual dining room incorporating fixtures and fittings supplied by Matsushita Electric Works Ltd. (Courtesy Division Ltd and Matsushita Electric Works Ltd)

Plate 11 Two views of a virtual supermarket. (Courtesy InSys Ltd and CWI plc)

Plate 12 How a *Jack* model can be used to assess reach distances and eye views. (Courtesy GMS Ltd and the University of Pennsylvania)

Plate 13 A virtual concept car. (Courtesy Division Ltd)

Plate 14 A single camera system being used with SimGraphics VActor Expression system. (Courtesy of Adaptive Optics Associates, Inc. and SimGraphics Engineering Corporation)

9a

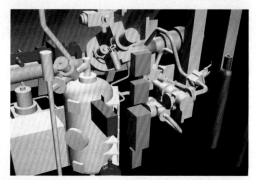

9b

11a

13

11b

14

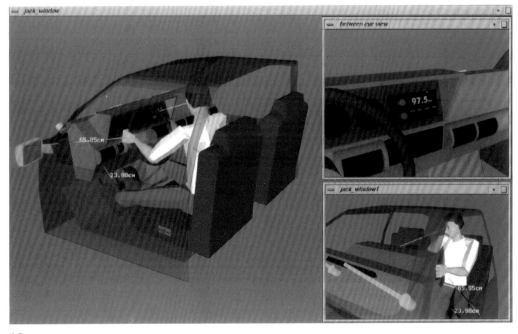

12

Plate 15 Immersive molecular modelling. (Courtesy Division Ltd, Glaxo Group Research and G. Tompkinson)

Plate 16 The CyberTron. (Courtesy StrayLight Corporation)

Plate 17 Two images illustrating real-world actions controlling a virtual face. (Courtesy Agnes Saulnier et al., Institut National de l'Audiovisuel, France)

15

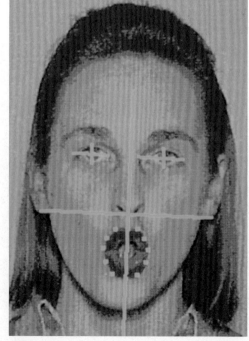

16

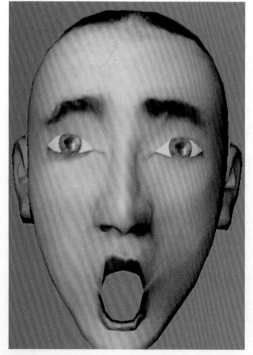

17a

17b

Plate 18 An internal view of a virtual reactor building. (Courtesy EDF and Division Ltd)

Plate 19 Volvo's safety simulator. (Courtesy Volvo (UK) Ltd and Division Ltd)

Plate 20 The Leclerc Tank Crew Training simulator. (Courtesy Thomson Training & Simulation Ltd)

18

19

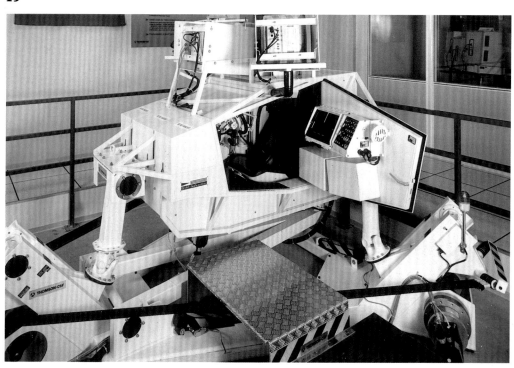

20

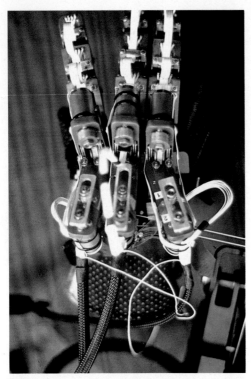

Plate 21 The ARTS Glove is capable of recording all the movements of the fingers and wrist. (Courtesy Scuola Superiore S. Anna)

Plate 22 The virtual hand is grasping an object under the control of the ARTS Glove. (Courtesy Scuola Superiore S. Anna)

21

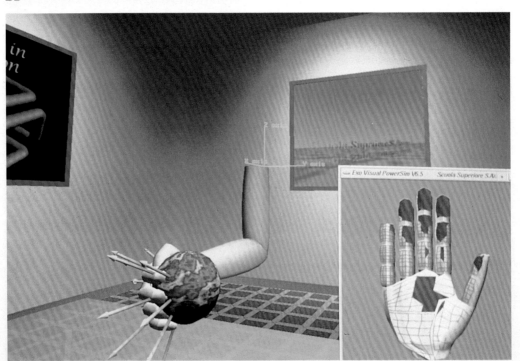

22

5.3 Instances

An important strategy in modern design and manufacturing methods is to minimize the number of different components used to construct an assembly or object. Significant savings in manufacturing processes, storage space, assembly procedures and maintenance costs are all possible if basic building blocks are used in different parts of a structure. For instance, a table can be constructed with four identical legs – there is no need for each leg to have a unique design. Similarly, the window frames for a large office complex might require only one or two designs.

When it comes to designing CAD systems that support such design activities, there is no need for the database to store repeated geometric descriptions for similar objects. For example, in the case of a table with four identical legs, a leg's geometry need only be stored once, and four references are made to this geometry in the table's description. The coordinates of the master leg are relative to the OCS, whereas the table's four legs require different positions, and possibly different orientations in the VE. However, the database can be organized such that the single leg is stored as a geometric entity, with a collection of matrix transformations. These are used to scale, rotate and translate this geometry to create the four legs in the correct positions, orientations and sizes. Such geometric elements are called *instances*, as they have no individual existence.

There are two major benefits for using instances: first, geometric descriptions are minimized, which keeps the database size under control; and second, if the attributes of the reference object, such as geometry, colour or texture, are altered, they are automatically propagated throughout the VE. Whereas, if every object had a unique definition within a database, it would be tedious to make repeated identical updates, and probably lead to errors and inconsistencies.

A simple table might require only a top and four legs, which means that we need to define the geometry of only the top and one leg.

5.4 Picking

In Chapter 3 we discovered how transforms are used to locate a virtual observer within a virtual environment. In particular, (3.13) showed that any point in the VE is transformed to the VO's frame of reference with four matrices: translate, yaw, pitch and roll. When these are concatenated, a single transform is available to perform this operation. The values of this transform are made available in real time by head-tracking hardware that permits a VR user to explore the VE with an HMD. The user's hand is also tracked with similar hardware. In this scenario we have three frames of reference: the virtual world space storing the VE, the virtual observer and the VO's hand.

Objects within the VE are modelled in their local frame of reference and positioned within the VE using modelling transformations such as translate, scale, reflect and rotate. By changing these transformations, an object can be moved about a VE according to some set of rules or procedure. But say the VO wishes to move an object with hand gestures – somehow the transform associated with the VO's hand must become associated with the object. At the end of the interaction, the transform describing the object's new position and orientation must be consistent with the original definition, as the VO may wish to interact with it again.

In order to cope with these different frames of reference, we need to introduce a notation that enables transform sequences to be manipulated with accuracy and confidence. The notation is based upon the paper by Holloway (1992).

5.4.1 Transform notation

If a single subscript is used to remind us of the local frame of reference, the notation P_O represents a point P in its Object space, while P_W represents a point in World space. The transform T_{WO} relates the two frames of reference sharing the two subscripts and is employed as follows:

$$P_W = T_{WO} \cdot P_O \qquad (5.56)$$

Notice the juxtaposition of the subscripts – the '$_W$' in P_W *mirrors* the '$_W$' in T_{WO}, while the '$_O$' in T_{WO} *mirrors* the '$_O$' in P_O.

If the transform T_{WO} converts points from the frame O to the frame W, the inverse transform T_{OW} performs the converse:

$$P_O = T_{OW} \cdot P_W \qquad (5.57)$$

Say we had three frames of reference A, B and C. A point in frame C is converted into frame B as follows:

$$P_B = T_{BC} \cdot P_C \qquad (5.58)$$

and a point in frame B is converted into frame A using:

$$P_A = T_{AB} \cdot P_B \qquad (5.59)$$

Therefore, a point in frame C is converted into frame A by the following:

$$P_A = T_{AB} \cdot T_{BC} \cdot P_C \qquad (5.60)$$

Once again, notice the mirroring or cancelling qualities of the subscripts.

With such a simple notation, we can immediately write expressions such as the following with considerable confidence:

$$P_A = T_{AB} \cdot T_{BC} \cdot T_{CD} \cdot T_{DE} \cdot P_E \qquad (5.61)$$

and

$$P_E = T_{DED} \cdot T_{DC} \cdot T_{CB} \cdot T_{BA} \cdot P_A \qquad (5.62)$$

The notation is very elegant and permits us to develop the transform strings to support object picking. However, before continuing with the 3D domain we will investigate a 2D example that will help our understanding of object picking.

5.4.2   Shape picking

Figure 5.14(a) shows a scenario where shape S is defined in its local frame O. This is located in the world frame W using the transform T_{WO}, such that:

$$P_W = T_{WO} \cdot P_O \tag{5.63}$$

and a similar transform T_{OW} relates points in the frame W back to the frame O as follows:

$$P_O = T_{OW} \cdot P_W \tag{5.64}$$

The same figure also includes a second frame of reference H which is related to W through the transform T_{WH}, such that:

$$P_W = T_{WH} \cdot P_H \tag{5.65}$$

and:

$$P_H = T_{HW} \cdot P_W \tag{5.66}$$

We can also see that the frames O and H arc related as follows:

$$P_H = T_{HO} \cdot P_O \tag{5.67}$$

and:

$$P_O = T_{OH} \cdot P_H \tag{5.68}$$

If we now wish to associate shape S with the movements of frame H, we can consider the action of this manipulation at two successive scene updates. Let the transform describing the current situation employ the above notation, while the transform describing the proposed movement be tagged with a prime ($'$). These two scenarios are shown in Figures 5.14(a) and 5.14(b).

If shape S is to share the behaviour of frame H, the transform must be identical to the previous transform T_{HO}. Therefore:

$$T'_{HO} = T_{HO} \tag{5.69}$$

In order to move shape S, the new transform T'_{WO} must be evaluated. Using the above notation we can write:

$$T'_{HO} = T'_{HW} \cdot T'_{WO} \tag{5.70}$$

and:

$$T_{HO} = T_{HW} \cdot T_{WO} \tag{5.71}$$

Using (5.69), we can write:

$$T'_{HW} \cdot T'_{WO} = T_{HW} \cdot T_{WO} \tag{5.72}$$

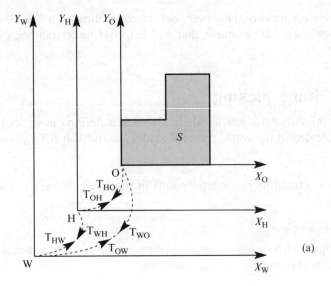

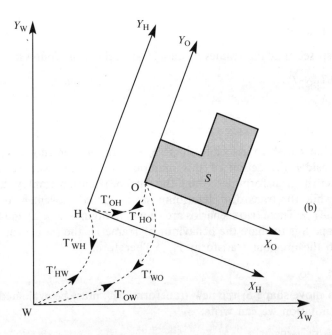

Figure 5.14 (a) The transforms describing the current scenario. (b) The transforms describing the next scene update.

Remembering that these are matrix transforms, we can remove T'_{HW} from the left-hand side by premultiplying both sides by T'_{WH}. Therefore, we have:

$$T'_{WO} = T'_{WH} \cdot T_{HW} \cdot T_{WO} \qquad (5.73)$$

and any point P_W can be evaluated as:

$$P'_W = T'_{WO} \cdot P_O \qquad (5.74)$$

or in its expanded form:

$$P'_W = T'_{WH} \cdot T_{HW} \cdot T_{WO} \cdot P_O \qquad (5.75)$$

We can examine the action of (5.75) with an example. Figure 5.15(a) shows the relationships between the three frames of reference O, H and W. The transform T_{WO} is given by:

$$T_{WO} = \begin{bmatrix} 1 & 0 & 2 \\ 0 & 1 & 2 \\ 0 & 0 & 1 \end{bmatrix} \qquad (5.76)$$

The transform T_{WH} is given by:

$$T_{WH} = \begin{bmatrix} 1 & 0 & 1 \\ 0 & 1 & 1 \\ 0 & 0 & 1 \end{bmatrix} \qquad (5.77)$$

therefore, the inverse transform T_{HW} is given by:

$$T_{HW} = \begin{bmatrix} 1 & 0 & -1 \\ 0 & 1 & -1 \\ 0 & 0 & 1 \end{bmatrix} \qquad (5.78)$$

Figure 5.15(b) shows the new transform for the hand T'_{WH} as:

$$T'_{WH} = \begin{bmatrix} 1 & 0 & 2 \\ 0 & 1 & 1 \\ 0 & 0 & 1 \end{bmatrix} \qquad (5.79)$$

Using (5.73), the transform T'_{WO} is:

$$T'_{WO} = \begin{bmatrix} 1 & 0 & 2 \\ 0 & 1 & 1 \\ 0 & 0 & 1 \end{bmatrix} \begin{bmatrix} 1 & 0 & -1 \\ 0 & 1 & -1 \\ 0 & 0 & 1 \end{bmatrix} \begin{bmatrix} 1 & 0 & 2 \\ 0 & 1 & 2 \\ 0 & 0 & 1 \end{bmatrix} \qquad (5.80)$$

which is equivalent to:

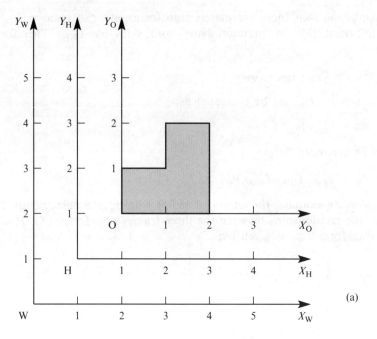

(a)

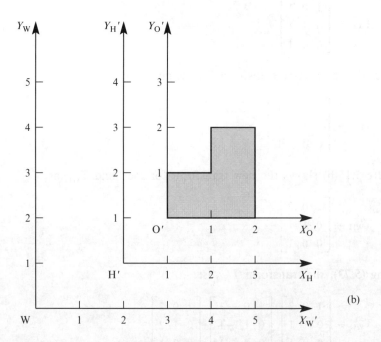

(b)

Figure 5.15   (a) The current relationship between the frames of reference W, H and O. (b) The relationships between the proposed frames of reference W, H′ and O′.

$$T'_{WO} = \begin{bmatrix} 1 & 0 & 3 \\ 0 & 1 & 2 \\ 0 & 0 & 1 \end{bmatrix} \tag{5.81}$$

Therefore, (5.81) is used to transform the shape coordinates as follows:

$$P'_W = T'_{WO} \cdot P_O \tag{5.82}$$

Inspection of (5.81) with Figure 5.15(b) shows that it effects a translation of (3,2), which is correct.

Although a simple translation has been used to illustrate the idea of transform sequences, any type of transform would have worked. We can now transfer these ideas to the 3D domain and consider object picking.

5.4.3 Object picking

As there was nothing special about the notation used for 2D shape picking, the same approach can be used for 3D object picking.

In order to describe the process of picking, flying (see Section 5.5) and scaling, it is convenient to isolate the virtual domain from the physical domain. In the following diagrams, the virtual domain is represented by the world frame, while the physical domain is the room frame, as illustrated in Figure 5.16. A transform T_{RW} relates the two frames together, but plays no vital role in picking. Nevertheless, it will be used in our calculations for consistency.

The tracker frame is located inside the room and has a default position with respect to the room's origin. The VO also has a transform relating the head with the tracker. There is a similar transform relating the 3D hand device with the tracker, and another transform relating an object with the origin of the VE.

These frames of reference are listed in Table 5.1, which shows the transform used to move from one frame of reference.

While object picking is in progress, the transform relating the hand and object is invariant. We can also assume that the tracker's position in the VE is constant, although we could imagine the VO flying through the VE picking objects on the fly. If the tracker is stationary, the transform T_{RT} is unaltered. Similarly, if the world is not moving relative to the room, the transform T_{RW} is unaltered, nevertheless they will be incorporated in the following transforms. We can now rewrite (5.70) and (5.71) as follows:

$$T'_{HO} = T'_{HT} \cdot T'_{TR} \cdot T'_{RW} \cdot T'_{WO} \tag{5.83}$$
$$T_{HO} = T_{HT} \cdot T_{TR} \cdot T_{RW} \cdot T_{WO} \tag{5.84}$$

While object picking is in progress, $T'_{HO} = T_{HO}$, therefore:

$$T'_{HT} \cdot T'_{TR} \cdot T'_{RW} \cdot T'_{WO} = T_{HT} \cdot T_{TR} \cdot T_{RW} \cdot T_{WO} \tag{5.85}$$

Premultiplying both sides of (5.85) by T'_{TH} produces:

$$T'_{TR} \cdot T'_{RW} \cdot T'_{WO} = T'_{TH} \cdot T_{HT} \cdot T_{TR} \cdot T_{RW} \cdot T_{WO} \tag{5.86}$$

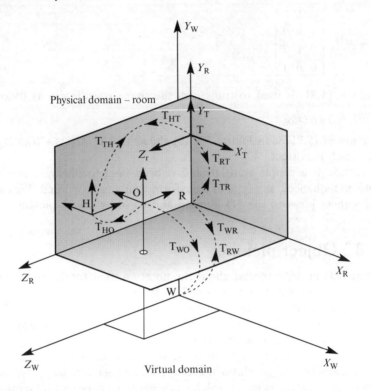

Figure 5.16   The transforms associated with object picking.

Table 5.1   Transforms needed to convert coordinates from one frame of reference to another frame.

		To				
		World	*Room*	*Tracker*	*Hand*	*Object*
	World	–	T_{RW}	T_{TW}	T_{HW}	T_{OW}
	Room	T_{WR}	–	T_{TR}	T_{HR}	T_{OR}
From	*Tracker*	T_{WT}	T_{RT}	–	T_{HT}	T_{OT}
	Hand	T_{WH}	T_{RH}	T_{TH}	–	T_{OH}
	Object	T_{WO}	T_{RO}	T_{TO}	T_{HO}	–

and premultiplying both sides of (5.86) by T'_{RT} produces:

$$T'_{RW} \cdot T'_{WO} = T'_{RT} \cdot T'_{TH} \cdot T_{HT} \cdot T_{TR} \cdot T_{RW} \cdot T_{WO} \qquad (5.87)$$

and finally, premultiplying both sides of (5.87) by T'_{WR} produces:

$$T'_{WO} = T'_{WR} \cdot T'_{RT} \cdot T'_{TH} \cdot T_{HT} \cdot T_{TR} \cdot T_{RW} \cdot T_{WO} \qquad (5.88)$$

Any point P_O associated with an object is transformed into world coordinates as follows:

$$P'_W = T'_{WO} \cdot P_O \tag{5.89}$$

If the room is coincident with the world frame, we can write (5.88) as:

$$T'_{WO} = T'_{WT} \cdot T'_{TH} \cdot T_{HT} \cdot T_{TW} \cdot T_{WO} \tag{5.90}$$

5.5 Flying

As travelling in the physical world can be very tiring, we need a simple technique of moving around the virtual domain that minimizes physical effort. This is achieved by *flying* through the VE, and requires the VO only to indicate the direction of flight and instruct the system to fly in this direction until the command is terminated. Effectively, what happens is that the VE is moved past the VO in the opposite direction to that indicated – as all motion is relative, the result is the same.

The flying direction is specified using a 3D mouse or an interactive glove, and the distance moved at each frame update can be a system-defined parameter, or a value determined interactively by the VO.

Figure 5.17 depicts what is happening when the VO flies through the VE. To begin with, the VO uses a 3D mouse to indicate the direction of flight. In this example, the z-axis of the hand frame of reference provides a direction vector, while the distance moved is a system-defined translation along the z-axis.

Flying is achieved by updating the transform T_{WR} relating the room to the world frame. Therefore, we need to find how far the room should be translated for each frame update, and then move the world in the opposite direction. As the translation is defined in hand coordinates, it can be transformed into room coordinates using the following:

$$T'_{RtranslateR} = T'_{RT} \cdot T'_{TH} \cdot T'_{HtranslateH} \cdot T'_{HT} \cdot T'_{TR} \tag{5.91}$$

and the invariant transform that can be applied repeatedly to effect flying is:

$$T'_{WR} = T_{WR} \cdot T'_{RtranslateR} \tag{5.92}$$

Therefore, substituting (5.91) in (5.92) produces:

$$T'_{WR} = T_{WR} \cdot T'_{RT} \cdot T'_{TH} \cdot T'_{HtranslateH} \cdot T'_{HT} \cdot T'_{TR} \tag{5.93}$$

As objects are transformed into the VO's head ($_{He}$) frame as follows:

$$T_{HeO} = T_{HeT} \cdot T_{TR} \cdot T_{RW} \cdot T_{WO} \tag{5.94}$$

the transform T'_{WR} must be inverted to produce T'_{RW}, and then substituted in (5.94).

We can easily verify the correctness of (5.93) by evaluating an example. For instance, let the following transforms be defined as:

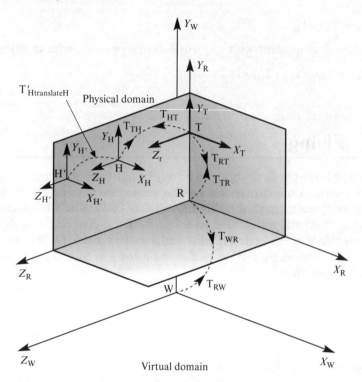

Figure 5.17   The transforms associated with flying.

- T_{WR} The room is translated $(1,1,1)$ relative to the world:

$$T_{WR} = \begin{bmatrix} 1 & 0 & 0 & 1 \\ 0 & 1 & 0 & 1 \\ 0 & 0 & 1 & 1 \\ 0 & 0 & 0 & 1 \end{bmatrix} \tag{5.95}$$

- T'_{RT} The tracker is translated $(0,1,0)$ relative to the room:

$$T'_{RT} = \begin{bmatrix} 1 & 0 & 0 & 0 \\ 0 & 1 & 0 & 1 \\ 0 & 0 & 1 & 0 \\ 0 & 0 & 0 & 1 \end{bmatrix} \tag{5.96}$$

- T'_{TH} The hand is translated $(0,0,1)$ relative to the tracker:

$$T'_{TH} = \begin{bmatrix} 1 & 0 & 0 & 0 \\ 0 & 1 & 0 & 0 \\ 0 & 0 & 1 & 1 \\ 0 & 0 & 0 & 1 \end{bmatrix} \tag{5.97}$$

- $T'_{HtranslateH}$ The hand indicates a translation of $(0,0,1)$:

$$T'_{HtranslateH} = \begin{bmatrix} 1 & 0 & 0 & 0 \\ 0 & 1 & 0 & 0 \\ 0 & 0 & 1 & 1 \\ 0 & 0 & 0 & 1 \end{bmatrix} \qquad (5.98)$$

- T'_{HT} The inverse of T_{TH} is:

$$T'_{HT} = \begin{bmatrix} 1 & 0 & 0 & 0 \\ 0 & 1 & 0 & 0 \\ 0 & 0 & 1 & -1 \\ 0 & 0 & 0 & 1 \end{bmatrix} \qquad (5.99)$$

- T'_{TR} The inverse of T'_{RT} is:

$$T'_{TR} = \begin{bmatrix} 1 & 0 & 0 & 0 \\ 0 & 1 & 0 & -1 \\ 0 & 0 & 1 & 0 \\ 0 & 0 & 0 & 1 \end{bmatrix} \qquad (5.100)$$

Substituting these transforms into (5.93) produces:

$$T'_{WR} = \begin{bmatrix} 1 & 0 & 0 & 1 \\ 0 & 1 & 0 & 1 \\ 0 & 0 & 1 & 2 \\ 0 & 0 & 0 & 1 \end{bmatrix} \qquad (5.101)$$

By comparing (5.95) with (5.101) we can see that the room has been translated a further $(0,0,1)$ with respect to the world, which is correct.

5.6 Scaling the VE

It is convenient to scale the VE up or down to obtain a new perspective. For example, by making it larger, the VO effectively becomes smaller, and can explore the world from the standpoint of a child. By making the VE smaller, the VO becomes larger, and can explore the world from the standpoint of a giant. What concerns us here is not so much the scaling factor, but what happens to the VO's view of the world when the scale is made. It would be rather disconcerting for the VO to be scaled down in a totally foreign part of the VE! Similarly, the VO could become so large that the VE became lost from view.

In order for the VO to become accustomed to the rescaling operation,

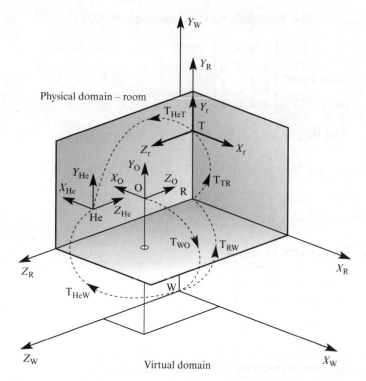

Figure 5.18 The transforms associated with scaling the VE.

it is effected over a period of seconds. This implies that the scaling factor will be slightly less than, or greater than, unity. A scaling factor of two, for example, would double the size of the VE at every frame update, and create massive worlds very fast.

Figure 5.18 shows the frames of reference involved in converting coordinates in the world frame to the head frame. The transform T_{HeW} is defined as:

$$T_{HeW} = T_{HeT} \cdot T_{TR} \cdot T_{RW} \tag{5.102}$$

As these transforms involve only translations and rotations, the VE will be transformed on a scale 1:1. However, should for any reason a scaling operation be introduced into the transforms, the VE will appear scaled too. T_{RW} is the only transform that lends itself to modification, and is the inverse of T_{WR} relating the room frame to the world frame. As the world frame is our master frame of reference, let us develop a value of T_{WR} and invert it when required. Therefore, we can write:

$$T'_{WR} = T_{WR} \cdot T'_{RscaleR} \tag{5.103}$$

which is invariant over successive scene updates, and can be used to effect the complete scaling operation. The problem with this approach is that the scaling is relative to the room's origin, and during scaling the VO sees the VE change size, and fly past!

If T_{WR} is a simple translation such as:

$$T_{WR} = \begin{bmatrix} 1 & 0 & 0 & 1 \\ 0 & 1 & 0 & 1 \\ 0 & 0 & 1 & 1 \\ 0 & 0 & 0 & 1 \end{bmatrix} \qquad (5.104)$$

and $T_{RscaleR}$ scales by a factor of two in all directions:

$$T'_{RscaleR} = \begin{bmatrix} 2 & 0 & 0 & 0 \\ 0 & 2 & 0 & 0 \\ 0 & 0 & 2 & 0 \\ 0 & 0 & 0 & 1 \end{bmatrix} \qquad (5.105)$$

then T'_{WR} becomes:

$$T'_{WR} = \begin{bmatrix} 2 & 0 & 0 & 1 \\ 0 & 2 & 0 & 1 \\ 0 & 0 & 2 & 1 \\ 0 & 0 & 0 & 1 \end{bmatrix} \qquad (5.106)$$

Therefore, the point $P_R(0,0,0)$, which has world coordinates $P_W(1,1,1)$, remains at $(1,1,1)$:

$$P'_W = \begin{bmatrix} 2 & 0 & 0 & 1 \\ 0 & 2 & 0 & 1 \\ 0 & 0 & 2 & 1 \\ 0 & 0 & 0 & 1 \end{bmatrix} \begin{bmatrix} 0 \\ 0 \\ 0 \\ 1 \end{bmatrix} \qquad (5.107)$$

$$= (1,1,1) \qquad (5.108)$$

confirming that the room's origin remains fixed in the world frame. However, the point $P_R(10,10,10)$ moves to $(21,21,21)$, and the VO sees the VE growing in size and translating through the room at the same time.

In order to stop the VO being translated during the scaling process, the centre of scale must be located inside the room, and preferably near to the VO. If we use the VO's head as the centre of scale, the world will appear to grow in all directions relative to the VO's viewpoint. This could be useful, however; something the VO might have been touching would either be scaled out of reach, or moved too near. If the VO's hand is the centre of scale, the world will grow in all directions relative to this point.

The VO's hand can become the centre of scaling by redefining T'_{WR} as follows:

$$T'_{WR} = T_{WR} \cdot T'_{RT} \cdot T'_{TH} \cdot T'_{HscaleH} \cdot T'_{HT} \cdot T'_{TR} \qquad (5.109)$$

If we use the transform values from Section 5.5, and make the $T'_{HscaleH}$ double in all directions, T'_{WR} becomes:

$$T'_{WR} = \begin{bmatrix} 2 & 0 & 0 & 1 \\ 0 & 2 & 0 & 0 \\ 0 & 0 & 2 & 1 \\ 0 & 0 & 0 & 1 \end{bmatrix} \tag{5.110}$$

The original position of the hand in room coordinates is $(0,1,1)$, which in world coordinates is $(1,2,2)$. And if the same point $(0,1,1)$ is substituted in (5.110), the world coordinates are still $(1,2,2)$, confirming that the centre of scaling is the origin of the hand frame of reference.

5.7   Collision detection

Collision detection between objects is important to many applications of VR. It is needed for basic operations such as picking or grabbing objects, and it is needed to detect when a virtual spanner intersects a virtual pipe. It is used in flight simulators to detect if the wingtips of the simulator craft touch buildings or other planes, and in surgical simulators to detect when a virtual scalpel has intersected some virtual tissue.

As VE can be built from polygons, patches, particles, voxels and CSG primitives, different strategies are required for each modelling modality. For this section we will consider only some of the ideas that are relevant primarily to polygons, but could be used with other modelling schemes.

One thing that is common to most aspects of modelling is the use of algorithms that can make clever decisions with minimum processing. To make such schemes possible, geometric data is extended with other artefacts such as bounding boxes and bounding spheres. However, let us begin first with the mini-max test for shapes.

5.7.1   Mini-max testing for shapes

Collision detection between 2D shapes is effected by comparing the minimum and maximum x- and y-extents for two shapes as shown in Figure 5.19. If shapes A and B have extents (x-min_a,x-max_a,y-min_a,y-max_a) (x-min_b, x-max_b,y-min_b,y-max_b) respectively, a horizontal overlap or touch condition is impossible if:

$$x\text{-}min_b > x\text{-}max_a \quad \text{or} \quad x\text{-}min_a > x\text{-}max_b \tag{5.111}$$

similarly, a vertical overlap or touch condition is impossible if:

$$y\text{-}min_b > y\text{-}max_a \quad \text{or} \quad y\text{-}min_a > y\text{-}max_b \tag{5.112}$$

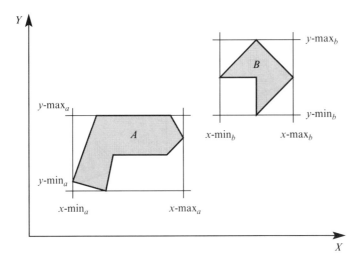

Figure 5.19 The mini-max test compares the x- and y-extents of two shapes as a first-level filter for rejecting trivial orientations.

Therefore, if the x- and y-extents do not overlap, neither can the reference shapes. On the other hand, if the x- and y-extents do overlap, there is a possibility that the shapes intersect or touch. This must be investigated by testing individual vertices of both shapes.

5.7.2 Bounding boxes

Extending the mini-max idea to 3D creates the idea of a bounding box enclosing an object. Figure 5.20 shows two such boxes associated with objects A and B. We can also reason that a horizontal overlap or touch condition is impossible if we extend (5.111) and (5.112) with:

$$z\text{-min}_b > z\text{-max}_a \quad \text{or} \quad z\text{-min}_a > z\text{-max}_b \qquad (5.113)$$

Therefore, if the x-, y- and z-extents do not overlap, neither can the enclosed objects. But if they do overlap, there is a possibility that the objects intersect or touch. This, too, must be investigated by testing individual vertices of one object against the surfaces of the other, and vice versa.

A variety of techniques are available to assist in proving that an edge intersects a polygon. For example, consider the situation shown in Figure 5.21 where $\mathbf{n}$ is the unit surface normal for the triangle. If $\mathbf{n} = [a,b,c]^T$ then the equation of the surface is given by:

$$ax + by + cz + d = 0 \qquad (5.114)$$

therefore, d can be determined by substituting (x_1, y_1, z_1) into (5.114):

$$d = -(ax_1 + by_1 + cz_1) \qquad (5.115)$$

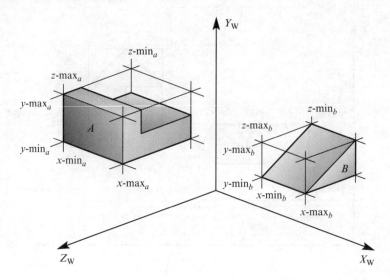

Figure 5.20 By comparing the extents of the bounding boxes, conditions under which collision or touching are impossible can be detected.

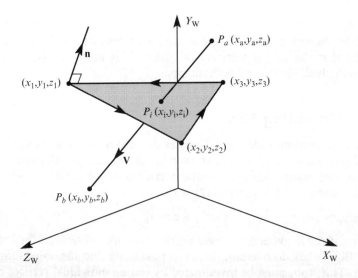

Figure 5.21 The vector **V** connects points P_a and P_b. P_i is where the vector intersects the triangle.

For any point $P(x,y,z)$ on the surface we can write:

$$ax + by + cz - (ax_1 + by_1 + cz_1) = 0 \tag{5.116}$$

therefore:

$$a(x - x_1) + b(y - y_1) + c(z - z_1) = 0 \tag{5.117}$$

If $P(x,y,z)$ is not on the surface, but in the half-space containing **n**, the left-hand side of (5.117) is positive. If P is located on the opposite half-space, the expression is negative.

In Figure 5.21 P_a is in the positive half-space, and P_b is in the negative half-space, therefore the line $\{P_a,P_b\}$ intersects the surface. The point of intersection P_i can be found as follows.

The vector **V** passing through the points P_a and P_b is given by:

$$\mathbf{V} = [\,(x_b - x_a),(y_b - y_a),(z_b - z_a)\,]^{\mathsf{T}} \tag{5.118}$$

Therefore, the point of intersection P_i must be of the form:

$$P_i(t) = P_a + t\mathbf{V} \tag{5.119}$$

where:

$$
\begin{aligned}
x_i(t) &= x_a + t(x_b - x_a) \\
y_i(t) &= y_a + t(y_b - y_a) \\
z_i(t) &= z_a + t(z_b - z_a)
\end{aligned}
\tag{5.120}
$$

Substituting (5.120) in (5.117) gives t as:

$$t = \frac{ax_a + by_a + cz_a + d}{a(x_b - x_a) + b(y_b - y_a) + c(z_b - z_a)} \tag{5.121}$$

which if substituted back into (5.120) provides the point of intersection P_i. What we do not know, however, is whether P_i is inside or outside the triangle. Berlin (1985) and Haines (1989) provide some solutions to this problem, but here is a technique that is very simple and easy to understand.

A point inside a triangle

Consider the triangle shown in Figure 5.22 containing the point P_i. The triangle's vertices have an anticlockwise order when viewed from the half-space containing its surface normal **n**. The projection of the triangle onto the planes $x = 0$, $y = 0$ and $z = 0$ produce 2D triangles whose vertex order is determined by the orientation of **n**. For example, if the y-component of **n** is larger than the x- and z-components, the projection onto the XZ-plane is also anticlockwise. Similarly, if the x-component of **n** dominates the y- and z-components, the projection onto the YZ-plane is anticlockwise. Thus, although the triangle's area is lost in the projection, the vertex sequence and juxtaposition of P_i are preserved.

In the example shown in Figure 5.22, the z-component of **n** is the dominant component, therefore the projection onto the $z = 0$ plane will also have an anticlockwise sequence. Furthermore, the projection of P_i is also inside the projected triangle.

Therefore, given a triangle $\{P_1,P_2,P_3\}$, its unit surface normal **n**, and associated reference point P_i, a 2D projection can be taken as described above. Let the vertices of the projected triangle be $\{T_1,T_2,T_3\}$ and the projected reference point be T_i as shown in Figure 5.23. If T_i is inside triangle $\{T_1,T_2,T_3\}$, the three smaller triangles $\{T_i,T_1,T_2\}$, $\{T_i,T_2,T_3\}$ and $\{T_i,T_3,T_1\}$

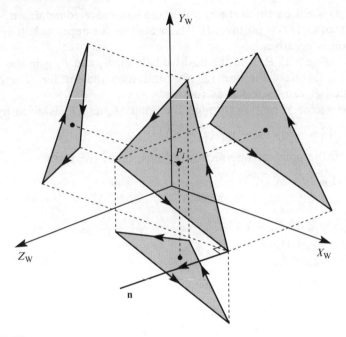

Figure 5.22 The 3D triangle can be projected onto the planes $x = 0$, $y = 0$ and $z = 0$. The vertex order of the projection is sensitive to the orientation of the surface normal **n**. The point P_i, which is inside the triangle, will also be inside the projections.

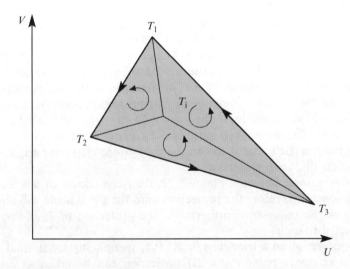

Figure 5.23 If the vertex sequence of a triangle is anticlockwise, the three triangles formed using an inside point are also anticlockwise.

will also be anticlockwise. If any one of these smaller triangles is clockwise, the point T_i must be outside the reference triangle. We now need a simple method for determining the vertex sense of a triangle.

Vertex sense of a triangle

The area of a triangle $\{T_1, T_2, T_3\}$ is given by:

$$\text{Area} = \tfrac{1}{2}[x_1(y_2 - y_3) + x_2(y_3 - y_1) + x_3(y_1 - y_2)] \tag{5.122}$$

However, the area is positive for anticlockwise vertices, and negative for clockwise vertices. Therefore, as the sign of the area is used to detect the vertex sequence of a triangle, the $\tfrac{1}{2}$ term can be dropped. Let us explore the action of this algorithm with an example.

Figure 5.24(a) shows a triangle $\{P_1(0,2,1),\ P_2(2,0,2),\ P_3(2,0,0)\}$ with vertices in anticlockwise sequence. The surface normal $\mathbf{n} = [0.7071, 0.7071, 0.0]^T$, and the reference point is $P_i(1,1,1)$. We can project onto either the $y = 0$ or the $x = 0$ plane. Let us take the $y = 0$ plane to create the triangle $\{T_1(1,0), T_2(2,2),\ T_3(0,2)\}$ shown in Figure 5.24(b). Note that the new x-coordinates come from the original z-coordinates, and the new y-coordinates come from the original x-coordinates. The projected reference point is $T_i(1,1)$.

The three areas are given by:

$$\begin{aligned}
\text{Area}_1 &= \tfrac{1}{2}[1(0 - 2) + 1(2 - 1) + 2(1 - 0)] = +0.5 \\
\text{Area}_2 &= \tfrac{1}{2}[1(2 - 2) + 2(2 - 1) + 0(1 - 2)] = +1.0 \\
\text{Area}_3 &= \tfrac{1}{2}[1(2 - 0) + 0(0 - 1) + 1(1 - 2)] = +0.5
\end{aligned} \tag{5.123}$$

As the signs of the areas are all positive, T_i is inside the triangle.

Let us test the algorithm for a known outside point. For example, let $P_o(1,1,0)$ be the reference point as shown in Figure 5.24(a). The projected point is now $T_o(0,1)$, and the three areas are given by:

$$\begin{aligned}
\text{Area}_1 &= \tfrac{1}{2}[0(0 - 2) + 1(2 - 1) + 2(1 - 0)] = +1.5 \\
\text{Area}_2 &= \tfrac{1}{2}[0(2 - 2) + 2(2 - 1) + 0(1 - 2)] = +1.0 \\
\text{Area}_3 &= \tfrac{1}{2}[0(2 - 0) + 0(0 - 1) + 1(1 - 2)] = -0.5
\end{aligned} \tag{5.124}$$

As Area_3 is negative, T_o is outside the triangle, therefore the original point $P_i(1,1,0)$ was outside the triangle $\{P_1, P_2, P_3\}$.

As mentioned earlier, there is no need to include the '$\tfrac{1}{2}$' term in the area calculation, only the sign is required. It is also worth noting that the same technique works for polygons, and the area for a polygon with n vertices is given by:

$$\begin{aligned}
\text{Area} = \tfrac{1}{2}[x_1(y_2 - y_n) + x_2(y_3 - y_1) + \ldots + x_{n-1}(y_n - y_{n-2}) + \\
x_n(y_1 - y_{n-1})]
\end{aligned} \tag{5.125}$$

5.7.3 Bounding spheres

Instead of enclosing an object within a box, it can be placed inside a sphere, the radius of which is adjusted to enclose all the vertices. Figure 5.25 illustrates

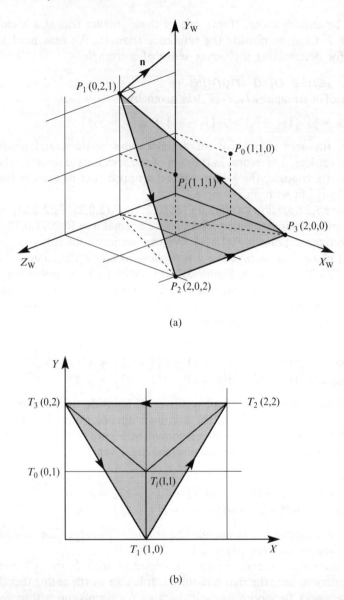

(a)

(b)

Figure 5.24   (a) The point P_i can be proved to be inside or outside the triangle by first projecting it onto the $y = 0$ plane. (b) The point T_i is inside the triangle if the areas of the inner triangles are positive.

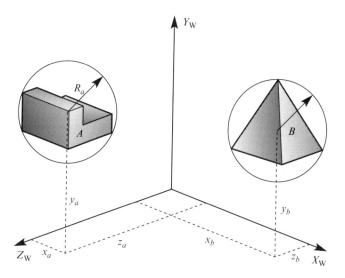

Figure 5.25 The two objects A and B may intersect if their bounding spheres intersect.

this idea with two objects. If the two spheres are located at (x_a, y_a, z_a) and (x_b, y_b, z_b), with radii R_a and R_b respectively, the distance between their centres is given by:

$$d = \sqrt{(x_a - x_b)^2 + (y_a - y_b)^2 + (z_a - z_b)^2} \tag{5.126}$$

If $d > R_a + R_b$ the two spheres cannot touch, therefore neither can the enclosed objects. When $d \leqslant R_a + R_b$, the two objects have to be investigated on a vertex-by-vertex basis as outlined above.

6

A Generic VR System

6.0 Introduction

Having explored relevant aspects of computer graphics, geometric modelling strategies and geometric transformations, we are now in a position to outline the building blocks for a generic VR system. This chapter identifies the central elements, describes their role and shows how they are coordinated to function as a coherent system.

Even though we have not yet explored the mechanics of VR technology, it will still be useful to pause at this juncture and prepare a system outline of a typical immersive VR system. There are four system elements to consider: the VE, the computer environment, VR technology and modes of interaction. The VE covers ideas such as model building, introducing dynamic features, physical constraints, illumination and collision detection. The computer environment includes the processor configuration, the I/O channels, the VE database and the real-time operating system. VR technology encompasses the hardware used for head-tracking, image display, sound, haptics and hand-tracking. Modes of interaction involve hand gestures, 3D interfaces and multi-participant systems. Figure 6.1 shows the connectivity between these elements. To begin with, let us consider the VE and its creation.

6.1 The virtual environment

The VE can take many forms, for example it could be a realistic representation of some physical environment such as the interior of a building, a kitchen, or even an object such as a car. Geometric accuracy is probably quite important, so too, perhaps, are the attributes of colour, texture and lighting.

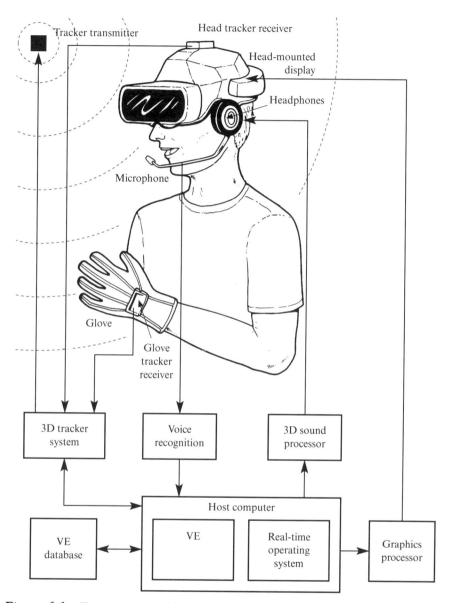

Figure 6.1 The integration of the various elements of a generic VR system.

Interactive 3D modelling software may be used to construct such an environment employing engineering drawings, architectural plans and the incorporation of important physical dimensions. The environment, or parts of it, may already exist as a CAD database – in this case some form of conversion software is required to translate it into a suitable format.

It could be that the VE does not have any physical basis at all. For instance, it might be a 3D database of a geographical, hierarchical network describing a multinational company. It could even be a multidimensional data set associated with stock transactions. Whatever the nature of the underlying data, a geometric model is required to represent atomic entities and their relationships with one another. This abstract model will still require construction, perhaps from geometric primitives such as spheres, cylinders and cubes. Colour, texture, transparency and even animated features could be used to translate system states, activities, processes and so on into a graphical visualization.

As another example, the VE could be used to evaluate some physical simulation, where the accuracy of physical behaviours are more important than visual fidelity. In the case of simulating the behaviour of molecules within electric fields, the behavioural dynamics of the atomic structures can be explored using simplistic models based upon coloured spheres, cylinders and twisted ribbons.

Whatever the application, a geometric database must be built to represent the environment, and stored such that it can be retrieved and rendered in real time when required.

6.1.1 Virtual objects

We describe objects in the real world using a rich vocabulary of adjectives. For example, we use words like 'round', 'flat', 'smooth', 'curvaceous', 'angular' and 'spherical' to describe shape and form. We also use terms like 'slippery', 'sticky', 'wet', 'dry', 'rough' and 'furry' to describe surface properties. Similarly, we have other words to describe an object's colour, texture and temperature. But when an object moves, or when we interact with it, an object can 'swing', 'spin', 'bounce' or 'slide'; and properties like 'weight', 'mass', 'inertia' and 'momentum' have to be used to account for its dynamic behaviour. Even an object's acoustic properties, such as 'deep', 'high', 'dull' and 'metallic', help us complete the overall description.

If we are to build virtual worlds with virtual objects, it is highly likely that many of the above attributes will have to be used. Thus the database storing the VE will have to include 3D geometry, colour and texture, dynamic characteristics, physical constraints and acoustic attributes.

A VR system provides a domain where a virtual world can be modelled, simulated, visualized and even experienced using immersive displays. Figure 6.2 is a diagrammatic representation of a generic system. The VE consists of a collection of objects and light sources which are manipulated by animation and physical simulation procedures. In parallel with these activities, collision detection algorithms monitor collisions between specified objects. The state of the VE is influenced by the input signals coming from the head trackers, hand trackers and any speech channel, while the outputs from the system are in the form of visual, audio and haptic data channels. Let us examine these elements in greater detail.

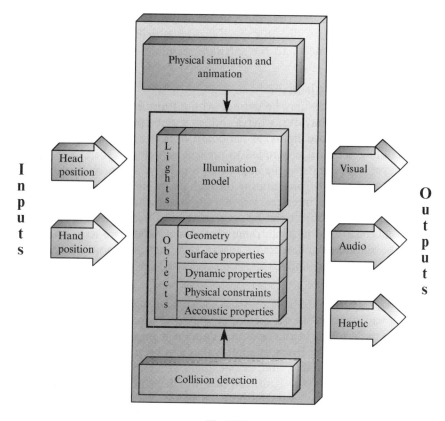

The VE

Figure 6.2 The inputs, processes and outputs in a generic VR system.

Static and dynamic features

In general, objects within a VE can be divided into two groups: static and dynamic. In the case of an architectural interior, the obvious static features are floors, walls, ceilings, stairs and so on, while the moving elements include objects such as doors, windows, cupboards, drawers and lids. When building such an environment, the database must reflect whether an object can be moved or not, otherwise this might lead to all sorts of geometric anomalies. For instance, imagine a virtual room where everything can be moved, including walls. If a wall were moved, its new position could intersect items of furniture! Although a z-buffered renderer could cope with this space sharing, the visual effect would be bizarre, and not very useful.

We can imagine other scenarios where the position of a door needs to be a dynamic feature. If this is the case, the 3D geometry describing the wall must adjust as the door is interactively positioned. This calls for special software to support this dynamic form of geometry, for the wall's geometry will require remodelling every time the door's position is altered. If the furniture has to move with the walls, this must also be anticipated and the necessary procedures incorporated into the software maintaining the database.

Physical constraints

Some dynamic objects may be defined without any constraints being placed upon their spatial behaviour, whereas others may be physically constrained to move within prescribed limits. A cupboard drawer can be constrained such that its sliding action is controlled to prevent its being pushed in too far, or pulled beyond the limits of the cupboard. Similarly, a door will require constraining to prevent it from rotating through its frame, or from being opened too far, causing it to intersect with an adjoining wall.

In general, an object can be constrained to limit translations and rotations about the axes of its local frame of reference. These are set as parameters within the database and used to ensure that matrix operations transform objects within desired limits.

Level of detail

Three-dimensional graphics is a compute-intensive application for computers, and when undertaken in the real-time domain it imposes severe constraints upon system designers. Every attempt is made to keep the system update rate running as high as possible, and, as one might expect, the physical complexity of the VE database plays a significant factor in determining this speed. Consequently, if there is any way the polygon count can be minimized without undermining the system's task, it has to be considered.

One such strategy involves storing within the database different levels of detail for specific objects. The real-time operating system automatically selects the model description that matches the current view and mode of operation. Higher levels of detail can then be accessed on a range basis. As the VR user approaches different objects, they might be introduced into the user's viewpoint for the first time, or their geometric description might be improved by making a model substitution. As the user withdraws from an object, the reverse occurs. Although this dynamic load-balancing provides an extra task for the real-time operating system, overall the benefits are worth while. Figure 6.3 shows a practical example of how the level of detail changes as the model is approached.

One drawback with model substitution is the sudden appearance or removal of a new feature, which, depending on the application, can be very distracting. In flight simulation, where visual fidelity plays an important training role, changes in level of detail are controlled using dynamic levels of transparency. This enables one model to be faded out while another model description is being faded in. When this is handled correctly it greatly improves this form of load balancing. The small price that must be paid for adopting this approach is that the image generator must have the capacity to store both model descriptions simultaneously while the fade level of detail is in progress.

Surface attributes

At some stage, objects within the VE will have to be assigned colours and perhaps textures. Colour parameters might be in the form of components of red, green and blue, or hue, saturation and value. Either way, it must be possible for the renderer to compute levels of light reflected from the objects. Furthermore, texture maps can be associated with surfaces to increase the level of realism. These require scaling and orientation parameters. Where a large dynamic viewing range is expected, a nest of maps (mip maps) will be needed to provide the range of textural information. It is unlikely that a single map will be able to cope with objects that are visible both near and far.

Acoustics

Sound can play an important role in virtual simulations. In a simple example, a digitized sound waveform can be triggered by some event, such as a collision. The collision could arise between two independent objects, in which case the accompanying sound could enhance the event with some suitable noise. The collision could be between the user's hand and some other object such as a virtual radio. In this case, the user could interactively switch the radio on or off. One can imagine many other sound-based scenarios that can be exploited using this type of interaction.

Where head-related transfer functions (see Section 6.3.5) are in use, the 3D location of the sound source is communicated to the sound hardware subsystem which then attempts to filter the sound signal to incorporate this spatial origin.

6.1.2 Virtual lights

The VE can be illuminated in various ways. One simple strategy takes advantage of the fact that in the real world light sources do not normally move – apart from the sun – and many objects are stationary. Under these conditions light intensities can be assigned to individual surfaces to exploit this fact, and the scene is rendered from these luminance values. Obviously this is not physically accurate as there is no mechanism to adjust the overall intensities needed to simulate different times of the day. Nevertheless, it removes the need to apply an illumination model for every frame.

A development of this idea subjects the environment to an off-line radiosity illumination model. When the radiosity algorithm has computed the discrete changes in light levels across the various surfaces, the VE database is prepared with this information. The VR user can now explore the environment in real time, with the obvious benefits of a radiosity illumination model,

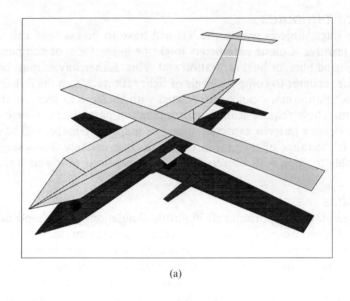

(a)

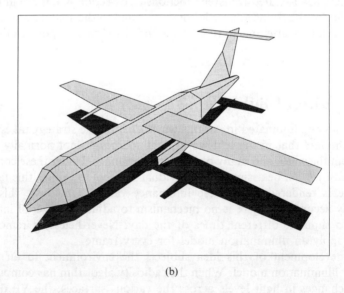

(b)

Figure 6.3 These four images show how the level of detail can help make the polygon count a function of the viewing distance.

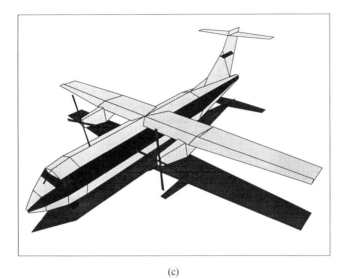

(c)

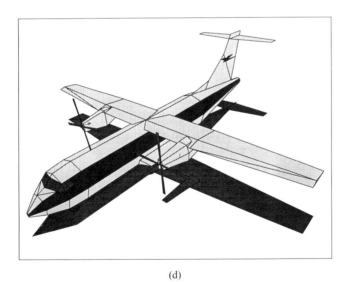

(d)

without incurring the normal computational overhead. However, as radiosity calculations are sensitive to the juxtaposition of surfaces, objects that are moved in the VE will still have the original radiosity parameters associated with them. This, however, should be regarded as a small price to pay for the superior realism. Plate 2 shows an example of a radiosity scene used in a VR application.

When extra computing power is available, it is possible to implement a complete illumination model incorporating several light sources. Moreover, the user can even explore the VE with a moveable light source to mimic the action of a handheld torch. Some VR graphics systems are even able to compute specular highlights that arise when moving about an environment.

6.1.3 Physical simulation

In the physical world we take for granted the regularity of a dripping tap, the apparent random motion of leaves blown by the wind, and the fact that most objects fall towards the ground. Such behaviours are the result of very complex interactions and are explored in Chapter 8.

In the last section we saw how a VE can be made to appear very realistic with the creative use of geometry, colour, texture and careful illumination. Even sound can be introduced to reinforce the illusion of interacting with virtual objects. However, if we are interested in simulating physical behaviours at a virtual level we must incorporate procedures that introduce such behaviours. These can demand significant levels of computation, and also introduce into the system further opportunities of increasing unwanted latency.

Computer animation has long been used to explore the simulation of various physical systems. Linked structures, fabrics, human motion and natural phenomena have all been animated with great accuracy. However, such dynamic simulations have had to be animated on a stop-frame basis. Creating these simulations in real time still presents a challenge to VR systems; nevertheless, some physical effects are easily simulated.

We must never lose sight of the fact that nothing will happen in a VE unless procedures are incorporated to support a particular type of behaviour. If objects are required to fall towards the floor they must be assigned the attribute of mass and a rate of acceleration must be available to evaluate the equations of motion. If an object is supposed to be falling through air, it will eventually reach a limiting velocity, just like a real object. Furthermore, objects tend to spin during their fall, which increases their kinetic energy in the form of angular momentum. This kinetic energy is converted into sound and heat on impact with the floor, and may even be used to overcome chemical bonds that result in the object's breaking into several pieces. After the impact, the motion of these pieces is influenced by their size, shape, spin and the elasticity of the floor. Even with this simple example we can see that simulating the physical world presents some daunting problems.

6.1.4 Animation

Chapters 7 and 8 describe the mathematical techniques used for moving objects about the VE and the mathematical procedures for simulating various physical behaviours. Some animations can be composed from translations and rotations which can be supported by matrix operations, whereas swinging and springing movements require a procedure. Evaluating such procedures in real time presents various problems, the most important being degraded latency in system response. A VR system that suffers from any significant delay between initiating an action and receiving a response can be very frustrating to use. Consequently, when insufficient computing power is available to evaluate the animation and simulation procedures, similar strategies to that used in fade-level-of-detail must be considered to resolve the problem.

In the case of certain animated sequences, a complex animation can be simulated without involving any extra mathematical procedures whatsoever. The technique requires that the animation is incorporated into the database as a sequence of discrete key models. In flight simulation, the wing flaps of an aircraft can be shown to descend from the wing by storing two or three dozen versions of the relevant structures in different positions. Figure 6.4 shows part of this sequence. At run time, the animation is triggered when the aircraft descends to a specified height. As the real-time software has access to all of the model definitions, it can construct the aircraft by animating them over a prescribed period of time. Like fade-level-of-detail, the image generator must have sufficient memory capacity to store this extra geometry (Longhurst, 1994).

6.1.5 Collision detection

Proving that two objects have collided is greatly simplified by the use of bounding spheres or bounding boxes. Either approach exploits the relatively simple mathematics used for testing intersections between two spheres or two boxes. The size of the sphere or box is such that it completely contains the object with which it is associated. Consequently, if there is no intersection at this level, it is impossible for the enclosed objects to intersect. On the other hand, if an intersection condition is detected, there is a chance that the enclosed objects intersect. To prove whether this has occurred or not, the objects' individual surfaces are compared for an actual intersection. If this is found to be the case, the event is communicated to the real-time operating system and other actions are initiated. This might result in a sound being issued; it might cause the two objects to become fused together; it could even cause an animation sequence to be initiated to simulate an explosion.

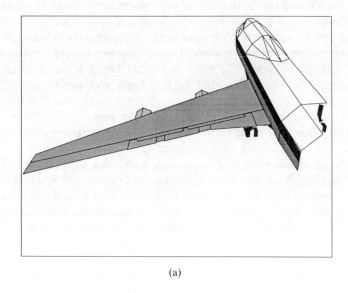

(a)

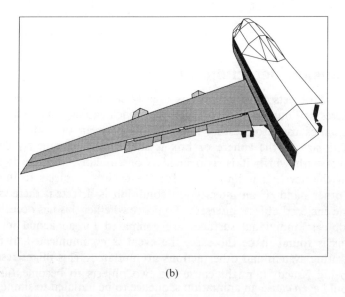

(b)

Figure 6.4 These three images are part of an animation sequence that simulates the lowering of the wing flaps.

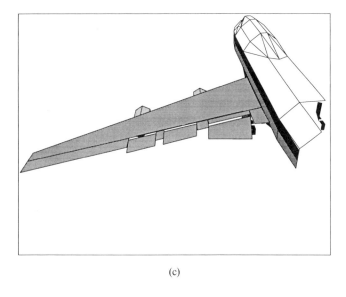

(c)

Figure 6.4 (continued)

One problem associated with collisions is their accurate detection within a discretely sampled system. If the sample frequency is too low, it is possible for one object to pass through another without the collision being detected. This would happen if one sample was made just before the time of impact, and the subsequent sample made just after the objects had passed through one another. Increasing the sample rate reduces the risk but increases the computation; however, colliding objects moving at even higher speeds would still go undetected. If we happen to know something about those objects that are likely to be involved in collisions, their trajectories can be continuously monitored. Collision events that would otherwise go undetected by the sampling process can be computed and reported upon.

6.1.6 User inputs

The basic user input signals consist of the position and orientation of the user's head and hand.

Head position and orientation

The user's head position and orientation are vital input signals to the system, as these determine the viewpoint from which the virtual world is rendered. Tracking hardware can provide this data at a rate of 100 Hz or more, with about 10 ms latency. However, this update rate deteriorates when the same controller is used to process the user's hand-tracking sensor.

Hand position and orientation

The user's hand position and orientation are used to interact with the VE. For instance, when an interactive glove is used, hand gestures can be used to initiate or terminate system processes. Similarly, a glove or a 3D mouse can be used to pick virtual objects and move them to different positions.

6.1.7 System outputs

The output signals from the VR system carry visual, audio and haptic information about the VE, and are supported by three independent subsystems working in parallel.

Visual signals

The primary output from the system is a visualization of the VE displayed upon the user's HMD. This may comprise of a single view displayed upon one display device, two identical views displayed upon two display devices, or binocular views displayed upon two display devices. The display devices are typically LCD panels or high-resolution CRTs.

Audio signals

The audio output signal is derived from the acoustic subsystem for simulating sound events in the VE. These signals can be preprocessed to incorporate information that allows the user to localize the sounds in space using headphones.

Haptic signals

The haptic channel carries signals describing forces to be transmitted back to the user's body. This assumes that the user is either wearing some sort of glove, holding a reactive joystick, or is attached to some force-feedback device.

6.2 The computer environment

The computers used to support a VR system range from simple PCs equipped with suitable graphics processors, to top-of-the-range graphics workstations working with multiple parallel processors or dedicated real-time image generators. In this text, the specific nature of these platforms is not considered, and no attempt will be made to compare the relative merits of the available commercial systems.

For the purposes of our generic VR system we require a computing environment that can coordinate the various inputs supplied by the user and output the necessary graphic, auditory and haptic data to the user. Let us explore some of these processes individually.

6.2.1   Input channels

Two primary input channels are used to input the position and orientation of the user's head and hand. The head data is used to control the dynamic behaviour of the VO within the VE, and determines the viewpoint of the computer-generated images returned to the user. The hand data supplies the position and orientation of a 3D mouse, or the individual positions of the user's fingers if an interactive glove is being worn.

At the start of an interactive session, the true physical height of the stationary head-tracker hardware must be available to the VR system. This ensures that when a user wears the mobile head-tracking component, a corresponding viewpoint of the VE is seen. Similarly, the 3D mouse or glove is monitored in real time and used to direct the movements of a virtual pointer icon, or a virtual hand within the user's view of the VE. With the aid of either of these input devices the user can point to features in the VE and undertake some form of interaction.

6.2.2   Output channels

Two primary output channels support graphics and sound. Ideally, the graphics channel provides two independent images for the user's left and right eyes so that a binocular view of the scene is perceived. The success of this integration is sensitive to matching the user's interocular distance to that employed in the perspective calculations. The system should enable this distance to be adjusted when necessary.

The sound channel provides the user with acoustic feedback relating to events taking place at a virtual level. With suitable convolving hardware it is possible to align spatially the perceived sound and visual sound stages.

6.2.3   The VE database

The VE database describing the virtual objects is stored on disk and loaded into main memory whenever required. The loading of this data may take only a few seconds, but when large numbers of texture maps are required the load can take considerably longer.

For very large databases, only that portion potentially visible to the user is loaded – the rest resides on disk and is copied in when needed. In high-performance IGs database management is handled automatically by real-time software, which ensures that the active database is always kept to a minimum size. A panoramic display system, as used in flight simulation, employs multiple IGs, each with a horizontal field of view between 40° and 50°. In a five-channel system the total field of view covers approximately 200°, which requires that a 360° view of the VE is always resident in the system's memory. This is necessary to cope with sudden horizontal rotations, as encountered in helicopter simulators.

During an interactive session it is highly likely that objects will be disturbed from their original positions. With some scenarios it will be necessary to reset the database to its original state so that an exercise can be repeated from a consistent start point. In other cases it might be necessary to continue a session from a point reached in an earlier exercise. If this facility is required, the user must have the option to save the database in its current status, and recover it at a later date.

Division, Ltd employs an open format for describing virtual objects and their attributes, such as constraints, physical properties, behaviour, geometry, materials and the hierarchical relationships between objects. This is called Virtual Data Interchange (VDI) format, and it is essential for the sharing of VEs between different users.

6.2.4   Run-time services

In many respects, the real-time run-time services are central to any VR system because their task is to coordinate all of the other system components and make them behave coherently. Typical duties include the management of the VE database, the input and output channels, collision detection, networking and processor resources. Somehow, they must undertake all of these tasks at the highest speed possible to maintain a real-time environment.

Parallelism

A natural way of implementing such a software environment is to divide the services into discrete elements which run in parallel on multiprocessor architectures. These autonomous processes include the discrete tasks of head-tracking, collision detection, audio, haptics, image generation, physical simulation, database management, hand gestures, 3D mice, networking and the user interface. Running these in parallel ensures the best performance on today's multiprocessors, and can reduce the opportunity of introducing unwanted latency, which undermines the whole concept behind virtual reality.

6.3   VR technology

VR technology embraces all of the hardware utilized by the user to support a VR task. Typically this includes head-mounted displays, head-coupled displays, 3D interactive devices, headphones and 3D trackers. As such a wide range of hardware exists in these categories, this section will examine only those relevant to our generic system.

6.3.1   3D trackers

Various techniques have been developed to monitor the position and orientation of objects in 3D space, but a popular method that has been used in VR systems for a number of years works electromagnetically. Typically, a stationary transmitter radiates electromagnetic signals that are intercepted by a mobile detector attached to the user's head. When these signals are received by the detector they are decoded to reveal the relative position and orientation between the transmitter and receiver. These signals are then passed on to the run-time system for transmission to the 3D graphics environment. The same principle is used for tracking the 3D mouse, whose signals are used to control an icon in the user's field of view.

Ideally, the system's overall update rate should operate at least at standard video refresh rates (25 Hz (UK) to 30 Hz (US)); preferably, this should be as high as possible. The 3D tracking system should operate at least at the visual update rate, with the lowest possible latency. Latency is a measure of the time it takes to make a sample, decode it and broadcast it throughout the computer environment. Even with a sample rate of 50 Hz, if the latency is 150 ms then the user will experience an unacceptable sensation of lag.

Very often the active range of electromagnetic trackers is restricted to 1–2 m, which restricts the VR user to a relatively small physical floor space to navigate the VE. The user is further restricted by the cable harness connecting the computer to the HMD. To compensate for this restriction, the user must navigate the VE in other ways. This might be achieved by requesting the system to fly the user through the VE in some specified direction or through *teleporting*. These are described in Section 6.4.1.

6.3.2   Head-mounted displays

An HMD isolates the user from the real world and substitutes binocular views of the VE. One approach to HMD design involves two small flat-panel liquid-crystal displays, in front of which are mounted optics to provide a comfortable focal point. When they are positioned such that their optical centres match the interocular distance of the user's eyes, the wearer should experience a stereoscopic scene.

In the real world our eyes are constantly converging and focusing as our attention is drawn from one point of interest to another. This is not possible with this type of HMD, which is fixed-focus and cannot exploit the natural eye activity we have mastered in the real world. Further technology is available to track the orientation of the user's eyes, and this is covered in Chapter 10.

6.3.3   3D mice

A handheld 3D mouse is employed by the user to direct an icon in the user's 3D graphic interface. Its position and orientation are also monitored similar to the method used for the user's head. The mouse also has various buttons whose status are continuously sampled and used to signal to the real-time operating system to move forwards or backwards within the VE. One button is always used to 'pick' a virtual object when it intersects with the 3D icon associated with the mouse. In this way the user can identify specific objects and manipulate them within the VE.

6.3.4   Gloves

The DataGlove developed by VPL can monitor the status of the user's fingers. This is achieved through the use of thin fibre-optics attached to the back of the glove's fingers. When the user's fingers are flexed, the optical characteristics of the fibre optics alters, which can be measured and scaled into an output signal. As the ability to control finger movements changes from person to person, the glove should be callibrated for an individual to ensure accuracy. A separate tracker is attached to the user's wrist to monitor its position and orientation.

6.3.5   Headphones

The acoustic domain of VR technology is still in its infancy, and research continues into the simulation of spatial localization cues and the real-time generation of synthetic audio cues. One approach to developing a virtual 3D sound stage is through the use of Head-Related Transfer Functions (HRTFs) measured in our ear canals. Ideally, these transfer functions should relate to an individual user's head, but very often they are derived from a population of individuals, resulting in an average set of characteristics. This data encodes how sound waves interact with our ears, and characterizes how we exploit signal propagation delays between our two ears to localize sound sources. When anechoic signals are processed by these HRTFs and are heard through conventional headphones, a realistic 3D sound stage arises. Research has shown that perceptual errors can cause problems with reversals in forward and rear localization, which are not helped when generalized HRTFs are used. Other erroneous cues can make it difficult to imagine the sound stage external from one's head.

Synthetic audio cues take advantage of the digital technology developed to support the popular music industry. Although digitized sound samples play an important role in these systems, it is the ability to shape a waveform and adjust features such as pitch, timbre, amplitude, phase and decay that make it an important technology for VR.

6.3.6 Haptic devices

'Haptics' is not a word used in everyday parlance, and is rare enough not to be mentioned in respectable dictionaries. Nevertheless, it has been embraced by the VR community to describe the human sensory domain of touch and force. Haptics encompasses the rich sensory information we glean from holding an object. This includes the ability to discern surface textures as well as attributes such as temperature, wetness, stickiness, tension and force.

As the user's hands play an important role in the VR interactive interface, it seems a natural requirement that when the hand effectively collides with a virtual object, the collision should not only be accompanied by an acoustic cue but also be complemented by a haptic cue. The mechanism of touch, however, is very complex, and today's haptic interfaces are very crude. Currently, they take the form of gloves fitted with pressure pads which can be dynamically inflated to stimulate the wearer's fingertips. Although they provide some form of tactile feedback, they are unable to communicate the wide bandwidth of sensory data we obtain from the real world.

Force feedback devices have been much more successful because their task is much simpler and well defined. Here a variety of devices such as reactive joysticks, exoskeletal hands and arms, and teleoperated mechanisms are available.

Because this technology is rather specialized, further technical details will be explored in Chapter 10.

6.4 Modes of interaction

Computers are, by their very nature, interactive machines. Throughout their 50 years of development a wide range of devices have been explored to identify new ways of simplifying the human–computer interface. Such devices have included paper-tape readers, punched-card readers, character recognition units, visual display units, touch screens, light pens, joysticks, thumbwheels, pressure-sensitive pens, tablets, digitizers, microphones and, recently, all the technology associated with VR.

With every new device, new interactive paradigms have been developed to support the extra features introduced into the interface. Ideally, these interfaces should couple the user efficiently and directly to the task in hand, yet at the same time remain as transparent as possible. One excellent example of such an interface is found on Quantel's Paintbox, where a cordless pressure-sensitive pen is used to direct a real-time painting system. Using natural hand gestures, the user selects screen-based menus from which colours are mixed and drawing modes selected. Pen pressure is used intuitively to control colour density and line thickness. With the minimum of training, users are able to master and exploit the wide range of sophisticated features.

VR systems provide a similar opportunity to develop transparent and intuitive interfaces, however these systems are application specific, and each application demands specific modes of operation. For instance, an immersive 3D VR painting system will be unable to use pressure-sensitive pens unless the user is able to hold a pen in one hand, and has access to a firm surface. Similarly, a virtual paint brush might not be an intuitive tool for applying paint in free space, as artists often exploit the physical interaction between the brush and canvas to create a painting effect. However, a virtual spray gun might be a useful tool for applying paint, but then a problem arises in defining the virtual surface, especially if the paint is intended to hang in space!

The design of VR interfaces will not be resolved overnight, it will take some years to perfect. This is not because the subject is intractable, but because it will be dependent upon the evolution of VR technology and the rate at which systems are embraced by commerce and industry.

6.4.1   Immersive interaction

A typical VR session begins by loading a VE from disk into the host computer's memory. Objects within the database take up their default positions and the computer graphics display processor provides binocular views of the VE. The initial view is determined by the resting position of the HMD relative to the stationary tracking system.

Flying

When the user dons the HMD, the display processor responds in real time to the new viewpoint. Once oriented, the user explores the VE by moving his or her head in different directions. As the user is physically restrained by the HMD's cable harness connecting it with the host computer, navigation of the VE is achieved by instructing the system to 'fly' the user's viewpoint in a specific direction. This is communicated to the operating system via the 3D mouse or a glove to identify both the direction of travel and when to start and stop the flight. Even the simplest of environments has to be navigated in this way, whether it be moving along a corridor, climbing a flight of stairs or moving to another point in a 3D dataset.

Teleporting

Flying long distances in a VE is not only time-consuming, but can also induce motion sickness. Flying can be avoided using the technique of 'teleporting'. This involves identifying a new location in the VE to which the operating system automatically transports the user without having to travel. The problem, however, is in specifying the destination. In flight simulation, the simulator is relocated to a new position by supplying the operating system with the longitude, latitude, height and heading. In another type of VE the destination could be identified using a map displayed in the user's interface. By pointing to the map the user can travel about the environment with great ease. Another method involves scaling the environment to a size whereby it can be viewed as a scale model. The user identifies the new location by pointing to the model and is teleported there by the system.

Object picking

A 3D mouse or an interactive glove can be used to explore and interact with any of the objects that have been assigned dynamic properties. For instance, if the VE contains a car, the car doors can be given dynamic properties and constrained to allow them to rotate about their hinges through a specified angle. The user opens a door by moving the icon of the 3D mouse towards the position of the door's handle. When a collision is detected, the user confirms the selection of the door by activating a button on the mouse. This is called 'picking'. If the user's hand is moved with a gesture to open the door, the system updates the rotation matrices associated with the door to cause it to rotate. Any attempt to rotate the door beyond the constraining angle stored within the database is prevented by the operating system.

If the door is now closed using similar gestures, a sound cue can be initiated at the point of impact. Sound can also be used to simulate the car's radio. In this case the mouse icon is positioned at the radio's controls, and when a collision is detected a digitized sound channel is activated. A similar gesture is used to switch the radio off.

If the VE contains objects that are totally unconstrained, the user can 'pick' them using the mouse icon. Once the selection has been confirmed by the user via a mouse button, the operating system arranges that from that point on, the object's motion is controlled by the position of the mouse. Thus the object goes wherever the user goes. The user can release the object by selecting the required button. At this point the object inherits the status of the last orientation and position matrix of the user's mouse. This might leave the object hanging in space, or the object might be subject to a behaviour that causes it to fall downwards. Any future behaviour depends upon the simulation environment to which the object is subject.

Gesture recognition

In principle, hand gestures appear to be an excellent VR interface; simply by tracking the user's hand position and finger joint angles it is possible to give commands through an accepted vocabulary of signs. Unfortunately, human hand gestures are not universal, and are used only to supplement other modes of communication, such as speech and facial expressions. Nevertheless, very simple gestures can be defined by combining together distinct states of the fingers and thumb.

As it is unlikely that a group of users will move their fingers and thumbs in identical ways, it is difficult to prepare a table of finger angle data that will hold for everyone. However, where hand gesture accuracy is vital, the system can be 'taught' to recognize the individual characteristics of a user by allowing the user to repeat the gestures until an average profile is obtained. Consequently, whenever the user makes a gesture, this table of data is automatically scanned to identify what action to take. Typically, a hand gesture will be used to pick objects, initiate or terminate an activity. Neural nets can also be used effectively to recognize hand gestures.

6.4.2 The user interface

The 2D user interface appears to have embraced the windows paradigm where menus, sliders and rulers are controlled using a consistent 'point and click' interaction. The universal nature of this interface has made it very easy to master new software packages with very little instruction.

The 3D VR interface, on the other hand, has a long way to go to adopt a similar paradigm, as there has been very little opportunity to explore and refine these tools. Hopefully, we will not abandon all of the ideas that have been developed for 2D systems.

Bryson (1994) defines his own principles of use as follows:

(1) Each object should have its own virtual controllers associated with it.

(2) Meaning of hand gesture depends on which object the hand is touching.

(3) Avoid global environment control directly through the hardware interface, that is, avoid gestures that have meaning all the time. It is too easy to make such commands unintentionally.

(4) Hide virtual controls as much as possible, but make them easy to get at.

He also argues that the user should have access to displays that reflect the state of the environment. Perhaps these objects could be in the form of probes that automatically display levels of light, pressure, sound or turbulence, for example. And there is no reason why such objects should not be allowed to move either autonomously or under hand control.

6.4.3 Through-the-window systems

Storage tubes and refresh displays have both played a key role in the development of computer graphics. Even the emergence of immersive VR systems does not mean that screen-based systems will disappear overnight. HMD technology is far from mature and it is highly unlikely that it will ever become a ubiquitous mode of interaction with computers.

There is a community that believes that if a VR system is not immersive, it is not VR. In the case of desktop screens, the viewer's head position and orientation can be used to control the viewpoint of the computer-generated images. This creates the impression of looking into a window, beyond which exists some volume of space. These systems are called 'through-the-window' and require only a graphics workstation and a simple head-tracker. The user can then interact with the VE via a Spaceball, a 3D mouse or an interactive glove and can achieve everything that is possible within an immersive environment, apart from experiencing the sensation of immersion.

6.4.4 Non-immersive VR systems

It cannot be denied that 3D immersion transcends all other modes of human–computer interaction. Actually to be *there* with the model or data, and to view it from any point of view, simulates the powerful sensory feedback we experience from living in the real world. Immersion integrates the user with a virtual model by providing object constancy. That is to say, in the physical world we learn through experience that when we move around another object such as a chair, it remains stationary no matter how we move. At a quantum level this is not so. The very act of observing something can disturb its behaviour! Nevertheless, being able to rely upon features of stability enables us to develop a consistent internal world model that supports various cognitive processes. Recreating object constancy, together with all of the other visual cues found in illumination, texture, shadows and so on reinforces our acceptance of the VE as a believable experience. The traditional graphics workstation, on the other hand, can be used to paint a *picture* of some 3D environment. Indeed, many workstations can render these images in real time, which allows the user to navigate through the environment using a joystick or Spaceball. In some respects the workstation is operating like an interactive television, where an animated scene provides us with a 2D window on some environment. At all times, the user is aware of looking at a picture rather than looking at an object. Now this non-immersive approach to 3D interaction is just as valid as any other form of interaction, and will probably always exist, and may even remain the dominant mode of graphical interaction for some time.

6.4.5 Multi-participant systems

Modern computer systems have always been able to support multi-users, and recent advances in video technology, especially in the area of real-time image compression, have made real-time collaborative working a reality.

The ability to support multiple participants in a logical and scalable way is a key issue for future VR systems. It requires the creation of a highly distributed model of computation that scales well to multi participants and guarantees adequate performance to individual users, while resolving any potential database conflicts. In principle, though, it is possible to network a group of people such that they can interact with one another in a virtual domain, and be aware of one another in their interaction.

6.5 VR systems

On no account should the description given in this chapter be interpreted as the only way a VR system can be configured. It has been used as a simple model to show how the various system elements can be configured to allow a user to interact with a virtual database. As VR technology evolves, totally new system approaches will appear. These might include multimedia interfaces, communication networks and hybrid configurations. For the moment, though, such developments are research projects, but they will eventually transform what we currently accept as VR.

7

Animating the Virtual Environment

7.0 Introduction

Associating a sense of mass or speed with a collection of hand-drawn lines is an essential skill in the world of traditional animation, and animators develop such skills through meticulous observation. They are interested in the complex movement of animals, humans and incidental things such as falling leaves, a dripping tap or curtains blowing in the breeze. When their visual memory fails them they resort to simulation and experimentation until they distil the essential dynamics that characterize a behaviour.

Within their own virtual worlds they can emphasize any behaviour to add an enhanced sense of fun, surprise or drama, which is why cartoons are so enjoyable. Computer animation, on the other hand, provides the animator with an alternative approach to the animation process. For example, the computer can be used to assist in the line drawing process and output frames to cel, which can then be back-painted and integrated with other hand-drawn elements. Another approach allows the image to be held within a frame store, rendered automatically by software and output to video tape. Perhaps the most exciting contribution computers offer the animator is the ability to create and animate 3D virtual objects.

Although 3D computer animation presents a powerful technological alternative to the traditional tools of pencil and paper, so far it cannot offer a complete substitute for animation. Perhaps one of the main problem areas for computer animation revolves around the human–computer interface. In cartoon animation the animator simply draws lines on paper, and when sufficient frames have been produced they are animated as a line test. Although the process is tedious, it is completely interactive and the animator is always in control.

However, with 3D computer animation, an animator works at a computer screen using a range of software tools. If a tool does not exist for a certain effect, then someone must write some extra code, which is often part of an animator's daily work. Animating objects in a VE presents similar problems, for the user can perform only those tasks anticipated by the supporting software.

The level of support needed to animate objects in a VE varies from application to application. In some cases the user will directly control the motion of objects through interaction, while in others the environment must behave autonomously to the user. For instance, a virtual clock must rotate its hands in unison with the current time. When simulating a gear train, gears are expected to rotate in the correct direction and at the right speed. In a car simulator application, windscreen wipers, electric windows and instruments must behave naturally, as must the virtual traffic. In a flight simulator, virtual aircraft land and take off automatically, and airport ground traffic moves convincingly along roadways. In a more esoteric application, the organs modelled inside a virtual human body are expected to behave and move like their real-world counterparts.

Behavioural control is already playing an important role in virtual environments. For example, when developing new handling procedures for robots, it is convenient to simulate this at a virtual level. This implies that the robot must be endowed with behaviours typical of its real-world counterpart. Operators can then be trained to handle the robot with safe and practical manoeuvres, without damaging a real robot or endangering themselves.

British Telecom are experimenting with behaviours associated with large multi-tier communication networks that may fail through random faults or sensitivity to network loads. A VR system is then used to explore how software reacts to these faults by redirecting messages around failed nodes.

As a last example, Colt International have developed VR software to simulate how groups of humans behave under emergency conditions. For example, in one scenario, up to 200 virtual humans are assigned one of a set of rules associated with vacating a building. As the simulation progresses, queues occur, exits are blocked and a potential disaster is seen forming. By redesigning access to exits, a building can be made safer without the lesson of a real disaster.

We will explore several schemes that will enable us to simulate a variety of physical behaviours using simple mathematical models. Unfortunately, the real-time domain poses a considerable challenge to the simulation of such behaviour with total realism. Nevertheless, we should aim at the highest possible realism, even though the final solution may be a compromise.

7.1   The dynamics of numbers

As a VE is nothing more than a complex numerical database, animating any of the attributes, be they physical or abstract, involves changing one number into another. The numerical envelope of the change is important, so too are the derivatives at any point in the operation. For example, if a ball has to be animated bouncing on a floor, the ball's centre could be used to guide its motion. To prevent the ball from passing through the floor we have to ensure that its centre point is never less than the ball's radius from the floor. Furthermore, if the ball's motion is to appear realistic, we have to simulate its downward acceleration in a gravitational field, and its deceleration after it bounces and moves upwards. To prevent the ball from bouncing indefinitely, some loss has to be introduced to attenuate the ball's energy. Such animation is a trivial exercise, but computing more complex behaviour requires non-trivial levels of computing power, and should not be underestimated.

Physically-based motion can be emulated by evaluating the relevant equations, but very often realistic motion can be simulated by numerical interpolation. For example, to simulate a door opening or closing we need to compute an angle of rotation at various instances in time. The dynamics of this angular value should reflect the object's inertia when its velocity changes, and incorporate the losses introduced by air resistance and friction. To compute the instantaneous angular rotation from first principles could be an unnecessary complication, especially if we can develop a simple interpolation procedure that produces a similar result.

To understand how such schemes work, the ideas of linear and non-linear interpolation will be developed and applied to various animation scenarios.

7.1.1   Linear interpolation

We can linearly interpolate between two values v_1 and v_2 using the following equation:

$$v(t) = (1 - t)v_1 + tv_2 \qquad \text{for} \quad 0 \leqslant t \leqslant 1 \tag{7.1}$$

When $t = 0$, $v(t) = v_1$, and when $t = 1$, $v(t) = v_2$. For intermediate values of t, $v(t)$ is linearly interpolated between v_1 and v_2. This can be used in a spatial context where it might be required to divide a straight line separating two points into an equal number of segments. For example, given two points $P_1(x_1,y_1,z_1)$ and $P_2(x_2,y_2,z_2)$, a point $P(x,y,z)$ can be positioned between P_1 and P_2 as follows:

$$
\begin{aligned}
x(t) &= (1 - t)x_1 + tx_2 \\
y(t) &= (1 - t)y_1 + ty_2 \\
z(t) &= (1 - t)z_1 + tz_2
\end{aligned}
\tag{7.2}
$$

If t takes on the values 0, 0.1, 0.2, . . ., 0.8, 0.9 and 1, the line between P_1 and P_2 is divided into 10 equal segments; and even if t assumes values outside of the range 0 to 1, the linear interpolation process continues in a consistent fashion.

Say it is required to move an object from its current position P_1 to another position P_2 in 10 equal steps. The matrix operation controlling this process can be described as:

$$
\begin{bmatrix} x' \\ y' \\ z' \\ 1 \end{bmatrix} = \begin{bmatrix} 1 & 0 & 0 & t_x \\ 0 & 1 & 0 & t_y \\ 0 & 0 & 1 & t_z \\ 0 & 0 & 0 & 1 \end{bmatrix} \begin{bmatrix} x \\ y \\ z \\ 1 \end{bmatrix}
$$

(7.3)

where:

$$
t_x = (x_2 - x_1)t
$$
$$
t_y = (y_2 - y_1)t
$$
$$
t_z = (z_2 - z_1)t
$$

(7.4)

where $P(x,y,z)$ is any vertex in the object, and $P'(x',y',z')$ is the translated vertex for $0 \leqslant t \leqslant 1$. Such a scheme can be used to move any point, whether it be a vertex, a control vertex for a Bézier curve, or the position of a light source. Furthermore, it could also be used to control colour changes, rotations, intensities, transparency, fog density or any other parameter. However, before examining some of these applications, let us consider non-linear interpolation.

7.1.2 Non-linear interpolation

We all know that an object accelerates as it falls to the ground. A rolling coin eventually falls over and comes to a complete rest. A short swinging pendulum will eventually lose its energy and come to rest. All of these movements are far from linear, as they involve some element of decay introduced by friction, the generation of heat or noise, or kinetic energy being converted into potential energy. Being exposed to such everyday phenomena is a powerful conditioning force. Furthermore, when we observe any linear motion, the first thing that springs to mind is that it is artificial and probably involves some sort of control mechanism.

In the world of traditional animation it is rare to see linear movements, and when they are seen they are very obvious and disrupt the visual continuity of the sequence. Animators use various tricks to avoid linear movement, which will not concern us here, apart from to note that such movements are referred to as 'faired' or 'cushioned'.

Let us return to the above example where an object was being moved from P_1 to P_2. Say this had to be achieved non-linearly such that initially the object moved very slowly away from P_1, accelerated, and then decelerated until it came to a complete rest at P_2. One simple way of controlling this movement is to employ part of a cosine curve. Figure 7.1(a) shows such a curve over the period $0 \leqslant \theta \leqslant 2\pi$. Figure 7.1(b) shows a similar curve $0.5(1 + \cos\theta)$ over the period $0 \leqslant \theta \leqslant 2\pi$. An interesting part of this curve exists over the range $\pi \leqslant \theta \leqslant 2\pi$ which grows non-linearly from zero, accelerates, and then

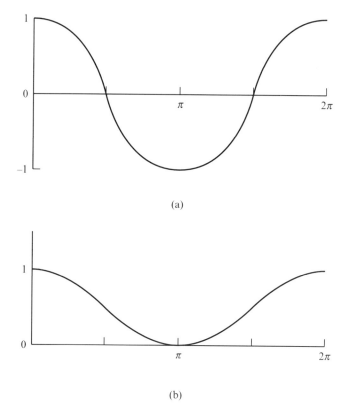

(a)

(b)

Figure 7.1   (a) The function $\cos\theta\,(0 \leqslant \theta \leqslant 2\pi)$. (b) The function
$0.5(1 + \cos\theta)\,(0 \leqslant \theta \leqslant 2\pi)$.

decays non-linearly to 1. A matrix operation can be developed to incorporate
faired movements as follows:

$$
\begin{bmatrix} x' \\ y' \\ z' \\ 1 \end{bmatrix} = \begin{bmatrix} 1 & 0 & 0 & t_x \\ 0 & 1 & 0 & t_y \\ 0 & 0 & 1 & t_z \\ 0 & 0 & 0 & 1 \end{bmatrix} \begin{bmatrix} x \\ y \\ z \\ 1 \end{bmatrix} \tag{7.5}
$$

where:

$$
\begin{aligned}
t_x &= (x_2 - x_1)f \\
t_y &= (y_2 - y_1)f \\
t_z &= (z_2 - z_1)f
\end{aligned} \tag{7.6}
$$

and

$$
f = 0.5(1 + \cos\theta) \tag{7.7}
$$
$$
\theta = (1 - t)\pi + t2\pi \qquad \text{for} \quad 0 \leqslant t \leqslant 1 \tag{7.8}
$$

Table 7.1   The first column shows how θ increases linearly, and the parameter t is influenced by the cosine function. The last two columns give the coordinates of the points between $P_1(1,1)$ and $P_2(2,3)$.

θ	t	x	y
180°	0.00	1.0	1.0
198°	0.024	1.024	1.049
216°	0.095	1.095	1.191
234°	0.206	1.206	1.412
252°	0.345	1.345	1.691
270°	0.5	1.5	2.0
288°	0.654	1.654	2.309
306°	0.794	1.794	2.588
324°	0.904	1.904	2.809
342°	0.976	1.976	2.951
360°	1.0	2.0	3.0

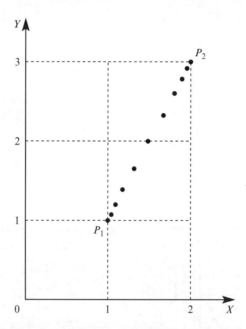

Figure 7.2   These points are plotted from the coordinates in Table 7.1.

If (7.5) is evaluated for a 2D example where $P_1 = (1,1)$ and $P_2 = (2,3)$, the interpolated values are as listed in Table 7.1, and as shown in Figure 7.2. The graph clearly shows that while the direction of the movement is linear, the speed is non-linear and provides some realistic fairing.

One major drawback with this technique is that it involves the evaluation of the cosine function, which consumes valuable processing time, especially in a real-time environment. One simple way to avoid such computation is to use a precomputed cosine table and linearly interpolate between a pair of entries. However, where an object is animated by cycling a sequence of objects in prepared states, the above function can be used to control their orientation – then at run time, their movement will appear faired.

7.1.3 Parametric interpolation

Although the above cosine function incorporates a natural curve for fairing movements, it possesses no mechanism to control its behaviour. For instance, it is not easy to make the acceleration part of the function different from the deceleration portion, because symmetry is the very essence of the cosine function. Nevertheless, a function can be developed that provides the required asymmetry using parametric interpolation.

Parametric interpolation provides a wide range of controllable functions without requiring excessive amounts of computation. Fortunately, they involve ideas covered in Chapter 4, namely the basis functions used for Bézier space curves.

Quadratic interpolation

For the moment, we will ignore the problem of controlling the fairing of movement and concentrate upon the issue of non-linear interpolation using paramctric tcchniqucs. To begin with, we know that a pair of numbers v_1 and v_2 can be linearly interpolated as follows:

$$v(t) = (1 - t)v_1 + tv_2 \qquad \text{for} \quad 0 \leqslant t \leqslant 1 \tag{7.9}$$

This can be extended into quadratic interpolation by introducing a control value v_c that determines the function's symmetry. The quadratic form is given as:

$$v(t) = (1 - t)^2 v_1 + 2t(1 - t)v_c + t^2 v_2 \qquad \text{for} \quad 0 \leqslant t \leqslant 1 \tag{7.10}$$

It can be seen that the terms in t are used in the definition of Bézier space curves, and the same matrix formulation can be used to define $v(t)$:

$$v(t) = [t^2 \quad t \quad 1] \begin{bmatrix} 1 & -2 & 1 \\ -2 & 2 & 0 \\ 1 & 0 & 0 \end{bmatrix} \begin{bmatrix} v_1 \\ v_c \\ v_2 \end{bmatrix} \tag{7.11}$$

If $v(t)$ is evaluated for $v_1 = 0$, $v_2 = 10$, and $v_c = 5$, for t over the range 0 to 1, we obtain a linear interpolation as shown in Table 7.2. If v_c is altered from 5 to 3, we notice that the interpolation is non-linear, with the distribution biased towards v_1. Furthermore, if v_c is set to 7, the distribution is biased towards v_2. These three distributions are shown in Figure 7.3. When v_c is halfway between v_1 and v_2, linear interpolation occurs. The quadratic interpolation can be accentuated by making $v_c < v_1$, but if this relationship is too great, the interpolated values will not lie within the numerical range v_1 to v_2; this, however, might be a desirable effect. The single control value v_c

Table 7.2   The first column shows values of the parameter t, while the last three columns list the corresponding values of v for different values of v_c.

t	$v_c = 5$ $v(t)$	$v_c = 3$ $v(t)$	$v_c = 7$ $v(t)$
0.0	0.0	0.0	0.0
0.1	1.0	0.64	1.36
0.2	2.0	1.36	2.64
0.3	3.0	2.16	3.84
0.4	4.0	3.04	4.96
0.5	5.0	4.0	6.0
0.6	6.0	5.04	6.96
0.7	7.0	6.16	7.84
0.8	8.0	7.36	8.64
0.9	9.0	8.64	9.36
1.0	10.0	10.0	10.0

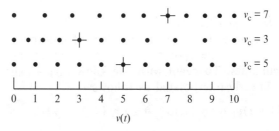

Figure 7.3   The rows of dots represent the distribution of the interpolated values v for values of t ranging from 0 to 1 in equal steps, for different values of v_c. The position of the control value is shown as a '+'.

provides the mechanism to adjust the quadratic distribution, and if a second control value is introduced a cubic distribution is created.

Cubic interpolation

Developing the ideas behind quadratic interpolation we can interpolate between two numbers v_1 and v_2 using two control values as follows

$$v(t) = (1 - t)^3 v_1 + 3t(1 - t)^2 v_c + 3t^2(1 - t)v_d + t^3 v_2 \qquad (7.12)$$

where v_c and v_d are the control values, and $0 \leqslant t \leqslant 1$. The same expression is used for computing cubic Bézier space curves and surface patches.

If $v_1 = 0$ and $v_2 = 10$, linear interpolation occurs when $v_c = 10/3$ and $v_d = 20/3$. This is shown in the second column of Table 7.3. If $v_c = 2$ and $v_d = 8$ the interpolation is cubic and symmetric about $t = 0.5$, but if $v_c = 1$ and $v_d = 8$, the interpolation is still cubic, but asymmetric. This can be confirmed from the distribution shown in Figure 7.4 where we can see that the closer the control value v_c comes to v_1, the tighter the interpolated values

Table 7.3   The first column shows the value of the parameter t controlling the cubic interpolation, while the remaining six columns are grouped into three pairs. The first column in each pair shows the interpolated value $v(t)$, and the second column of the pair gives the increment in v. Note that with $v_c = 10/3$ and $v_d = 20/3$, the interpolation is linear. The two other cases illustrate symmetric and asymmetric cubic interpolation.

t	$v_c = 10/3$ $v_d = 20/3$		$v_c = 2.0$ $v_d = 8.0$		$v_c = 1.0$ $v_d = 8.0$	
	$v(t)$	Δv	$v(t)$	Δv	$v(t)$	Δv
0.0	0.0	–	0.0	–	0.0	–
0.1	1.0	1.0	0.712	0.712	0.469	0.469
0.2	2.0	1.0	1.616	0.904	1.232	0.763
0.3	3.0	1.0	2.664	1.048	2.223	0.991
0.4	4.0	1.0	3.808	1.144	3.376	1.153
0.5	5.0	1.0	5.0	1.192	4.625	1.249
0.6	6.0	1.0	6.192	1.192	5.904	1.279
0.7	7.0	1.0	7.336	1.144	7.147	1.243
0.8	8.0	1.0	8.384	1.048	8.288	1.141
0.9	9.0	1.0	9.288	0.904	9.261	0.973
1.0	10.0	1.0	10.0	0.712	10.0	0.739

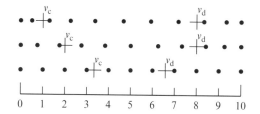

Figure 7.4   The rows of dots represent the distribution of the interpolated values v for values of t ranging from 0 to 1 in equal steps, for different pairs of control values. The position of the control values is shown as a '+'.

become. Similarly for v_d and v_2. When translated into movement, this results in progressive acceleration and deceleration respectively. Note that v_c may be set less than v_1, and v_d may be greater than v_2. The matrix operation for this form of cubic interpolation is as follows:

$$v(t) = \begin{bmatrix} t^3 & t^2 & t & 1 \end{bmatrix} \begin{bmatrix} -1 & 3 & -3 & 1 \\ 3 & -6 & 3 & 0 \\ -3 & 3 & 0 & 0 \\ 1 & 0 & 0 & 0 \end{bmatrix} \begin{bmatrix} v_1 \\ v_c \\ v_d \\ v_2 \end{bmatrix} \tag{7.13}$$

and is identical to that used for a cubic Bézier space curve.

Hermite interpolation

Hermite interpolation is particularly useful when specific rates of change are required at the start and end of a transition. The algorithm requires the start and finish values together with their derivatives at these points. In matrix terms the interpolated value $v(t)$ is given by:

$$v(t) = \begin{bmatrix} t^3 & t^2 & t & 1 \end{bmatrix} \begin{bmatrix} 2 & -2 & 1 & 1 \\ -3 & 3 & -2 & -1 \\ 0 & 0 & 1 & 0 \\ 1 & 0 & 0 & 0 \end{bmatrix} \begin{bmatrix} v_1 \\ v_2 \\ R_1 \\ R_2 \end{bmatrix} \qquad (7.14)$$

where R_1 and R_2 are the two derivatives at the starting and finishing values v_1 and v_2 respectively. For example, if v_1 and v_2 are 0 and 10 respectively, and the associated derivatives are both equal to 1, then the matrix operation becomes:

$$v(t) = \begin{bmatrix} t^3 & t^2 & t & 1 \end{bmatrix} \begin{bmatrix} 2 & -2 & 1 & 1 \\ -3 & 3 & -2 & -1 \\ 0 & 0 & 1 & 0 \\ 1 & 0 & 0 & 0 \end{bmatrix} \begin{bmatrix} 0 \\ 10 \\ 1 \\ 1 \end{bmatrix} \qquad (7.15)$$

which becomes:

$$v(t) = \begin{bmatrix} t^3 & t^2 & t & 1 \end{bmatrix} \begin{bmatrix} -18 \\ 27 \\ 1 \\ 0 \end{bmatrix} \qquad (7.16)$$

$$v(t) = -18t^3 + 27t^2 + t \qquad (7.17)$$

Evaluating (7.17) over the range $0 \leqslant t \leqslant 1$ we obtain the value shown in Table 7.4. The graph of the equation is shown in Figure 7.5.

7.2   The animation of objects

In the real world objects possess mass, potential energy and kinetic energy in the form of linear and angular momentum. We also associate attributes, such as a centre of gravity and a moment of inertia, which enable us to predict an object's behaviour under various dynamic conditions. Newton's laws of motion provide a useful framework to compute these predictions, and such scenarios can be simulated within a VE. This form of physical simulation will be examined later in this chapter. For the moment, we will restrict ourselves to the simple linear animation of objects.

Table 7.4 For every value of t, $v(t)$ represents a Hermite interpolation between 0 and 10, with start and end derivatives of 1.

t	$v(t)$
0.0	0.0
0.1	0.352
0.2	1.136
0.3	2.244
0.4	3.568
0.5	5.0
0.6	6.432
0.7	7.756
0.8	8.864
0.9	9.648
1.0	10.0

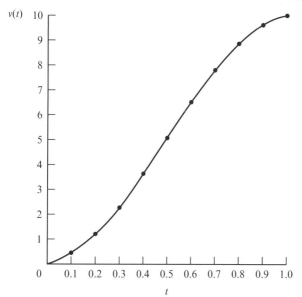

Figure 7.5 A Hermite interpolation between values 0 and 10 with both derivatives set to 1. Note that the t-axis is scaled by a factor of 10, which is why the starting and finishing slopes do not appear correct.

7.2.1 Linear translation

If the system's update rate is F Hz, then the time slice t between each update is $1/F$. For example, if $F = 25$ Hz, each frame is separated in time by 40 ms. If we now wish to show a virtual object moving at a speed S, it must be displaced a linear distance St between each update. In the case of something moving at an approximate walking pace, for example 100 cm s^{-1} with a 25 Hz update rate the object must be displaced 3.66 cm for every update.

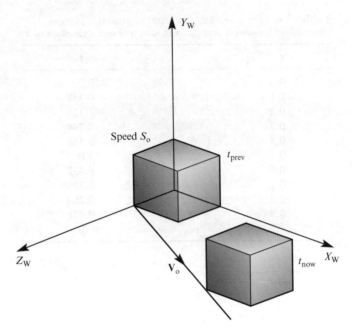

Figure 7.6   The displacement of an object can be computed by the product of its component velocity and the time $t = (t_{\text{now}} - t_{\text{prev}})$.

Unfortunately, we cannot rely upon a consistent update rate frequency, which means that the system's real-time clock must be interrogated to determine the actual time that has elapsed since the last update. Therefore, the time slice t must be derived by subtracting the previous time t_{prev} from the actual time t_{now}.

Figure 7.6 shows an object located at the VE's origin and assigned a speed S_0 across the XZ-plane. To simulate this sliding movement the x- and z-coordinates of the object must be modified by the corresponding components of the vector $(t_{\text{now}} - t_{\text{prev}})\mathbf{V}_0$. The velocity $\mathbf{V}_0$ can be defined as the scalar S_0 representing the linear speed, and a unit vector for the direction. If the object in Figure 7.6 is travelling across the XZ-plane at an angle of 45°, its unit vector is $[0.707, 0.0, 0.707]^T$. The increments made to the x- and z-coordinates are then $0.707 S_0 (t_{\text{now}} - t_{\text{prev}})$.

To contain the object within specified boundaries, we can automatically compute the object's new velocity after bouncing off the boundary. For example, Figure 7.7 shows a plan view of the XZ-plane with a point object moving with a linear speed S_0 and direction $\mathbf{V}_0$. We can see that eventually the point will collide with the right-hand boundary at P. For simple elastic collisions, the angle of reflection equals the angle of incidence θ. The direction of the point $\mathbf{V}_0'$ after the reflection is given by $[-V_{ox}, V_{oy}, V_{oz}]$ where the sign of the x-component of $\mathbf{V}_0$ has been reversed, and the other two components are preserved. The reversal of the x-component is only because the

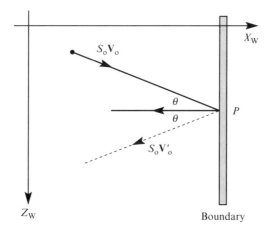

Figure 7.7 The point object is moving with a linear speed of S_o in a direction given by the unit vector V_o. Where it hits the boundary at P, it bounces off at an angle equal to the angle of incidence θ.

boundary was orthogonal to the x-axis. The computation of elastic collisions for any arbitrary planar boundary is covered in Section 8.4.2.

If an object's kinetic energy is required to decay with time, a parameter can be used to reduce the linear speed either by a constant amount or by a fraction of its current speed at each frame update. In the first case, the new speed S_o' is given by:

$$S_o' = S_o - \Delta s \tag{7.18}$$

where S_o is the previous speed and Δs is the constant reduction. S_o' must be prevented from going negative. In the second case, the new speed is given by:

$$S_o'' = kS_o \tag{7.19}$$

where k is some suitable decay constant. Table 7.5 shows the two approaches with an initial speed of 36, $\Delta s = 3$ and $k = 0.8$.

7.2.2 Non-linear translation

In Section 7.1.3 we examined three interpolation techniques – quadratic, cubic and Hermite – which can now be used to control the non-linear motion of objects. As an illustration, we will develop the controlling matrices to move an object using a cubic interpolation.

Say, for example, it is required to move an object along the x-axis in 1 second, pause momentarily, and then return it to its original position in 2 seconds. Both movements have to be non-linear and controllable, and can be simulated by computing the x-translation as a function of time.

Table 7.5   The left-hand column shows the linear decay in speed caused by reducing the current speed by a constant value. The right-hand column shows the non-linear decay caused by reducing the speed by a constant proportion.

S_o'	S_o''
36.0	36.0
33.0	28.8
30.0	23.0
27.0	18.4
24.0	14.7
21.0	11.8
18.0	9.4
15.0	7.6
12.0	6.0
9.0	4.8
6.0	3.9
3.0	3.1

If the real-time clock is in units of seconds, then at time T_1 the translation can begin. At time T_2, that is $(T_1 + 1)$, the object pauses momentarily and then begins its return journey, and at time T_3, that is $(T_1 + 3)$, it comes to rest at its original position. A parameter t, such that $0 \leqslant t \leqslant 1$, is used to control the two interpolations and is defined as follows:

$$t = T - T_1 \qquad\qquad \text{while } T_1 \leqslant T \leqslant T_2 \qquad\qquad (7.20)$$
$$t = (T - T_1 - 1)/2 \qquad \text{while } T_2 \leqslant T \leqslant T_3 \qquad\qquad (7.21)$$

where T is the current time.

Two control values, c_a and c_b, are used to control the non-linearity during the first slide, and two further values, c_c and c_d, are used on the return slide. The interpolants can now be defined as follows:

- For the period $T_1 \leqslant T \leqslant T_2$

$$i(t) = \begin{bmatrix} t^3 & t^2 & t & 1 \end{bmatrix} \begin{bmatrix} -1 & 3 & -3 & 1 \\ 3 & -6 & 3 & 0 \\ -3 & 3 & 0 & 0 \\ 1 & 0 & 0 & 0 \end{bmatrix} \begin{bmatrix} 0 \\ c_a \\ c_b \\ 1 \end{bmatrix} \qquad (7.22)$$

- For the period $T_2 \leqslant T \leqslant T_3$

$$i(t) = \begin{bmatrix} t^3 & t^2 & t & 1 \end{bmatrix} \begin{bmatrix} -1 & 3 & -3 & 1 \\ 3 & -6 & 3 & 0 \\ -3 & 3 & 0 & 0 \\ 1 & 0 & 0 & 0 \end{bmatrix} \begin{bmatrix} 1 \\ c_c \\ c_d \\ 0 \end{bmatrix} \qquad (7.23)$$

Table 7.6 The first column shows the passage of time starting at
$T = 10$ and finishing at $T = 13$. The second column shows the value of
the interpolant t at any time T, and the last column shows the value of
the translated vertex x'.

T	$i(t)$	x'
10.0	0.0	1.000
10.1	0.028	1.056
10.2	0.104	1.208
10.3	0.216	1.432
10.4	0.352	1.704
10.5	0.500	2.000
10.6	0.648	2.296
10.7	0.784	2.568
10.8	0.896	2.792
10.9	0.972	2.944
11.0	1.000	3.000
11.2	0.994	2.987
11.4	0.925	2.850
11.6	0.809	2.618
11.8	0.662	2.325
12.0	0.500	2.000
12.2	0.338	1.675
12.4	0.191	1.382
12.6	0.075	1.150
12.8	0.006	1.013
13.0	0.000	1.000

The interpolant $i(t)$ can now be incorporated to control the x-translation as
follows:

$$
\begin{bmatrix} x' \\ y' \\ z' \\ 1 \end{bmatrix} = \begin{bmatrix} 1 & 0 & 0 & i(t)t_x \\ 0 & 1 & 0 & t_y \\ 0 & 0 & 1 & t_z \\ 0 & 0 & 0 & 1 \end{bmatrix} \begin{bmatrix} x \\ y \\ z \\ 1 \end{bmatrix}
\tag{7.24}
$$

where (x,y,z) is a vertex in the object; t_x, t_y and t_z are the translations; and
(x',y',z') is the translated vertex. If this process is evaluated with the
following data, we obtain the results shown in Table 7.6, and the graph in
Figure 7.8.

$$
\begin{aligned}
&T_1 = 10, \quad T_2 = 11, \quad T_3 = 13 \\
&c_a = 0.0, \quad c_b = 1.0, \quad c_c = 1.1, \quad c_d = -0.2 \\
&t_x = 2.0 \\
&x = 1.0
\end{aligned}
\tag{7.25}
$$

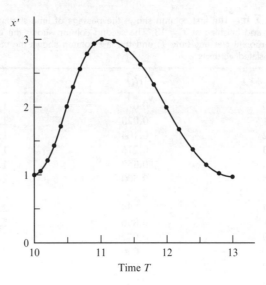

Figure 7.8 The relationship between the x-coordinate x' and time T. During the period $10 \leqslant T \leqslant 11$ the translation increases, and during the period $11 \leqslant T \leqslant 13$ the translation decreases. The individual values are found in Table 7.6.

Note that the values of c_a, c_b, c_c and c_d have been carefully chosen to ensure that there is a smooth acceleration and deceleration at the start and end of each movement.

As can be seen from Table 7.6, the x-coordinate x' alters from 1.000 at $T = 10$, reaches 3.000 at $T = 11$, and returns to 1.000 at $T = 13$. The graph in Figure 7.8 confirms that the interpolation is non-linear, and that the two movements are asymmetric.

7.2.3 Linear angular rotation

In Chapter 3 we saw that the VO's gaze orientation can be specified using direction cosines, *XYZ* fixed angles, *XYZ* Euler angles or quaternions. The same techniques can also be used to control the rotational animation of objects, although some are more useful than others. In this section we will consider *XYZ* Euler angles and quaternions.

XYZ Euler angles

XYZ fixed angles achieve a compound rotation by applying three individual rotations about the OCS's fixed three axes, whereas *XYZ* Euler angles achieve the rotation about an axial system that rotates with the object. To illustrate their use, consider the problem of animating an object such that it rotates once about its local y-axis, and twice about its x-axis every second.

The rotation about the y-axis is a yaw rotation, while the rotation about the x-axis is a pitch rotation, and they are specified by the following matrices:

$$\begin{bmatrix} \cos yaw & 0 & \sin yaw \\ 0 & 1 & 0 \\ -\sin yaw & 0 & \cos yaw \end{bmatrix} \quad \begin{bmatrix} 1 & 0 & 0 \\ 0 & \cos pitch & -\sin pitch \\ 0 & \sin pitch & \cos pitch \end{bmatrix} \quad (7.26)$$

where *yaw* and *pitch* are the yaw and pitch angles respectively.

The values of *yaw* and *pitch* could easily be computed if the angular rotations were fixed for each frame update. However, there is no guarantee that a precise update rate can be maintained in a real-time VR system. Consequently, we will use the real-time clock to ensure that the original rotational requirement is met.

If the current time is given by T, and T_1 is the event when the rotation was initiated, then *yaw* and *pitch* can be defined as:

$$yaw = 360° (T - T_1) \quad (7.27)$$
$$pitch = 720° (T - T_1) \quad (7.28)$$

These assume that the system clock value is in seconds. The complete matrix operation is given by:

$$\begin{bmatrix} x' \\ y' \\ z' \end{bmatrix} = [yaw][pitch] \begin{bmatrix} x \\ y \\ z \end{bmatrix} \quad (7.29)$$

where $[yaw]$ and $[pitch]$ are their respective matrices and must be updated at each system update. Even though the angular rotations are themselves constant about their axes, the distance covered by any point varies during the rotation (Vince, 1992).

Quaternions

Section 3.2.4 describes how a single quaternion can represent the product of three individual quaternions q_{yaw}, q_{pitch} and q_{roll}. Encoded within this single quaternion are the axis of rotation and the angle of rotation as follows:

$$q_{ypr} = [\cos \theta/2, \sin \theta/2 \, u] \quad (7.30)$$

where θ is the angle of rotation and u is a unit vector representing the axis.

It was also shown earlier with (3.75) how q_{ypr} can be represented by a single matrix:

$$\begin{bmatrix} M_{11} & M_{12} & M_{13} \\ M_{21} & M_{22} & M_{23} \\ M_{31} & M_{32} & M_{33} \end{bmatrix} \quad (7.31)$$

where:

$$M_{11} = 1 - 2(y^2 + z^2)$$
$$M_{12} = 2(xy - sz)$$
$$M_{13} = 2(xz + sy)$$
$$M_{21} = 2(xy + sz)$$
$$M_{22} = 1 - 2(x^2 + z^2)$$
$$M_{23} = 2(yz - sx)$$
$$M_{31} = 2(xz - sy)$$
$$M_{32} = 2(yz + sx)$$
$$M_{33} = 1 - 2(x^2 + y^2)$$

(7.32)

and:

$$s = \cos yaw/2 \cos pitch/2 \cos roll/2 + \sin yaw/2 \sin pitch/2 \sin roll/2$$
$$x = \cos yaw/2 \sin pitch/2 \cos roll/2 + \sin yaw/2 \cos pitch/2 \sin roll/2$$
$$y = \sin yaw/2 \cos pitch/2 \cos roll/2 - \cos yaw/2 \sin pitch/2 \sin roll/2$$
$$z = \cos yaw/2 \cos pitch/2 \sin roll/2 - \sin yaw/2 \sin pitch/2 \cos roll/2$$

(7.33)

If we repeat the above example where the roll rotation is zero, the values of *s*, *x*, *y* and *z* become:

$$s = \cos yaw/2 \cos pitch/2$$
$$x = \cos yaw/2 \sin pitch/2$$
$$y = \sin yaw/2 \cos pitch/2$$
$$z = -\sin yaw/2 \sin pitch/2$$

(7.34)

Evaluating *s*, *x*, *y* and *z* for interpolated values of *yaw* and *pitch*, we discover that the speed of any point varies slightly with time, just like *XYZ* Euler angles. This can be overcome, but before addressing this problem let us examine the effect of interpolating quaternions.

The quaternion equivalent to zero rotation is the identity quaternion $q_0 = [1,[0,0,0]]$, and if we interpolate between q_0 and q_{ypr}, we obtain a quaternion that changes its rotation from zero to θ. To begin with, let us explore the possibility of linearly interpolating the individual components as follows:

$$q = (1 - t)q_0 + tq_{ypr} \quad \text{for } 0 \leqslant t \leqslant 1$$

(7.35)

The quaternion **q** can then be used to rotate a point *P* using $\mathbf{P'} = \mathbf{qPq}^{-1}$. Table 7.7 shows the effect of subjecting the point (1,0,0) to a yaw rotation of 90° using this type of interpolation.

We can see from the values in Table 7.7 that the point (0,1,1) is correctly rotated to (1,1,0) but the interpolated point accelerates and then decelerates. This interpolant is non-linear as it ignores the underlying spherical geometry behind rotations. To develop a linear interpolant we will derive one from first principles.

In two dimensions, a unit circle is the locus of points that satisfies the relationship $x^2 + y^2 = 1$, and the shortest route between two points is an arc.

Table 7.7   The effect of using an interpolated quaternion to rotate the point $(0,1,1)$ through a yaw rotation of $90°$. The first column shows the status of the interpolant t; columns s, x, y and z give the interpolated quaternion; *dist* represents the linear distance travelled at each step.

t	s	x	y	z	*dist*
0.0	0.0	0.0	1.0	1.000	–
0.1	0.0	0.145	1.0	0.989	0.145
0.2	0.0	0.294	1.0	0.956	0.153
0.3	0.0	0.441	1.0	0.897	0.159
0.4	0.0	0.581	1.0	0.814	0.163
0.5	0.0	0.707	1.0	0.707	0.165
0.6	0.0	0.814	1.0	0.581	0.165
0.7	0.0	0.897	1.0	0.441	0.163
0.8	0.0	0.956	1.0	0.294	0.159
0.9	0.0	0.989	1.0	0.145	0.153
1.0	0.0	1.0	1.0	0.000	0.145

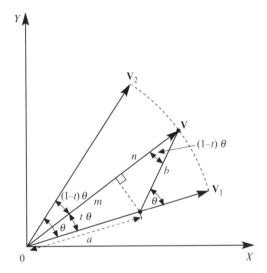

Figure 7.9 V_1, V_2 and V are unit vectors. V is an interpolated vector such that $V = aV_1 + bV_2$. The text derives values for a and b based upon $(1 - t)\theta$ and $t\theta$.

In three dimensions, a unit sphere is a surface satisfied by the relationship $x^2 + y^2 + z^2 = 1$, where the shortest route between two points is a great circle, a so-called orthodrome, as used in ship navigation. In four dimensions, the unit hypersphere is a data set satisfied by the relationship $x^2 + y^2 + z^2 + s^2 = 1$, and the shortest route is a 4D arc. We can develop a single interpolant for all three structures by investigating the 2D case.

Consider two unit vectors V_1 and V_2, as shown in Figure 7.9, separated by an angle θ. The interpolated unit vector V can be defined as:

$$\mathbf{V} = a\mathbf{V}_1 + b\mathbf{V}_2 \tag{7.36}$$

To ensure that $\mathbf{V}$ is controlled by a specific angle between the two vectors, the angle between $\mathbf{V}_1$ and $\mathbf{V}$ is defined as $t\theta$, and the angle between $\mathbf{V}$ and $\mathbf{V}_2$ is $(1 - t)\theta$. From Figure 7.9 we can see the following relationships:

$$\frac{a}{\sin(1 - t)\theta} = \frac{b}{\sin t\theta} \tag{7.37}$$

$$
\begin{aligned}
m &= a\cos t\theta \\
n &= b\cos(1 - t)\theta \\
m + n &= 1
\end{aligned}
\tag{7.38}
$$

Therefore:

$$b = \frac{a\sin t\theta}{\sin(1 - t)\theta} \tag{7.39}$$

and:

$$a\cos t\theta + \frac{a\sin t\theta \cos(1 - t)\theta}{\sin(1 - t)\theta} = 1 \tag{7.40}$$

Solving for a we obtain:

$$a = \frac{\sin(1 - t)\theta}{\sin\theta} \quad \text{and} \quad b = \frac{\sin t\theta}{\sin\theta} \tag{7.41}$$

The final interpolant becomes:

$$\mathbf{V} = \frac{\sin(1 - t)\theta}{\sin\theta}\mathbf{V}_1 + \frac{\sin t\theta}{\sin\theta}\mathbf{V}_2 \tag{7.42}$$

Interpolating between two unit vectors $\mathbf{V}_1$ and $\mathbf{V}_2$ separated by 60° we obtain the data shown in Table 7.8. The first column shows the status of the interpolant t, and the second and third columns list the x- and y-components of the interpolated unit vector $\mathbf{V}$. The fourth column shows the linear distance *dist* travelled between each interpolation, and its constant value confirms that the angular rotation is uniform.

Interpolating between two arbitrary unit vectors, the angle θ would be derived from the 2D dot product:

$$\cos\theta = \mathbf{V}_1 \cdot \mathbf{V}_2 \tag{7.43}$$

The very nature of this inner product infers that θ has a range $0° \leqslant \theta \leqslant 180°$. Our interpolant, however, involves a $\sin\theta$ term in the denominator, which means that it can be used only for two linearly independent vectors. Thus the range of the interpolation is limited to $0° < \theta < 180°$.

The same interpolant can be used for 3D vectors, and we will confirm this with another example. Consider the two unit vectors $\mathbf{V}_1 = [0.0, 1.0, 0.0]^T$ and $\mathbf{V}_2 = [0.707, 0.0, 0.707]^T$ shown in Figure 7.10. Their angular separation is 90° and we want to interpolate linearly between them to derive a vector $\mathbf{V}$, where:

Table 7.8 The x- and y-components of a vector derived from interpolating two reference vectors. The first column shows the linear interpolating parameter t, and the last column confirms that the linear distance between successive points is constant at 0.105.

t	x	y	*dist*
0.0	1.0	0.000	–
0.1	0.995	0.105	0.105
0.2	0.978	0.208	0.105
0.3	0.951	0.309	0.105
0.4	0.914	0.407	0.105
0.5	0.866	0.500	0.105
0.6	0.809	0.588	0.105
0.7	0.743	0.669	0.105
0.8	0.669	0.743	0.105
0.9	0.588	0.809	0.105
1.0	0.500	0.866	0.105

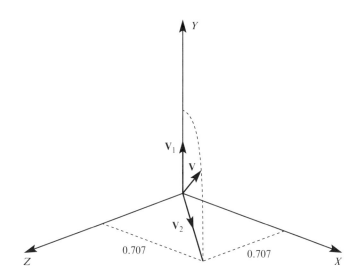

Figure 7.10 V_1, V_2 and V are unit vectors, where V is interpolated between V_1 and V_2 using the interpolant described in the text.

$$V = \frac{\sin(1-t)\theta}{\sin\theta}V_1 + \frac{\sin t\theta}{\sin\theta}V_2 \qquad (7.44)$$

If V is evaluated for $\theta = 90°$, and $0 \leqslant t \leqslant 1$, we obtain the data shown in Table 7.9. Again, the *dist* column confirms that equal distances are travelled for equal changes in the interpolant t.

Now we can return to the problem of interpolating between a pair of quaternions. Given two quaternions q_0 and q_{ypr} an interpolated quaternion q is derived as follows:

Table 7.9   The *x*-, *y*- and *z*-components of a vector derived from interpolating two other reference vectors. The first column shows the linear interpolating parameter *t*; the next three columns list the point's coordinates; and the last column confirms that the linear distance *dist* between successive points is constant at 0.157.

t	*x*	*y*	*z*	*dist*
0.0	0.000	1.000	0.000	–
0.1	0.111	0.988	0.111	0.157
0.2	0.219	0.951	0.219	0.157
0.3	0.321	0.891	0.321	0.157
0.4	0.416	0.809	0.416	0.157
0.5	0.500	0.707	0.500	0.157
0.6	0.572	0.588	0.572	0.157
0.7	0.630	0.454	0.630	0.157
0.8	0.672	0.309	0.672	0.157
0.9	0.698	0.156	0.698	0.157
1.0	0.707	0.000	0.707	0.157

Table 7.10   The effect of using an interpolated quaternion to rotate the point (0,1,1) through a yaw rotation of 90°. The first column shows the status of the interpolant *t*; the columns headed *s*, *x*, *y* and *z* give the interpolated quaternion; and *dist* represents the linear distance travelled at each step.

t	*s*	*x*	*y*	*z*	*dist*
0.0	0.0	0.000	1.0	1.000	–
0.1	0.0	0.156	1.0	0.988	0.157
0.2	0.0	0.309	1.0	0.951	0.157
0.3	0.0	0.454	1.0	0.891	0.157
0.4	0.0	0.588	1.0	0.809	0.157
0.5	0.0	0.707	1.0	0.707	0.157
0.6	0.0	0.809	1.0	0.588	0.157
0.7	0.0	0.891	1.0	0.454	0.157
0.8	0.0	0.951	1.0	0.309	0.157
0.9	0.0	0.988	1.0	0.156	0.157
1.0	0.0	1.000	1.0	0.000	0.157

$$q = \frac{\sin{(1-t)\theta}}{\sin\theta} q_0 + \frac{\sin t\theta}{\sin\theta} q_{ypr} \qquad (7.45)$$

Using the original values of rotating the point (0,1,1) through a yaw angle of 90° we obtain the data shown in Table 7.10. The *dist* column data confirms that the interpolant functions correctly as the distance moved at each step is constant at 0.157.

7.2.4   Non-linear angular rotation

Angular rotations are not always linear. A spinning top loses energy and slows down from the moment it is set down, and a pendulum swings about

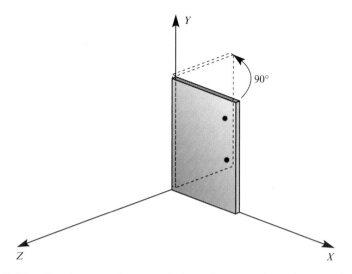

Figure 7.11   The door is to be rotated about the y-axis through an angle of 90°.

its pivot and comes to rest unless it receives some external source of energy. To imitate such behaviour we need to control precisely the angle rotated at each frame update, and we will consider the use of *XYZ* fixed angles and quaternions in this role.

XYZ fixed angles
The *XYZ* fixed angles are often referred to as roll, pitch and yaw, and they perform individual rotations about the fixed *z*-, *x*- and *y*-axes respectively. They can be used in any sequence, however a popular sequence is roll, followed by pitch, followed by yaw. In matrix form this is represented by:

$$\begin{bmatrix} x' \\ y' \\ z' \end{bmatrix} = [yaw]\,[pitch]\,[roll]\begin{bmatrix} x \\ y \\ z \end{bmatrix} \tag{7.46}$$

where (x,y,z) is the point to be rotated, and (x',y',z') is the rotated point.

Let us take a simple example involving a yaw rotation, where we have to rotate a door through 90°, but with a faired movement. Figure 7.11 shows the geometry. As this is a simple yaw rotation we can represent the operation by:

$$\begin{bmatrix} x' \\ y' \\ z' \end{bmatrix} = \begin{bmatrix} \cos yaw & 0 & \sin yaw \\ 0 & 1 & 0 \\ -\sin yaw & 0 & \cos yaw \end{bmatrix}\begin{bmatrix} x \\ y \\ z \end{bmatrix} \tag{7.47}$$

where $yaw = f(t)$.

Table 7.11   The value of the function *hermite* for both derivatives set zero over the range $0 \leqslant t \leqslant 1$.

t	*hermite*
0.0	0.000
0.1	0.028
0.2	0.104
0.3	0.216
0.4	0.352
0.5	0.500
0.6	0.648
0.7	0.784
0.8	0.896
0.9	0.972
1.0	1.000

If $f(t)$ is a function linearly dependent upon the system clock, the door will appear to open with constant angular velocity. However, we can introduce a non-linear interpolant to fair the movement. For example, let us define a function *hermite* that returns a value between 0 and 1. The input parameters to *hermite* are the derivatives at the start and end values, together with the interpolating parameter t. The function is defined as:

$$hermite(R_1,R_2,t) = [t^3 \quad t^2 \quad t \quad 1] \begin{bmatrix} 2 & -2 & 1 & 1 \\ -3 & 3 & -2 & -1 \\ 0 & 0 & 1 & 0 \\ 1 & 0 & 0 & 0 \end{bmatrix} \begin{bmatrix} 0 \\ 1 \\ R_1 \\ R_2 \end{bmatrix} \qquad (7.48)$$

where R_1 and R_2 are the derivatives at $t = 0$ and $t = 1$, respectively.

For instance, if both R_1 and R_2 are set to zero, the function definition becomes:

$$hermite(0,0,t) = [t^3 \quad t^2 \quad t \quad 1] \begin{bmatrix} -2 \\ 3 \\ 0 \\ 0 \end{bmatrix} \qquad (7.49)$$

$$hermite(0,0,t) = -2t^3 + 3t^2 \qquad (7.50)$$

If this is evaluated for $0 \leqslant t \leqslant 1$, $hermite(0,0,t)$ takes on the values shown in Table 7.11. The graph in Figure 7.12 shows that the function is symmetric and includes some subtle fairing. If we now define *yaw* as a function of *hermite* as follows, our door will open with a non-linear rotation:

$$yaw = 90\,hermite(0,0,t) \qquad \text{for } 0 \leqslant t \leqslant 1 \qquad (7.51)$$

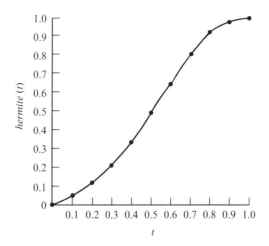

Figure 7.12 The value of *hermite* (*t*) over the range $0 \leqslant t \leqslant 1$.

Quaternions

The *hermite* function could also be used to interpolate quaternions non-linearly. For example, if the linear interpolation between quaternion $\mathbf{q}_1$ and $\mathbf{q}_2$ is given by:

$$\mathbf{q} = \frac{\sin(1-t)\theta}{\sin\theta} \mathbf{q}_1 + \frac{\sin t\theta}{\sin\theta} \mathbf{q}_2 \qquad (7.52)$$

a hermite interpolation can be achieved by:

$$\mathbf{q} = \frac{\sin(1-h)\theta}{\sin\theta} \mathbf{q}_1 + \frac{\sin h\theta}{\sin\theta} \mathbf{q}_2 \qquad (7.53)$$

where $h = hermite\ (R_1, R_2, t)$. The arguments for *hermite* retain their original definition.

7.3 Shape and object inbetweening

7.3.1 Shape inbetweening

One of the techniques used to speed up the process of creating artwork in the cartoon industry is that of *inbetweening*. This is a process where 'inbetween' drawings are derived from two key images drawn by a skilled animator. These key images may show an object or character in two different positions, called key frames, which require extra inbetween images if they are to animate smoothly. Rather than give this task to the animator, the extra drawings are produced by an 'inbetweener' who prepares them by interpolating between the two key drawings. The number and positions of these interpolated images determine the dynamics of the final animation.

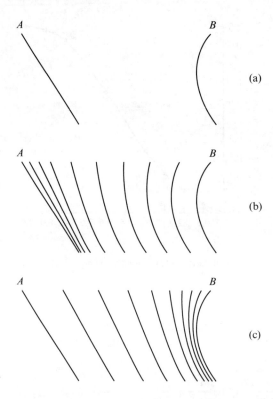

Figure 7.13   (a) Contour *A* is to be animated into contour *B* by introducing extra inbetween lines. (b) Placing the inbetween lines close to *A* creates an accelerated movement. (c) Placing the inbetween lines close to *B* creates a retarded movement.

Figure 7.13(a) shows two simple key contours labelled *A* and *B* which are to be interpolated. If the inbetween lines are drawn as shown in Figure 7.13(b), and are animated, contour *A* will transform into contour *B* with an accelerated motion. But if the inbetween lines are drawn as shown in Figure 7.13(c), *A* will still transform into *B*, but the dynamics will be reversed. The movement introduced into the final animation is called fairing or cushioning. If the inbetween lines are distributed evenly, then the animated motion appears as a constant velocity.

This process of inbetweening lends itself to a computer solution, where both contours are stored as lists of coordinates which are then interpolated using one of the mathematical techniques previously described. For example, let us consider the action of interpolating two 2D lines *A* and *B* as shown in Figure 7.14. Both lines are separated by a short distance and have two vertices. If we linearly interpolate the *x*- and *y*-coordinates of each corresponding vertex, and draw the inbetween lines, we obtain the extra lines as shown. An inbetween vertex (x_i, y_i) is computed as follows, where (x_a, y_a) and (x_b, y_b) are the two vertices of *A* and *B* respectively:

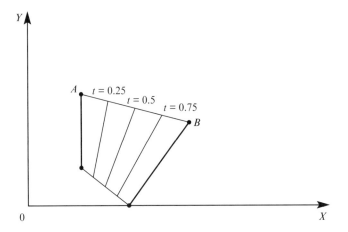

Figure 7.14 Linearly interpolating between lines A and B produces the three inbetween lines where the interpolant t has values 0.25, 0.5 and 0.75.

$$\left.\begin{aligned} x_i &= (1 - t)x_a + tx_b \\ y_i &= (1 - t)y_a + ty_b \end{aligned}\right\} \quad \text{for } 0 \leqslant t \leqslant 1 \qquad \begin{aligned} &(7.54) \\ &(7.55) \end{aligned}$$

When the interpolant t equals 0.5, the inbetween line has its end points half-way between the end points of lines A and B. We can see from Figure 7.14 that the end points of the inbetween lines lie on straight lines joining the two key contours.

If we employed a quadratic instead of a linear interpolant, the lines would still be the same, but the interpolant would control their spacing. For example, if the following interpolant were used:

$$\left.\begin{aligned} x_i &= (1 - t)^2 x_a + 2tx_b - t^2 x_b \\ y_i &= (1 - t)^2 y_a + 2ty_b - t^2 y_b \end{aligned}\right\} \quad \text{for } 0 \leqslant t \leqslant 1 \qquad \begin{aligned} &(7.56) \\ &(7.57) \end{aligned}$$

when $t = 0.5$, an inbetween x-coordinate is positioned three-quarters of the distance separating B from A, whereas with linear interpolation, it is positioned halfway.

We could extend this idea to work with contours having any number of vertices, and, so long as they shared the same number of vertices, it would be possible to interpolate open or closed complex shapes. In fact, there is no need for the key shapes to share the same number of vertices, for a procedure can be designed that maps a vertex of one shape to an equivalent position on the second shape.

7.3.2 Object inbetweening

By inbetweening the z-coordinate, the above technique can be applied to 3D contours. However, 3D object descriptions are not arbitrary collections of

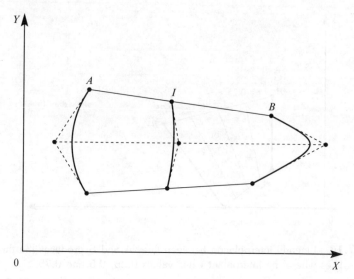

Figure 7.15   Bézier curves *A* and *B* can be inbetweened by interpolating their control points. At a halfway point, the curve labelled *I* is the corresponding inbetween shape.

contours: they are constructed from a coherent set of surface elements, and we cannot expect to interpolate between two different complex objects and expect that the inbetween objects are geometrically consistent. For example, a four-sided tetrahedron cannot be inbetweened into a six-sided cube without losing part of the surface geometry. Nevertheless, given suitable geometric definitions, it is possible to transform one object into another and create subtle animations.

7.3.3   Parametric line inbetweening

Although the technique of Section 7.3.1 has an immediate application to explicit shapes and objects, there is no reason why it should not be applied to the control points of implicit parametric lines. For instance, in the case of a quadratic Bézier curve, the two end points and associated control vertex could be inbetweened with a similar set belonging to a second curve. Such a situation is shown in Figure 7.15 where the control vertices of curve *A* are interpolated with those of curve *B*. At each stage of the interpolation a curve can be computed from the status of the inbetween vertices. At the halfway point, the inbetween control points are halfway along their journeys joining *A* to *B*, and are used to develop the curve labelled *I* in the same figure.

   More complex shapes can be processed by employing piecewise curves, and although curves with identical numbers of line segments are easier to process, dissimilar curves can be processed by introducing phantom segments of zero length.

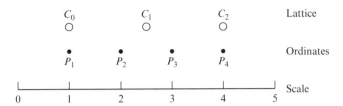

Figure 7.16 P_1, P_2, P_3 and P_4 are four ordinates with values determined by the bottom scale. The three control values C_0, C_1 and C_2 form a 1D lattice that can be used to alter the spatial distribution of the four ordinates.

7.3.4   Parametric surface patch inbetweening

The elegance of parametric techniques enables line-based procedures to be extended to incorporate surface patch descriptions. In the case of Bézier surface patches, two sets of control meshes are inbetweened, which involves two sets of nine control points for quadratic patches, or sixteen control points for cubic patches. Even multi-patched objects can be inbetweened, but a consistent level of patch correspondence must be maintained between the two key objects.

7.4   Free-form deformation

Free-Form Deformation (FFD) is a technique for modelling and animating objects. It works by surrounding an object with a 3D lattice of control points that can be used to deform the object by deforming the enclosed volume of space. Its action can be understood by first considering its application to a 1D set of ordinates, then a 2D shape and finally a 3D object.

7.4.1   Deforming 1D ordinates

Consider the problem of altering the spatial distribution of the four ordinates P_1, P_2, P_3 and P_4 shown in Figure 7.16. The FFD approach is to associate these numbers with a 1D lattice of control values which, when moved, will disturb the positions of the original ordinates. If the Bernstein polynomials are associated with the control values, then three control values effect a quadratic distribution, while four values effect a cubic distribution.

In the case of the four ordinates in Figure 7.16, two control values C_0 and C_2 are positioned at P_1 and P_4 respectively, and a third value C_1 is placed halfway between P_1 and P_4. Any ordinate P can now be moved to a new position P' as follows:

$$P' = (1 - u)^2 C_0 + 2u(1 - u)C_1 + u^2 C_2 \qquad \text{for } 0 \leqslant u \leqslant 1 \qquad (7.58)$$

Table 7.12   The first column identifies the values of the original ordinates for P. The next column gives the value of the parameter u, and the last column shows the value P'. Note that the four values of P' are identical to the original values.

	P	u	P'
P_1	1.0	0.000	1.0
P_2	2.0	0.333	2.0
P_3	3.0	0.666	3.0
P_4	4.0	1.000	4.0

Table 7.13   By changing the central control value C_1 from 2.5 to 3.5, the value of P_2 has changed from 2.0 to 2.44, and P_3 has changed from 3.0 to 3.44.

	P	u	P'
P_1	1.0	0.000	1.00
P_2	2.0	0.333	2.44
P_3	3.0	0.666	3.44
P_4	4.0	1.000	4.00

where the parameter u is defined as:

$$u = \frac{P - P_1}{P_4 - P_1} \tag{7.59}$$

From Figure 7.16 we see that $P_1 = 1$, $P_2 = 2$, $P_3 = 3$ and $P_4 = 4$. The control values C_0, C_1 and C_2 equal 1, 2.5 and 4 respectively. If u is computed for each point and used to compute P', then Table 7.12 shows the results.

The table confirms that the four values of P' are identical to the original values of P_1, P_2, P_3 and P_4; this is because of the special values assigned to C_0, C_1 and C_2. However, if we change C_1 from 2.5 to 3.5, a new distribution is created as listed in Table 7.13. Although the values of P_1 and P_4 remain unchanged, P_2 moves from 2.0 to 2.44 and P_3 moves from 3.0 to 3.44. If more points were evaluated, we would see that they exhibited a quadratic distribution.

If, instead of moving the central control value, one of the boundary values were moved, the distribution of the original ordinates would become compressed or stretched. For instance, let us change C_0 from 1.0 to 2.0, and keep $C_1 = 2.5$, and $C_2 = 4.0$. The new distribution given in Table 7.14 shows that P_1 has moved with the value of C_0, while P_2 and P_3 have been distributed on a quadratic basis. Perhaps it is now clear that the distribution of the original ordinates can be manipulated by altering any arbitrary number of control values. Moreover, if a greater degree of control is needed, a 1D lattice of four control values can be used to effect a cubic distribution. P' is computed as follows:

$$P'(u) = (1 - u)^3 C_0 + 3u(1 - u)^2 C_1 + 3u^2(1 - u)C_2 + u^3 C_3 \tag{7.60}$$

Table 7.14 By changing C_0 from 1.0 to 2.0, the new distribution of P_1, P_2, P_3 and P_4 is compressed into the range 2.0 to 4.0 with an internal quadratic distribution.

	P	u	P'
P_1	1.0	0.000	2.0
P_2	2.0	0.333	2.44
P_3	3.0	0.666	3.11
P_4	4.0	1.000	4.0

where C_0, C_1, C_2 and C_3 are the four control values. This could also be written as:

$$P'(u) = \sum_{i=0}^{3} B_{i,3}(u)c_i \qquad (7.61)$$

7.4.2 Deforming 2D shapes

If the distribution of ordinates can be controlled using a 1D lattice of control values, it is a natural extension to control a family of 2D coordinates with a 2D lattice of control values. Figure 7.17(a) shows a 2D lattice of nine control vertices that can be used to deform the enclosed space with a quadratic distribution, and any point $P'(u,v)$ can be computed as follows:

$$P'(u,v) = \begin{bmatrix} (1-u)^2 & 2u(1-u) & u^2 \end{bmatrix} \begin{bmatrix} C_{00} & C_{01} & C_{02} \\ C_{10} & C_{11} & C_{12} \\ C_{20} & C_{21} & C_{22} \end{bmatrix} \begin{bmatrix} (1-v)^2 \\ 2v(1-v) \\ v^2 \end{bmatrix} \qquad (7.62)$$

where:

$$u = \frac{x - x_{min}}{x_{max} - x_{min}} \qquad (7.63)$$

$$v = \frac{y - y_{min}}{y_{max} - y_{min}} \qquad (7.64)$$

The above expression for $P'(u,v)$ can also be written as:

$$P'(u,v) = \sum_{i=0}^{2} B_{i,2}(u) \sum_{j=0}^{2} B_{j,2}(v)c_{i,j} \qquad (7.65)$$

The values of x_{min}, x_{max}, y_{min} and y_{max} are the minimum and maximum values of the control points. If C_{01}, C_{12}, C_{21} and C_{10} are positioned at the centre of their edges, and C_{11} is at the centre, no deformation occurs. This is shown in Figure 7.17(a). However, if one or more points is moved, the enclosed space is distorted. For example, Figure 7.17(b) shows the effect of moving C_{22} from (3,3) to (4,4).

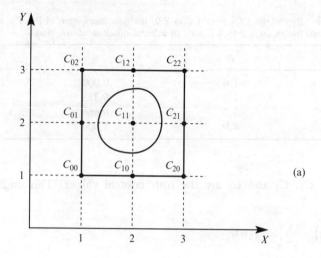

(a)

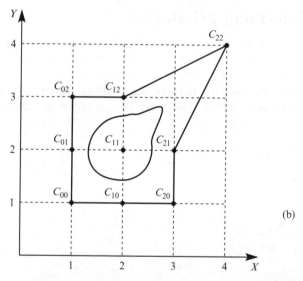

(b)

Figure 7.17   (a) The relaxed nine control points enclosing some shape. (b) The enclosed area is deformed when C_{22} is moved to (4,4).

7.4.3   Deforming 3D objects

In the 3D case a volume of space can be enclosed by a lattice of $3 \times 3 \times 3$ control points as shown in Figure 7.18. Moving one or more of the surface control points causes some deformation to the enclosed volume. Any point $P'(u,v,w)$ within the lattice is defined as:

$$P'(u,v,w) = \sum_{i=0}^{2} B_{i,2}(u) \sum_{j=0}^{2} B_{j,2}(v) \sum_{k=0}^{2} B_{k,2}(w)c_{i,j,k} \qquad (7.66)$$

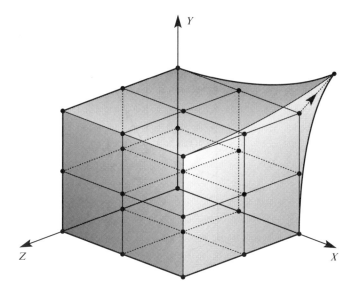

Figure 7.18 The organization of control points for deforming a 3D object. When one or more of the control points is moved, the enclosed volume is deformed.

where:

$$u = \frac{x - x_{min}}{x_{max} - x_{min}} \qquad v = \frac{y - y_{min}}{y_{max} - y_{min}} \qquad w = \frac{z - z_{min}}{z_{max} - z_{min}} \qquad (7.67)$$

Although in the above description we have employed a quadratic deformation, there is nothing preventing the technique from working with different degrees of the Bernstein polynomials.

7.5 Particle systems

Particle systems (Reeves, 1983) provide a powerful technique for modelling natural phenomena such as water, rain, fire, grass and trees. As the name suggests, the technique involves the modelling of fuzzy objects from very large numbers of discrete points or particles. Bill Reeves used them for creating very realistic images of trees.

Although their creative use produces photo-realistic images, their discrete nature requires efficient anti-aliasing, which leads to long rendering times. Nevertheless, they are also very useful as an animation tool to indicate complex motion. For example, imagine the problem of visualizing in real time a virtual wind tunnel. Fluid dynamics software would evaluate flow lines around a test object, and particles could be injected to move along them. For each frame, the particles are moved a distance proportional to their simulated

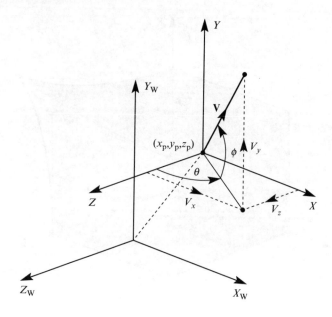

Figure 7.19   The vector $\mathbf{V} = [\,V_x\ V_y\ V_z\,]$ and is defined in terms of the angles θ and ϕ. The source of the particles is (x_p, y_p, z_p).

speed and the lapsed time. When a particle has traversed a flow line, it is injected into another flow line and used again.

There is no need to model the particles from polygons – a single coloured point is sufficient. Consequently, their storage is minimal, and they are generally held as a table. Each entry in the table holds the particle's current position in the VE and its colour. Other attributes might include transparency, the time the particle was born, and the time allocated to the particle's life. The birth and extent of the particle's existence are useful in animating flows, and showing a tail of previous positions.

As a practical example, consider the problem of simulating a source of sparks emanating from a point (x_p, y_p, z_p) in space. The sparks emerge from this point with a random velocity and direction. Their colour starts as white and decays to blue during their lifetimes.

A random velocity can be assigned to each spark using a pseudo-random number generator *rand* as follows:

$$V = rand(V_{\min}, V_{\max}) \qquad \text{where } V_{\min} \leqslant V \leqslant V_{\max} \tag{7.68}$$

Figure 7.19 shows that the direction of V is fixed by the angles θ and ϕ where:

$$\theta = rand(0, 2\pi) \tag{7.69}$$
$$\phi = rand(-\pi/2, \pi/2) \tag{7.70}$$

The vector components of V are given by:

$$V_x = V \cos \phi \cos \theta$$
$$V_y = V \sin \phi \tag{7.71}$$
$$V_z = V \cos \phi \sin \theta$$

and the position of a particle after the elapsed time t is given by:

$$x = x_p + V_x t$$
$$y = y_p + V_y t - \tfrac{1}{2} g t^2 \tag{7.72}$$
$$z = z_p + V_z t$$

where g is the acceleration due to gravity.

If each particle has an individual random life time of t_{life} then:

$$t_{\text{life}} = rand(t_{\min}, t_{\max}) \qquad \text{where } t_{\min} \leqslant t_{\text{life}} \leqslant t_{\max} \tag{7.73}$$

and its primary colour components p_{red}, p_{green} and p_{blue} will change as follows:

$$\left.\begin{aligned} p_{\text{red}} &= 1 - \frac{t}{t_{\text{life}}} \\[2mm] p_{\text{green}} &= 1 - \frac{t}{t_{\text{life}}} \\[2mm] p_{\text{blue}} &= 1 \end{aligned}\right\} \qquad \text{where } 0 \leqslant p_{\text{red}}, p_{\text{green}}, p_{\text{blue}} \leqslant 1 \tag{7.74}$$

The above parameters for each particle can be stored as a table that is updated on a frame-by-frame basis. When the special effect is initiated, the table is updated and rendered for each frame. The values of V_x, V_y and V_z could be kept constant to avoid the evaluation of the sine and cosine functions.

If this special effect is animated within a VE, one migh want to consider the interaction of the particles with other objects, With the above description, the particles will pass through other objects, rather than bounce off them.

8
Physical Simulation

8.0 Introduction

Over recent centuries the scientific approach has revealed various systems of laws to describe the dynamics of objects, electromagnetic phenomena, atomic forces and cosmological models for the universe. Each domain has its own set of laws, and for this chapter we will restrict the examples to some of the simple behaviours of objects related to our own human scale. In particular, we will investigate the motion of objects in a gravitational field, collisions with other objects, and other simple dynamic systems.

It was mentioned at the start of Chapter 7 that traditional animators rely upon a mixture of visual memory and drawing skills to simulate various physical behaviours. When a line test reveals that the animation is not correct, it is redrawn and retested until it satisfies the animator. Unfortunately, such techniques cannot be used in real-time computer graphics. If we want realism, we must rely upon deterministic procedures that encode knowledge of the physical world. Such procedures may be based upon either empirical laws or techniques that have been 'tweaked' to mimic a particular physical behaviour. Both approaches have their advantages and disadvantages: on the one hand, numerical techniques can be made very realistic and efficient, but may have limited application; whereas empirical laws accurately describe physical behaviour and enjoy a wide domain of applications, but may require significant levels of computation. In the circumstances, we must be prepared to use the best techniques for the right application and use our experience to decide how and when to make this choice.

When considering the motion of objects we cannot ignore Newton's contribution to this domain. Newton's laws of motion provide us with the primary behaviours of theoretical particles having mass but no size. These laws, however, can be employed to describe the motion of very large objects without introducing significant errors.

Newton's first law of motion states that 'the momentum of a particle is constant when there are no external forces'. This law reminds us that an object moves in a straight line unless disturbed by some force. In reality, the universe is awash with force fields, be they gravitational, electric, magnetic or atomic, and in general it is only when we move away from the earth that objects begin to obey this law.

Newton's second law of motion states that 'a particle of mass m, subjected to a force F, moves with acceleration F/m'. This law is also called the equation of motion of a particle, and reminds us that work has to be done whenever an object is accelerated.

Newton's third law of motion states that 'If a particle exerts a force on a second particle, the second particle exerts an equal reactive force in the opposite direction'. This law is useful when considering collisions between objects. Let us now examine how these laws can help us simulate some simple physical behaviours.

8.1   Objects falling in a gravitational field

When an object is moved away from the earth's surface it is attracted back through a gravitational force. This force is called the object's *weight* and is equal to mg, where m is the object's mass, and g is the acceleration due to gravity. Generally, g equals $9.81 \, \mathrm{ms}^{-2}$, but is 0.3% smaller at the equator and 0.2% larger at the poles. As the vertical y-axis represents positive offsets from the origin, upward velocities are defined positive and downward velocities negative.

In general, if a particle has an initial vertical velocity of v and acceleration a, the distance d travelled after time t is given by:

$$d = vt + \tfrac{1}{2}at^2 \tag{8.1}$$

If the particle has an initial vertical velocity of v_0 and is acceleration under the influence of gravity, the distance d becomes:

$$d = v_0 t - \tfrac{1}{2}gt^2 \tag{8.2}$$

In Figure 8.1 a particle is positioned at point P_0, at a distance h_0 above the ground plane. If the particle is allowed to fall under the action of gravity, after time t it will be at P_1 having fallen a distance d:

$$d = -\tfrac{1}{2}gt^2 \tag{8.3}$$

Its height h_1 above the ground plane is given by:

$$h_1 = h_0 + d = h_0 - \tfrac{1}{2}gt^2 \tag{8.4}$$

Calculating h_1 after any time t is trivial. But say we want to identify the point in time when the particle collides with the floor – this requires further analysis.

If the status of the particle is sampled at various time intervals, the point

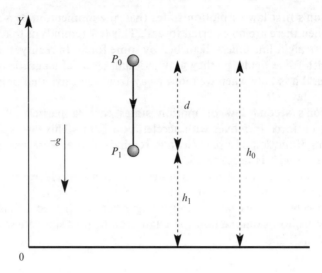

Figure 8.1 If a particle P is dropped from a height h_0, after time t it will have travelled $\frac{1}{2}gt^2$ downwards. Therefore, its new height h_1 is $h_0 - \frac{1}{2}gt^2$.

of collision with the floor is detected when the particle's height is zero. Because of the sampling process we will not automatically discover this condition. It is much more likely that the particle's height becomes negative and the point of intersection has to be computed. This can be implemented by maintaining a record of the particle's velocity and height at the previous sample.

Let the following parameters be used for the simulation:

h is the particle's height above the ground plane
v is the particle's velocity
t is the time at the sample point

When the status of the particle is sampled, it will produce values h_{now} and v_{now} at t_{now}, while the previous values will be h_{prev} and v_{prev} at t_{prev}. The values of h_{now}, v_{now}, and t_{now} become t_{prev}, h_{prev} and v_{prev} when the next sample is made. Figure 8.2(a) shows this situation. If $t = (t_{\text{now}} - t_{\text{prev}})$ the velocity v_{now} is given by:

$$v_{\text{now}} = v_{\text{prev}} - gt \tag{8.5}$$

while the new height h_{now} is given by:

$$h_{\text{now}} = h_{\text{prev}} + v_{\text{prev}}t - \frac{1}{2}gt^2 \tag{8.6}$$

If $h_{\text{now}} > 0$, the particle is still falling. If $h_{\text{now}} = 0$, the particle has just hit the floor, and with a perfect elastic collision will bounce upwards with its velocity reversed (see Figure 8.2b). If $h_{\text{now}} < 0$, the particle has passed through the floor as shown in Figure 8.2(c). When this occurs we can take various actions:

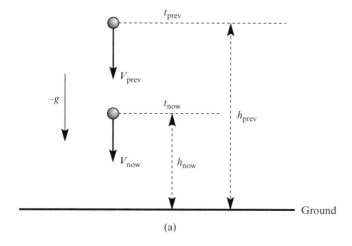

(a)

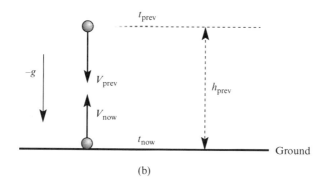

(b)

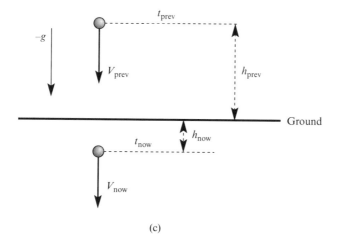

(c)

Figure 8.2   (a) The particle is still falling, therefore $h_{now} > 0$. (b) The particle has hit the ground, therefore $h_{now} = 0$. (c) The particle has effectively intersected the ground plane, therefore $h_{now} < 0$.

(1) If the sample rate was high and the velocities low, we could ignore the point of collision and reposition the particle on the ground plane with its velocity reversed.

(2) We could assume that the conditions were such that a collision has occurred and the particle has bounced and starts its upward journey at h_{prev} with a reversed velocity of v_{prev}.

(3) We could compute the precise time of the collision by solving a quadratic equation, compute the particle's velocity on impact and derive its new position and velocity as it bounces upwards during the remaining time interval!

The choice we take depends upon the level of realism we want to simulate.

If we do wish to compute the precise moment of impact and reposition the particle accurately, then the following equations can be used.

The time t_g it takes for the particle to strike the ground after the previous time sample t_{prev} is given by:

$$t_g = \frac{v_{prev} \pm \sqrt{v_{prev}^2 + 2gh_{prev}}}{g} \tag{8.7}$$

There are two roots to this equation and we must take the positive one. The particle's velocity v_g when it strikes the ground is given by:

$$v_g = \sqrt{v_{prev}^2 + 2gh_{prev}} \tag{8.8}$$

This time we take the negative root. Therefore, at a time $(t_{prev} + t_g)$ the particle strikes the ground at a speed of v_g.

The next stage in the computation is to reverse the sign of the velocity as it starts its upward journey. The particle still has $(t_{now} - t_{prev} - t_g)$ seconds to travel with this starting velocity, and by substituting these time and velocity values in (8.9) and (8.10) we can determine its final velocity and height v_{now} and h_{now} as follows:

$$v_{now} = v_g - gt \tag{8.9}$$

$$h_{now} = v_g t - \tfrac{1}{2}gt^2 \qquad \text{where} \quad t = t_{now} - t_{prev} - t_g \tag{8.10}$$

In the above calculations the particle has a radius of zero. This can easily be introduced into the collision detection by effectively shifting the particle's frame of reference vertically by the radius r. The time t_g to collide with the ground now becomes:

$$t_g = \frac{v_{prev} \pm \sqrt{v_{prev}^2 + 2g(h_{prev} - r)}}{g} \tag{8.11}$$

8.1.1   Temporal aliasing

The above example raises a fundamental problem associated with all discrete sampling systems, namely, aliasing. Figure 8.3 shows diagrammatically what

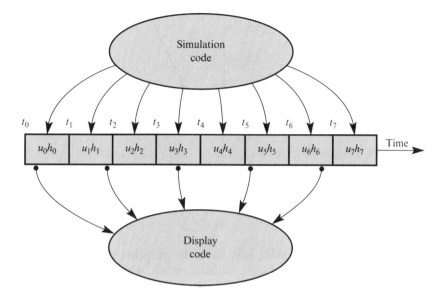

Figure 8.3 Temporal aliasing arises when any continuous system is discretely sampled. In this situation, the simulation code computes parameters and different points in time. The display code may sample this data on a regular basis, which introduces irregular temporal sampling.

is occurring. The simulation code is evaluating a numerical model at a particular sample rate that probably varies in time. At any time t_n, values of v_n and h_n are computed. Meanwhile, the display code is updating the display processor with the latest version of the simulated model at a different rate. Even though this update rate is regular, the sampling process results in an inconsistent display of the simulation producing temporal aliasing. A practical way of minimizing this phenomenon is to increase the sample rate of the simulation code.

8.1.2 Restitution

Theoretically, the bouncing particle should continue indefinitely, however, the way the collision calculation is handled determines the level of error introduced into the model. Practically, the particle should come to rest because of imperfections in the physical system, and the conversion of kinetic energy into heat and sound. This can be effected through a coefficient of restitution e which relates the separation speed v_s to the approach speed v_a as follows:

$$v_s = ev_a \quad \text{where} \quad 0 \leqslant e \leqslant 1 \tag{8.12}$$

In the bouncing particle scenario we could attenuate the bouncing cycle by

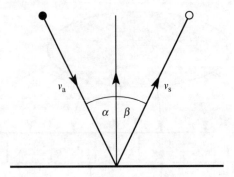

Figure 8.4   When a particle strikes a rigid surface, the separation speed and angle are influenced by the coefficient of restitution.

introducing a value of $e = 0.95$, say, when the particle's velocity is reversed. By keeping $e = 1$, a perfectly elastic collision occurs, while a perfectly inelastic collision is created when $e = 0$.

Figure 8.4 shows a particle striking a smooth rigid surface with an approach speed v_a at an angle α, and a separation speed of v_s at an angle of β. The component of its velocity tangential to the surface remains constant, whereas the magnitude of the normal component is influenced by the coefficient of restitution as follows:

$$v_s \sin \beta = v_a \sin \alpha \qquad \text{(tangential component)} \tag{8.13}$$

$$v_s \cos \beta = ev_a \cos \alpha \qquad \text{(normal component)} \tag{8.14}$$

Therefore:

$$e \tan \beta = \tan \alpha \tag{8.15}$$

and:

$$v_s^2(\sin^2 \beta + \cos^2 \beta) = v_a^2(\sin^2 \alpha + e^2 \cos^2 \alpha) \tag{8.16}$$

Therefore:

$$v_s = v_a\sqrt{\sin^2 \alpha + e^2 \cos^2 \alpha} \tag{8.17}$$

and:

$$\beta = \tan^{-1}((\tan \alpha)/e) \tag{8.18}$$

8.2 Rotating wheels

In Chapter 7 we saw how rotational movements are achieved using matrix techniques, so let us now examine some of the practical issues of simulating rotating elements in a VE.

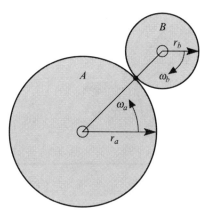

Figure 8.5 If wheel A is rotating at ω_a [rad s^{-1}], wheel B will rotate in the opposite direction at a rate proportional to r_a/r_b.

8.2.1 Gear trains

Consider the problem of animating the rotational speed of a wheel in contact with some driving wheel. Figure 8.5 illustrates two wheels A and B, with radii r_a and r_b, and rotational rates ω_a and ω_b rad s^{-1} respectively. At the point of contact P, the angular speed of wheel A is $\omega_a r_a$, which must be the same for wheel B, that is if we assume zero slip between the two wheels. However, as wheel A is rotating anticlockwise, wheel B is driven in the opposite direction, therefore the following relationship holds:

$$\omega_b r_b = -\omega_a r_a \tag{8.19}$$

and:

$$\omega_b = \frac{-r_a \omega_a}{r_b}\ [\text{rad s}^{-1}] \tag{8.20}$$

If t seconds is the elapsed time from some reference time, wheel A will rotate $\omega_a t$ radians and wheel B will rotate $-\omega_a t r_a/r_b$ radians which can then be substituted into the relevant matrix used to rotate wheel B.

8.2.2 Combined linear and rotational motion

If a wheel or ball rolls across a surface, there is a simple relationship linking the linear and rotational speeds. Figure 8.6 shows a wheel of radius r whose centre is travelling at a speed v. The linear distance d travelled after t seconds is given by:

$$d = vt \tag{8.21}$$

The angle θ turned by the wheel is:

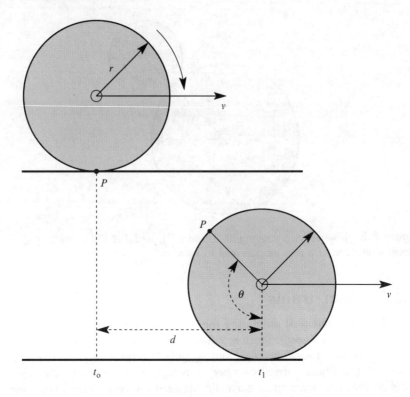

Figure 8.6   If a wheel of radius r is rolling with a linear speed of v, the distance travelled in time t is vt, which must equal the arc length rolled by the wheel. The angle θ turned by the wheel equals vt/r [radians].

$$\theta = d/r\,[\text{radians}] \tag{8.22}$$

therefore:

$$\theta = vt/r\,[\text{radians}] \tag{8.23}$$

Now consider a wheel of radius r modelled as shown in Figure 8.7(a) with its centre coincident with the origin of its OCS. It can be animated to roll along the x-axis of the VE by applying suitable rotation and translation matrices. If at time t_0 the wheel has an instantaneous linear speed of v, then at time t_1, it will have rotated $\theta = v(t_1 - t_0)/r$ radians and moved a linear distance $d = v(t_1 - t_0)$. Therefore, the translation matrix is:

$$\begin{bmatrix} 1 & 0 & 0 & d \\ 0 & 1 & 0 & r \\ 0 & 0 & 1 & 0 \\ 0 & 0 & 0 & 1 \end{bmatrix} \tag{8.24}$$

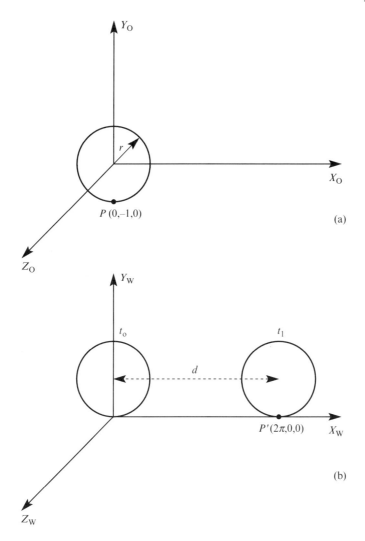

Figure 8.7   (a) A wheel of radius *r* is modelled such that its centre is at the origin of the OCS. (b) During one revolution the point $P(0, -1, 0)$ is transformed to $P'(2\pi, 0, 0)$.

(Note that the *r* term lifts the wheel in the *y*-direction by its radius) and the rotation matrix is:

$$
\begin{bmatrix}
\cos(-\theta) & -\sin(-\theta) & 0 & 0 \\
\sin(-\theta) & \cos(-\theta) & 0 & 0 \\
0 & 0 & 1 & 0 \\
0 & 0 & 0 & 1
\end{bmatrix}
\tag{8.25}
$$

(Note that the angle of rotation θ is negative, because the wheel rotates clockwise relative to the OCS), which simplifies to:

$$\begin{bmatrix} \cos\theta & \sin\theta & 0 & 0 \\ -\sin\theta & \cos\theta & 0 & 0 \\ 0 & 0 & 1 & 0 \\ 0 & 0 & 0 & 1 \end{bmatrix} \qquad (8.26)$$

and the two matrices concatenate to:

$$\begin{bmatrix} \cos\theta & \sin\theta & 0 & d \\ -\sin\theta & \cos\theta & 0 & r \\ 0 & 0 & 1 & 0 \\ 0 & 0 & 0 & 1 \end{bmatrix} \qquad (8.27)$$

For instance, say $v = 2\pi r$, $(t_1 - t_0) = 1$ and $r = 1$. The distance travelled is $d = 2\pi$, and the rotated angle is $360°$. Substituting these values in (8.27) produces:

$$\begin{bmatrix} 1 & 0 & 0 & 2\pi \\ 0 & 1 & 0 & 1 \\ 0 & 0 & 1 & 0 \\ 0 & 0 & 0 & 1 \end{bmatrix} \qquad (8.28)$$

which confirms that a point $P(0,-1,0)$ is transformed to $P'(2\pi,0,0)$ after 1 second, as shown in Figure 8.7(b).

8.2.3 A steerable wheel

Let us now consider simulating a steerable wheel that can roll about the ground plane under the control of some external agent. This will probably be the VO who is controlling the wheel's speed and direction through some interface. The system samples the wheel's linear speed v, and steering angle ϕ, at some frequency, which hold until the next sample is made.

The wheel is modelled as shown in Figure 8.8(a) with its centre at the origin of the OCS, and rotates about the Z_O-axis. Three matrices are needed to position the wheel in the VE: the first matrix rotates the wheel about the Z_O-axis of the OCS by the accumulated roll angle α (Figure 8.8b); the second matrix rotates the wheel about the Y_O-axis by the current steering angle θ (Figure 8.8c); and the third matrix translates the wheel (x,r,z) in the VE. At time t_0 the wheel is located in the VE as shown in Figure 8.9, with the following conditions:

r is the wheel's radius

α is the accumulated angle rolled by the wheel

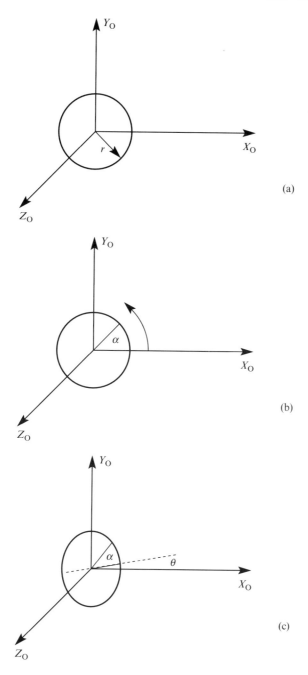

(a)

(b)

(c)

Figure 8.8   (a) A wheel, radius r, is modelled with its centre at the origin of the OCS. (b) It is rotated α about the Z_O axis to simulate rolling. (c) It is then rotated θ about the Y_O axis to simulate the steering angle.

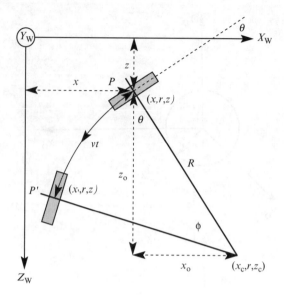

Figure 8.9 This plan elevation of the VE shows two views of the wheel at P and P'. Initially the wheel has a steering angle of θ, a linear speed v and an incremental steering angle of ϕ. These parameters are used to roll it to its next position at P'.

θ is the steering angle turned by the wheel

$P(x,r,z)$ is the current position of the wheel's centre

ϕ is the incremental steering angle ($\phi \neq 0$)

v is the linear speed of the wheel

Both ϕ and v are always available to the real-time system, and note that ϕ is assumed to be non-zero.

If at time t_0 the wheel is at position P (Figure 8.9) with a linear speed v and an incremental steering angle ϕ, then at time t_1, the wheel will be at P', having rolled a linear distance $v(t_1 - t_0)$. The wheel will therefore roll through an angle $v(t_1 - t_0)/r$ radians. The geometry in Figure 8.9 shows that the wheel is steered about a point (x_c,r,z_c) with a turning radius R. Therefore, the following conditions exist:

$$R\phi = v(t_1 - t_0) \tag{8.29}$$

$$R = v(t_1 - t_0)/\phi \tag{8.30}$$

$$x_o = R \sin \theta \tag{8.31}$$

$$z_o = R \cos \theta \tag{8.32}$$

$$x_c = x + x_o = x + R \sin \theta \tag{8.33}$$

$$z_c = z + z_o = z + R \cos \theta \tag{8.34}$$

We now have sufficient information to develop the three matrices that will be applied to every wheel vertex in the following order:

$$\begin{bmatrix} x' \\ y' \\ z' \\ 1 \end{bmatrix} = [\textit{translate}] \, [\textit{steer}] \, [\textit{roll}] \begin{bmatrix} x \\ y \\ z \\ 1 \end{bmatrix} \tag{8.35}$$

Roll matrix

The roll matrix rotates the wheel about the Z_O-axis of the OCS, by an angle α. This angle, however, increases by the rolled angle between each update, therefore:

$$\alpha \leftarrow \alpha + \frac{v(t_1 - t_0)}{r} \tag{8.36}$$

The roll matrix is:

$$\begin{bmatrix} \cos \alpha & -\sin \alpha & 0 & 0 \\ \sin \alpha & \cos \alpha & 0 & 0 \\ 0 & 0 & 1 & 0 \\ 0 & 0 & 0 & 1 \end{bmatrix} \tag{8.37}$$

Steer matrix

The steer matrix rotates the wheel about the Y_O-axis of OCS by an angle θ. However, this angle increases by the incremental steering angle ϕ between each update:

$$\theta \leftarrow \theta + \phi \tag{8.38}$$

Therefore, the steer matrix becomes:

$$\begin{bmatrix} \cos \theta & 0 & \sin \theta & 0 \\ 0 & 1 & 0 & 0 \\ -\sin \theta & 0 & \cos \theta & 0 \\ 0 & 0 & 0 & 1 \end{bmatrix} \tag{8.39}$$

Translate matrix

The translate matrix translates the wheel into the VE by the new position of the wheel, which is obtained by rotating the previous position (x,r,z) about $(x_c, 0, z_c)$ by the incremental steering angle ϕ. In matrix terms, this is expressed as:

$$\begin{bmatrix} \textit{translate} \\ (x_c, r, z_c) \end{bmatrix} [\textit{rotate } \phi \textit{ about Y-axis}] \begin{bmatrix} \textit{translate} \\ (-x_c, 0, -z_c) \end{bmatrix} \tag{8.40}$$

$$\begin{bmatrix} 1 & 0 & 0 & x_c \\ 0 & 1 & 0 & r \\ 0 & 0 & 1 & z_c \\ 0 & 0 & 0 & 1 \end{bmatrix} \begin{bmatrix} \cos \phi & 0 & \sin \phi & 0 \\ 0 & 1 & 0 & 0 \\ -\sin \phi & 0 & \cos \phi & 0 \\ 0 & 0 & 0 & 1 \end{bmatrix} \begin{bmatrix} 1 & 0 & 0 & -x_c \\ 0 & 1 & 0 & 0 \\ 0 & 0 & 1 & -z_c \\ 0 & 0 & 0 & 1 \end{bmatrix} \tag{8.41}$$

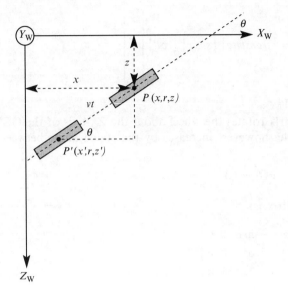

Figure 8.10   This plan elevation of the VE shows two views of the wheel at P and P'. The wheel has a steering angle of θ, a linear speed v and an incremental steering angle of zero. Its new position at P' depends only upon v, t and θ.

The above geometric reasoning holds only for non-zero values of ϕ. If the controlling agent sets this input value to zero, it implies that the wheel should continue forward in the current direction defined by θ. For this to occur, the wheel is still subjected to the roll and steer matrices, but the translation matrix is modified. Figure 8.10 shows the relevant geometry. If at time t_0 the wheel is at $P(x,r,z)$, travelling at a speed v with a steering angle θ, then at time t_1 the wheel will be at $P'(x',r,z')$, having rolled a linear distance $v(t_1 - t_0)$. Therefore:

$$x' = x - v(t_1 - t_0) \cos \theta \tag{8.42}$$
$$z' = z + v(t_1 - t_0) \sin \theta \tag{8.43}$$

These values are then substituted into the translate matrix (8.41) as before.

There are some interesting features of this example worth exploring. To begin with, the above matrices provide the basis for developing a steerable vehicle that can be driven inside a VE. The vehicle could be controlled by an agent in the real world, with the vehicle's movements observed on a computer display. The vehicle could even be controlled by a VO immersed in the VE using a control device similar to that used for radio-controlled model cars. The VO could be positioned inside the vehicle and experience the changing views of the VE as the vehicle moves about. The latter scenario could form the basis for a VR-based car simulator.

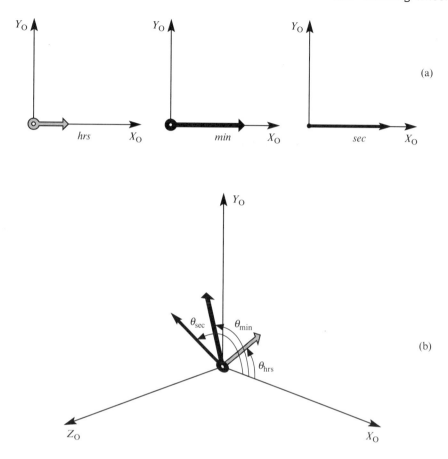

Figure 8.11 (a) The hour, minute and second hands. (b) The three angles θ_{sec}, θ_{min} and θ_{hrs} are used to rotate the individual hands about the Z_O-axis.

8.2.4 Clocks

Consider the problem of animating a clock to show the current time. Basically, we need to develop the matrices to rotate the clock's hour, minute and second hands. These hands are modelled as shown in Figure 8.11. For this example we will assume that the current time is available in the form of (hrs, min, sec), which will be used to derive $(\theta_{hrs}^{\circ}, \theta_{min}^{\circ}, \theta_{sec}^{\circ})$. As the second hand is initially pointing at the '15 second' position, θ_{sec}° is given by:

$$\theta_{sec}^{\circ} = 90 - 6\,sec \tag{8.44}$$

As the minute hand is pointing at the '15 minute' position, θ_{min}° is given by:

$$\theta_{min}^{\circ} = 90 - 6\,min - sec/10 \tag{8.45}$$

Similarly, θ_{hrs}° is given by:

$$\theta^{\circ}_{\text{hrs}} = 90 - 30\,hrs - min/2 - sec/120 \tag{8.46}$$

If these angles are substituted into the matrix for rolling objects and applied to the clock hands for each frame, the clock will always display the current time. We should also remember to translate each hand forward slightly along the z-axis so that the hands do not intersect one another.

8.3   Elastic collisions

Most collisions between real objects are complex physical interactions. For instance, the objects may have irregular boundaries; the individual surfaces may have different coefficients of friction; their densities may be non-homogeneous; the objects may possess angular momentum; and the objects might be travelling across an irregular surface which itself introduces non-linear frictional forces. Simulating such phenomena is possible but beyond the scope of this chapter.

8.3.1   Direct impact of two particles

Principle of the conservation of momentum
The simplest collisions to simulate involve two imaginary particles with mass and velocity but no size. When two such particles collide, their new velocities are controlled by the principle of the conservation of momentum and the principle of relative motion. The momentum of a particle is the product of its mass and velocity, and, given two particles with mass m_a and m_b, and associated velocities v_a and v_b, then:

$$m_a v_a + m_b v_b = \text{constant} \tag{8.47}$$

The principle of relative motion
The principle of relative motion states that the relative velocity after an impact equals the relative velocity before the impact multiplied by the coefficient of restitution. Therefore, if the respective velocities of the two particles after the collision are u_a and u_b, then:

$$u_a - u_b = -e(v_a - v_b) \tag{8.48}$$

where e is the coefficient of restitution.

When two bodies collide, the interaction is assumed to take place during a short time interval. The forces generated during the collision are assumed to be much larger than any external forces such as gravity and wind resistance. Furthermore, any two particles are assumed to move in the same straight line connecting their centres. Such collisions are called 'direct impact'.

To illustrate the principle of the conservation of momentum and relative velocity, consider the case of particle A with mass m_a and velocity v_a striking particle B with mass m_b and velocity v_b, travelling in opposite directions. Their total momentum is given by:

$$\text{Momentum} = m_a v_a + m_b v_b \tag{8.49}$$

If the following conditions prevail:

$$m_a = 5 \qquad v_a = 2 \qquad m_b = 3 \qquad v_b = -4$$

and the velocities of A and B after the impact are u_a and u_b, then:

$$m_a v_a + m_b v_b = m_a u_a + m_b u_b \tag{8.50}$$

and, using the relative velocities for a perfect elastic collision:

$$u_a - u_b = -(v_a - v_b) \tag{8.51}$$

Therefore:

$$(5 \times 2) + (3 \times -4) = 5u_a + 3u_b \tag{8.52}$$

$$-2 = 5u_a + 3u_b \tag{8.53}$$

and, using (8.51) we have:

$$u_a - u_b = -(2 - (-4)) = -6 \tag{8.54}$$

From (8.53) and (8.54) we discover that $u_a = -2.5$, and $u_b = 3.5$.

8.3.2 Oblique impact of two particles

Figure 8.12 shows two particles A and B positioned at c_a and c_b at the time of impact. Their respective approach velocities are v_a and v_b at angles α and β relative to the line connecting their two centres.

The components of velocity perpendicular to the line $c_a c_b$ are unaltered by the collision, and are given by $v_a \sin \alpha$ and $v_b \sin \beta$ respectively. The components of velocity parallel to the line $c_a c_b$ are subject to the conservation of momentum because the particles' masses are accelerated. Therefore:

$$m_a v_a + m_b v_b = m_a u_a \cos \alpha + m_b u_b \cos \beta \tag{8.55}$$

By Newton's law of relative motion,

$$u_a - u_b = -e(v_a \cos \alpha - v_b \cos \beta) \tag{8.56}$$

where e is the coefficient of restitution. Substituting (8.56) in (8.55) we have:

$$u_a = \frac{(m_a - em_b)v_a \cos \alpha + m_b v_b \cos \beta (1 + e)}{m_a + m_b} \tag{8.57}$$

$$u_b = \frac{(m_b - em_a)v_b \cos \beta + m_a v_a \cos \alpha (1 + e)}{m_a + m_b} \tag{8.58}$$

The final velocity of each particle and its direction of motion is found from the perpendicular and parallel components.

If particle B is at rest, the final velocities are given by:

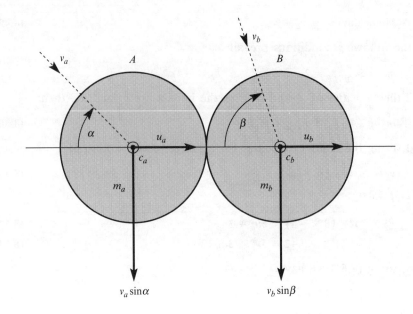

Figure 8.12 When two particles A and B collide with velocities v_a and v_b, at angles α and β to the line joining their two centres, the components of velocity perpendicular to the line are unaltered. The tangential components are determined by applying the principle of the conservation of momentum.

$$u_a = \frac{(m_a - em_b)v_a \cos \alpha}{m_a + m_b} \tag{8.59}$$

$$u_b = \frac{m_a v_a \cos \alpha (1 + e)}{m_a + m_b} \tag{8.60}$$

Furthermore, its velocity after impact must be directed parallel to the line $c_a c_b$ as its perpendicular velocity component was zero.

If the new direction of the colliding particle A is defined in terms of an angle β relative to the line $c_a c_b$, then:

$$\begin{aligned} \tan \theta &= \frac{v_a \sin \alpha}{u_a} \\ &= \frac{(m_a + m_b) \tan \alpha}{m_a - em_b} \end{aligned} \tag{8.61}$$

If the two particles have the same mass, then:

$$\tan \theta = \frac{2 \tan \alpha}{1 - e} \tag{8.62}$$

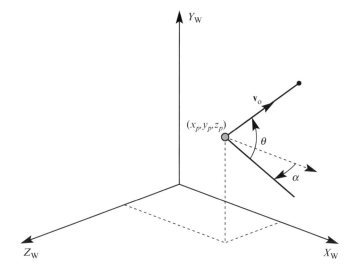

Figure 8.13 The source of the projectiles is (x_p, y_p, z_p), and two angles α and θ are used to position the exit vector.

8.4 Projectiles

Shells and bullets are the first things we associate with projectiles, but any object projected into the air is a projectile, be it a coin, stone or table. An inflated balloon, however, cannot be considered as a projectile as its buoyancy and air resistance are significant factors influencing its motion. For the following analysis it will be assumed that the frictional force due to air resistance is insignificant, and that the earth's gravitational force is constant at all heights.

8.4.1 The motion of a projectile

In order to develop a general solution to the trajectory of a projectile, let us employ the scenario shown in Figure 8.13, where an object is projected from the position (x_p, y_p, z_p) with velocity v_o and orientation angles θ and α.

The initial velocity components are given by:

$$v_x = v_o \cos \theta \cos \alpha \tag{8.63}$$

$$v_y = v_o \sin \theta \tag{8.64}$$

$$v_z = v_o \cos \theta \sin \alpha \tag{8.65}$$

After time t after projection, the velocity components are given by:

$$v_x = v_o \cos \theta \cos \alpha \tag{8.66}$$

$$v_y = v_0 \sin \theta - gt \tag{8.67}$$

$$v_z = v_0 \cos \theta \sin \alpha \tag{8.68}$$

The position of the projectile (x,y,z) after time t is given by:

$$x = x_p + v_0 t \cos \theta \cos \alpha \tag{8.69}$$

$$y = y_p + v_0 t \sin \theta - \tfrac{1}{2} gt^2 \tag{8.70}$$

$$z = z_p + v_0 t \cos \theta \sin \alpha \tag{8.71}$$

Using (8.69), (8.70) and (8.71) we can translate an object to position (x,y,z) as the elapsed time progresses. The resulting path is parabolic constrained within a vertical plane. The influence of a cross-wind can be introduced by defining the wind's speed and direction as a vector and adding the components to (8.66), (8.67) and (8.68).

8.4.2 Collision with the ground

Earlier in Section 8.1 we investigated the problem of detecting when a falling object struck the ground. It was shown that different strategies could be adopted depending upon the level of accuracy required. The same applies in this situation. If we maintain the status of the projectile at each sample, we can identify the precise moment in time when the projectile's height becomes zero. At this point we can determine the impact velocity. Rather than repeat this analysis again, we will continue and consider the behaviour of the projectile if it bounces off the surface.

As the ground plane is a specific case, an arbitrarily oriented surface will be used to derive the bounce vector. Figure 8.14 shows a surface whose orientation is specified by its normal vector $\mathbf{N}$. The incident unit vector is $\mathbf{V}_i$ and the bounce unit vector is $\mathbf{V}_b$. If restitution is ignored, the angle of incidence θ equals the angle of bounce. From Figure 8.14 it can be seen that the surface normal vector $\mathbf{N}_u$ is given by:

$$\mathbf{N}_u = -\mathbf{V}_i + \mathbf{V}_b \tag{8.72}$$

$$-\mathbf{V}_i \cdot \mathbf{V}_b = \cos 2\theta = 2 \cos^2 \theta - 1 \tag{8.73}$$

$$\frac{|\mathbf{N}_u|}{2} = |-\mathbf{V}_i| \cos \theta \tag{8.74}$$

but as $\mathbf{V}_i$ is a unit vector:

$$|\mathbf{N}_u| = 2 \cos \theta \tag{8.75}$$

Using the dot product definition:

$$-\mathbf{V}_i \cdot \mathbf{N} = \cos \theta \tag{8.76}$$

Therefore:

$$|\mathbf{N}_u| = 2(-\mathbf{V}_i \cdot \mathbf{N}) \tag{8.77}$$

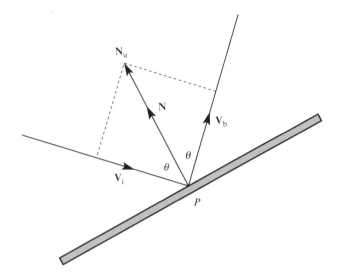

Figure 8.14 The relationship between the incident unit vector V_i, the unit surface normal vector N and the unit bounce vector V_b.

but:

$$N = \frac{N_u}{|N_u|} = \frac{-V_i + V_b}{2(-V_i \cdot N)} \tag{8.78}$$

and:

$$2(-V_i \cdot N)N = -V_i + V_b \tag{8.79}$$

Therefore, the bounce vector is given by:

$$V_b = V_i + 2(-V_i \cdot N)N \tag{8.80}$$

It is left to the reader to implement this geometry and introduce the effect of restitution.

8.5 Simple pendulums

It can be shown that a simple pendulum exhibits approximate simple harmonic motion if it consists of a heavy concentrated mass suspended by an inextensible cord and restricted to a swing of up to $\pm 14°$. To simulate this behaviour dynamically we must analyse the forces shown in Figure 8.15. In this figure we see that the mass of the pendulum, m, is supported by a cord of length L. If the mass is displaced from its upright position by an angle θ radians, a restoring force $m \sin \theta$ will attempt to re-establish equilibrium. The acceleration a produced by this restoring force is given by:

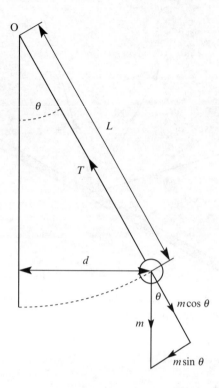

Figure 8.15   When a pendulum is displaced by an angle θ from the vertical position, a restoring force $m \sin \theta$ attempts to re-establish equilibrium. The future position of the pendulum is determined by computing its velocity and acceleration from this force.

$$a = \frac{m \sin \theta}{m/g} \tag{8.81}$$

$$a = g \sin \theta \tag{8.82}$$

If the angle of swing does not exceed $\pm 14°$, $\sin \theta$ is approximately equal to θ radians. Therefore, we can write:

$$a = g\theta \tag{8.83}$$

But for these small angles:

$$\theta = \frac{d}{L} \tag{8.84}$$

Therefore:

$$a = g\frac{d}{L} \tag{8.85}$$

At any point in time t, the pendulum has displacement d, velocity v and acceleration a. Therefore, at time $t + \Delta t$ the new displacement d' is given by:

$$d' = d - v\Delta t \tag{8.86}$$

The acceleration is given by:

$$a = g\frac{d}{L} \tag{8.87}$$

and the new velocity v' by:

$$v' = v + a\Delta t \tag{8.88}$$

If the equations for the displacement, velocity and acceleration are iterated, the pendulum's motion is simulated. The pendulum is animated by rotating the object description through and angle θ relative to the upright position, where $\theta = d/L$.

8.6 Springs

The motion of an object attached to a spring or a piece of elastic can be simulated by analysing the dynamic forces acting upon the object. Figure 8.16 shows a spring of length l hanging from a rigid fixing. If an object of mass m is attached to the free end of the spring, it will bounce up and down with simple harmonic motion. Two laws are used to describe the active forces, namely Newton's second law of motion, and Hooke's law. Hooke's law states that the tension T in a spring is given by:

$$T = \lambda\frac{e}{l} \tag{8.89}$$

where λ is the modulus of the spring and e is the extension of the spring. While the object is moving up and down, its motion is controlled by:

$$ma = mg - T \tag{8.90}$$

where m is the mass of the object, a is the acceleration of the object and g is the acceleration due to gravity.

If at any time t, the mass has position y, velocity v and acceleration a, at a time $t + \Delta t$ its new position y' relative to the top of the spring is given by:

$$y' = y + v\Delta t \tag{8.91}$$

The extension e is given by:

$$e = y - l \tag{8.92}$$

and if this is substituted into (8.93):

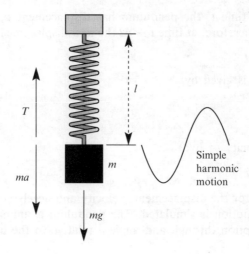

Figure 8.16   If a mass m is attached to a light spring it will oscillate with simple harmonic motion.

$$ma = mg - \lambda \frac{e}{l} \tag{8.93}$$

the acceleration a is equal to:

$$a = g - \lambda \frac{e}{lm} \tag{8.94}$$

and the new velocity v' of the mass is equal to:

$$v' = v + a\Delta t \tag{8.95}$$

If this value of v' is substituted back into (8.91) to develop a new value for y, and continuously repeated, the trace of y is simple harmonic. The value of y can then be substituted into a matrix to subject an object to this motion. Perhaps one of the most useful features of this approach is that the model can be dynamically modified while it is running. Any of the above parameters can be interactively changed, resulting in an almost instantaneous change in the motion.

8.6.1   Restitution

As there is no loss in this model, the simple harmonic motion continues indefinitely. If the motion is required to decay to zero, a restitution term k_d can be introduced in (8.95) as follows:

$$v' = k_d v + a\Delta t \qquad 0 \leqslant k_d \leqslant 1 \tag{8.96}$$

When $k_d = 1$, the motion continues unchecked, but when $k_d < 1$, the motion decays away.

8.6.2 Moving springs

Figure 8.17(a) shows a spring of length *l* connected to a wheel which can travel over a surface. On top of the spring is a mass *m*. If the spring's restitution is less than unity, when the mass is placed on the spring it will oscillate and settle down to some state of equilibrium. The mass will oscillate only if it is subjected to some external force.

One way of introducing a force is to roll the wheel over an undulating terrain as shown in Figure 8.17(b). As the wheel rises and falls, the spring is compressed and stretched, modulating the spring tension transmitted to the mass. The extra spring compression *h* is the difference between the terrain height sampled at $t + \Delta t$ and t. Initially *h* is set to zero and is introduced into the spring extension equation as follows:

$$e = y - l - h \tag{8.97}$$

where *y* is the height of the spring before the mass was added.

The new set of equations then become:

$$y' = y + v\Delta t$$
$$e = y - l - h$$

$$a = g - \lambda \frac{e}{lm} \tag{8.98}$$

$$v' = k_d v + a\Delta t$$
$$h' = h_{new} - h$$

Where h_{new} is the next value of *h* sampled at $t + \Delta t$. When this algorithm is implemented, it produces very realistic motion.

8.6.3 Elastic structures

We saw in Section 7.4 how free-form deformations (FFDs) are used by animators to form flexible objects. But if a sense of elasticity has to be introduced into the animation, the control points of the FFDs must be moved with suitable dynamics. We can use the dynamic model of a spring to create this effect, but the ideas developed below have also been applied to model flexible objects such as flags, carpets, curtains and tablecloths (Miller, 1984; Scanlon, 1990; Terzopoulos and Witkin, 1988; Weil, 1986).

Fabrics can be modelled as a matrix of mass points connected together in a mesh, where each mass is connected to a neighbouring mass using springs, as shown in Figure 8.18. The forces acting on the springs can be related to the masses they act upon using Newton's second law of motion.

To illustrate the technique we will analyse the 2D case, and it will be left to the reader to extend the ideas to the 3D domain, with reference to the papers cited.

Consider the dynamic simulation of an elastic thread fixed at both ends.

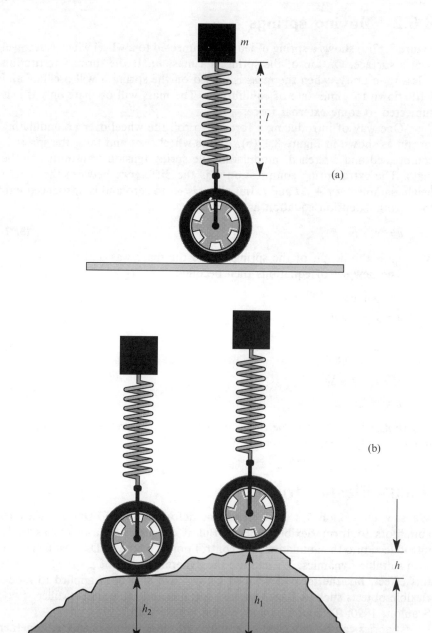

Figure 8.17   (a) If a mass m is attached to a light spring it will move with simple harmonic motion and settle down to a state of equilibrium. (b) As the wheel rises and falls, the mass attached to the free end of the spring will subject the spring to extra forces caused by accelerating the mass.

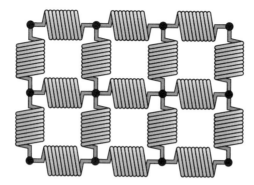

Figure 8.18 Fabric can be represented as a mesh of mass points connected to one another by stiff springs. The forces acting through these springs can be computed and used to move the mass point positions to simulate the behaviour of material under the forces of gravity.

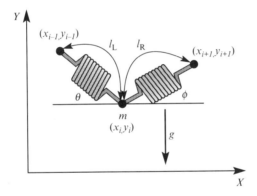

Figure 8.19 Given three mass points falling under the action of gravity (g), their changing positions in space can be determined by resolving the horizontal and vertical force components.

This can be represented approximately by a sequence of mass points m connected to their neighbours with springs of length l. Now imagine that the middle of the thread has been raised and allowed to fall under the action of gravity. Hooke's law implies that the spring's extension is proportional to the applied force. It is these forces that need to be calculated, but first the spring extension has to be computed.

Figure 8.19 shows the positions of the three mass points whose positions are specified by:

$$(x_{i-1}, y_{i-1}) \qquad (x_i, y_i) \qquad \text{and} \qquad (x_{i+1}, y_{i+1}) \tag{8.99}$$

The left- and right-hand lengths l_L and l_R will be:

$$l_L = \sqrt{(x_{i-1} - x_i)^2 + (y_{i-1} - y_i)^2}$$ (8.100)

$$l_R = \sqrt{(x_{i+1} - x_i)^2 + (y_{i+1} - y_i)^2}$$ (8.101)

and the left- and right-hand spring extensions e_L and e_R will be:

$$e_L = l_L - l \quad \text{and} \quad e_R = l_R - l$$ (8.102)

With the spring extensions known, we need to identify the horizontal and vertical components of the forces, which requires a knowledge of the spring's angles. These are:

$$\cos \theta = (x_i - x_{i-1})/l_L \quad \sin \theta = (y_i - y_{i-1})/l_L$$ (8.103)

and

$$\cos \phi = (x_{i+1} - x_i)/l_R \quad \sin \phi = (y_{i+1} - y_i)/l_R$$ (8.104)

As the force exerted by a spring is proportional to its extension and stiffness S, the horizontal forces acting on the ith mass, using Newton's second law of motion ($F = ma$), are:

$$ma_h = S(e_R \cos \phi - e_L \cos \theta)$$ (8.105)

therefore:

$$a_h = \frac{S}{m} \left[\frac{(l_R - l)(x_{i+1} - x_i)}{l_R} - \frac{(l_L - l)(x_i - x_{i-1})}{l_L} \right]$$ (8.106)

and a similar expression can be derived for the vertical acceleration:

$$a_v = \frac{S}{m} \left[\frac{(l_R - l)(y_{i+1} - y_i)}{l_R} - \frac{(l_L - l)(y_i - y_{i-1})}{l_L} \right] - g$$ (8.107)

(8.106) and (8.107) describe the horizontal and vertical accelerations of the central mass point, and we now require to determine values of the x- and y-coordinates that satisfy them. Euler's method for numerical integration is useful for solving this type of problem, and assumes that the mass points move small discrete distances in equally small time intervals.

Acceleration is a measure of the rate of change of velocity, which in turn is a measure of the rate of change of displacement with time. On an incremental basis, the horizontal acceleration can be defined in terms of the horizontal velocity as follows:

$$a_h = \frac{v_h(t + \Delta t) - v_h(t)}{\Delta t}$$ (8.108)

where t is any point in time, and Δt is a small increment in t. The velocity at time $t + \Delta t$ is therefore:

$$v_h(t + \Delta t) = v_h(t) + \Delta t a_h$$ (8.109)

but the velocity can also be defined as:

$$v_h(t) = \frac{x(t + \Delta t) - x(t)}{\Delta t} \qquad (8.110)$$

therefore the new horizontal position for the mass point (which is what we require) is given by:

$$x(t + \Delta t) = x(t) + \Delta t v_h(t) \qquad (8.111)$$

At t_0, when $t = 0$, the horizontal velocity and acceleration are zero:

$$v_h(t_0) = 0 \qquad \text{and} \qquad a_h(t_0) = 0 \qquad (8.112)$$

Therefore, we evaluate (8.106) relating horizontal forces with acceleration to discover the initial acceleration. This is substituted into (8.109) using some suitable value of Δt and an initial velocity $v_0(0)$ of zero. The new velocity $v_h(t + \Delta t)$ is substituted in (8.111) to reveal the new position of the mid mass point. A similar process is applied to (8.107) to derive the vertical displacement. When both the x- and y-displacements are known, the position of the mid mass point is updated and the cycle repeated. Values of the stiffness S, the gravitational acceleration g, and the mass m will have to be selected to create the desired movement.

When this algorithm is implemented, we discover that the central mass bounces around with a realistic sense of elasticity. In fact, as there is no opportunity for energy loss, the system refuses to decay; however, this can be introduced by a restitution term in (8.109), similar to that used in (8.96).

8.7 Flight dynamics of an aircraft

Hopefully, it requires little convincing that simulating the dynamic behaviour of a 100 ton aircraft taking off, flying and landing is a non-trivial exercise. Nevertheless, it is possible, and is a central component of a flight simulator. However, in this example we will not attempt to reproduce an actual flight simulator model, but will develop a simple flight model that could be used to fly an aircraft within a VE.

The numerical models used to simulate the forces acting upon the frame of an aircraft are complex and address the effects of the craft's aerodynamic characteristics, engines, the atmospheric environment, undercarriage and hydraulic/mechanical control system used by the pilot to fly the aircraft (Rolfe, 1991).

The aerodynamic characteristics are affected by the vehicle's weight, speed, altitude, centre of gravity, angle of attack, flight surface geometry and ground proximity effects. The forces transmitted through the undercarriage during take-off and landing are determined by the mechanical, hydraulic and pneumatic assemblies associated with these structures. Apart from simulating these effects, the mathematical model may even include the dynamic behaviour of brakes, tyres and the nose-wheel steering system.

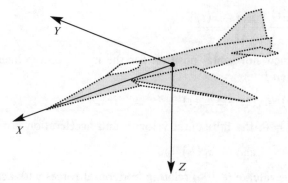

Figure 8.20 The traditional method of representing the axial system for an aircraft is a right-handed system with the Z-axis pointing downwards.

Different types of aeroengines possess different dynamic characteristics. They have varying thrust profiles and capacities; they burn fuel at different rates; they have differing temperature/efficiency characteristics and differing response patterns.

The atmospheric model reflects the variation of air density and temperature with height. Wind speed must be included as it can significantly affect a plane's true ground speed, as well as modify the craft's behaviour during landing and take-off. Wind shear, which creates highly dangerous flying conditions, must be modelled, and even the turbulence caused by large planes must be simulated as it can seriously affect the aerodynamics of planes following in their wake.

The mathematical techniques used to simulate such a complex system can be only an approximation of reality. But our understanding of these numerical simulation models is such that their accuracy and fidelity allow them to play a significant role in flight simulators. As this level of detail is relevant only to flight simulation, let us examine a simple first-order aircraft model.

8.7.1 A simple aircraft model

Figure 8.20 shows the traditional method of representing the axial frame of reference for an aircraft. It is right-handed, with the z-axis directed downwards. For the sake of consistency the axial system will be modified to conform with the examples in the rest of the book.

A first-order model for approximating an aircraft assumes that it is a point without mass, travelling with speed v in its body-fixed z-axis, and velocities v_x and v_y in the x- and y-axes respectively, as shown in Figure 8.21(a). The heading ϕ is specified by the angle between the z-axes of the aircraft and the WCS, as shown in Figure 8.21(b). For the moment, the aircraft is not allowed to yaw, pitch or roll.

Given the aircraft's position (x,y,z), speed v, acceleration a, and heading

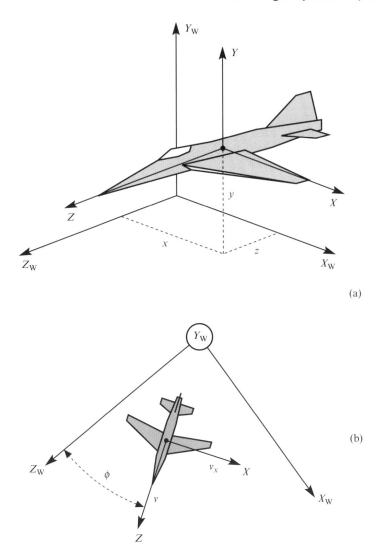

(a)

(b)

Figure 8.21 (a) A first-order flight model for an aircraft assumes that the craft is a point without mass, with instantaneous velocites v, v_x and v_y. (b) This plan elevation shows the definition of the heading angle ϕ.

ϕ, its new position (x',y',z'), after time Δt can be computed as follows. The incremental distance Δd moved forward is given by:

$$\Delta d = v\Delta t + \tfrac{1}{2} a\Delta t^2 \qquad\qquad\qquad \textbf{(8.113)}$$

The corresponding increments Δx and Δz in the x- and z-axes are given by:

$$\Delta x = \Delta d \sin \phi \qquad\qquad\qquad \textbf{(8.114)}$$

$$\Delta z = \Delta d \cos \phi \tag{8.115}$$

then:

$$x' = x + \Delta x \tag{8.116}$$
$$z' = z + \Delta z \tag{8.117}$$

In order to compute a new altitude, air speed and heading, we can assume that an agent, such as an autopilot, is regularly providing a new demand altitude y_d, demand speed v_d and demand heading ϕ_d.

Altitude

The new altitude y' can be computed by first determining the altitude error y_{err}:

$$y_{err} = y_d - y \tag{8.118}$$

The new vertical velocity v_y' then becomes:

$$v_y' = k_v y_{err} \qquad -V_{des} \leqslant v_y' \leqslant V_{cli} \tag{8.119}$$

where k_v is some gain factor; $-V_{des}$ is the maximum descent rate, and V_{cli} is the maximum climb rate. If y_{err} is below some threshold value, altitude acquire is disabled. The change in altitude is then given by:

$$\Delta y = v_y \Delta t \tag{8.120}$$

and the new altitude y' becomes:

$$y' = y + \Delta y \tag{8.121}$$

Acceleration

The new acceleration a' can be computed by first determining the airspeed error v_{err}:

$$v_{err} = v_d - v \tag{8.122}$$

The new acceleration in the direction of travel then becomes:

$$a' = k_a v_{err} \qquad -A_{dec} \leqslant a' \leqslant A_{acc} \tag{8.123}$$

where k_a is some gain factor, $-A_{dec}$ is the maximum deceleration permitted, and A_{acc} is the maximum acceleration rate permitted. If v_{err} is below some threshold value, airspeed acquire is disabled. The new airspeed is given by:

$$v' = v + a \Delta t \tag{8.124}$$

Heading

Finally, we come to the new heading ϕ'. Again we establish the error between the current heading and the demand heading

$$\phi_{err} = \phi_d - \phi \tag{8.125}$$

The new lateral velocity v_x' becomes:

$$v_x' = k_\phi \phi_{err} \qquad -V \leqslant v_x' \leqslant V \tag{8.126}$$

where k_ϕ is some gain factor and V is the maximum lateral velocity, given by $V = v\tan(M\Delta t)$, where M is the maximum turn rate (3° per second for standard turns). The change in heading is then given by:

$$\Delta\phi = \tan^{-1}\left(\frac{v_x}{v}\right) \tag{8.127}$$

and the new heading ϕ' becomes:

$$\phi' = \phi + \Delta\phi \tag{8.128}$$

After time Δt the aircraft has position (x',y',z'), speed v', acceleration a' and heading ϕ'. These become the new values of (x,y,z), v, a and ϕ respectively for the next time period Δt.

This flying model makes many assumptions. To begin with, the aircraft has no mass, it cannot rotate about any of its axes, and there is nothing in the model to simulate the action of landing and taking-off.

One simple mechanism for introducing a banking angle is to roll the aircraft about its z-axis by an angle proportional to the heading angle error ϕ_{err}. It is left to the reader to develop the model further by introducing pitch, yaw, mass and gravity.

In reality, the Euler equations of a rigid body moving in a vacuum are used as a starting point for a flight simulator model. These are sensitive to the aircraft's mass, the moments of inertia about the centre of gravity and the forces acting along the axes. Readers wishing to pursue this approach are forewarned of their relative complexity, and the axial notation used, which is different to that used above.

9

Human Factors

9.0 Introduction

It is ironic that the vast majority of computer users operate their systems via terminals that were designed for mechanical typewriters at the turn of the last century. But apart from this mechanical anomaly, computer keyboards have keys marked 'Ctrl', 'Alt', 'Esc' and 'Alt Gr', whose meaning is known only by computer engineers! All that typical users know is that if they simultaneously press the keys 'Ctrl', 'Shift' and 'W', the current word is underlined! It is difficult to imagine that anyone could have designed an interface with a greater disregard for human factors. However, the very idea of designing an interface to replace the current one is almost unthinkable, as there are just so many machines around the world and software packages in use that we have no choice but to continue with these keyboards.

Many keyboards in use do not even take into account the way humans sit at a table and hold their hands over the device. This is a problem for people who spend most of their working life as keyboard operators, and are now discovering the effects of *repetitive strain injury* (RSI). Similarly, we know very little about the long-term effects of working at computer screens for long periods of time – and only time will tell if, and how, we have been ignoring certain human factors in these vital areas of design.

VR proposes a totally new interface for human–computer interaction. An interface where the keyboard is replaced by interactive gloves and 3D mice, and the computer screen is replaced by a head-slaved, head-mounted display. As we have the chance of starting from scratch, there are no excuses for getting it wrong. We are under no obligation to incorporate out-of-date technologies or concepts unrelated to the task in hand.

If VR is to be successful, system designers cannot afford to ignore vital aspects of human physiology, details of which are available from any modern medical textbook. It is highly unlikely that early VR systems will incorporate all such ideas, but in the long term they must not be forgotten.

For a variety of reasons, designing and implementing an optimum VR system today may not be possible. To begin with, certain technologies may not be adequately mature; and if they do exist, they may be too expensive. A possible solution may meet every requirement of the design specification, but not be capable of withstanding the day-to-day knocks from continuous usage. There are many more valid excuses, but let us continue and examine various human factors relevant to VR systems. Four areas of human physiology are examined: the eye, the ear, somatic sensations and the sense of equilibrium.

9.1 The eye

A knowledge of the eye is very important if we are to understand how its abuse can be minimized by VR display technology. The eye is a highly developed organ and its action is well documented. But for this diversion we will explore only those features and characteristics relevant to the design of display systems.

Figure 9.1 shows a diagrammatic cross-section of the human eye identifying the cornea, the aqueous humor, the crystalline lens, the vitreous humor and the retina. All of these play an important role in forming an image that starts the process of seeing. Apart from the retina, they collectively provide an optical element that refracts light from an external object such that it is focused onto the retina upside-down and inverted. This double 'twist' to the image seems to cause no problem for the brain, which is able to integrate it with other sensory mappings of the external world.

The refractive power of an optical element is measured in units of dioptres, where a 1 dioptre lens can focus a beam of parallel light at a distance of 1 metre. The refractive power of the human eye is about 60 dioptres, which implies that all of the compound elements of the eye can be replaced by a single *virtual lens* 17 mm in front of the retina. What is surprising about the eye's action is that the refractive power of the lens is only 20 dioptres. Most of the refractive power comes from the boundary of the cornea with air.

9.1.1 Accommodation

A young and healthy crystalline lens is flexible, and its refractive power can be continuously varied by about 14 dioptres by tensioning or relaxing the ciliary muscle attached to its periphery. This is called *accommodation* or *focusing*, and it provides the mechanism for obtaining clear images from distant objects, as well as those close to. With age, the lens becomes larger and thicker and, unfortunately, less flexible. It is not uncommon for the power

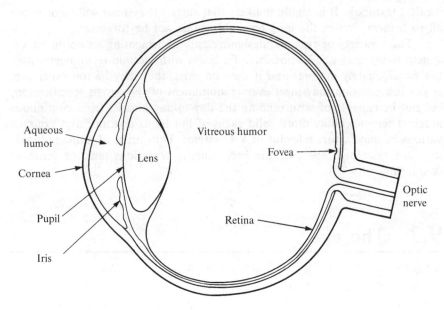

Figure 9.1 Cross-section of the human eye.

of accommodation to reduce to 2 dioptres by the age of 50, and zero by the age of 70! This is called *presbyopia*, and results in a person having to focus at a constant distance.

When we focus upon a moving object, an automatic feedback mechanism attempts to keep the image in focus by dynamically changing the refractive power of the crystalline lens. Although there is no definitive explanation for this process, it has been found that the lens is permanently oscillating slightly up to 2 Hz. This results in an image that continuously moves in and out of focus. It is thought that this modulation of the lens plays some part in the nervous system's hunting for a clear image.

Although we possess this extraordinary skill to focus upon objects at different distances, it is not exploited in HMDs. However, our ability to keep parts of a scene in clear focus while others are blurred is an excellent filtering mechanism, as it allows us to concentrate upon a specific zone of our field of view (FOV) without being unduly distracted by activity outside this area. Most HMDs provide two images, permanently focused between 2 and 3 metres. This would be acceptable if the image content corresponded to this spatial depth of field, which is rarely the case.

A similar problem is encountered in the panoramic displays used in flight simulators, where the image is collimated such that it appears to be located many metres beyond the device. When a computer-generated distant scene is viewed, the human visual system accepts the scene for what it is – everything in the image is in focus, which is what would happen in reality. However, when a close object, such as a cup, is introduced into the same scene, a conflict occurs. We are now faced with viewing a scene containing near and far objects in clear focus, with all the light rays parallel. This conflict of information makes it impossible to resolve the scene, and the cup appears to be a colossal object located in the distance. The reverse happens in an HMD that is collimated to 2 metres or so. But as typical virtual worlds are local environments, such as rooms, the conflict is not so acute. Furthermore, head- and hand-tracking in a VR system provide the necessary motion parallax cues one would expect between near and far objects, and although the entire scene is in clear focus, it is something that can be tolerated.

9.1.2 The pupil

The iris is a pigmented opaque structure positioned in front of the crystalline lens, and it contains a hole through which light passes. The hole, or *pupil*, changes in size under different conditions. The size variation is between approximately 1.5 mm and 8 mm in diameter, which gives an area ratio of 1:30. As the eye has a sensitivity to light in the order of 1 000 000:1, the pupil size has little effect on controlling the amount of light entering the eye. Gregory (1979) points out that the principal functions of the iris are to:

(1) Increase depth of field for near vision by contracting.
(2) Confine incoming light to the central and optically best part of the lens by contracting.
(3) Maximize eye sensitivity by opening.

If light levels are low, pupil size increases with a corresponding loss of depth of focus.

9.1.3 The retina

The retina is the light-sensitive surface attached to the rear of the eye, and is several hundred microns thick, with 10 distinct layers. Light incident on the cornea passes through the aqueous humor, the lens, the vitreous humor and finally strikes the retina. It then has to traverse 8 of the retina's 10 layers before it is absorbed by the *rod* and *cone* photoreceptors. The rod photoreceptors are responsible for low-acuity, monochrome, night vision, while the cones are for high-acuity, colour, day vision. It takes 25 ms to turn light into electrical signals, which then have to be interpreted by the brain's visual cortex. This latency does not appear to cause us any problems with everyday life, but there are occasions when this time delay prevents us from responding to certain events. Take, for example, a tennis player serving a ball at 200 kph. In 1 s the ball travels 55.5 m, and in 25 ms it travels 1.4 m. This means that if we ignore all other delays in the visual system, the tennis ball is 1.4 m away from where we see it, which makes hitting it rather difficult!

As the action of rods and cones has already been covered in Section 3.7

it will not be repeated again. Nevertheless, it is worth completing this description with some information on the fovea. This is the highly sensitive central part of the retina and accounts for the high-resolution portion of our FOV. Its existence is easily confirmed by staring at a particular word on a page of text. Here it can be observed that surrounding text is difficult to read unless the eye is moved. What is happening is that the eye is being rotated by motor reflexes to capture on the fovea the light rays from a required point in space. As the fovea is only 0.1 mm in diameter and contains the highest density of cones in the retina, only the centre part of our FOV is seen in high resolution. The remainder of the image is projected onto the surrounding retina which contains a mixture of rods and cones with a lower spatial resolution.

Not only are the cones packed closer together at the fovea, but they are finer than the cones distributed over the rest of the retina. This also contributes to the extra visual acuity of the fovea. Although the fovea provides us with high-resolution colour vision, the existence of rods, albeit at a reduced distribution, provides a consistent image field for night vision.

As the fovea is so small, it accounts for only approximately 1° of our FOV. This has been exploited in the display systems of some military dome simulators, where the pilot's head and eye are tracked to identify the central field of view. A single projector forms a high-resolution elliptical image on the dome's surface to cover the pilot's foveal area completely, while other projectors display the remainder of the scene in a lower resolution. This reduces the rendering load on the image generators, but does require head- and eye-tracking hardware, and the careful integration of the two image formats.

9.1.4 Visual acuity

Like any other optical system the eye has limitations, and one that is important to display systems concerns *visual acuity*. The eye's ability to distinguish between two external points of light is limited to approximately 1.5–2 mm at a distance of 10 m. This measure of visual acuity is often specified in terms of the angle subtended to the eye by the light points. For the average eye this is about 40 seconds of arc, and corresponds to a separation of 2 microns on the retina.

9.1.5 Light and dark adaption

The luminous sensitivity of the eye is automatically adjusted by slight changes in concentration of the photosensitive chemicals in the rods and cones. We notice this phenomenon when we move from bright sunlight into a dark room. Although we appear to become accustomed to the new ambient light quickly, it can take as long as 40 minutes before we are completely adapted. This is called *dark adaption*. Moving from a dark room back into bright sunlight, the reverse happens – this is called *light adaption*. The relative change in eye sensitivity through adaption is in the order of 25 000:1. Rods can take in excess of an hour to adapt fully to a high sensitivity, whereas cones cease adapting after several minutes. Thus when we don an HMD, we quickly adjust to the new light level.

9.1.6 Peripheral vision

The retina is not just a passive photosensitive surface. Its structure, especially the connectivity of the rods and cones to the ganglion cells, provides us with a range of useful image processing functions. For instance, some ganglion cells are excited by *changes* in light intensity, which helps direct our attention to moving objects in our visual field. This feature is available right across the retina, and although image resolution is poor at the periphery, anything that moves in our peripheral vision is very noticeable. As the distribution of rods is much higher at the periphery, their extra sensitivity, which is 300 times greater than that of cones, complements the detection of movement with extra visual sensitivity.

By the time signals are travelling along the one million axons down the optic nerve they encode the attributes of colour, motion, shape and retinal stimulus derived from the 100 million photoreceptors. The visual cortex still has the considerable task of placing some sort of visual interpretation on this data, as well as integrating it with similar data from the other eye.

9.1.7 Persistence of vision

The electrochemical nature of the retina introduces a reaction time into the visual process, such that when a very short pulse of light is observed, the rod receptor potential reaches a peak in approximately 0.25 s. Cones react about four times faster. Their combined action introduces the phenomenon of *persistence of vision*.

Persistence of vision is fundamental to the display technology of cinema, television, computers and even VR. Our ability to integrate a rapid succession of discrete images into a visual continuum takes effect at the *Critical Fusion Frequency* (CFF) which can be as low as 20 Hz – much depends upon image size and brightness.

Television images are refreshed at a rate of 50 Hz fields for the United Kingdom, and 60 Hz fields for the United States, whereas cinema employs a frame rate of 24 frames per second, which is then interrupted by a three-bladed shutter to increase it to 72 images per second. Some IGs operate nominally at two speeds: 30 Hz for night scenes, and 60 Hz for day scenes. The associated projector must also be able to switch between these two modes. An IG, like a television, may still generate one frame in the form of two fields, which also helps to reduce the rendering task, as half the number of pixels have to be computed in a given time period. As the eye's sensitivity to flicker is proportional to scene brightness, for dusk and night scenes the refresh rate can be reduced to 30 Hz. However, if the scene contains any bright zones, such as white patches, they flicker noticeably. On the other hand, small bright lights do not flicker when refreshed at the same rate. When bright day scenes are projected, especially upon large screens, the refresh rate is increased to 60 Hz (and higher), to minimize flicker.

Sensitivity to flicker is also related to where it appears in our FOV. A display screen that appears stable in the centre of our FOV can appear to flicker when seen out the corner of our eyes, which is another human factor that influences the design of panoramic visual displays.

9.1.8 Stereopsis

In order to derive a stereo perspective projection, Section 3.4 included a brief review of monocular and binocular depth cues. We will now expand upon some of these ideas and see how they influence VR display technology.

By using random dot stereograms, Bela Julesz (1971) proved that stereo perception was independent of object recognition. When we view two identical patterns of random dots through a stereoscope, that is exactly what we perceive, without any sensation of depth. However, Julesz showed that if a portion of one pattern is displaced horizontally, and the stereogram viewed again, the disparity between the two images tricks the brain into believing that it is viewing a 3D structure. The result appears as though the displaced part of the scene is in front of the rest.

Recently, computer graphics techniques have been used to create single images from random textures, which, when viewed with a fixation point beyond the image, give rise to scenes with startling depth. Not everyone is able to see the encoded 3D scene, indeed, it appears that at least 10% of the population is unable to enjoy stereo depth perception. Such people rely upon motion parallax and perspective to make judgements of depth.

What these and other experiments show is that stereopsis and the compelling sensation of depth perception arise from the image disparity on the two retinas. When our eyes converge to fixate upon an object, those features on the object that fall upon corresponding parts of the retinas are fused into one. Those parts of the object that lie in front or behind the fixation plane fall on disparate retinal points, and provide the brain with a measure of depth. Through experience, and other cues such as the eye's convergence angle, the brain learns how to judge distances in space.

Thus to perceive a stereoscopic effect with an HMD, the two images must not only contain different aspects of a scene, but also overlap one another. The 6.5 cm, or so, distance between our eyes enables each eye to obtain a slightly different view of the world. Within the high-acuity foveal region, depth perception is fading at 150 m, whereas outside of this region 100 m is the norm. At these distances, however, stereopsis is not the most useful of cues to judge depth. Motion parallax and perspective can be much more useful.

9.1.9 Visual field

The binocular visual field extends approximately ±100° horizontally and ±60° vertically, with a horizontal overlap of 120° where stereopsis occurs. Reproducing a display system with a similar specification might seem impossible, but collimated panoramic displays can produce a visual field of ±100° horizontally and ±30° vertically. When seated within such a system, the sense of immersion is very powerful. Moreover, even though there is no stereoscopic information, the depth cues from motion parallax and perspective more than compensate for this deficiency.

9.1.10 Synthetic images versus reality

Although it is always dangerous to predict the future, it seems highly unlikely that any form of HMD and IG will ever be able to fool the eye and brain into believing that they are immersed in the real world. The fundamental technological stumbling blocks are daunting, and concern resolution, colour gamut, ficld of view, depth of ficld, dynamic range, optical distortion and overall sense of immersion. Nevertheless, HMDs will improve dramatically over the next few years, so too will IG performance. The quest for realism of synthetic images will also progress, and even though we will always be able to distinguish a real-time synthetic visual experience from the real world, that should not concern designers of VR systems. The real design thrust should be towards developing lightweight, incongruous HMDs that can be worn without fatigue, and also allow the user to undertake the task in hand as efficiently as possible.

9.2 The ear

The ear, like other sense organs, provides us with another interpretation of the physical world, and although there exists an incredible body of knowledge about its action, there are still many features that we know little about. This section reviews some of the basic principles associated with sound transmission, the ear's action and how we localize sounds in 3D space. This last topic is rather special to VR systems as it is useful to complement images of VEs with auditory cues. Such cues could be transmitted via loudspeakers or headphones, but, as we shall see, they require different types of signal manipulation.

9.2.1 Sound

At the turn of the last century attempts were made to identify the medium for the transmission of light. It was thought that an all-pervading substance called the *lumeniferous ether* enabled light to be propagated over any distance. Even empty space was full of ether and it was imagined that planets were able to pass through it without any resistance. Only after Michelson and Morley demonstrated in 1881 that the ether did not exist, was it accepted that a medium was unnecessary, and that light was an electromagnetic phenomenon. Today, we tend to continue with this belief, and accept that light can also be thought of as particles called *photons*, that have no mass and travel at $300\,000$ kms^{-1}.

Sound, on the other hand, does require a transmission medium, whether it be a gas, liquid or solid. For us, the most useful medium for sound is air, while fish and certain mammals depend upon water. And as sound is nothing more than a compression wave that propagates through a medium, its velocity is sensitive to the medium's density. In the case of air at $0\,°C$, sound travels at $331\,ms^{-1}$, while at $20\,°C$ its speed increases to approximately $344\,ms^{-1}$. It can be shown that the velocity of sound in a gas varies inversely as the square root of its density. The velocity of sound varies dramatically in pure gases. For example, in carbon dioxide its velocity is $257\,ms^{-1}$, and in hydrogen it is $1286\,ms^{-1}$.

A liquid transmits sound much faster than a gas, and, like a gas, the velocity is sensitive to density and temperature. A typical value for the sea is $1453\,ms^{-1}$ at $1\,°C$, which varies with altitude and salinity. The speed of sound in a solid, such as a cast iron bar, is around $3500\,ms^{-1}$. So it is impossible to talk about the speed of sound without specifying very precisely the nature of the medium.

The range of frequencies relevant to human hearing is approximately 20 Hz to 20 kHz. This is typical of a young healthy person, but this spectrum reduces with age, especially with the higher frequencies.

If we take the velocity of sound to be $344\,ms^{-1}$, the wavelength λ at 20 Hz is 17.2 m, whereas at 1 kHz, $\lambda = 34.4$ cm, and at 10 kHz, $\lambda = 3.44$ cm. This wide range of wavelengths is very important in the design of theatres and concert halls, as unwanted reflections and standing waves can seriously compromise sound quality. Furthermore, as the human ear is in the order of 7 cm high, which is the wavelength of sound at 5 kHz, it is bound to influence the collection of sound in this frequency range.

Although the effect is small, the very action of listening to something modifies the perceived sound; this is because our bodies interact with the pressure wavefronts. Such interference has a significant effect on the quality of sound in a concert hall when the hall is empty or full. When it is empty, an orchestra sounds 'bright' due to the interreflections of frequencies above 1 kHz. However, introduce 1000 people dressed in wool suits, dresses and cardigans, and these frequencies are significantly attenuated through absorption and random reflections.

With very high frequencies, for example 10^{12} Hz, sound waves can be used to scatter light. As the corresponding wavelength is very small, like light, it can be described as a particle called a *phonon*.

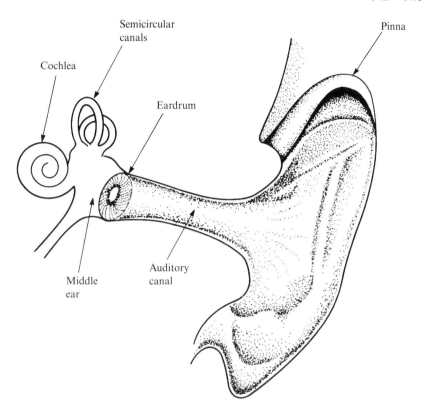

Figure 9.2   Simple diagram of the human ear showing the outer ear (pinna and auditory canal), the middle ear (behind the eardrum), and the inner ear (the cochlea).

9.2.2   Sound perception

Although we have been talking as though sound actually exists in the real world, 'sound' is the brain's interpretation of the pressure wave that impinges upon the ear. The real world is completely quiet, yet is awash with vibrations.

Figure 9.2 shows the three distinct parts of the ear: the outer ear, middle ear, and the inner ear. The outer ear helps direct an incident sound wave into the middle ear. In so doing, it acts as a filter and modifies the captured sound. You can easily discover how the perceived sound is sensitive to the *pinna*'s shape by placing a cupped hand behind the ear. Not only is the sound quality altered, but the ambient background noise also changes.

The pressure wave travels along the ear canal and eventually strikes the *tympanic membrane* (eardrum) which oscillates in sympathy with the changes in pressure. Movements of the membrane are then transmitted through a system of small bones called the *ossicular system*. The pressure changes incident on the eardrum are increased twenty-fold by the time they are propagated to the cochlea, which achieves an efficient form of impedance matching. In order to cope with sudden bursts of high-level sound, a reflex action automatically stiffens the entire ossicular system to attenuate the sound transmission through to the cochlea, and protects it.

9.2.3   Frequency range

Three coiled tubes form the cochlea and are separated by two membranes called *Reissner's membrane* and the *basilar membrane*. When vibrations enter the cochlea they stimulate the 20 000 to 30 000 stiff hairs on the basilar membrane, which in turn vibrate and generate electrical signals that travel to the brain and become 'sound'. The basilar membrane resonates at different rates which provides the mechanism for identifying sound frequencies. For high frequencies the standing wave in the cochlea is short and stimulates the hairs only at the start of the cochlea, whereas medium frequencies create standing waves within the cochlea's centre, and low frequencies at the far end.

9.2.4   Sound intensity

The intensity of sound is a direct translation of the amplitude of the basilar membrane into the excitation of the hair cells, which in turn fire at higher rates. It is also reinforced by the number of hair cells firing, and other hairs that move only with high-amplitude vibrations.

9.2.5   Sound direction

It is widely believed that the time lag between the sound paths to the two ears and the difference in amplitude in the signals are used by the brain to localize the source of a sound. When a person is facing a sound source, the intensities and sound paths for the left and right ears are equal; therefore there are no differential cues. If, however, the person turns to the left such that the right ear is nearer the sound source, that ear will hear the sound louder and before the left one. Assuming that the distance between the two paths is around 20 cm, this produces a time delay of approximately 0.6 ms, which is detected in the auditory cortex. The brain obviously finds these cues useful: however they do not explain how we localize a sound source in the vertical plane.

9.2.6   The sound stage

When we listen to a stereo sound recording through a pair of loudspeakers it is possible to recreate a credible sound stage that has both breadth and depth. The sound stage appears to be between the two speakers. It might also appear in front or behind them, much depends upon the type of speaker and their juxtaposition with the room's walls. Not all audio recordings manage to capture the ambience that is present at the time of recording; this is often due to the use of multiple microphones which are electronically mixed. Sometimes extra ambience is artificially introduced by accentuating the reverberation level electronically. This can be effective, but can also confuse clarity and definition.

9.2.7 Head-related transfer functions

When we listen to a stereo recording through headphones, the left and right ears hear the sounds only from the individual transducers. This is called binaural hearing. There is, however, some sound transmission through the skull from one ear to another. In the case of loudspeakers, each ear hears the sound emanating from both loudspeakers. Obviously, the perceived sound heard with headphones cannot be the same as that heard via loudspeakers. What is more, the sound stage appears to be located somewhere within the listener's head.

It was Lord Rayleigh (1907) who proposed that we localized sound sources by exploiting intensity and phase differences between the signals from the left and right ears. He suggested that the phase differences were useful at low frequencies, while the intensity differences were effective at high frequencies. Since then further research has shown that this theory does not account for all types of sound localization. For even when binaural sounds contain phase and intensity cues, the perceived sound is still within the listener's head, rather than localized externally. Research by Shaw (1974) demonstrated that the pinna has a significant influence on shaping the spectral envelope of incident sound. Furthermore, this spectral shaping is dependent upon the spatial origin of the sound source. Thus the brain learns to extract spatial information from the unique 'earprint' the pinnae impress upon the incoming pressure waves.

Work by Plenge (1974) confirmed that the shaping of incoming sound by the pinnae was responsible for creating an external rather than an internal sound stage. And as headphones, especially the small type that plug directly into the middle ear, ignore or destroy the action of the pinna, the perceived sound stage is internal. This leads to the idea that if the left and right channels driving the headphones can be artificially shaped electronically, the brain can be tricked into thinking that the sounds have an external reality. To achieve this, we must discover the spectral shaping, or transfer function, introduced by the left and right pinnae. These transfer functions are bound to be personal attributes as we all have ears and heads of different sizes and shapes. The role of the head cannot be ignored in these functions as its shape will also interact with the pinna's own action. Therefore, the transfer functions are known as *Head-Related Transfer Functions* (HRTFs). In fact, the influence of the head, shoulders and body must be taken into account when computing accurate HRTFs.

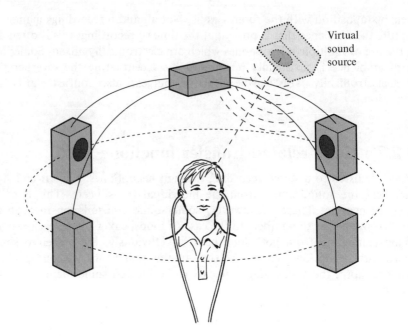

Figure 9.3   The five loudspeakers are driven with different signal strengths to create a virtual sound source. Small microphones in the ears monitor the sound pressure waves incident at the eardrums.

9.2.8   Measuring HRTFs

The spectral shaping that takes place in the vicinity of the ear can be discovered by measuring the spectral difference between an external sound and that incident on the eardrums. These measurements need to be made inside an anechoic chamber to remove any spurious reflections.

The subject is placed at the centre of a hemispherical configuration of loudspeaker driver units, which, when driven with signals of different intensities, cause a sound to be heard from a specific direction in space. Figure 9.3 shows this configuration. For each position of a sound source, the perceived signal is measured using a small microphone placed as near as possible to each eardrum. The signal is in the form of an impulse response which covers the required frequency spectrum.

In the NASA AMES 3D Auditory Display Project, 144 equidistant sample pairs were taken for a subject. The microphone data was then processed to compensate for the non-linear frequency responses of the audio test equipment. The HRTFs were then derived to provide the filters that are convolved with a sound source to drive a set of headphones. As the headphone signals already incorporate the acoustic earprints caused by the pinnae, the brain is provided with the necessary localization cues.

Do not assume from the above simple explanation that HRTFs are the only answer to creating 3D sound fields. Many problems still remain, and recent research is only the beginning of a programme of study that will continue for some time.

9.2.9 Ambisonics

An alternative approach to making a 3D sound stage was developed in the 1970s called *Ambisonics* (Gerzon, 1970). This technique employs a single point *Soundfield* microphone to record 3D soundfields. As the Soundfield microphone captures accurate pressure information at a point in space, it can be coded into multiple signals such that, when they drive a system of speakers, the original soundfield is created. The B-format signal assumes a configuration of four speakers, which, when placed at the corners of a square, create a horizontal soundfield, whereas eight speakers placed at the corners of a cuboid provide a full 3D soundfield.

By varying the signal strengths to the individual speakers, the perceived sound can be localized anywhere within a horizontal circle, for four speakers, and anywhere within a sphere, for eight speakers. Furthermore, once signals are coded into a B-format form, multiple sounds can be combined together to develop complex acoustic scenarios. Conventional matrix operations can be applied to the vector components of the B-format signals to subject the sound-stage to yaw, pitch and roll rotations (Fellgett, 1974).

More recently, Ambisonic techniques have been considered to provide 3D sound stages for VR systems, using either loudspeakers or headphones (Malham, 1993).

9.3 The somatic senses

Whereas the visual and auditory senses are stimulated by light and sound waves, the somatic senses collect data from our own body and tell us about its state and relationship with its immediate surroundings. For instance, when I close my eyes and touch some blotting paper in front of me, my fingertips can detect the roughness of the paper's surface, and the fibrous nature of the paper at the frayed edges. When my fingers accidentally brush against torn edges of the paper, a tickle sensation is recorded. When I press the paper between my thumb and first finger, I can estimate the paper's thickness. My fingers can also sense the temperature of the paper. If I now explore the computer screen facing me I can feel the roughness of the ubiquitous plastic employed by the computer industry and, without any confusion, recognize the smooth glass screen. My fingertips can easily detect the edge of the plastic moulding surrounding the glass screen and, still with my eyes closed, I can follow the contour of this edge, and let my fingers guide my arm around its shape. If I touch the back of my left hand with the fingers of my right hand, my fingers detect the warmth of my hand. They also detect a slight stickiness due to skin moisture and, if I press slightly, I can discern internal veins and bones. Meanwhile, my left hand records that something warm is touching it as hairs are accidentally brushed. If I hold my arms out in front of me I become aware of my biceps working against the force of gravity. And if I blow gently over my hands I can sense the flow of air, its temperature and even its direction.

Such simple experiments remind us how powerful the sense of touch is, and also how difficult it is going to be to simulate the same range of sensory feelings in a VR system. However, in spite of these obstacles, it is worth exploring the mechanisms of the somatic senses to see how technology can be effectively applied.

9.3.1 Somatic sensations

Somatic sensations are associated with how we sense surface roughness, vibrations, movements against the skin, position, pressure, pain and temperature. The brain's somatic sensory cortex translates signals received from receptors distributed over the body's surface, and within deep tissue, into a rich variety of sensory feelings. Brodmann's mapping of the somatic cortex, Figure 9.4, shows how various parts of the body are related to the surface topology of the cortex. The mapping shows that the different parts of the body are related in the following sequence: genitals, toes, foot, leg, hip, trunk, neck, head, shoulder, arm, elbow, forearm, wrist, hand, fingers, thumb, eye, nose, face, lips, teeth, mouth, tongue, pharynx and abdomen. The lips consume the largest area, whereas the lower part of the body has the smallest area, relatively speaking.

The sensations that arise from stimulating different parts of our bodies can be classified into four groups: *deep*, *visceral*, *proprioceptive* and *exteroceptive*.

Deep sensations
Deep sensations provide us with information about the status of joints, bones, tendons, muscles and other tissues. These are experienced as internal pressures, pain and vibrations. Receptors within these structures are activated when muscles are contracted and relaxed, so that we know the spatial status and condition of limbs and their extremities. Muscle tone is also important – when it is in good condition it can respond quickly to negotiate a new posture in the earth's gravitational field. When it is out of condition, an upright posture is difficult to maintain and the nervous system's feedback mechanism becomes influenced by latency.

Visceral sensations
The viscera organs are the large internal organs in the abdomen and chest such as the intestines and liver. In general, the sensations we experience from these organs are in the form of pain, to signal that something is amiss.

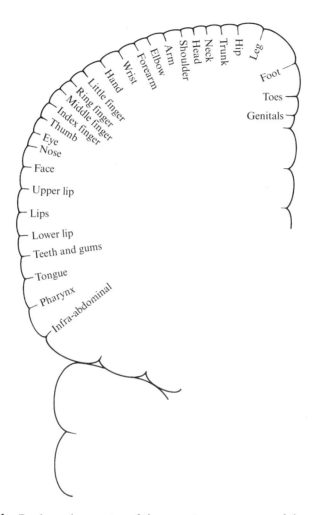

Figure 9.4   Brodmann's mapping of the somatic sensory area of the cortex.

Proprioceptive sensations

Proprioceptive sensations encode the physical state of the body such as its position, equilibrium and muscle sensations. They also provide us with information when we are in contact with other structures, such as standing on floors, lying on a bed, or leaning against a wall.

Exteroceptive sensations

Exteroceptive sensations are the touch sensations we experience over our body surface.

9.3.2   Pain

Pain sensations are warning signals about the state of our body, especially if it is damaged in some way, or being abused. Similarly, if it is poisoned, either by an external toxic substance, or by an internally generated toxin, the brain is warned with pain signals, or registers some form of discomfort, such as nausea.

The skin surface and other tissues contain pain receptors in the form of free nerve endings. When these are stimulated by excessive heat, or by the chemical messenger *bradykinin*, intense pain is felt. It is also thought that when blood flow is blocked to a muscle, the resulting pain is caused by bradykinin or *lactic acid*.

9.3.3   Tactile sensations

The sensations of touch, pressure and vibration are all detected by the same types of receptors. The sensation of touch generally arises from the stimulation of receptors in the skin and neighbouring tissue; the sensation of pressure arises when the skin and deeper tissues are deformed; and the sensation of vibration arises when receptors are subject to a cyclic stimulus. Tactile receptors may be *free nerve endings*, *Meissner's corpuscles*, *Iggo dome receptors*, *hairs*, *Ruffini's end-organs*, and *pacinian corpuscles*.

Free nerve endings

Free nerve endings respond to touch, pressure and also to pain. They are located throughout the skin and other tissues and tell us about the things with which we come in contact. For instance, to distinguish between various surface textures, special receptors are required to adapt quickly to a stimulus. This ensures that the receptors fire in response to small changes in surface features. At the other extreme, we require receptors that do not adapt, and continue to fire with the same stimulus. A splinter or a rose thorn may enter the skin with hardly any sensation, but within a few seconds, its presence triggers off a continuous response that abates only when the foreign object is removed.

Meissner's corpuscles

Meissner's corpuscles account for the sensation of touch in the fingertips, and enable us to discern with great accuracy precisely which area of the skin is stimulated. Because they adapt very quickly to any stimulus, they play a vital role in the detection of small changes in pressure. For instance, when we pass our fingertips over a rough surface, the small changes in surface pressure are recorded by Meissner's corpuscles.

Iggo dome receptors

The Iggo dome receptor is formed from a collection of *Merkel's discs*. This is another type of receptor, but, unlike Meissner's corpuscle, when a Merkel disc receptor is stimulated, it responds with a strong signal and continues to fire as it slowly adapts to the stimulus. Iggo dome receptors play an important role in the way we locate the position of a stimulus, and the nature of the surface being touched.

Hairs
Hairs also behave as a touch receptor, and whenever one is brushed by something, it stimulates the nerve located at its base. As they adapt rapidly to a stimulus they are particularly useful in detecting the movement of small objects.

Ruffini's end-organs
Ruffini's end-organs are receptors located in the deeper layers of the skin and deep tissue, and because they do not adapt to any extent, they fire in direct response to a stimulus. Thus if an object is pressed against our bodies such that skin and tissue are deformed, Ruffini's end-organ receptors act as a sensor or pressure and continue to fire until the object is removed. These receptors are also used to monitor the status of bone joints, and relay to the brain joint pressure and active angle.

Pacinian corpuscles
Pacinian corpuscles have a very fast response time, in the order of hundredths of a second, and are used to respond to vibrations. For example, these receptors are activated when we touch a working mechanism such as a food mixer or an electric drill. The receptors are found just beneath the surface of the skin and some deep tissues, and respond to frequencies in the range of 30–700 Hz.

Itching and tickling
It is thought that the itch and tickle response arises through very sensitive free nerve endings located on the outer layers of skin. Such receptors are activated by very small stimuli, such as an ant walking across our body, or an insect preparing to bite us.

9.3.4   Proprioceptive senses

The proprioceptive senses are concerned with monitoring the static and dynamic position of the body, and exploit receptors located within joints, muscles and deep tissues. Joint angulation, however, is not just a question of receptors that fire in response to joint angle – we use signals from different receptors located in skin, tissue, joints, tendons and muscles. Collectively, this data is used to gather information about various joints, and if they are static or moving, and whether they are being moved outside their safe operational envelope.

9.3.5   VR haptic technology

This cursory glance at the somatic senses illustrates the incredible range of receptors used to monitor the body's response to touch and position. It is evident that we will never be able to simulate with total fidelity similar physical sensory responses to virtual objects. To begin with, the majority of tactile data we experience from everyday activities comes from skin in direct contact with the air and our immediate surroundings. When we don gloves, for whatever reason, we immediately restrict our hands' access to a rich source of sensory data. Thus any form of interactive glove that incorporates pressure pads to stimulate contact with a virtual object can be regarded only as a crude interpretation of the meaning of 'touching'.

There is no doubt that the haptic interface to the virtual domain presents an incredible technological problem. However, if we ignore the idea of aspiring to recreate a virtual equivalent of the real world of haptics, then we will succeed in developing suitable interfaces. Today, various gloves are available that feed back pressure cues to the user's fingertips. Such gloves can be used to complement a variety of visual and audio cues such as touch conditions. Force feedback joysticks, force-reflecting exoskeleton hands and robotic arms with force feedback have also been used. This technology is examined in Chapter 10.

9.4   Equilibrium

There are obvious reasons why this chapter includes sections on the eye, ear and somatic sensations, but the inclusion of a section on equilibrium may not be immediately obvious. Its importance stems from experience gained in the flight simulation industry over the past two decades, especially in the area of motion sickness. Some pilots who spend long periods training inside a simulator suffer from motion sickness. In some cases, it is so severe that affected personnel are restricted from flying or driving for at least 24 hours until they have completely recovered from symptoms such as sweating, pallor, vertigo and disorientation.

The induced nausea has no one cause, but is often attributed to conflict between visual and vestibular information. For example, a fighter aircraft simulator is usually constructed from a fixed-base cockpit with a dome, inside which are projected panoramic computer-generated scenes. When the simulator is operational, the pilot flies over very realistic virtual environments performing acrobatic manoeuvres typical of the simulated craft. This might entail 360° rolls, flying upside down, and turns that would normally induce g-forces that can be as high as $8g$. Although the IG is capable of generating the images associated with such manoeuvres, if there are no complementary physical motion cues, the vestibular system is not excited and the brain receives conflicting signals concerning the body's status. On the one hand, there is substantial visual evidence to convince the brain that it is being subjected to violent motion, and on the other hand the sense of equilibrium confirms that the pilot's head is vertical. Furthermore, the somatic sense of position also supports the vestibular system to suggest that, in spite of what the visual sense is indicating, the body is stationary.

Because the projected images are so realistic, and encompass the pilot's visual field of view, the brain is easily tricked into believing it is in motion. However, under normal circumstances it would expect vestibular information supporting this conclusion. As this does not happen, for some reason, an area of the brain called the *chemoreceptor trigger zone* is excited to induce the vomiting response. This zone is normally activated by irritative impulses from the gastrointestinal tract, but it can also be activated by certain drugs such as apomorphine and morphine, or by rapid changes in motion. Prior to the act of vomiting the body passes through a warning period of nausea, sweating, loss of equilibrium, pallor, eye strain and a general feeling of being unwell. If this cannot be controlled by conscious action, the vomiting centre of the medulla is excited and vomiting occurs within 3 to 5 minutes. It could be that this automatic response is a signal to the body to stop doing what appears to be a life-threatening action. Human beings were never intended to move at high velocity or spin upside down. Basically we are ground-based creatures used to limited amounts of running and swimming. Furthermore, as we have been engaged in these acrobatic activities only for a century or so, evolutionary forces have not had time to adjust to this behaviour pattern.

A full-flight simulator incorporates a motion platform to create the onset motion cues associated with ground-based and in-flight aircraft manoeuvres. Basically, it is used to recreate the forces that arise through changes in the craft's velocity. The hydraulic rams that move the simulator have a limited range of travel, which determines the operational envelope over which they can be used. Most modern simulators are equipped with motion systems that provide six degrees of freedom, that is, they can perform translations along any of the three Cartesian axes, and rotations about any axis. The translational modes of travel are often referred to as heave, sway and surge, while the rotational movements are yaw, pitch and roll.

To simulate the forces of acceleration experienced when taking off, the motion system responds with a surge movement and then leans the simulator backwards. The pilot is not conscious of what is actually happening to the simulator, and believes that the force on his/her body is due to the acceleration of the craft, when in reality it is due to gravity. In this situation, the brain receives convincing visual data that is supported by realistic body forces. Unfortunately, the sense of equilibrium sends back contradictory signals that indicate that the pilot's body is stationary and leaning backwards! Although this subterfuge is effective to a point, some people are very sensitive to these sensory conflicts, and suffer terrible motion sickness.

Another aspect of simulator sickness is concerned with the accurate synchronization of motion cues with visual cues. Here, we expect that forces induced by motion coincide exactly with the motion cues encoded in the real-time images. If this does not occur with any accuracy, another opportunity arises for generating conflicting sensory signals.

In order to understand why this sensory conflict occurs, we will explore the body's mechanism for equilibrium – the *vestibular system*.

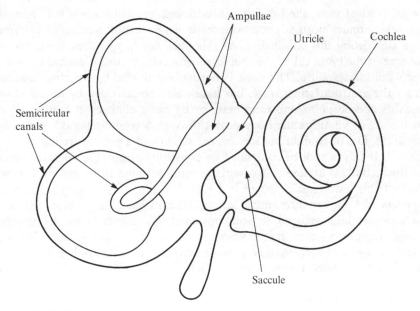

Figure 9.5 The vestibular system.

9.4.1 The vestibular system

The vestibular system is located on both sides of the head, very close to the inner ear, and is the organ that registers the head's state of equilibrium. It consists of a system of membranes and tubes that monitor the direction of gravity, head orientation, linear acceleration, head rotation and static equilibrium. Figure 9.5 shows the important components.

9.4.2 Sensing equilibrium through gravity

A pendulum is an excellent device for identifying the direction of gravity, and although this mechanism is not used in the vestibular system, it is replaced by something similar. In fact, two areas of small and large hair cells, called the *macula*, are randomly oriented in the *utricle*, and are used to sense the direction of gravity. The hairs are covered in a gelatinous layer of calcium carbonate crystals which provide a degree of damping. Whenever a new head position forces the smaller hairs, called *stereocilla*, to lean towards the large hairs called *kinocillium*, sodium ions are released causing associated nerve fibres to fire more rapidly. When the stereocilla are in a quiescent state, pointing vertically, the nerve fibres fire at about 100 Hz. When they lean towards the kinocillium they fire at several hundred cycles. When the stereocilla lean in the opposite direction, the nerve firing rate falls rapidly. By monitoring these nerve signals, the brain has a very efficient control mechanism for sensing equilibrium.

9.4.3 Sensing equilibrium and head rotation

The semicircular canals comprise the *anterior*, *posterior* and *horizontal ducts*, and are arranged at right angles to each other, like a system of Cartesian axes. At the end of each duct is a chamber called the *ampulla*, which contains a gelatinous mass called the *cupulla*, which in turn, rests on hair cells that stimulate local nerves. The ducts contain a viscous fluid which flows against the cupulla depending upon the nature of the rotation. Signals from the local nerves are used by the brain to decode how the head has been been rotated, or whether it is in a state of equilibrium. Whenever the head is suddenly rotated, the cupulla responds by triggering a signal burst, which decays exponentially over 20 seconds. This is because it takes this period of time to restore itself to its neutral state. The semicircular ducts are sensitive enough to detect angular accelerations of $1° \, s^{-2}$.

9.4.4 Sensing linear acceleration

If we arc suddenly pushed forward without any warning, the head's inertia and mechanical coupling through the neck pushes it back relative to the body. This action accelerates the maculae, which signal to the nervous system that the body has moved out of equilibrium. As a response to this we feel that we are falling backwards and attempt to correct the situation with a new body posture. It is highly likely that an automatic postural reflex is initiated in the form of moving our legs and arms to anticipate a fall. Our body posture is altered until the maculae register an acceptable state of equilibrium.

9.4.5 Coupling between the vestibular and visual systems

Apart from sensing head equilibrium, the vestibular system is closely coupled to the visual system. This ensures that when the head is suddenly rotated, the retinas continue to record a reasonably stationary image. Without such a reflex, we would have to be stationary before we could register a clear picture, which would not be a useful survival strategy. This 'hardwiring' between the senses of vision and equilibrium accounts for the eye strain and dizziness associated with simulator sickness. For when someone is enclosed within a simulator and subjected to conflicting visual and vestibular cues, the brain attempts to adapt to this new environment. When the person exits the simulator, they find themselves within an environment that does not match their newly acquired skills. This can result in staggering, disorientation and vertigo. It has been suggested that the brain's interpretation of this behaviour is that the stomach has been poisoned, and proceeds to take quick action to correct the situation!

As the vestibular system monitors head equilibrium, the body cannot be directed to adopt a corrective attitude unless the relative orientation between the head and body is known. To allow this, the neck proprioceptors are used by the nervous system, in conjunction with vestibular signals, to derive a correcting signal.

Although the vestibular system plays a central role in maintaining equilibrium, people who have lost this apparatus through an accident, or otherwise, are still able to move about without falling over. They must, however, keep their eyes open and move very slowly.

9.5 Conclusions

Hopefully, this review of human factors has identified some of the issues that need to be kept in mind in the design of VR peripheral devices. Many of them are very obvious, for example that head-mounted displays should be adjustable to the user's interocular distance. Others are not so obvious, such as the subtle causes of nausea that result when immersed for long periods of time.

Unfortunately, very little is known about the long-term effects of working with VR systems. What we do know is that humans are very adaptable and can tolerate extraordinary levels of abuse. We can work in poorly lit offices, breathe contaminated air, sit for hours in chairs that offer no support and work with computer screens that force us to stoop forward to read their contents. Sadly, we accept all of these as part of everyday working life.

Recent research at the Defence Research Agency (Regan, 1994) has investigated the side-effects on the users of immersive displays. In particular, it looked at the causes of nausea experienced by some users. Previous work by Mon-Williams *et al.* (1993) suggested that wearers of HMDs suffered stress because they were unable to utilize eye convergence and accommodation when viewing virtual objects at different distances. Similar research by the DRA had shown that if a person's interocular distance did not match the distance between the optical centres of the HMD, this too caused uncomfortable eye strain. In fact, if the subject's eyes had to diverge, rather than converege, to fuse a 3D scene, this aggravated the problem even further.

Some people are very sensitive to unfamiliar motion stimuli. The motion of cars, boats, trains, planes, swings and roundabouts are familiar causes of motion sickness. Even astronauts report bouts of nausea when they are subjected to gravity-free environments (Jennings, *et al.*, 1988). Hypersensitive people experience nausea if they spend only a few minutes seated with their backs towards the direction of motion.

As many pilots suffer from motion sickness when flying real planes, it is not surprising that they also experience similar symptoms when flying a simulator. This could be interpreted as a measure of the fidelity that can be created within a modern simulator. It could also be hiding inherent faults in simulator design. Fortunately, most pilots adapt to the unusual motions of their craft, but simulator sessions can still cause loss of balance, eye strain, visual flashbacks and out-of-body experiences (Ungs, 1989).

Against this historical background, Regan conducted a series of experiments to investigate whether VR posed similar problems of motion sickness to those found in simulators. Out of a test group of 150 subjects, 8 subjects withdrew after experiencing severe nausea or dizziness. The remaining subjects completed the experiment which consisted of a 20 minute immersive session. At 5 minute intervals, subjects were asked to report on their physical status. The results showed that 22% of the the subjects reported symptoms after 5 minutes, 32% after 10 minutes, 40% after 15 minutes, 45% after 20 minutes, 36% after 5 minutes' post-immersion, and 27% after 10 minutes' post-immersion.

Although this and other research confirms that current immersive systems can arouse nausea, it is still not certain what the actual cause is. A popular belief is that the conflict theory proposed by James Reason (1974) to explain motion sickness is also behind the symptoms experienced in simulators and VR systems. This theory proposes that the vomit trigger zone is stimulated when the brain receives simultaneous conflicting signals from the vestibular system and the visual system. Most modern VR systems still exhibit latency in image generation, tracking and computing physical simulations, therefore there are plenty of opportunities for conflict. If this is the cause of the symtoms, faster processors will help resolve these issues. Other techniques such as predictive algorithms may help synchronize the virtual visual system with the physical vestibular system.

10

Virtual Reality Hardware

10.0 Introduction

Photographs of early computers reveal racks of hardware bristling with meters, valves, switches and lights held together with exposed runs of electrical cable. They were nursed by teams of operators who teased the delicate machine to run for a few minutes before a thermionic valve blew, a relay jammed or a mercury delay line failed. I suppose that scientists working on such machines imagined that these complex devices were never going to run for more than a few minutes at a time. And the idea of building a computer that could be carried in a pocket never even entered their heads.

Today's computers bear no relation to these laboratory experiments, yet we have quickly adjusted to carrying digital diaries, palm-top computers, portable fax machines and communicating to other computers on the other side of the world. Could it be, though, that in 50 years' time, a future generation will look at photographs of today's technology and ask themselves, 'How did they ever cope with such slow computers?' or, 'Did they actually have to write their own programs?' There is no doubt that digital technology will continue to evolve at an incredible pace. Circuits will become even smaller, and much faster, which will enable them to be integrated into everyday artefacts such as telephones, televisions, cars, light switches, door locks, watches, radios, HMDs and games systems.

Only a few years ago, a computer rated at 1 MIPS was considered fast, but already machines exist that operate at speeds in excess of 100 GFLOPS. In 1991, the MP Linpack (massively parallel linear package) benchmark record was established by the Concurrent Supercomputing Consortium's Intel Touch-stone Delta system with a throughput of 13.9 GFLOPS. In August 1993, the world record was set at 124.5 GFLOPS by Fujitsu's Numerical Wind Tunnel.

In June 1994, this record was broken again by an Intel Paragon XP/S 140

Supercomputer running at about 143.4 double-precision GFLOPS, using the MP Linpack.

Fortunately, processor speeds are advancing at both ends of the processor spectrum, and any problems encountered with today's VR systems that are due to processor performance are temporary, and will be quickly resolved. Needless to say, other problems will surface to take their place, and they will probably be associated with software.

So against this backdrop of a rapidly evolving technological world, this chapter reviews some of the hardware currently available to the VR community.

10.1 Sensor hardware

When interacting with a virtual environment, various sensors and transducers are needed to monitor a user's actions and feed back signals that reflect the status of something within the environment. For instance, an interactive glove must be tracked in three dimensions, finger positions may be monitored and the glove may even incorporate pressure pads that inflate when a virtual touch condition is detected. To monitor the glove's position, a sensor is needed to provide the x-, y- and z-coordinates relative to some physical frame of reference, which is complemented by orientation angles, such as yaw, pitch and roll. Finally, the pressure pads must give a tactile stimulus when activated.

Designing sensors to capture this data is not fundamentally a difficult problem. What is difficult is making these devices reliable, repeatable, accurate, portable, fast, safe, non-invasive, robust and low cost. Attempting to satisfy all of these design criteria is no mean task. Nevertheless, a range of products are commercially available, and new ones appearing every day.

This section reviews some of the important sensors that are being integrated into today's VR systems.

10.1.1 Tracking sensors

A central requirement of any immersive VR system is the accurate tracking of the user's head in terms of its position and orientation. Various methods have been employed for head-tracking including: ultrasonics, low-frequency a.c. electromagnetic fields, pulsed d.c. electromagnetic fields, mechanical coupling, optical, image processing and the earth's magnetic field. Kalawsky (1993) has reviewed these technologies in great depth.

The user's hand is also tracked using identical sensor technology. In the case of a glove, the sensor is attached to the back of the glove, while a 3D mouse has the sensor encapsulated within the device.

Update rate and latency
Apart from the obvious need to provide accurate spatial and angular reference information, a tracking system must operate in real time and provide at least

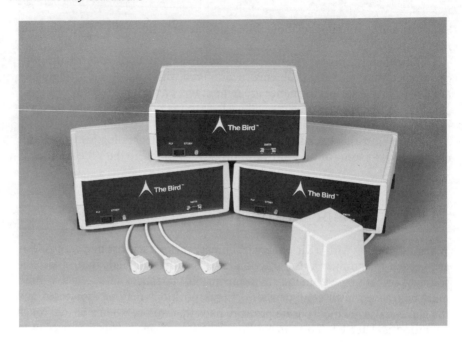

Figure 10.1 Flock of Birds.

50 updates per second. This does not seem to present a real technological problem, as the Polhemus Fastrak updates at 120 Hz and the Ascension Flock of Birds (see Figure 10.1) works at 144 Hz. What has been a problem, however, and is much more important to any real-time system, is latency. This is the time delay between when the sample is taken, and when data is available for processing. It is true that a system updating at 100 Hz makes a sample every 10 ms, but if there is a 100 ms system latency before the information becomes usable, the high update rate contributes little to real-time tracking. Both the Polhemus Fastrak and the Ascension Flock of Birds have a latency quoted at less than 10 ms. For a 30 Hz visual update rate, this is quite acceptable if the data can be processed and delivered to the IG in less than 10 ms, giving a total latency of 20 ms.

Range

Range is a measure of the active tracking distance for determining translation and orientation within the operational specification. Both range and linearity of a.c. electromagnetic systems are influenced by conductive metals such as stainless steel and aluminium in the vicinity of the tracker. This is due to the eddy currents that are induced by the alternating electromagnetic fields, which in turn set up new field patterns that distort the original field. Ferrous metallic structures in the fabrication of floors, walls and ceilings are also a problem. However, an alternative approach is to employ d.c. magnetic fields which do not cause these continuous eddy currents.

In general, trackers work reliably up to a radius of 2-3 m in a perfect environment, but, in practice, this range is reduced by local electromagnetic noise and metallic objects. Translational accuracy is in the order of 2.5 mm, and translational resolution 0.8 mm. Angular range covers ±180° of yaw and roll, and ±90° of pitch, with an accuracy of approximately 0.5°.

ADL-1

The ADL-1 from Shooting Star Technology is a six DOF tracking system that employs mechanical coupling. The user wears an adjustable headband which is connected to a fixed mounting via two jointed lightweight arms. Two potentiometers are used to measure joint angles in these arms, which provides the data to specify the position and orientation of the user's head. The output of the control box is an RS-232c serial interface with 300 updates per second, and a typical latency of 2 ms. Positional resolution is quoted at 0.625 mm, and a maximum angular resolution of 0.3°. The work volume is a half-cylinder, approximately 90 cm diameter, and with a height of 45 cm.

Logitech Head Tracker

The Logitech Head Tracker, manufactured by Logitech, Inc., measures absolute position and orientation using ultrasonic speakers and microphones. Three speakers are mounted in a large fixed triangle, while three microphones are housed in a small mobile triangle that is normally attached to the user's head. The technique of triangulation enables the position of the mobile triangle to be specified relative to the fixed triangle. Because ultrasonic sound is used, the sensor microphones must be within line of sight of the speakers.

Dextrous HandMaster

The Dextrous HandMaster was developed in 1986 at ADL, Inc. under the direction of Dr Beth Marcus, and is now marketed by EXOS, Inc. under license from ADL. The device is a sensor-lined exoskeleton attached to the user's wrist, thumb and three fingers. Each sensor causes small changes in the magnetic field intersecting a Hall element. As the terminal voltage of a Hall element is proportional to the magnetic flux, joint angles are measured with great accuracy. These signals are easily interfaced to any computer system where they can control real or virtual robots.

Spaceball 2003

The Spaceball 2003 is manufactured by Spaceball Technologies, Inc. and is an input device for measuring simultaneous translations and rotations about the X-, Y- and Z-axes. When the ball is gripped by the user, forces and torques are measured and input to a host computer. The approximate force range is 0.5–20 N, and the approximate torque range is 15–600 N mm. The ball's radius is 60 mm. The Spaceball is illustrated in Figure 10.2.

BioMuse

BioControl Systems, Inc. manufacture the BioMuse, a biolectric signal controller. This accepts input of brain electrical activity, muscle signals and eye

Figure 10.2 Spaceball.

movement, captured through a headband and small skin sensors. The output channel can be used to activate events in a computer system. The BioMuse receives data from four main sources of electrical activity in the human body: muscle activity (EMG signals), eyemotion (EOG signals), the heart (EKG signals) and brain waves (EEG signals). The vertical and horizontal eye movements are used by the BioMuse to create an eye-controlled joystick, and it can also be configured to measure eye convergence.

10.1.2 Force feedback sensors

EXOS, Inc. have pioneered a range of products for sensing real-time hand gestures and the feedback of force information from a virtual environment. A simple touch response can be generated by a low-frequency electromagnetic transducer which is small and lightweight. However, where large torques are involved, careful design is required to minimize the weight of the actuators and not interfere with the natural movements of the user. Thus the system must be light and freely backdrivable, by either active or passive means.

TouchMaster

The TouchMaster is a non-reactive, tactile feedback device which provides a sense of contact when activated. The sensors consist of voice coil transducers driven at approximately 200 Hz, and they are attached to the user's thumb and first finger. When interfaced via a control unit to a host computer, an event derived by a virtual collision can activate the sensors, creating a tactile sensation.

SAFiRE

The SAFiRE system measures the torques developed at the user's wrist, thumb, index and middle fingers, which can then be used to control some virtual process. The same control mechanism reflects back through an exoskeleton, torques to the active joints using small d.c. motors. The thumb and index finger are each actuated with three DOF, and the middle finger with two DOF. SAFiRE can be used in a variety of simulation exercises where forces exerted by the user play an important part of the manipulation. The torque feedback also tells the user how much force is being exerted by the simulated mechanism.

Force ArmMaster

The Force ArmMaster develops the SAFiRE system to engage the arm and shoulder, and is capable of passively monitoring, or actively driving, the forearm, elbow and shoulder with respective torques of 2 cm kg, 8 cm kg and 36 cm kg.

Force Feedback Master

In applications such as surgical simulation or molecular modelling, there is a requirement to track and feed back forces relating to the orientation of a handle or probe. Such information is processed by EXOS's four DOF Force Feedback Master. The basic device works with the following angular ranges: 140° of yaw, 140° of pitch and 350° of roll. The vertical heave is 10 cm, but can be configured for other distances. The forces active at the device's handle are 0.23 kg for the three angles, and 0.14 kg of vertical heave.

PowerStick

A similar device to the Force Feedback Master is the EXOS PowerStick which is a joystick to sense and create forces in pitch and roll. The continuous force is approximately 0.45 kg in all directions, and the peak force is 2.36 kg. It is also capable of creating a peak force of 7.5 kg in selected directions.

10.1.3 The GLAD-IN-ART project

GLAD-IN-ART stands for Glove-like Advanced Interface for the Control of Manipulative and Explorative Procedures in Artificial Realities, which is a research project at the Scuola Superiore S. Anna, managed by Massimo Bergamasco. The objective of the project has been the development of an advanced interface system capable of replicating forces to the human operator's hand.

At the centre of the system is the ARTS glove, developed by Scuola Superiore S. Anna, capable of recording all the movements of the fingers and wrist, an arm exoskeleton and a hand exoskeleton, for the replication of forces at the level of the human arm and hand respectively. The system also includes proprioceptive and force feedback interface software modules, developed by the Technology Application Group, UK.

The arm exoskeleton is a force-replicating device attached to the user's arm. It possesses seven DOF which correspond to the joints in the human arm from the shoulder to the wrist. The hand force feedback system is a set of mechanical exoskeleton structures covering the fingers. Each exoskeleton is capable of recording the movement of each joint of the finger, and, at the same time, exerting forces in correspondence of the central part of the palmar surface of each phalanx. The phalanges of each finger are attached to the links of the exoskeleton structure, which is connected to a glove. Plate 21 shows the ARTS Glove and Plate 22 illustrates how it is used to grasp an object in a virtual environment.

10.2   Head-coupled displays

Ever since Sutherland's research work on HMDs in the late 1960s, attempts have been made to develop new systems for a range of specific applications. Today, this work still continues, but the VR community has a reasonable range of products to choose from at different costs and specifications.

HMDs have been developed for military pilots for integrating navigational and tactical data with out-of-the-cockpit scenes, and for the commercial market, there exists a wide range of HMDs, booms and specialist display products, some of which are examined below.

10.2.1   Military HMDs

The technical specification for military HMDs is a primary consideration, followed by the secondary one of cost. In an avionics application, a military pilot is unable to wear any headgear that could cause high *g*-forces. Consequently, any display system must have minimal impact upon the weight of the pilot's helmet. At the same time, the pilot requires high-resolution information to be displayed upon an optically accurate and rugged display. Designers have explored the use of cockpit-mounted displays coupled to the pilot's helmet through flexible coherent fibre optic bundles. The displays are full colour with a horizontal resolution of at least 1000 lines. Computer-generated images are then superimposed over the pilot's view of the real world using off-axis optics.

A typical specification provides a field of view of 60° horizontal, by 55° vertical, with about 45° binocular overlap. The specification also addresses features such as minimum aberrations, peripheral vision, exit pupil, eye relief,

Figure 10.3 Sim Eye.

optical transmission, scene collimation, helmet slippage, chromatic correction, interocular adjustments and optical mapping functions. It is not a surprise that such high-performance HMDs are expensive, and cannot be considered for non-military applications. Figure 10.3 shows a view of the Sim Eye HMD.

10.2.2 General-purpose HMDs

General Reality's CyberEye is a lightweight monoscopic, or stereoscopic, HMD that can fit to the user's forehead without interfering with normal vision. When gazing upwards into the HMD, the user sees a collimated view of the displayed images. For increased degrees of immersion, the display is lowered into the natural gaze direction of the user. The display system is a dual active matrix LCD with a resolution of 420 × 230 pixels (triads) per eye, with a FOV of approximately 30°. This is equivalent to looking at a 2.13 m TV about 3.65 m away. It also incorporates stereo audio channels and an optional tracking system.

Datavisor
n-Vision's Datavisor HMD employs a pair of miniature CRT displays fitted with liquid crystal shutter devices. The shutters are electronically switchable

light filters that allow only one primary colour to pass at any instant. Synchronizing the shutter with the miniature CRT, red, green and blue components of each full-colour frame are displayed in rapid succession to produce full-colour images inside the HMD. The CRTs and shutters are balanced at ear level on the sides of the head and project high-contrast polarized images into the HMD relay optics. The output of each assembly is an infinity-focused exit pupil 12 mm in diameter with a FOV of 50°. The interocular distance is adjustable between 58 mm and 75 mm.

The video formats supported by the Datavisor are: 1280 × 960 at 30 Hz, 800 × 600 at 55 Hz, and 640 × 480 at 60 Hz. Stereo headphones are included with the HMD system as standard.

MRG2

The MRG2 HMD manufactured by Liquid Image employs a single, full-colour, 14.5 cm TFT-LCD display element with a resolution of 240 × 240 triads. The FOV is 84° horizontally and 65° vertically. It also incorporates stereo headphones. The lighter MRG4 employs a 10 cm display element, with 234 × 160 pixels with a horizontal FOV of 61°, and vertical FOV of 46°.

VIM

The VIM (Visual Immersion Module) HMD is manufactured by Kaiser Electro-Optics, Inc., and employs their patented cholesteric Pancake Window. This consists of a cholesteric liquid crystal panel, a half-silvered concave mirror, a $\frac{1}{4}$ wave plate and an LCD panel. The combined thickness is about 12 mm and weights about 32 g. The VIM Personal Viewer has a vertical FOV of 30° and a horizontal FOV of 100°. It is expected that the technology can be used to achieve a full peripheral vision system with 220° horizontal FOV by 128° vertical FOV, and 90° of stereo overlap.

Visette 2

The Visette 2 from Virtuality, Ltd is a lightweight (600 g) HMD. The horizontal and vertical FOVs per eye are 60° and 46.8° respectively. Each eye has a manual focus adjustment of ±4 dioptres, and there is a motorised inter-pupilary range of 58–70 mm. The video format is NTSC/PAL with a resolution of 60K pixel triads. Visette 2 also incorporates stereo earphones.

VR4

The VR4 from Virtual Research is a lightweight (0.935 kg) HMD using twin 3.3 cm diagonal Active Matrix LCDs. The resolution per eye is 742 × 230 colour elements, which is equivalent to 56 887 triads. The field of view depends upon the degree of overlap: 60° at 100% overlap and 67° at 85% overlap. The interocular distance is adjustable between 52 and 74 mm, and the eye relief is adjustable between 10 and 30 mm. The HMD employs Sennheiser HD440 digitally compatible headphones.

Figure 10.4   Private Eye. Courtesy Reflection Technology.

10.2.3   Boom devices

Fakespace, Inc. supply three BOOM devices: BOOM, BOOM2C and BOOM3C. BOOM is a monochrome device; BOOM2C uses a colour space based on red and green; and BOOM3C is a full-colour device. All three display devices are stereo using CRT technology. There are six joints in the supporting counter-balanced arm, enabling the user to move the BOOM within a sphere of approximately 2 m radius. The arm joints contain sensors that enable the position and orienation of the BOOM to be computed. There are two buttons mounted on the ends of the grip handles which can be programmed to perform any task in a VR application. Plate 3 shows one of the BOOM devices in action.

10.2.4   Virtual screens

Reflection Technology manufacture the Private Eye (see Figure 10.4) which is a compact display device attached to the user's head and viewed by one eye. Although the viewing distance is adjustable to 25.4 cm, the virtual image can be adjusted to appear about 30 cm wide when collimated to form a virtual screen at 60 cm (24 in) from the eye. The display resolution is 720 × 280 pixels, which can be formatted as 25 lines with 80 characters per line. The device is particularly useful when computer-generated information, such as maintenance manuals, electronic books or remote displays, is required to aid a person working in some physical environment.

10.3 Acoustic hardware

10.3.1 Crystal River Engineering, Inc.

Crystal River Engineering, Inc. provide specialist support in 3D sound with their Convolvotron, Beachtron, Acoustetron and Alphatron products.

Convolvotron

The Convolvotron is a digital audio signal processing system which creates real-time 3D sound over conventional headphones, controlled from any RS-232 interface. Using 74 HRTF filters, with 256 coefficients per ear, the Convolvotron can produce four independent virtual sound sources at an update rate of 33 Hz. The acoustic reflection model provides transmission-loss modelling, several reflective surface materials, up to six programmable reflection paths, and independent gain and directional controls for each source.

Beachtron

The Beachtron is like the Convolvotron, but is configured for PCs. It creates two independent virtual sound sources at an update rate of 22 Hz, and the HRTFs provide only 75 coefficients per ear.

Acoustetron

The Acoustetron is an integrated 3D audio workstation incorporating Convolvotron and Beachtron processors. Inputs can be from any traditional audio system, such as microphones, amplifiers or CD players, from which it can create up to sixteen 3D anechoic (non-reflective) virtual sound sources, and four 3D echoic sound sources with six reflective surfaces (walls). An associated software library enables the user rapidly to prototype complex acoustic environments that include reflective objects and Doppler shifts.

Alphatron

The Alphatron is a recent product. It plays back two sounds (wavefiles) and allows the user to locate them anywhere in 3D space. It, too, employs HRTFs which have 256 coefficients per ear; the update rate when both sound channels are operating is 44 Hz, with an average latency of 23 ms.

10.4 Integrated VR systems

Early VR systems bear little relationship to today's commercial products. They were little more than programming environments where researchers could investigate solutions to many of the problems described in previous chapters. Whereas today, anyone wanting to explore an application for VR can either purchase a fully-immersive development system, or different combinations of VR toolkits working on workstations or PCs. They can all be described as 'integrated', as they provide a coherent system where a virtual world can be created, simulated, vizualised and, if necessary, experienced through immersion.

The following brief descriptions identify some of the configurations that are currently available, and also reflect important trends in the way future VR systems are evolving.

10.4.1   Division, Ltd

Division's PROVISION 100 system is based on the Intel 80x86 architecture and the EISA bus. The CPU is a 66 MHz i486 (optional Pentium) with 16 Mb or 32 Mb RAM, and standard EISA cards provide SCSI disk interface, super-VGA video display, and Ethernet support. Special accelerator cards support I/O, collision detection, 3D audio and stereo image generation.

A single plug-in board provides I/O processing for the acquisition of tracker data, and collision detection using two dedicated I/O channels. Motion data from trackers, such as the Polhemus Fastrak, is communicated through a dedicated high-speed link to the graphics subsystem. This minimizes interference from the EISA bus and minimizes latency degradation. An additional floating-point processor provides continuous real-time collision detection between stationary or moving objects in the VE.

The Beachtron audio board, from Crystal River Engineering, provides audio synthesis and 3D spatialization, and is configured to spatialize two independent sound sources at a sustained update rate of 22 Hz.

Three options are available for supporting stereo graphics: VRX, VPX (single pipe) and VPX (dual pipe). The VRX option is a low-cost system which delivers up to 80K z-buffered triangles per second without texture mapping. The VPX (single pipe) option provides 555K z-buffered, flat-shaded triangles per second, which reduces to 162K with texture mapping. The dual pipe version doubles this specification. The VPX system is based upon the Pixel-Planes graphics engine.

The PROVISION 100 uses Division's dVS VR operating environment described in Chapter 11. Figure 10.5 shows one of Division's immersive systems.

10.4.2   Sense8 Corporation

Five development licences are available for Sense8's WorldToolKit. World-ToolKit-Windows runs on any computer that runs Windows 3.1 or NT. A recommended configuration is a 486DX or Pentium PC, 8 Mb RAM, and a VGA or SVGA graphics board. WorldToolKit-PC/i860 requires DOS 3.X or

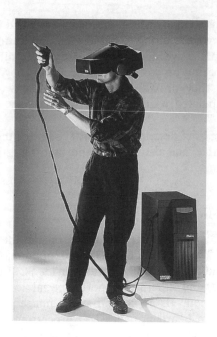

Figure 10.5 A virtual reality user.

greater, and a high-performance PC equipped with a graphics board. One PC with two graphics boards can be used to generate stereo views, or two PCs with single graphics boards. WorldToolKit-SGI works on any Silicon Graphics workstation that supports IRIX 4.0.5 or greater, and GL 4.0. WorldToolKit-SUN runs on SPARC2, SPARC10 or SPARC20 workstations equipped with the SX or optional ZX graphics accelerator. The WorldToolKit-DEC/Denali is optimized to run on DEC's Alpha Unix workstation family, along with the Denali graphics system from Kubota Pacific Computer. Chapter 11 contains a complete description of the software, together with the interactive devices supported.

10.4.3 Superscape, Ltd

The Superscape VRT and Superscape Visualiser software products require a PC to support the real-time VR environment. The recommended configuration is a 486DX/66 MHz or Pentium with 8 Mb of RAM, although lower specifications are possible. The system supports a variety of proportional, sound and graphics devices. The proportional devices include: Ascension Flock of Birds, Logitech 3D Mouse, Polhemus Fastrak, Spaceball and Spacemouse. Sound devices include: Ad Lib Gold 1000, Music Quest MIDI, Sound Blaster 2 and Sound Blaster 16 ASP. Graphics cards can have the following standards: MCGA, SVGA and TIGA.

10.4.4 Virtuality, Ltd

Since the early 1990s, Virtuality, Ltd has pioneered integrated immersive games systems. The Series 2000 comes in two configurations: a stand-up version (2000SU) where the participant stands inside a console interacting with a 3D mouse, and a sit-down version (2000SD) where the participant sits in a chair-like console and interacts through a joystick. The 2000SU system is designed for games where 360° interaction is exploited, while the 2000SD is for cockpit-based or driving experiences. Both systems are immersive and employ the Visette 2 headset. Other accessories include a Vocalizer, and a replay station. The Vocalizer is an audio processing device which allows players to take on the voices of their chosen characters within the virtual experience, while the replay station is used to view highlights of the game. The processing hardware is based upon an industrial PC fitted with RISC-based multiprocessor PC cards. The graphics system includes texture mapping, and the audio system uses CD ROM technology.

The V-PC is also manufactured by Virtuality, Ltd but is a general-purpose VR system, and is shown in Plate 4. The central processor is IBM's ValuePoint 6492 PC, and graphics is provided by dual MC88110 45 MHz RISC engines. A complete system includes a PC, a Visette 2 headset, a portable deskstation with self-contained tracker, an LCD display and a V-Flexor. The last is a handheld device which provides proportional pressure finger inputs, as well as hand tracking. With one graphics card the performance is quoted as 53K Gouraud-shaded polygons per second, and with six graphics cards the throughput increases to 212K Gouraud-shaded polygons per second. When the polygons are shaded and texture mapped, the throughput capacities are 36K polygons per second (one card), 144K polygons per second (six cards). V-Space is an object-oriented software development system for V-PC, and includes facilities for 3D modelling, designing textures, object hierarchies, importing external databases, animation with spline paths, forward and inverse kinematic animation, and the capture of real-world motion.

11

Virtual Reality Software

11.0   Introduction

Any effective computer system depends upon the successful integration of hardware, software and the user interface. VR pushes these three domains to their technical limits, which makes it a potential candidate for failure – though this has not happened.

One reason for VR's success concerns the building blocks used to configure a system, which, in general, employ off-the-shelf technologies. Workstations, personal computers and graphics boards provide an adequate range of real-time hardware platforms. HMDs exploit LCD elements from the television and camcorder markets. VR software exploits two decades of CAD and computer graphics development, and even tracking hardware is based upon well-established electromagnetic techniques. Perhaps the weakest link in the system chain is the user interface, which will evolve as VR is applied to different application areas.

Integrating these system elements does not pose any unusual technological problems, but what is challenging is making them run in real time. Minimizing latency and maximizing update rate are the prime considerations of the system designer. Both parameters decide whether a VR system will serve a useful purpose, or will simply frustrate the user.

Although there are hard digital connections between these system elements, it is software that performs the ultimate integration. Software determines the overall framework for coordinating events within the processing envelope of the hardware, and as multiple processors and parallel processing are becoming common features of today's systems, software is also reflecting the level of complexity required to make these systems function in real time without compromising reliability.

We will now examine the VR software environment and, in particular, look at modelling tools for building virtual worlds, and simulating physical behaviours and how this environment is supported when subjected to real-time interaction. In this review, reference will be made to various commercial systems, however no comparisons will be made.

11.1 Modelling virtual worlds

As every application brings with it its own peculiar set of problems, it is impossible to lay down hard and fast rules about VR modelling systems. It may be that a simple environment, such as a kitchen, can be constructed from polygonal objects constrained to move like drawers and doors. Another scenario, such as an airport, requires models to be viewed over distances ranging from a few metres to several kilometres. This calls for objects modelled to different levels of detail that are automatically selected depending upon their range. A medical application might call for voxel-based models that have to be rendered by making transparent those voxels with a specific attribute. Thus one will never find an interactive modelling environment to cater for all of these different applications and modelling data types. We will have to depend upon a range of different systems to address these various applications, and there is a good chance that for some applications, original modelling tools will have to be designed in-house.

11.1.1 Imported models

As CAD has had a substantial head-start over VR, there is a very large collection of virtual environments waiting to be explored in a VR mode. Model formats such as AutoCAD, 3D Studio, Wavefront, Alias, Multigen, Pro-Engineer and Computer Vision can normally be imported into most VR systems, saving considerable rebuilding time. It would be wrong to imply that it is possible to import models that exploit all of a modelling system's features. For example, models constructed from NURBS (Non-Uniform Rational B-Splines) will have to be triangulated if they are to be manipulated and rendered in real time. Polygonal models, however, pose few problems, and are readily converted into other formats.

11.1.2 Modelling toolkit features

Libraries

Modelling systems must provide the user with a variety of tools to select shapes and objects from a system library. A shape library holds parametric definitions of circles, ellipses, arcs, parabolas, triangles, squares, rectangles and polygons, while an object library contains cubes, boxes, spheres, cylinders, cones and Platonic objects. Interactive commands are available to delete or insert vertices, reverse a vertex sequence in a facet, or delete a facet. Standard tools such as extruding and sweeping are also used to construct more user-specific objects.

Superscape's VRT system has an extensive library of virtual objects that includes everything for building an office, a house and outside environments.

Object sorting

In order to speed up the rendering process, some modelling environments make the modeller determine the rendering sequence of the facets and objects. Thus at rendering time, the renderer is not engaged in any form of sorting process to determine visibility. A common ploy in flight simulation is to include within the database a system of Binary Separating Planes (BSPs) to partition objects into discrete half-spaces. When the objects and separating planes are stored as a binary tree, the tree is rapidly traversed to reveal an optimum rendering sequence. Moving objects are then held separately and integrated with the static elements using a z-buffer.

Surface attributes

Objects can be coloured in a variety of ways. One colour could be assigned to the entire object, or each facet could be given a different colour. Colours could even be assigned to vertices and interpolated across the facet when it is rendered. A facet could be given two colours – one for each side – or it could even be given a degree of translucency.

Facets can be decorated using texture maps scanned in from photographs. These require positioning, scaling and orientating, and some rendering systems may be able to process a nest of texture maps (mip maps) to cope with very large viewing ranges.

Lighting

The VE will have to be illuminated by a mixture of ambient light and individual light sources. As already seen, these could be directional, point or spot lights. It may be that a light source is held by the user and used to explore the VE. One could also imagine a design application where the user needs to adjust interactively every parameter associated with the lights. Lights may be used to illuminate the entire environment or specific objects.

To avoid the use of virtual light sources, the virtual world can be prelit by colouring objects with colour intensities that suggest a directional light source. For example, to simulate an overhead ceiling light, all surfaces pointing towards the ceiling are made bright, while others are made darker depending on their vertical orientation.

If a radiosity model is used to illuminate the environment, then illumination levels can be integrated into the database, and there is no need for any extra lights. It does mean, however, that the renderer must be able to cope with this hybrid mixture of geometry and illumination.

Dynamic vertices

The Superscape system supports *dynamic points* which allow vertices to be animated between two extremes. At the modelling stage, the modeller identifies the points that remain static, and those that will move. An inbetweening procedure determines a sequence of inbetween shapes which, when rendered in sequence, creates an animated effect. This is particularly useful for animating levers and instruments, and does not involve any geometric processing.

11.2   Physical simulation

In Chapter 8 we explored some simple ideas for simulating physical behaviours. Although most of the procedures are mathematically trivial, the real problems arise in designing an interface where such behaviours can be associated with arbitrary geometric databases.

Computer animation systems such as Wavefront, Alias and Softimage take this type of problem in their stride, because that is their domain. A VR system, on the other hand, must work in real time and will not be able to support every type of physical behaviour used in stop-frame animation. Obviously this will change as processor performance improves, but for the moment it is not possible to interact with a complex VE in real time and expect every object to behave like its physical counterpart. Nevertheless, designers of VR software are including procedures that animate the VE with credible simulated behaviours.

11.2.1   Division, Ltd

Division's dVISE environment employs the concept of *actors* (servers) that are responsible for various system activities. For instance, there are actors to support collision detection, audio, tracking and image generation. In keeping with this system philosophy, a 'physics' actor is responsible for implementing an extensible group of physics-based functions. The physics actor uses Newton's second law of motion ($F = ma$) to compute the forces acting upon an object and how the object's behaviour changes, especially in collisions. All calculations employ metric (SI) units: length (metres), time (seconds), mass (kilograms), force (newtons), torque (newton metres) and angles (radians).

Rigid bodies

The physics actor implements a Newtonian model involving rigid bodies. Deformable models are to be included when processor performance can support their simulation in real time.

Mass

Homogeneous, symmetric objects are often represented as a point mass, where the object's inertial mass is assumed to be concentrated at a point. If this model is used for non-homogeneous, irregular objects, then the physical simulation is far from accurate. The dVISE physics actor supports point and extended masses, where the latter simulates distributed mass. This requires the evaluation of an inertial tensor from the six equations describing the linear and angular accelerations.

Forces due to fields

A pseudo-gravitational field is supported by the physics actor, and always creates a vertical downwards force in a Cartesian frame of reference. Strictly speaking, the force due to the earth's gravitational field should take into account the spherical nature of the earth, by accelerating objects towards the earth's centre. This is why dVISE refers to it as a pseudo-gravitational field. However, for most simulations the error is negligible. Objects can be subjected to forces derived from other fields, which are accumulated to derive a resultant force.

Forces due to direct intervention

External forces can also be applied to an object at any point in its frame of reference, together with torques about an object's centre of mass. Forces that do not pass through the origin of a frame of reference cause a torque about that origin.

Forces due to collisions

The physics actor implements simple reflective collisions using a coefficient of restitution to simulate energy loss. The conservation of momentum calculations also ensure the correct distribution of energy.

Dead reckoning

Dead reckoning information is available to other actors interested in the dynamic status of an object. This consists of an object's linear position, velocity and acceleration, angular position, velocity and acceleration, and a scale factor.

Collision detection

Various types of collisions can be supported by the physics actor and involve interactions between polygons, edges and vertices. All the interactions are subject to a user-defined tolerance level. A collision involving a polygon against a polygon implies that one or more coplanar polygons of one object intersect with a group of coplanar polygons from another object. When this occurs, the point of collision is taken as the centroid of the plane figure. A collision of an edge with a polygon implies that the edge lies in the plane of the polygon, and the point of collision is taken as the centre of the edge. One of the most frequent types of collisions involves a polygon against a vertex. In this case, the collision point is the location where the vertex lies within the polygon. A collision involving two edges creates two possible collision points: when the edges are coincident, the point of collision is taken as the centre of the line segment common to both edges; otherwise, it is where the edges intersect. A collision with an edge and vertex creates a precise point of contact along the edge. Finally, two objects can collide vertex against vertex.

Steady-state behaviour

At the start of a VR session the physics actor is initialized and then exhibits a steady-state behaviour. This consists of the following steps:

(1) Lock the database.

(2) Extract all the information in which the actor is interested, updating the local copies as necessary.

(3) Unlock the database.

(4) Simulate the physics for the next time step.

(5) Simulate the collision detection code for the first change in collide status that occurred during the physics time step.

(6) Report the change in collision to the rest of the database.

(7) Rewind the simulation to the time of the change in collision state. Adjust the physics model to account for the change in collision status, recalculate the remainder of the time step.

(8) Repeat Steps 4 to 7 until the entire time period is used up.

(9) Check the dead reckoning positions of all the objects with changed local positions to see if they are still within an acceptable tolerance of the current positions. If not, update the positions in the database for those objects that have unacceptable dead reckoning positions.

(10) Repeat Steps 1 to 9 for ever.

The physics library

The physics library provides a range of functions to set an object's physical properties. This includes inertial mass, centre of mass, inertial tensor, translate tensor, gravitational mass, gravitational field, restitution, mass and external forces.

11.2.2 Jack

Another type of physical simulation used in virtual environments concerns the human body. Various attempts have been made at modelling the human form – some just for computer animations, and others for ergonomic applications. Boeing Corporation were using 3D computer-generated characters in the 1960s to assess their new cockpit designs. Today, the most sophisticated system commercially available is Jack, developed by the Center for Human Modeling and Simulation at the University of Pennsylvania.

Jack is a general-purpose interactive environment for manipulating articulated geometric figures. One popular application is to import into Jack a geometric database from a CAD system, and then to introduce an articulated human figure to explore the database for fit, reach, movement, strength and view analyses. Jack includes a wide range of articulated figures with revolute and prismatic joints. A general-purpose constraint engine uses iterative inverse kinematics to manipulate the joints into different positions, and a behavioural control regime manages the articulation and constraint envelopes. As the software includes goal-directed animation procedures, commands such as: 'move arm', 'bend torso', 'place hands on hips', can be issued interactively to produce human-like behaviours.

Jack's articulated figures are based upon the Anthropometric Survey (ANSUR) of the US Army in 1988. The survey, which included males and females, captured data on joint limits, body segment dimensions and strength values. The data also includes moment of inertia. A figure can have 73 joints, with a total of 136 degrees of freedom. A typical model is shown in Plate 5. Some joints are grouped together, such as the torso and shoulder, and can be manipulated as a coherent structure. The model's spine, which contains 17 vertebrae, is simultaneously controlled by the position of the waist and lower neck. Because the database is based upon a very large sample, it is possible to select any percentile figure.

One of the most powerful features offered by Jack is the ability to explore in real time the physical behaviours of articulated figures. Thus when a Jack figure is instructed to lift a heavy object, the iterative inverse kinematics software evaluates whether the figure becomes unstable at any stage. If this does occur, the figure can be programmed to fall over or respond in some other way.

The key features of a Jack figure include articulated hands, ability to reach and grasp, collision detection, collision avoidance, anthropometric scaling, walking behaviours, balance control, field of view, joint torque and sensor channels:

- **Articulated hands** A Jack hand possesses 16 joints and is preprogrammed with three grip methods. Other hand positions can be designed inter-actively or based upon external data channels derived from interactive devices.

- **Reaching** A Jack figure is often used for assessing reach limits in ergonomic exercises. This can be achieved by constraining various parts of the figure and then instructing it to reach for some object in space. If the figure is instructed to reach in a standing position, the reach exercise can be constrained to preserve body balance.

- **Grasping** The articulated hand can be instructed to grasp an object within its reach. The fingers and palm wrap around the object using collision detection to prevent them from intersecting. If the object moves for any reason, the Jack figure automatically takes up a new orientation to maintain the grasp. However, the hand is released if the object moves out of reach.

- **Collision detection**   Collision detection is an important feature of Jack. It detects collisions between the figure and the environment, and any collisions between the figure's own body segments.

- **Collision avoidance**   Jack's collision avoidance is a powerful physical behaviour that simulates how a person would move to avoid being hit by an object. For instance, if an object is thrown at a figure's head, the entire body manoeuvres into a new position to avoid the collision.

- **Anthropometric scaling**   As the body segments are derived from a population of several thousand people, a figure can be selected from any percentile group – male or female. A spreadsheet interface enables segment dimensions, joint limits, moment of inertia and strengths to be individually selected.

- **Walking behaviours**   A Jack figure can be animated to mimic walking behaviours which can then be interpolated into other states such as jogging, running and standing still.

- **Balance control**   As body segments have mass and a centre of mass, a figure can be made to search for a balance condition by implementing different strategies. These include moving the arms, body or legs to new positions.

- **Field of view**   A figure's viewpoint can be set at either eye or at a central point between the two eyes, and as the eyes are articulated (socketed), it is possible to explore the visual FOV without moving the head or body.

- **Joint torque**   Every joint possesses a joint torque captured at the original survey. This enables a figure to be assessed for possible strain conditions when it is programmed to perform a physical task such as lifting an object.

- **Sensor channels**   Jack supports Ascension Technology's Flock of Birds six DOF sensors to capture natural motion of the body.

Another aspect of the Jack system that shows great potential concerns the modelling of the figure's interior. This has been created with a level of accuracy that opens up all sorts of applications for medical training. Plate 6 shows a view of some of the internal structures currently included in the database.

Further information on Jack can be found in Badler *et al.* (1993). The iterative inverse kinematic technique is described in the technical report by Zhao and Badler (1989). Posture interpolation and collision avoidance are covered by Badler *et al.* (1994).

11.2.3   Superscape, Ltd

Objects in Superscape's VRT can be given a range of dynamic features that mimic the dynamics of objects in the real world. They include gravity, fuel, climbing and falling, friction, restitution, driving velocity, external velocity, maximum velocity, angular velocity and whether an object can be pushed or not. Time can be defined in terms of absolute time, or based upon the scene update rate.

- **Gravity**   Gravity is entered as units which alter an object's Y-velocity at a rate of g per frame^2 downwards (where g is the acceleration due to gravity), thus accelerating the object towards the ground. In practice, g is given a default value of 98 mm per frame^2 for a frame update rate of 10 frames per second.

- **Fuel**   Fuel is an attribute that can control an object's behaviour. For example, using Superscape's control language SCL, an object's fuel attribute can be used to determine the intensity of a light source, or the velocity of an object. And if the fuel attribute is reduced over time, this in turn will attenuate the light source or slow the object down.

- **Climbing**   The climbing attribute specifies how high an obstacle is allowed to be before a collision occurs and restitution is applied. An object, for example, may be moving in a straight line on a horizontal surface. If it has a climbing value of 20 and meets an obstacle on the same surface which is only 10 units high, then the moving object will rise 10 units over the obstacle and continue with none of its velocity values changed. If the object hits any obstacle that rises more than 20 units above surface, then this is interpreted as a collision.

- **Falling**   The falling attribute specifies the maximum distance that an object can fall without its being 'damaged'. If an object falls by a distance greater than that specified by the falling value, then it is stopped and flagged as having fallen 'too far'. This flag can be accessed with the control language SCL.

- **Friction**   In VRT, friction is an attribute of a moving object rather than of the virtual surfaces it moves over, and it is expressed as the percentage reduction in the object's external velocity per frame on the horizontal plane.

- **Restitution**   Restitution is described in Chapter 8 and is associated with collisions between objects. Basically, when objects collide, their velocity is changed. When hitting a wall, for example, a car will come to a halt, but a ball will bounce off. The amount of 'bounce' in a collision is measured by the restitution attribute. Superscape's VRT permits an object to be given horizontal and vertical restitution attributes. When an object hits a surface, the object's current velocity is multiplied by the restitution, and the direction of the velocity is reversed.

- **Driving velocity**   The driving velocity is a constant velocity assigned to objects as they move about the VE. It is unaltered by friction, and is associated with one or a combination of the X-, Y- or Z-directions.

- **External velocity**   An object's external velocity is acquired through external events such as collisions with other objects.

- **Maximum velocity**   The maximum velocity parameter restricts the velocity of an object to some upper limit.

- **Angular velocity** The angular velocity updates an object's rotation attribute and turns the object through a given angle every frame.
- **Pushable** The pushable attribute allows an object to respond to collisions with other objects. Thus walls, floors and ceilings would have this attribute switched off.

Apart from the above physical attributes, Superscape's VRT includes facilities for animations, bending, viewpoints and paths.

- **Animations** An object is animated by preparing at the modelling stage a sequence of cels that show the object in different states. At run time, these are activated at a specified rate, resulting in a smooth animation. Sequences can consist of a linear pass, a cyclic repeat, a bounce (the animation runs forwards and then backwards), include pauses and combinations of all the modes.
- **Bending** Bending, like animation, alters the position of vertices in an object, which in turn influence the position of facets. The bend is made about an existing point, and is effected by selecting a collection of points in the object and specifying a bend angle. This is shown in Figure 11.1: part (a) shows the initial position of a shape; part (b) shows how a group of vertices are rotated; and part (c) shows how a second bend is introduced.

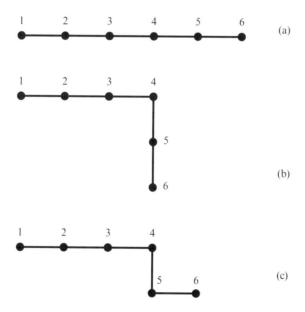

Figure 11.1 An object can be bent about one of its vertices to create new shapes. (a) The original object. (b) Bending part of the object about vertex 4. (c) Bending part of the object about vertex 5.

- **Viewpoints** As the virtual observer (VO) is treated as an object in the VE, and controls the viewpoint, it is a simple process to attach the viewpoint to any other object. For example, a VE might have one viewpoint attached to, and controlling, a moving car. This can be steered using a Spaceball, while the viewpoint provides a view as seen from the driver's seat. Other viewpoints can be established external to the car that are either moving with the car or stationary.

- **Viewpoint paths** A viewpoint can be moved through a VE along a predefined path. The path is a closed loop, defined by a few set positions of key frames. The viewpoint moves between the key frames at a speed set by the number of frames between them. At the end of the sequence, control returns to the beginning again. Each key frame can define the position of the viewpoint, its rotation, or both. There are several different options for each of these. Positions may move along a straight line between key frames or they may follow a smooth curve through them. Rotations may be set relative to the rotation of the object to which the viewpoint is attached, targeted to look at another object, or looking forward along a defined path.

11.3 VR toolkits

A simple computer graphics problem may involve only the drawing of few lines, circles and some relevant text, and can be achieved either by a small C or Pascal program, or with a desktop package. A computer animation application introduces the dimension of time, and there is always the problem of having to make something move, or achieve some goal by a particular frame. This type of problem can also be solved by writing high-level programs, but is generally helped by a computer graphics library. It is, however, much easier to employ an integrated computer animation system where objects are modelled and animated in one environment. A VR problem is even more complex, as it is 3D, animated, interactive and runs in real time.

VR is not just concerned with moving about a VE to gain a different view of a model, VR is about the interaction that can occur with all aspects of the virtual domain. This might involve the touching of objects, moving objects to new positions, measuring angles, changing light levels, evaluating reach envelopes, acoustics, or exploring shadow extents. Such tasks cannot take place unless software is available to support them.

If an environment is to be modified in real time by user commands, the virtual world must be closely coupled to the system software. Vertex, edge and polygon tables, surface normals and texture maps must all be immediately accessible and easy to modify. Similarly, if a virtual object is supposed to behave like its physical counterpart, the procedure that simulates this behaviour must be able to modify the virtual description without introducing excessive latency. To meet such requirements, VR toolkits have become commercially available and provide a coherent software environment to support a wide range of VR applications.

Central to these toolkits is the control language used to support all aspects of interaction, animation and physical simulation. We will now examine three such systems to gain some insight into the level of programming support for a VR system. No attempt is made to compare the systems, but each toolkit is used to explore the total range of features that are required to support a VR application.

11.3.1 Division's dVISE environment

dVISE is a virtual world simulation and authoring tool and is built on top of Division's dVS run-time environment. It is based upon a simple model in which a virtual world is composed of a number of objects, each with user-defined attributes such as colour, movement constraints, behaviours and audio characteristics. Objects can be designed using a range of commercial CAD and modelling systems and then animated by dVISE.

World authoring

dVISE provides two modes of authoring or editing a world. There is a 3D interface that allows the user to modify virtual objects while immersed in a virtual world, and a conventional 2D window interface where objects are represented iconically and controlled using a mouse and keyboard.

dVISE file format

The dVISE file format is called MAZ, and is an ASCII text file which may be edited using a simple text editor. Any virtual world will ultimately have a MAZ file description, and converters exist to import geometry descriptions from other formats such as Autodesk's DXF file description. A MAZ file is executed by an actor (server) in dVS.

MAZ command summary

MAZ commands are used to control collision detection, illumination, acoustics, update rate, and the size, position and orientation of objects. A complete description is shown in Table 11.1.

Each command addresses a specific attribute of the world, such as an object's size and position, and whether it is seen or heard. In the case of **COLLISION**, this assigns a collidable attribute to an object, and has the following syntax:

> **COLLISION** { 〈 specifier__list 〉 }
>
> 〈 specifier__list 〉 ::
> VOLUMES   '〈 filename 〉'
> COLLIDE   on | off

For an object to be picked up, COLLIDE must be enabled. The collision boundary is automatically derived from the **VISUAL** GEOMETRY file, and

Table 11.1   The MAZ command summary.

Command	Description
AUDIO	Defines the acoustic attribute of an object.
COLLISION	Assigns a collision attribute to an object.
CONSTRAINTS	Assigns a movement constraint to an object.
EVENT	Handles external events.
FRAME_RATE	Defines the animation rate of a scene.
ICON	Defines the visual creation icon of an object.
LIGHT	Defines a light source.
OBJECT	Defines a definition or an instance of an object.
ORIENTATION	Sets the orientation of an object.
POSITION	Sets the position of an object.
SCALE	Sets the scale of an object.
SCENE	Defines the context of a world.
VISUAL	Defines the visual attribute of an object.

is formed from the bounding volume occupied by the contained model. The **VISUAL** command has the following syntax:

VISUAL { ⟨specifier_list⟩ }

```
⟨specifier_list⟩ ::
GEOMETRY       '⟨filename⟩'
F_TEXTURE      '⟨filename⟩'
B_TEXTURE      '⟨filename⟩'
F_COLOUR       (⟨red⟩, ⟨green⟩, ⟨blue⟩)
B_COLOUR       (⟨red⟩, ⟨green⟩, ⟨blue⟩)
F_SPECULAR     ⟨ks⟩⟨power⟩
B_SPECULAR     ⟨ks⟩⟨power⟩
VISIBLE        on|off
```

The **VISUAL** attribute is defined within the context of an OBJECT and defines the rendering characteristics of a 3D polygonal model. One can see in the specifier list obvious references to texture, colour, specularity and whether the object is visible or not.

The following example shows how a frying pan is positioned within an environment such that it can be picked up:

```
OBJECT pan {
  VISUAL {
    GEOMETRY  'frying/pan.biz'
  }
    POSITION     (−86,41,24)
    COLLISION {
      COLLIDE        on
    }
}
```

dVISE is written in C and users are able to extend the system to support activities associated with a particular area of application.

The actor concept

The main objective in the design of dVS was to create a distributed model for VR simulation. This stemmed both from the need to simplify the process of defining complex VEs, and from the need to optimize the performance of the final experience. A parallel model of the 3D user interface is a natural one, and helps to control the complexity of the resulting system and provides a very powerful development paradigm.

The distributed model is one in which different servers or actors can mediate different elements of the overall simulation. The functions of these actors can be broadly divided into three groups:

(1) Sensing of the real environment, such as the tracking of head, hand and body attitudes.

(2) Control of the virtual environment, such as the movement of objects and the sounds they make.

(3) Display of the virtual environment, such as the visual and acoustic rendering of the VE.

Figure 11.2 shows the relationship between the different actors, and how they are charged with controlling a specific part of the real and virtual environments. The 'visual' actor provides a visual display, an 'audio' actor provides an acoustic display, a 'collision' actor provides collision detection services, and a 'Tracker' actor provides 3D positions.

A shared data space

Given a model in which different elements of the overall user interface are provided by separate servers (actors), it is necessary to create an efficient infrastructure through which these servers can communicate. In traditional client–server architectures, a set of messages are defined to encapsulate all possible server functions, then the client then addresses the server through either local or remote procedure calls. However, this does not scale to a multiserver system, in which different parts of the interface are handled by different servers. Neither does it adequately address the needs of multiuser systems, in which multiple servers need to arbitrate state changes to maintain consistency.

dVS therefore adopts a more abstract object model. Instead of each actor establishing direct connections to other actors, a shared data space is created into which actors may place shared objects called *elements*. Different actors monitor these elements and respond to global changes in the environment. Actors essentially communicate through these shared objects, and the structure of these objects defines the functionality of the system. Access to the environment is provided by a library of access routines called VL. This provides low-level functions to create, delete, extract and update elements and instances. The environment is, in effect, the VL database.

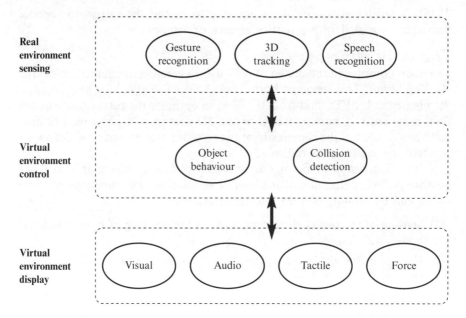

Figure 11.2   The visual, audio, tactile and force actors are responsible for specific activities in the system. They are sensitive to events such as collision detection and object behaviour.

The standard elements

The overall functionality of the system is defined by the elements that an environment contains. Although the VL database is totally general and can maintain any element, there are a set of standard elements which are supported by the standard actors which form part of the dVS run-time release. These elements are essentially the components of a VE. The standard elements include VCObject, VCAudio, VCBoundary, VCConstraints, VCLight and VCVisual. Their names describe their roles.

The dVS run-time system

A set of standard actors is provided in the dVS run-time. These actors interpret the standard elements described above. The user application actually communicates with the run-time system through the VL database.

- The VIZ actor provides a visual representation of the environment. It is affected by VCObject, VCVisual, VCLight and a number of other special elements. Then as other actors create VCLight, or VCVisual, instances, it renders them using the current viewpoint of the user from the BODY actor.

- The SOUND actor provides an acoustic representation of the environment. It is affected by VCObject, VCAudio and various other special elements. Then as other actors create VCAudio instances, it uses them to generate sounds, and spatializes these sounds where required.

- The TRACKER actor is a low-level device actor. It takes input from a range of 3D tracking devices, such as Polhemus Fastrack, and creates a number of TRACKER instances, which can then be used by the BODY actor, and attached to hands, heads and so on.

- The BODY actor represents the user. It creates a VCObject to define the user in space, giving both visual and audio features, and so on. It then uses regular updates from the VCTracker instances and overloads these positions into the position of head, hand and so on.

- The COLLIDE actor provides constant collision detection for all VCBoundary instances. It monitors the environment for VCBoundary changes and detects the intersection of VCBoundary instances. Once a VCBoundary intersects, it creates an update which can then be used by any actor interested in that VCBoundary. The BODY actor, for example, creates VCBoundary instances for all parts of the body, such as hands and head, so that collisions between the body and other objects in the world are automatically detected.

VCToolkit

The VCToolkit is a collection of high-level C routines that create and manipulate virtual objects. It allows the programmer to create virtual objects and to arrange these within a spatial hierarchy. Routines are provided to manipulate the visual, acoustic and physical properties of objects. There are functions to create, delete and modify all the standard elements, and a flexible callback system to process events which result from VL updates made by actors within the dVS run time, or other user code.

11.3.2 Sense8's WorldToolKit

Sense8's WorldToolKit (WTK) is a library of C functions that can be used to write C programs for developing and interacting with virtual worlds. The user writes a C program referencing the functions, which then becomes a WTK application.

A typical program consists of an initialization phase followed by a simulation loop. Initialization consists of setting up the interactive and tracking sensors, identifying the objects, configuring the illumination, initializing the viewpoint and so on, while the simulation loop supports an interactive VR session. The update rate of the display depends on how many times the simulation loop is evaluated per second.

A universe of objects

WTK employs the class universe which is a collection of WTK objects, where the class objects includes: 3D objects, sensors, lights, animation sequences, paths, polygons and windows. Thus any WTK program begins by a call to the function **WTuniverse__new** which performs an initialization task.

Initially, 3D objects are known by name, but in order for them to be manipulated by WTK functions, a pointer is required – which is achieved using **WTuniverse__name2object**. Similar pointer functions are available for sensors, lights, animations and so on.

Parallel universes

It is possible to construct a number of *parallel universes* and move from one to another using a WTK *portal*. Portals are doorways in space that connect the currently displayed universe with another universe. Only one universe is ever displayed at a time, and crossing a portal causes the connected universe associated with the portal to be displayed. Each portal is associated with a polygon at the time of creation. When the current viewpoint is moved through the plane of the polygon associated with a portal and within the polgon extents, the connected universe for that portal is automatically loaded. For instance, the interior and exterior of a house model may be different universes, with the door to the house established as a portal connecting the two universes. When the viewpoint is outside the house, none of the features of the interior are considered for rendering. When the viewpoint crosses through the door, the universe for the house interior is current, with the outside detail of the house ignored.

Modelling

WTK includes a library of parametric objects such as a block, cone, cylinder, sphere and hemisphere. Other objects can be imported using Autodesk's DXF format, Wavefront's OBJ format, 3D Studio's 3DS 'mesh file' format and VideoScape's GEO files. There is also a neutral file format for communicating between other systems. Text is also easily converted from a text string into 3D polygonal objects.

In WTK, the front face of a polygon is the side of the polygon for which the vertices are ordered anticlockwise. It is also the side from which the surface normal points.

Models can be organized into hierarchies to create articulated structures. For example, the function **WTobject__setpivot** sets the point about which an object is to be rotated, and the function **WTobject__attach** connects two objects into a hierarchy. Therefore, if the pivot points for the rectangular blocks lower, middle and effector are at one end, they can be connected to base to form a simple robotic arm using the following instructions:

> **WTobject__attach** (base, lower)
> **WTobject__attach** (lower, middle)
> **WTobject__attach** (middle, effector)

Plate 7 shows a manipulator arm built with WTK for Hermes, the European Space Shuttle.

Collision detection

As 3D objects can be static or dynamic, those objects that move can be tested for intersection with other objects in the universe using the function **WTuniverse__intersect**. The object's bounding box (rather than its polygons) is tested against the polygons of the other 3D objects. As this function only returns a TRUE or FALSE answer, another function can identify the polygons involved in the collision. **WTuniverse_intersect** identifies only the possibility of an intersection, but the function **WTpoly_intersectpoly** can accurately determine whether two polygons intersect or not. However, the system's update rate would suffer if the function were applied to every polygon in a world.

Terrain

WTK provides function calls enabling the creation of three types of terrain objects: flat chessboards, random altitude meshes and user-defined terrain inported from a file. There is also a facility to support 'terrain following', where objects are positioned according to the terrain geometry.

Sensors

Coping with the ever-increasing collection of position, motion and orientation sensors has to be addressed by anyone working in VR, and is taken very seriously by WTK. Software support is provided for a mouse, Spaceball, CiS Geometry Ball Jr, Polhemus Isotrak and Fastrak, Ascension Technology Bird and Flock of Birds, Logitech 3D Mouse and Head Tracker, Stereo-Graphics CrystalEyes VR LCD shutter glasses, Fakespace BOOM, BOOM2C and BOOM3C, PC joysticks and the Advanced Gravis MouseStick optical joystick.

Stereo viewing

Various functions are available to support viewpoint management. One group in particular concerns stereo viewing. For instance, **WTviewpoint_setparallax** sets the distance between the user's eyes, while **WTviewpoint_setconvergence** sets the horizontal offset in pixels that is applied to both the left and right eye images. Another function, **WTviewpoint_setasymmetric**, enhances the 3D effect in stereoscopic viewing by skewing the images horizontally.

Networking

WTK includes a networking capability where applications can asynchronously communicate over Ethernet between several PCs and UNIX workstations. The time it takes for a change in the distributed simulation (such as changing the appearance of a remote object) to propagate through the entire simulation is a function of the number of nodes in the simulation, the current packet traffic, the frame rate of the slowest node in the net and the network's communication bandwidth and latency.

11.3.3   Superscape's VRT

Superscape's VRT is an integrated VR system consisting of several editors, the most of important of which are the Shape Editor and the World Editor. The Shape Editor provides interactive tools for building polygonal objects, while the World Editor organizes the construction of virtual worlds from these objects. Other editors are available for customizing screen layouts, editing texture and sound, and controlling menus and dialogue boxes.

Shape Editor

The Shape Editor uses vertices and facets to create 3D objects which can be coloured, duplicated, transformed and animated. A bounding cube is always associated with an object and is used by VRT to sort objects in the VE. As mentioned earlier, VRT employs the concept of dynamic points, which can be animated when the object is eventually displayed. This dynamic attribute and others, such as colour, lighting, colour palettes and holes, are set with this editor.

World Editor

The World Editor uses object descriptions from the Shape Editor to build virtual worlds organized as a tree of objects. An object may contain other objects (its children), where two or more children with the same parent are called siblings. Their positions are given not in absolute terms, but relative to the origin of their parent. This means that moving the parent will move all the children with it.

The World Editor is also used to assign the physical attributes such as velocity, fuel, gravity, climbing and restitution. It also organizes animation cels from the Shape Editor into animation sequences that will occur when the scene is rendered.

VRT detects collisions using bounding cubes or collision boxes. A bounding cube is one cube containing the entire object, which may be irregular. If this is the case, some collisions will not appear as though a true contact has been made. To overcome this, extra collision boxes may be attached to individual elements of an object.

Bending, viewpoints, viewpoint paths and moveable objects are all controlled by the World Editor. So, too, is the feature of replacements, which arranges for the automatic replacement of low-detail objects as their distance from the observer increases.

The Visualiser

After the objects have been created and given all of their necessary attributes and functions, the Visualiser is used to display the world, move around it and interact with it. When used as a desktop VR system, a Spaceball (or other proportional device) is used to control the picking of objects and the user's viewpoint.

The control language

The Superscape control language, SCL, is similar in many respects to the C programming language. It is used to control objects within a VE, performing actions that are not undertaken by automatic system routines. Each object can have its own attached SCL program, which is executed once per frame. A simple method is provided to allow SCL programs to continue execution over several frames.

SCL semantics

Programs are constructed from constants and variables, with support for arrays, pointers, functions, arithmetic expressions, input/output, control and conditional structures. Objects are referenced by their names in single quotes, such as 'Pyramid', and can be interrogated and manipulated by a library of procedures and functions. The library includes the control of colour, size, position, rotation, bending, flags, markers, counters, sorting, collisions, animations, windows, viewpoints, textures, movement and lighting.

For example, the **setcol** procedure sets a facet of an object to a particular colour, while the functions **xpos**, **ypos** and **zpos** return the current x-, y- and z-offsets of an object. The function **grav** associates a rate of acceleration with an object, and the logical function **hit** returns a TRUE value if the referenced object has been hit by another object.

SCL syntax

SCL code is organized into procedures which are compiled for interpretation at run time. If the following procedure is repeated four times, it makes the object 'Buggy' move in a square:

```
resume(1,0);
/* Stop, rotate buggy 90 degrees (10 steps of 9) */
yangv(me) = 9;
zdrive('Buggy') = 0;
waitfs(10);
/* Stop rotns, move 4000 units (20 × 200) forward */
yangv(me) = 0;
zdrive('Buggy') = 200;
waitfs(19);
```

This script illustrates the similarity to C code, even with the comment lines. The commands **yangv** and **zdrive** alter the Y angular velocity and Z driving velocity, respectively, and **waitfs** instructs the system to wait 10 frames before proceeding. No attempt will be made to describe the syntax to any deeper level, the example simply illustrates the scripting that is necessary to make any environment active.

Animation

Simple animations can be implemented by a series of individual textures. Such textures are not necessarily photographs of real-world scenes, but perhaps drawings or outlines. For example, if an animation has to be simulated showing a cartoon figure moving on a display screen, the sequence is prepared as a sequence of still frames. SCL then activates these textures, and displays them over any period of time, and even cycles them as a closed loop. The sequence is activated by initiating some event such as touching a button, or colliding with an object.

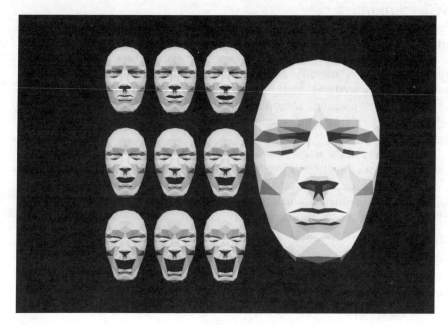

Figure 11.3 A sequence of faces that could be used in an animation sequence. (Courtesy of Superscape, Ltd).

Procedural models

SCL can also be used to construct 3D objects using procedures. For example, a flag could be built from a mesh of triangles, using an SCL procedure, and modulated by a sinusoidal function. If the function included a phase delay, the wave function could be made to move across the flag. By storing several frames of the flag in different cels, SCL can animate the flag at run-time by cycling the models. Figure 11.3 shows a sequence of models that can be used in an animation sequence.

Waiting for frames

Normally, the SCL programs associated with object are executed once per frame, with the frame redraw occurring after all of them have finished executing. To split the execution of a program over several frames, SCL contains the commands **waitf** and **resume**. **Waitf** suspends execution until the next frame, storing the position in the program and various other data. SCL procedures on other objects can then execute. **Resume**, when executed, resumes execution at the last **waitf**, restoring the stored information and carrying on as if nothing had happened. In the meantime, the VE has been displayed and SCL code on other objects has had a chance to be executed.

11.4 Summary

As mentioned earlier, the objective of this chapter was not to undertake a comparative study of VR software systems, but to illustrate the attention to detail that must be given to every aspect of a VR application, from the definition of a single polygon, to the storage of a quaternion from a tracking sensor.

Like any other computer system, a VR application requires a clear system specification before it can be built. Like any other project, there is no reason why the design implementation should be trouble-free. VR systems are complex, and there are plenty of opportunities for things to go wrong. Objects may refuse to move, collisions may go undetected, latency may be erratic, or the virtual world recedes as the user approaches. Such errors must be located and corrected as with any program. Fortunately, this is simplified by the high-level nature of VR toolkits, which means that application programs are not too unmanageable.

12

Virtual Reality Applications

12.0 Introduction

It has been said that VR is a technology looking for an application. Who ever coined this phrase might have been justified at the time, but today it is no longer true. VR is not so much a technology, but more a mode of computer interaction – and as computers are now firmly integrated into every facet of modern society, VR is here to stay and will become a natural feature of computer systems.

It is very easy to go overboard with ambitious predictions as to how VR systems will be used, but this would serve no real purpose. What is useful is to examine practical applications that are being explored today, and stand a reasonable chance of success. The long-term predictions are reserved for Chapter 13, when we look towards the future.

Virtual environments have played a significant role in flight training over the past two decades, and they will continue to do so in the future. Their use has demonstrated that they possess distinct advantages over physical scale models, and there is no way that the flight simulation industry could ever return to model making. Models still play an important role in various industries such as architecture, aero engine design, aircraft design, medicine and car design. Although it is hard to imagine that these industries will abandon all forms of physical models in the future, there are obvious reasons why virtual models should be used for visualizations, simulations and assessing new servicing and manufacturing strategies.

Once a virtual object exists, it can be subjected to many forms of manipulative procedures. For example: it can be decorated with colour and texture; illuminated with different lighting configurations; and dimensions can be adjusted to satisfy optimum layouts. The user can explore the environment to obtain an insight into how it would look if it existed. The ramifications of this approach to design create endless possibilities for stage designers, interior designers, lighting design, animators and car designers. Introduce a fully jointed virtual human figure such as Jack, and the environment can be evaluated for a wide range of ergonomic conditions.

A VE can be subjected to Finite Element Analysis (FEA) techniques to identify areas of stress. It can be subjected to Computational Fluid Dynamics (CFD) techniques to discover air or fluid flow around the object, and surface temperature profiles. The VE can even be subjected to other mathematical procedures that can be used to predict its behaviour under different physical conditions. All of these techniques are familiar operations in the world of computer graphics, and they are rapidly becoming part of the world of VR where parameters can be adjusted in real time and the user is part of the environment.

Not all applications demand that the user be immersed within a VE. Total immersion will have invaluable benefits in some areas, partial immersion in others, and desktop systems will serve another community. Obviously it would be 'exciting' to stand next to a virtual human mannequin as it attempted to reach inside an aero engine to access an oil filter casing, but if immersion does not provide any advantages over a non-immersive system, then there is no need to use it.

The following applications for VR have been divided into four groups: engineering, entertainment, science and training.

12.1 Engineering

The virtual domain is not new to the engineering community: for two decades they have successfully applied CAD and CAM techniques to design and manufacturing processes. Preparing 2D schematics of wiring diagrams, floor layouts, designs for PCBs and ASICs are everyday activities in engineering industries. Similarly, 3D CAD systems have been used to design everything from a shoe to an oil rig.

The computer has now become the most powerful design tool ever created. This is not just because of its speed or its ability to display images – it is because of the computer's flexibility to change its role. It can be used to process text and organize documents; but the same machine can be used to develop line drawings, and even construct 3D objects. Geometric information from these objects can be used to control lathes and milling machines, and, with the process of stereo-lithography, create a real physical representation.

For these systems, the virtual domain has been nothing more than a framework for storing descriptions of 2D and 3D entities, and the workstation screen has just been a convenient projection space to view them. VR provides another role for the computer, whereby the virtual domain becomes a

3D space that can be explored by the user. Descriptions of engineering components that have been viewed as lifeless drawings or static perspective projections can now be visualized as animated objects. VR has opened a door to a virtual engineering space where objects can be manufactured, inspected, assembled, tested and subjected to all sorts of simulations.

The full potential of VR cannot be enjoyed today as hardware and software tools are still under development. Nevertheless, certain industries have seen the light and are developing their own systems. The following examples are just some of the projects being tackled by the engineering community.

12.1.1   Aero engine design

An aero engine involves years of design, and its operational lifetime is often measured in decades. The engines are designed to withstand incredible forces during operation, and must function in all types of weather, and over incredible ranges of temperature and atmospheric conditions. In the pursuit of safety, they are regularly removed from aircraft, serviced and replaced. Such operational procedures play an important factor in their purchase, and any reputation arising through difficulty of servicing is a serious cost disadvantage.

Although aero engines are designed with the latest CAD systems, full-size prototypes still play an important role in investigating all aspects of servicing. In 1994, McDonnell Douglas acquired a ProVision 100 VPX system to evaluate how an immersive environment could aid the design of new engine types. Initially, the system is to be used to explore procedures for installing and removing engines, especially for detecting potential interference with other components.

Removing an engine from an aircraft is a complex process, nevertheless, it can be simulated in a virtual environment. An engineer in the VE opens the engine door bay, positions a trailer under the engine bay, and jacks the trailer up to the proper height. Using virtual tools, the engineer removes the bolts securing the engine to its housing. The engine is connected to the trailer, then lowered and removed for service. Installation is a similar process performed in reverse. When removed, the virtual engine can be used to evaluate the ease with which certain components can be accessed and removed. Collision detection is a powerful technique for discovering whether specific tools can access certain engine parts, and discovering whether components can be easily removed.

The tangible benefits of introducing a VR system are fewer mock-ups and prototypes, earlier design testing and reduced costs.

Rolls-Royce: aero engine maintenance
Rolls-Royce use ComputerVision's CADDS4X system to design products such as their Trent aero engine. They also rely upon physical mock-ups to assess maintenance issues, before commencing the engine's manufacture. Although

these physical mock-ups do not function, their construction must be sound and accurate, which makes them very expensive to build. In 1992, Rolls-Royce approached ARRL (Advanced Robotics Research Laboratory, Salford, UK) now renamed InSys, Ltd, to see whether VR technology could remove the need to construct replicas of their engines.

The first stage in the feasibility study involved an investigation of the portability of the CADDS4X files of the Trent 800 civil engine onto ARRL's VR platform – Division's SuperVision system. This was a non-trivial exercise, owing in part to the solid modelling nature of CADDS4X. However, by using the CADDS4X stereo-lithography processing option, the first port of the Trent engine casing and lower bifurcation pipe assembly was achieved in the form of simple flat-shaded groups of polygons. Recent work has identified a more efficient and robust CADDS data conversion path, which is being refined at the time of writing.

A series of polygon optimization programs were written to improve the 'fly-through' speed of the virtual models. Additional routines were then written to colour-code individual pipe routes selectively, and to segment pipes into groups of objects, thereby allowing detail switching and their removal and manipulation by engineers. Plate 8 shows two views of the Trent 800 aero engine.

The feasibility study culminated in a successful demonstration of the VR system, and the work continues.

12.1.2 Submarine design

Vickers Shipbuilding and Engineering Limited (VSEL)

VSEL specialize in submarine design and refit planning, and employ physical models to investigate maintenance and ergonomic issues. Even though their models are one-fifth scale, when the original is a Trident nuclear submarine, the model remains a substantial structure. Model human figures are also used to evaluate how real humans cope with working in the confined spaces associated with submarines.

Like Rolls-Royce, VSEL approached ARRL to undertake a feasibility study to see if physical models could be replaced by VR technology. The system for the project included a Virtual Research Flight Helmet, a Polhemus Fastrak hand and head tracking system and a CyberGlove glove controller.

'Flying' through the virtual submarine did not seem to be be a realistic method of moving about the environment, and in the absence of an extended 3D tracking system, the concept of a 'cherry picker' was implemented. This consisted of a virtual gantry or crane to manoeuvre the VR user through the submarine. Although such a mechanism could not be used in practice, the metaphor was ideal for the feasibility study. While immersed, the user can look down to bring a simple virtual control panel into view, 'mounted' on the front rail of the cherry picker. By touching the controls on this panel, the user is able to move relative to the environment. In addition, the controls govern the level of detail presented to the user.

The use of virtual tools is being investigated in order to permit the release of bolt and bracket fittings, thereby unconstraining the pipe geometry and permitting further manual handling to occur. With the selected pipe free to move, collisions with surrounding pipework can be detected in real time, using an in-house collision preprocessor which greatly reduces the computational power required for collision detection.

Although an immersive experience provided valuable insight into the submarine's interior, by far the most successful portrayal of this particular geometry involved stereoscopic projection using Sharp LCD video projectors. The vision at VSEL is to use stereoscopic projection for group inspections and technical meetings, complemented by immersion when more detail is required to check that operational and ergonomic criteria have been satisfied, or when verification of the model is necessary to ensure optimum access and equipment removal. Plate 9 shows two interior views of the virtual submarine.

12.1.3 Architecture

CAD systems

Architectural design is a natural application for computers, and even in the early days of CAD, when software could cope only with 2D elevations, the benefits were very worth while. CAD systems play a central role in all major architectural practices, and provide architects with plans, sections, elevations, line perspectives and full-colour, rendered visualizations of interiors and exterior views. Apart from the obvious benefits of computer graphics, computer systems introduce the concepts of integrated databases, data exchange and scheduling tools, all within an interactive multi-user environment.

The marriage of form, function and space determine the design success of any architectural project – and, apart from computers, today's architects enjoy the benefits of modern building materials such as plastic, fibreglass, steel, aluminium, composites and reinforced concrete which enable them to explore for the first time new techniques for suspended ceilings, cantilevered structures and impressive glass atriums.

Architects have always been interested in the internal spaces of their buildings, and the way supporting structures can be exploited to sculpt these spaces. Free-hand sketches and perspective drawings were the only tools available to architects prior to computers. Now, most CAD systems can provide sophisticated diagrams and visualizations of any of the data associated with a building project.

VR systems

Now that architects are accustomed to working with interactive workstations, VR is a natural technological progression that brings them even closer to their virtual designs. Immersive displays will provide a much more accurate method for assessing the success of their designs. They will be able to walk through their buildings in real time and explore at first hand the vistas they envisaged during the building's conceptual design.

Illumination

Lighting plays a vital role in complementing a building's internal aesthetic, and architects have a very difficult task in predicting illumination levels on walls, ceilings and work surfaces. The orientation of a building, the juxtaposition of windows, external glass walls and lighting fittings all have to be taken into account in making these predictions.

Radiosity, which has always been a tool of architects, is now a familiar global illumination model in computer graphics. Even though the first attempts to render interiors of buildings took many hours for one image, modern algorithms are bringing radiosity into the real-time domain. VR systems already exist that are capable of exploring complex interiors that incorporate precomputed radiosity levels. The Real Light software system from ATMA Rendering Systems is a radiosity-based renderer that is easily integrated into a VR system. Plate 2 shows a typical view of a 3D interior that can be explored in real time.

Eventually, it will be possible to explore a virtual environment and adjust internal light fittings for position and intensity, and there is no reason why a virtual light meter should not be used to measure the new illumination levels.

Acoustics

The acoustic properties of buildings are extremely difficult to predict, and architects often turn to consultants specializing in this field. They in turn rely upon their professional experience and various mathematical tools for determining reverberation times, decay profiles and how electronic audio systems can be used to balance the frequency characteristics of a large auditorium.

The work on HRTFs has shown how audio signals can be processed to create binaural sound channels. When incorporated into a VR system, the user is able to associate these sounds with the visual virtual environment. Further sound processing algorithms can simulate the acoustic effects of reflections, reverberations and even how certain building materials influence the sound-proofing of rooms.

Matsushita Electric Works (MEW) have investigated the use of large display screens to immerse an audience of 30 people in a walk-through of a house. The house has several rooms, which can be explored in real time. The simulation environment provides accurate data on lighting, ventilation and acoustics. A filter model of sound for walls, doors and windows is used to simulate the normal transmission of sound through air. The model is evaluated at specific points throughout the virtual building, and filter parameters are interpolated during the walk-through. Plate 10 shows a view of the dining room that incorporates fixtures and fittings supplied by MEW.

Supermarket design

Founded in 1844, the CWS is a major UK business with a turnover of £3.25 billion, excluding its activities in banking and insurance. As a leading retailer of both food and non-food products they are continuously involved in the design of supermarkets and planning new interior layouts – a costly process. The position of a product cannot be left to chance, and, as there may be several thousand items to choose from, every device must be used to ensure that the shopper's gaze is enticed to explore the entire product range.

At a time when retail margins are tight and competition is high, the use of technologies such as VR can be seen as key to the continuing profitability and success of a business, such as the CWS. To assess the potential of VR, the CWS approached ARRL to implement a system for visualizing super-market interiors and shelf layouts. This was successfully completed and gave managers, product buyers and space planners a totally new framework for implementing their projects.

Another system concerned the ergonomics and 'context' prototyping of a new design of checkout for the CWS chain of Late Shops. As in the first project, initial database geometry and parent–child hierarchy definition activities were carried out using Superscape's VRT system. In close consulta-tion with the CWS point-of-sale manager, successive refinements to the model were made (using an in-house windows-based GUI) until the style, size and layout details were acceptable. The model was then ported into Division's dVS, implemented on an SGI Onyx computer. Plate 11 shows two views of the virtual supermarket.

The code developed by InSys accesses databases that contain geometric and textural information based upon internationally standardized Universal Product Codes (UPCs). Hence the demonstrator has been developed with existing industry standards well in mind. While each brand on sale has a unique texture (generated from digitized images or pattern catalogues), around 20 base geometries are thought sufficient to describe every product available. The retail industry actually recognizes a much smaller number (for example, cube, bottle, roll, pyramid, bag) for the purpose of space filling. These geometric constraints actually ease the porting of large numbers of products (rather than large product geometries) between different platforms and soft-ware architectures, promoting subsequent enhancements for real-time inter-active walk-throughs, such as detail management, object replacement and so on.

12.1.4 Human factors modelling

Jack

The human figure has always posed a tantalizing problem area for computer animation. It is very difficult to model, and to endow it with true-to-life animated behaviour is a daunting task. Although the animation community set themselves these problems as interesting challenges in the 1980s, the research is now finding another application in human factors modelling. The challenge today is to develop interactive environments where a fully jointed human figure can be used to evaluate virtual 3D worlds. Jack (see Section

11.2.2) is probably the most well-known system available today, and was developed by the Center for Computer Graphics Research, at the University of Pennsylvania.

Physical attributes

Jack is a virtual 3D human model incorporating 68 joints – 16 of which are in one hand. The torso is segmented and constrained to move within the limits associated with real humans. Joints can be positioned by translations and rotations within predefined constraints, and limb segments possess attributes such as centre of mass and moment of inertia. With these qualities, the model can be subjected to dynamic simulations to reveal its behaviour under changes in velocity. Apart from these powerful dynamic features, Jack's anthropometry can be based upon a particular individual or male or female percentiles. An internal database of human characteristics was derived from the General Forces Data ANSUR-88, compiled from 10 000 people.

Inverse kinematics

Jack is animated using inverse kinematics and possesses various motor reflexes such as grabbing, reaching while retaining balance, direction stepping and re-orienting behaviours. Thus if instructed to lean forward to grasp an object, it will automatically attempt to retain its balance by adjusting its centre of gravity.

When grabbing an object, collision detection is used to ensure that Jack's hand does not penetrate the object being grasped. When its hands are attached to a steering wheel, for example, and the wheel is turned, the entire body will adjust to accommodate the wheel's new orientation.

Ergonomics

When Jack is placed inside a virtual environment, it is possible to explore human factors such as reach space, field of view, joint torque load and collision. Thus it can quickly be established whether it can reach controls and see specific parts of moving machinery. It is also possible to discover if the body is placed under any painful strain. This is possible as realistic loadings are known for the joints and limbs, and during any virtual exercise these forces and torques can be monitored for potential overload conditions. Plate 12 shows Jack being used to evaluate the ergonomics of a car interior.

Collision avoidance

Collision avoidance is a property where Jack automatically moves to avoid being hit by a moving object. For instance, if a ball is thrown at the head, Jack will automatically take avoiding action. Furthermore, Jack can be set walking within an environment and instructed to avoid obstacles such as walls or furniture. It can even be endowed with 'virtual sight' that enables it to search out an object hidden away behind a wall. This is implemented by 'force fields'. The hidden object emits an attractive field, while obstructing objects emit a repulsing field.

We can imagine many scenarios where Jack could be used to evaluate the suitability of an interior for future human use, or the practicality of servicing a complex mechanical structure. Environments that come to mind include the design of cockpits, cars, kitchens, aero engines, ships, spacecraft and military vehicles. In fact, anywhere ergonomic issues are important.

Jack has recently been evaluated as a virtual soldier for training military personnel in various combat duties. When projected onto large video screens, Jack is animated in real time to mimic behaviour patterns associated with weapon handling. Real soldiers can then train with Jack to develop appropriate combat skills.

Perhaps it will not be long before we have a virtual assistant to help us undertake a whole range of virtual experiments. Why, for example, should it not be possible to assemble a structure with the aid of someone like Jack? We could even instruct a team of Jacks to collectively solve a problem for us!

Whatever the future holds, virtual humans will play an important role in VR applications, and today we are only at the beginning of a very exciting era of computer simulation.

12.1.5 Industrial concept design

In terms of choice, the car industry has moved from one extreme to another. Henry Ford's secret was mass production of one model type, with one colour. Today's car industry prides itself on its ability to give customers exactly what they want, even to the choice of seat covering, alloy wheels and type of CD player!

To provide this level of flexibility requires complex systems support, and manufacturing a continuous range of car body shapes requires a constant evaluation of concept designs. Fortunately, computers are part of both activities, which is why VR is perceived as a complementary technology.

All sorts of techniques are used to visualize concept designs, from artists' impressions and scale models, to life-size working replicas. VR provides another approach, and although it still requires some form of modelling, it does remove the need for any physical representation.

Researchers at the Computer Aided Industrial & Information Design Centre at Coventry University are working in collaboration with Division Ltd on an immersive VR system for use in industrial concept design and evaluation. This collaborative project will investigate how designers can interact with virtual concept cars, and how such designs can be evaluated for functional correctness, ease of assembly and even maintainability. In the later stages of the project, the research team expect to use VR to check assembly and fit of their designs in moving or articulated components such as doors. It will also be possible to determine if a mechanic can actually reach certain components. It is hoped that the cost savings VR will bring over conventional mock-up development will allow earlier trials to be performed, increasing design quality and efficiency. Plate 13 illustrates a concept car design that can be explored within an immersive VR system.

12.1.6 Telecoms engineering

BNR Europe manufacture and supply telecommunication equipment and services. In the past, planning the installation of a new system has been carried out using a CAD system to design the new products, then building physical models and placing all the equipment into the available space. Using a desktop VR system, they are able to visualize the allotted room and all the equipment, and then make decisions about possible layouts, cable runs and maintenance access.

12.2 Entertainment

The success of an arcade game has normally been measured in the income derived per hour per unit area of floor space it requires. Hidden within this figure is the game's ability to induce a player to return over and over again to achieve a higher score. During this process the player is kept interested and involved in the game, and is willing to pay for this pleasure. The lifetime of some games extends beyond a year, and more than covers the initial development costs.

Designing these games is a skilled business, and requires an intimate knowledge of the psychological make-up of the typical player. It is not necessarily about technology, for some very exciting racing games employ simple graphics, and yet are so compelling that there is always time to have just one more go!

In a busy arcade centre, dead time means lost revenue; therefore the time required to restart the game for the same or next customer must be minimal. A game should also be enjoyed by the passive watching crowd, as hopefully they will be induced to try their skill and propagate the game's attraction.

Using a game for the first time must exploit the player's intuitive skills. Cluttered screen layouts or complex controls are quickly shunned by the experienced player, and the game soon becomes an isolated feature of the arcade centre.

Against this backdrop of money, noise, excitement, obsessive behaviour and a knowledgeable customer base, the introduction of VR posed some new problems for the industry. Arcade owners had to consider questions such as: how could expensive HMDs be introduced into a busy, physical environment? What games would succeed? What game strategies would attract the player back? What were the health risks, if any? How could the immersive experience be enjoyed by a watching audience? What sort of customer throughput could be expected? Perhaps the most important question of all to the client was: how long does it take before the system is making a profit?

These were all realistic questions to ask of a revolutionary technology that surfaced at the start of the 1990s. Today, many of the questions have been answered, and both arcade games and VR have progressed. There is no doubt in anyone's mind that entertainment is destined to become a massive market for virtual reality. Like most applications however, this will not happen overnight, as it will depend upon the growth of other technologies and consumer market forces.

It is noteworthy that parallel with the development of single user, immersive VR systems – motion theatres – are providing an alternative scenario for entertaining groups of people. Although they are large, and have an initial high cost, their throughput, which is several hundred people per hour, has attractive financial strengths. Traditionally, these simulator rides are passive, and each group of people receives the same experience. However, interactive rides exist, where individuals can interact with real-time computer graphics.

The future, then, looks very exciting. VR technology will continue to stimulate new game formats, where single and networked users will compete with one another, while sophisticated motion theatres will provide an alternative experience.

12.2.1   Computer animation

Over the past 20 years or so, animators have used computer graphics techniques to recreate historic events, tell stories about modern life and take us forward in time to futuristic space cities. Their imaginative storyboards kept advancing the frontiers of computer graphics, and resulted in new algorithms for modelling environments and animating objects. This has played an important role in the development of VR systems, as it has demonstrated the wealth of imaginary objects and landscapes that can be stored in a computer system.

However, we must be very careful in making comparisons between computer animation and virtual reality. To begin with, computer animation sequences are developed on a frame-by-frame basis, which entails laying down on video or film single frames, which, when played back at a suitable speed, create the desired animation. VR, on the other hand, is a real-time environment, where animated movement is a natural feature of the experience. Many of the behaviours associated with objects in computer animation, such as walking, facial expression, bouncing balls, falling objects and sea states, are often the result of sophisticated procedures, or the painstaking adjustment of parameters on individual frames. This is why weeks or months are needed to create an animated sequence that may last only a minute or so.

Rendering times of 10 minutes per frame is a ratio of 15 000 : 1 when compared to real-time rendering, but this does not mean that there is no place for VR technology in computer animation. In fact, it has already been demonstrated that VR could have a dramatic influence upon the future of computer animation.

Take, for example, the problem of imparting a 3D cartoon character with human-like behaviour, such as walk cycles, hand gestures, or facial expressions, that remain in synchronization with a soundtrack. Non-VR techniques used to solve these problems have included inverse kinematics for walking and runing (Girard and Maciejewski, 1985), muscle models for facial expression (Waters, 1987) and free-form deformation, which can bend and twist an object into new orientations.

Although these solutions have provided interesting research projects, they have not resulted in an intuitive tool set that can be used by the animation community. Instead of writing software procedures, the VR approach couples the animator directly to the real-time virtual domain. For example, the output channels of an interactive glove can be used to control specific parts of a 3D polygonal model in real time. These movements can be practised until the desired motion is obtained. The successful motion parameters can then be stored within the animation system and integrated with other elements of the animation script.

By monitoring the motion of specific human joints with trackers such as Ascension's Flock of Birds, a virtual character can be given very lifelike behaviours. Making the character walk or dance or perform any other movement can then be simulated, and is limited only by the ability of the human model. The digital nature of the tracking data means that it can be further modified by software to shorten, lengthen, introduce pauses, emphasize, reverse and edit it with other sequences.

Adaptive Optics Associates manufacture the Multi-Trax real-time motion capture system. This uses near-infrared CCD cameras to detect the motion of reflective markers attached to an animator's body. Twin cameras monitor the animator and output the 2D image coordinates of the markers to a host computer. From this data it is possible to compute the 3D position of the original markers. As this data is output at the rate of 30 Hz, it can easily be used to control the motion of a virtual body. This means that computer animation can be created at the time of broadcast, and integrated with conventional video images. Plate 14 shows the FaceTrax single camera system being used with SimGraphics' VActor Expression real-time animation software running on an SGI system.

The work of Saulnier, Viaud and Geldreich (1994) has shown that it is possible to extract facial control parameters from a live video signal. In their approach, a subject is monitored by a video camera. From these images it is possible to determine head movements and mouth deformations, which are then used to animate some virtual clone. The computer graphics clone may be either symbolic, in which case it is based on a geometric model, or realistic, in which case it is endowed with a muscular basis. In the latter case, the facial surface is represented by a network of springs. Each muscle is modelled by forces, and muscular deformations are calculated by solving dynamic equations for the given system. The muscular deformations are then precalculated to obtain a system capable of real-time display. Finally, facial texture is mapped onto the polygonal representation of the face. Plate 17 shows the animator and the computer-generated face in action.

12.2.2   Games systems

CyberTron

CyberTron is an immersive VR game manufactured by StrayLight Corporation. The player wears an HMD and stands inside a gyro mechanism, which moves in sympathy with the user's body weight and inertia. Players must 'fly' themselves through obstacles, tunnels and mazes, while facing clever virtual opponents, gathering treasure and solving puzzles. The hardware platform is from SGI, and the CyberTrons can be networked to support multi-player games. Current game software consists of Wing-Nuts, Cozmik-Debris and Bonk. Plate 16 shows a CyberTron system.

Head Mount Based Theatre

In 1994, StrayLight Corp. designed a 26-seat immersive theatre including individual high-resolution HMDs for each viewer. The theatre was built for CableTron, Inc. as part of a presentation at their Interop + Networld trade show booth. The theatre can handle in excess of 300 people per hour, and incorporates sanitary head mounts for the HMDs.

Virtuality Entertainment Ltd

Virtuality Entertainment Ltd. have pioneered the development of VR game systems, and today their products are found throughout the world. Their current systems include the Series 2000 which are described in Section 10.4.4.

The VR games include X-treme Strike, Virtuality Boxing and Zone Hunter. They are all 3D immersive games, with texture-mapped graphics and 32 channel stereo sound. X-treme Strike immerses the player in an inter-galactic warfare game; Virtuality Boxing is a world boxing game for one or two players; and Zone Hunter is a race against time in the 21st century.

12.2.3   Television

The television industry has over 50 years' experience in building 'virtual' worlds out of wood and canvas. When painted and illuminated they pass as acceptable substitutes for the real thing, but, like the real thing, they require considerable storage space. The flight simulation industry had a similar problem with the manufacture and storage of the scale models used in their early visual systems. Such models are no longer used, and modern flight simulators rely totally upon virtual environments.

For many years, television designers have used DVE (Digital Video Effects) to composite an image from different video sources. Chromakey, with its ubiquitous blue backgrounds, plays an important role in the integration of these images, especially in news and current-affairs programmes. Digital Chromakey can use any colour, although blue is still prevalent. In recent years, real-time computer graphics has been used to illustrate news items, where, for example, ground vehicles and aircraft are animated over 3D terrain.

These sequences, though, have not been integrated with any other form of image source. However, moves are afoot to change all of this.

Real-time computer cartoons

The Media Lab in Paris has developed a technique where a computer cartoon character is animated at transmission time by a puppeteer. The puppeteer is fitted with various sensors that, like any tracking system, can be used to modify a computer 3D model. A similar system is used by the BBC with 'Ratz the Cat', where a cat's head is animated in real time during a live presentation.

Virtual sets

The use of virtual sets in TV is not new but, up to now, such sets have been nothing more than a 2D backdrop against which live actors could move. Multi-layering techniques have enabled actors to be masked by intermediate layers of 2D video scenery to create a sense of depth, but this has been used in the cartoon industry for decades.

Significant advances are now being made where the motion and orientation of a TV camera has been used to integrate virtual objects with real scenes. The Institut National de l'Audiovisuel (INA) has already demonstrated such a system. To understand the process, imagine a real TV camera located in a simple set containing walls and pillars. A replica of the set and the camera are modelled at a virtual level. If the virtual camera possesses a knowledge of the optical characteristics of the real camera's lens, then any computer-generated image should match the real camera's image. Furthermore, if the real camera is tracked in 3D, its motion and orientation can be used to control the virtual camera. If a virtual object, such as a plane, is now animated in the virtual world, as there is an accurate overlap, the real and virtual images can be integrated with the those from the virtual camera. Any occultation that occurs at a virtual level will result in the virtual object being masked by any real object, so long as that object exists in the real world.

This pioneering work is paving the way for various techniques where virtual and real 3D worlds can be integrated in real time. For example, the MONA LISA (MOdelling NAturaL Images for Synthesis and Animation) project is already investigating the tools needed for using virtual sets with TV.

The ramifications of these developments for the TV industry are immense, as it could revolutionize the whole process of set building. Although it is difficult to imagine virtual sets replacing all physical sets, it is not difficult to see how virtual sets could play a valuable role in many TV productions.

TV training and rehearsal environments

As with other training scenarios, it is often necessary to construct a physical replica of an operational environment, whether it be a submarine, tank or an air-traffic control tower. Images external to the submarine, tank or control tower have to be created to complete the illusion, and normally can be simulated at a virtual level. Translating these established techniques to a television scenario suggests that a virtual studio could be used for rehearsals and training personnel without any dependence upon a real studio.

At the heart of this environment would be a virtual studio, equipped with flats, tables, chairs, cycloramas, staircases and so on. Other studio artefacts, such as cameras, lights, boom stands, monitors and microphones would complete the environment. Using interactive VR tools, a studio could be configured to create a typical production environment.

Real-time graphics engines could then render views of the virtual studio from the viewpoint of one of the virtual cameras using virtual lights. The virtual studio could be used for evaluating camera moves involving tracking, panning and zooms, investigating lighting strategies and exploring shadow footprints. There is no reason why virtual actors should not be introduced to recreate realistic human behaviours. This would provide the opportunity to rehearse camera positioning, lining up shots, fades, dissolves and lens depth-of-field.

When used as a production resource, the virtual cameras could be slaved to real cameras shooting actors against blue backgrounds and the two locked images integrated using Chromakey.

12.3 Science

Scientific visualization is a well-defined domain of computer graphics, where various types of data are interpreted using images. For example, an aero engine's turbine blade subjected to an FEA simulation is a natural candidate for visualizing stresses using false colours. Indeed, such tools are an essential part of any modern CAD system. Scientific visualization encompasses such techniques and embraces many more that address the complex, multi-dimensional data sets being created by computer simulations.

Scientific visualization is used to interpret static and animated 2D and 3D data sets from the worlds of cartography, remote sensing, archaeology, molecular modelling, medicine, oceanography and CFD. It is only through the development of powerful graphics workstations that some of the images in these domains can now be rendered in real time. Thus when a parameter is adjusted within a simulation exercise, an immediate response appears in the image. The closed loop created by the user, simulation software and visualization package provides a very efficient problem-solving environment.

If the user is now interfaced to the images through the immersive technology of VR, even more benefits are possible, for being located in the virtual domain means that the user's actions are interpreted as actual 3D events, rather than as cursor movements on a screen-based display device. VR visualization software tools are already under development. Some will overlap with other subject areas such as medical imaging, but others will create a paradigm shift where the user becomes part of the simulation process.

Any computer user needs little convincing about the benefits of real-time interactive systems. A delay, whether it is measured in minutes, seconds or milliseconds, is frustrating, as it disrupts the flow of interaction. A true real-time VR system simply makes the user a natural part of the computational process – not a passive observer, but someone who interactively modifies parameters and observes the resulting action.

If we develop this ideal scenario with a simulation model, we create a powerful environment where a concept can be simulated, observed and tested, all in one process. Placing the user within the virtual domain is not just to make the exercise interesting, but provides a viewpoint for revealing new insights, new relationships and new patterns that could have remained hidden without this advantage.

Future VR visualization tools will transform the way we process and interpret data, whether it be from laboratory instruments such as X-ray machines, engineering test machines or wind tunnels, or from real-time data acquisition, space exploration, CFD, FEA or remote sensing. That we can be part of the simulation or data collection, and can react to events that would have hitherto gone unnoticed, will increase our understanding of natural and artificial processes.

12.3.1 Computational neuroscience

Computational neuroscience uses simulation models of single neurons or networks to discover how the nervous system works. Visualization plays an important part in this process, and VR is being investigated at the University of Illinois at Chicago as a suitable tool (De Schutter, 1992).

The research group opted for a non-immersive system, as the long-term use of an HMD caused too much discomfort. Their system is essentially a 'fish tank' VR system, with stereo images displayed upon a workstation and the user's head tracked with a Logitech ultrasonic tracker. Stereographics glasses, with a synchronizing infra-red emitter, provide the stereo images.

The software environment is GENESIS (GEneral NEural SImulation System) developed at Caltech. GENESIS was developed as a research tool to provide a standard and flexible means of constructing realistic simulations of biological neural systems, from subcellular components to whole cells and networks of cells.

Projects have included the visualization of electric fields in freshwater fish (*apteronotus leptorhynchus*), simulations of the piriform cortex and the complex spike in a cerebellar Purkinje cell.

Visualization of electrical fields
In the freshwater fish project, the VR system was used to understand how the fish uses the phase and amplitude information from the electric organ discharge for electrolocation and communication. In real life, when the fish swims by an object, the object perturbs the current distribution, therefore casting an 'image' onto the fish's surface, which is detected by an electro-receptor array. The VE contains a model of the fish surface and midplane in which the electric organ discharge potential is simulated by a number of current sources. In the visualization, a virtual object is interactively inserted

into the midplane where the perturbation to the electric field is calculated. The object image is then displayed on the fish's surface, representing the difference between the potential on the skin with and without the object present.

Visualization of a piriform cortex simulation

The piriform cortex is a three-layered cortical area which receives its input from the olfactory bulb, which in turn receives signals from the nose. The principal neuron of the piriform cortex is the pyramidal cell that receives afferent input from the bulb and makes connections with other local and distant pyramidal cells within the piriform cortex. The simulation model employs 135 pyramidal cells organized in a 15×9 array, partitioned into 5 compartments. Each compartment receives a distinct kind of synaptic input and is located in a different sublayer of the cortex. The visualization shows the array of cells with membrane potential or synaptic conductance, and, as random inputs are triggered, waves of activity can be seen to propagate throughout the network.

Visualization of a complex spike in a cerebellar Purkinje cell

The Purkinje cell is the largest neuron in the cerebellar cortex and is its only output element. A detailed model was created upon an Intel Touchstone Delta supercomputer and used for simulations. Data from this model was then visualized on the 'fish tank' VR system to allow the membrane potentials to be investigated using a virtual electrode. The system also allowed the user to load other neuron structures and their corresponding firing data.

The main thrust of these projects has been to explore the use of low-cost VR systems as a visualization tool. Head tracking and stereo images create a credible 3D virtual space that simplifies the interpretation and understanding of very complex data sets.

12.3.2 Molecular modelling

Although quantum mechanics has transformed the way physicists visualize atomic particles and their interactions, molecular structures can still be accurately visualized using simple 3D geometric forms. In fact, chemists still employ a 2D notation for explaining how valency bonding controls molecular structures.

Spatial connectivity provides a powerful tool for predicting new molecular compounds, and recently Glaxo Group Research, the University of York and Division Ltd have collaborated to explore how VR can help in this role.

The traditional approach to molecular modelling is through the use of a workstation and an interactive graphics system. The VR approach is to immerse the scientist such that he or she can interact directly with the graphical representation of the molecule.

The aim of this work is to design systems using existing stereo imaging facilities, which can be developed to use VR systems. Laboratory workers will then be able to use the more intuitive user interface of VR systems to understand the structure of macromolecules and how their structure relates to their function.

Under the project, three molecular modelling systems will be developed: a system for building models of macromolecules that satisfy 'low resolution' experimental and other constraints; a protein visualization system for natural and effective representation and analysis of protein structure; and a system for exploring similarities between molecules, in terms of both structure and friction. It is hoped that this will provide a greater insight into the space configurations that influence the ability to engage new atoms into a molecular structure. Plate 15 illustrates how a scientist can be visualized when interacting with a virtual molecule.

12.3.3 Phobias

A phobia is an intense irrational fear of something, such as a snake or spider, or of an environment, such as a lift or large room. Some people who suffer from agoraphobia (the fear of open spaces) can be so traumatized by the condition that they rarely leave their homes, and eventually become housebound. The treatment of these anxiety-based behaviours requires sensitive handling over a long period of time. At each stage of the programme, the patient slowly learns to tolerate increasing levels of exposure to the relevant problem, until the anxiety disappears and confidence returns.

The Communication Research Group at Nottingham University and the Institute of Psychiatry have investigated the use of a VR system to cure different phobias. Early trials have been used to cure people with a phobia of spiders. The model for the cure is to allow the patient to wear an HMD which displays a virtual spider in a form that can be tolerated without causing any fear. After each exposure to the virtual creature, its realism is increased until the patient's tolerance level is sufficient to cope with the real thing.

Virtual therapy

Acrophobia is the abnormal fear of heights, and it prevents sufferers from driving over bridges, looking out from tall buildings and travelling inside glass-enclosed lifts. Treatment for this condition requires sensitivity and considerable patience on the part of the therapist. However, VR could open up totally new ways of treating this phobia.

The Kaiser-Permanente Medical Group in Marin County, California, USA, have developed a trial system which evaluates the use of VR in the treatment of acrophobia. Research, headed by Dr Ralph Lamson, has been shown to help over 90% of participants to reach self-assigned treatment goals. These include walking over a narrow plank and crossing a suspension bridge spanning a deep gorge.

According to Dr Lamson:

> Virtual reality gives the individual an opportunity to approach the thing they are
> fearful of in a VE. Being immersed in a virtual, feared situation is very close

to the real situation. After the virtual therapy, participants feel as if they have already had a success in overcoming their fear. This is a strong confidence builder.

After successfully 'surviving' their virtual encounter with heights and depths, 32 participants faced 2 real-world goals, and over 90% were successful.

12.3.4   Telepresence

A Telepresence-controlled Remotely Operated Vehicle (TROV) is being used by NASA to explore 240 metres below the surface of McMurdo Sound near Ross Island. The modified mini-submarine is steered by remote control, and its on-board cameras are guided by head movements of the land-based crew member. A second team of scientists based at the NASA Ames laboratory at Moffett Field, California, can also control the TROV directly, or by computer. Sense8's WorldToolKit has been used to model underwater terrain of Antartica, which is used as a reference model to steer the TROV.

12.3.5   Ultrasound echography

Ultrasound echography is a non-invasive technique for obtaining real-time views of the interior of the human body. Typically, it is used to view the progress of a foetus in a pregnant woman, and although ultrasound is relatively safe compared with other imaging modalities such as X-rays, there are still doubts about its total safety for the unborn baby.

In practice, the patient's abdomen is scanned with a handheld probe and the data is displayed upon a monochrome monitor. Because ultrasound imaging has a low signal to noise ratio and poor spatial resolution, the final image requires careful analysis and skilled interpretation. Even though the displayed image is a 2D view of the patient's interior, it is possible to derive information about the shape and size of various features, and the existence of any abnormalities.

Dr Olaf von Ramm's group at Duke University is developing a real-time 3D scanner (Von Ramm *et al.*, 1991) which will capture volumetric data from the body's interior, similar to that obtained from a CT scan. In anticipation of this device, Bajura *et al.* (1992) have developed an experimental HMD system that permits the viewing of this data superimposed over the patient.

The system will have access to a collection of 2D ultrasound data slices that form a 3D volume. An image generator then renders a view of this data set from a viewpoint determined by the position and orientation of an HMD worn by the medical practitioner. These synthetic images are then video mixed with images relayed from two miniature cameras attached to the HMD. The result is a composite image that creates the effect of seeing inside the patient's body. The critical aspects of this technology concern display resolution, rendering speed, lag, tracking range and visual cues:

(1) The display resolution of HMDs needs to be in the order of 0.5 to 1 million pixels per eye if the technique is to provide real benefits to the medical community.

(2) Very powerful rendering engines are needed to convert the volumetric data into stereoscopic views.

(3) System lag destroys the illusion created by the image composition. On the one hand, the video cameras are supplying images in real time, while on the other, the synthetic images are subject to the tracking lag and the latency of the rendering engine's pipeline. A possible solution is to delay the video signals electronically before the edit is made, and another concerns the use of predictive tracking for the HMD.

(4) Tracker technology still imposes restrictions on the range, stability and sensitivity to local metallic structures, which, in turn, creates problems in the accurate integration of the two image types.

(5) The research project has already identified important visual conflicts introduced by compositing two video images. Although this is a standard practice in the television industry, it has taken many years to develop the right technology. We now know that edge quality, colour balance, contrast ratios and shading all influence the ease with which the brain can accept multiple images as one.

Recent work by Nelson and Elvins (1993) demonstrates that ultrasound data acquisition will play an important role in the future of medical imaging. Their work has addressed the visualization of these 3D data sets and, in particular, the problems of multiplanar slicing, surface fitting and volume rendering.

12.4 Training

Training is an important part of everyone's life – whether it is learning to drive a car, use a computer, fire a missile or master laparoscopic surgery. Some aspects of training can be acquired in a classroom or from a book, but there is no substitute for training with the real thing. Or is there?

The training/simulation industry believes that there are some excellent substitutes for the real thing, and have been using them for many years. Training simulators are used for planes, submarines, power plants, tanks, helicopters, ships, cranes, trains, surgery, endoscopes and air traffic control. Such simulators use a replica of the real operational environment and real-time computers to model its dynamics.

Training through simulation provides significant benefits over other methods. For example, a hazardous environment, such as a nuclear power station, or an aircraft landing in fog can be accurately simulated without any danger to the trainee. Computer software provides the flexibility to structure training programmes and even monitor and measure the progress of a training session. Because simulators are so forgiving in the way they tolerate mistakes, trainees can experience first-hand why certain procedures must not be used in the real world.

Many simulators employ computer-generated images as part of the training process, and the concept of a virtual environment is nothing new to the industry. However, immersive VR systems will provide new training paradigms for existing and new training applications, which are already appearing. The following are just some of the exciting projects being investigated.

12.4.1   Fire Service College

The Fire Service College at Moreton in the Marsh, United Kingdom, is using Superscape's desktop VR system as a training tool. In particular, the system is being used to demonstrate the principles of fire engineering, escape strategies, fire modelling, human behaviour and spatial awareness of complex buildings. Prior to this system, training methods were based upon diagrams and slide presentations.

In conjunction with the VR system, the college is using the VEGAS (Virtual Egress Analysis and Simulation) software system from Colt VR, Ltd. VEGAS provides a means of modelling human behavioural response under different emergency conditions. Fires can then be started in a virtual building, and the user can assess how people would react, and whether or not the risk can be lessened by alternative positioning of escape routes.

VEGAS can handle the following parameters: the physical size of the occupants, people's speed of movement during escape; the level of aggression (pushing and resiliency) during escape; people's reaction to the fire and other people (for example, survivalist or behaving as a family group); the size and location of the fire itself and, hence, the formation of barriers such as smoke and fumes; smoke and toxic fume exposure limits; the escape routes; and barriers such as furniture and doorways.

12.4.2   Flight simulation

The flight simulator shown in Plate 1, provides a training environment where pilots can acquire flying skills to convert from one plane to another. For example, a pilot familiar with flying a Boeing 737 can learn to fly a Boeing 747, 767 or 777 by training in a simulator.

To achieve this, the simulator must look and behave like the real plane, which requires that it incorporates a cockpit identical to that used in reality. The cockpit is enclosed in a cabin mounted upon a motion system driven by hydraulic rams. The pumps actuating the rams are in turn driven by signals derived from the software flight model.

It is possible to purchase from the aircraft manufacturer a numerical database describing the dynamic behaviour of the craft when taxiing on the ground, or flying in the air. Similar data is available from the manufacturers of the aero engines. Collectively, this data describes characteristics such as the rate of climb, banking angles, yaw characteristics, descent rates, moments of inertia, engine temperatures and fuel burn rates. The flight model uses this reference data and the positions of the flight controls to simulate the behaviour of the plane.

It is not difficult to imagine a pilot seated in a simulator moving the flight controls and seeing the instruments show realistic changes in airspeed, altitude, horizon angle, fuel temperature and consumption. If this is complemented with realistic force feedback on the flight controls, and other forces generated by velocity changes in the simulated plane, the pilot can easily become immersed in the experience. Flying, however, also depends upon visual contact with the outside world, especially during landing and taking-off scenarios.

In early flight simulators, model boards were used as part of the visual display system. A scale model was built to represent a generic airport that included terminal buildings, runways, taxiways, surrounding terrain, roads and buildings. A video camera was moved over the model to mimic the motion of the simulated plane, and the video images were projected upon a screen positioned in front of the cockpit. Although this was reasonably effective, there were many disadvantages with physical models.

In the 1980s, with the arrival of real-time computer graphics, physical models were replaced by virtual models that provided a new approach to image generation and display systems. Today, a customer can purchase a simulator and a variety of virtual environments for specific international airports such as London Heathrow, Dallas or Hong Kong. These 3D models are loaded into an image generator which can fly over them with a scene update rate of 60 Hz.

As cockpits are fitted with forward-facing and side-facing windows the simulator must provide images that can be viewed through all of these windows. An efficient method of achieving this is to place a panoramic spherical mirror around the cockpit to provide 200° of horizontal view and 50° of vertical view. Computer-generated images are then projected upon a spherical back-projection screen situated above the cockpit and out of view of the pilot. When the pilot gazes into the mirror, he or she sees the image formed on the screen, and is completely immersed in the VE. As the runway is the nearest object seen by a pilot in a plane, the images are collimated to appear as though they are located at infinity. In reality this cannot be achieved and collimation is about 20 m. Figure 12.1 shows a cut-away view of a simulation display system.

There are many advantages of working in the virtual domain, some of which are as follows:

- *Accuracy* The airport models can be built with great accuracy as they are based upon plans and CAD data used to construct the airport in the first place. They can also be easily updated as airports are developed with extra runways and terminal buildings.

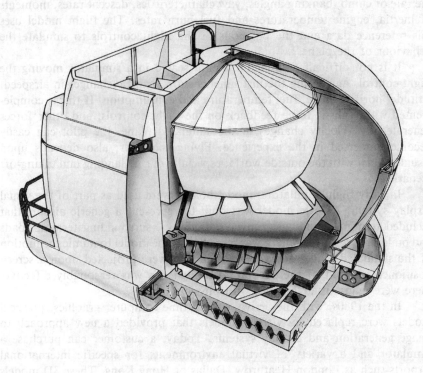

Figure 12.1 This cut-away view of a simulator's display system shows the spherical back-projection screen above the cockpit, and the spherical mirror which encloses the cockpit. (Courtesy Thomson Training & Simulation.)

- *Interaction* As with many virtual environments, we often require to know about collisions with objects. In the case of flight simulation, the pilot needs to know when the simulated craft touches the runway, and also if its wing tips touch another craft or buildings while taxiing. Another form of interaction concerns the runway landing lights which change their colour depending on the approach angle of the plane.

- *Animated features* The VE can be animated to include other planes, ground vehicles, marshallers and motorway traffic. Animated sequences are used to show rotating radar dishes, the lowering and raising of landing gear and sea states.

- *Weather effects* Something that was impossible with physical scale models was the simulation of weather effects. In the virtual domain it is possible to recreate rain, snow, lightning, clouds, fog, ground mist and scud with effective realism.

- *Time of day and year* Simply by changing a few parameters in the database it is possible to alter lighting conditions from bright sunlight to dusk, and to night-time conditions. With the aid of texture maps, a model can be overlaid with photographic textures that reflect seasonal changes.

The modern full-flight simulator has shown that very high levels of realism are possible using virtual environments. Furthermore, it is possible to integrate vision, sound, force feedback and motion to great effect. This, however, is only commercially viable in an industry regulated to maintain high levels of safety, and is a cost that can be spread over a large international community.

12.4.3 Medicine

Medicine has always found excellent uses for computer graphics, whether it has been in the use of paint programs for predicting the effects of plastic surgery, or in the use of volume rendering to visualize CT data. With the progress of both disciplines, more esoteric applications have emerged, and there is no doubt that we are now moving towards an era where very advanced ideas are being considered.

Today, virtual reality technology creates the possibility of developing training simulators where surgeons can develop surgical skills without harming animals or human beings. Systems are being investigated where real-world images are overlaid with 3D data sets derived by real-time scanners which will provide physicians with 'X-ray vision'. Head-coupled endoscopes have already been used to assist surgeons in laparoscopic operations, and work has already begun to develop miniature robots that will help surgeons perform operations through telepresence.

It will be impossible to investigate all the developments taking place in medicine, therefore this section concentrates on an endoscopic and a laparoscopic simulator.

Colonoscopy

Colonoscopy concerns the investigation of the human colon with an endoscope. The colonoscopist, the endoscope operator, must be skilled in the use of the endoscope if the patient is to have a pain-free examination, and not be put at any risk. A trainee colonoscopist can practise on mechanical teaching models, which, unfortunately, do not accurately reproduce the pathology of the human body. Often the teaching models are transparent, which creates an artificial environment for acquiring the skill base. They are further limited by the one model of the colon.

A computer-based simulator has been under investigation for several years to see whether the virtual domain could overcome the disadvantages associated with mechanical models. Gillies and Williams (1987) investigated the modelling of a colonoscope using splines. This model was extended by Poon *et al.* (1988) to incorporate the concept of an articulated body constructed from rigid linear links. Further work by Poon (1991) incorporated the modelling of the colonoscope as an articulated chain, which enabled a kinematic and/or dynamic model to specify its motion. The acceleration of each link was calculated to provide the forces and torques acting on the links, and numerical integration was used to derive the velocity and positions of each link.

Simulating the colon presents some non-trivial modelling problems. To begin with, it is elastic and very flexible; it lengthens and shortens depending on how the endoscope is moved; it is constrained to remain in position by various attachments inside the abdominal cavity; and it contains flexible loops. Such a structure requires a model that can support non-rigid and deformable bodies. Furthermore, it must be possible for the structure to be analysed to provide the physical simulation dynamics in real time. This can be used to provide the information for force feedback to the operator. For the moment, the research continues. But as our understanding of modelling human tissue progresses, there is real hope for a training simulator based upon a virtual environment.

A laparoscopic simulator

The medical community has witnessed countless changes over the past two decades, and has included advances in medicines, non-invasive views of the body's interior and minimally invasive surgical techniques. Endoscopic techniques have their origins in the eighteenth century, and, two centuries later, it has become an everyday surgical procedure to view the interior of the body through a flexible fibre optic cable and video camera.

It was probably a natural development from endoscopic procedures to attempt to pass surgical instruments through the abdominal cavity and undertake simple operations. Such laparoscopic surgery is standard practice throughout the western world for the removal of gall bladders. These procedures, however, require surgeons to perform their surgery by looking at video images relayed to monitors from an endoscope. Some of their instruments are based upon traditional instruments fitted with long thin extensions. The instruments are passed through a special sheath that directs them into the body's interior, which is inflated using carbon dioxide. The actual hole in the skin and tissue is in the order of 1–3 cm wide – hence the name 'key-hole surgery'. The surgeon operates the instruments by closely monitoring the images displayed on a monitor.

The use of a video monitor means that the surgeon sees a magnified view of the patient's interior together with the laparoscopic instruments. Typically, an endoscope provides a 110° field of view, with a depth of field that extends between 1 cm and 10 cm. Thus small movements of the instruments give rise to large changes in the video image. Furthermore, as the surgeon has lost the ability to view the body's interior directly as in open surgery, there is no stereopsis and no head-based motion parallax, and a vital loss of depth perception. The surgeon has to rely upon experience and careful exploratory manoeuvres before making any vital incision.

Acquiring these skills has been achieved through the use of cadavers, live and dead animals, mechanical simulators and the general public. Cadavers work up to a point, but tissue texture changes rapidly with rigor mortis and fails to simulate live human tissue with any realism. There are natural ethical reasons why live animals should not be used for this training, but even though this continues in some countries, animals provide neither the anatomical accuracy nor the range of pathology necessary for training.

The general public has always been involved in medical experimentation, either voluntarily or without knowing. Furthermore, recent accidents in laparoscopic operations have drawn attention to the potential dangers of the procedure when performed by untrained surgeons.

A short-term solution to this quandary is for surgeons to practise on physical models where no damage can be done. However, the level of realism is minimal, as the models cannot exhibit the dynamic properties associated with living tissue. It is hoped that a longer term solution will be found in VR. In such a system, a surgeon will be able to interact with a virtual environment representing a specific part of the human anatomy. It will be texture mapped using photographs of real organs and tissue, and move with the natural behaviours associated with their physical counterparts. Virtual tissue will have to bleed when cut, and react to gravity when decoupled from supporting skin and tissue.

There are, however, four major problems that have to be solved before such simulators begin to have an impact upon surgical training: image fidelity, accurate virtual anatomical models, realistic physical behavioural models and force feedback. Image fidelity is already at an advanced stage and simple experimental training simulators have been demonstrated with some success (Stanger, 1994). Accurate anatomical models are being developed by a number of groups around the world, so too are the physical behaviour models. Force feedback has already been incorporated into some experimental systems. Integrating these systems into a coherent real-time system will be no mean feat, but when it happens, medicine will take a significant step forward.

12.4.4 Military training

Training, whether it be for a military application of otherwise, involves the transfer of skills. The training process is often configured as a programme of integrated tasks, where each task builds upon previously learned information. It must be possible to measure the success of the training, otherwise there is no feedback to determine the effectiveness of the training procedures, or the suitability of the training to the trainees. When large numbers of trainees are involved, the above considerations become even more important; and when human lives are at stake, a second attempt to retrain may not be an option to the trainees – especially when they are soldiers.

Computer Based Training (CBT) techniques are now well established, and provide an environment where multimedia tools can be used to create a wealth of interactive interfaces, and passive system software can monitor every response made by the trainee. This total control of the training environment implies repeatability, reliability, accuracy and confidence in information obtained from assessment studies.

It is a natural progression to extend these training methods into the 3D virtual domain, and already VR techniques are being explored to evaluate how today's soldiers can master new weapons and tactical procedures without the support of physical environments. It is hoped that the virtual domain will eventually be able to offer all the realism associated with the real domain, without the obvious drawbacks of cost, organization, weather, time of day and so on. The virtual domain is repeatable, interactive, 3D, accurate, reconfigurable and networkable, and will become an important medium for military training.

Infantry training

The US Army Research Laboratory (ARL) at Aberdeen Proving Grounds is currently conducting research in the application of VR in infantry training. The trainees wear high-resolution HMDs and traverse a VE using a 'stair-stepper'. The resistance of the stair-stepper is adjusted according to the steepness of the terrain. The VE is based upon a townscape containing enemy tanks and paratroopers, and trainees have to navigate the environment and defend themselves using semi-automatic and anti-tank weapons.

The VR system consists of an SGI Onyx RealityEngine, and Division's dVS and dVISE software.

Military simulators

Although traditional mechanical weapons still play an important part in modern warfare, today's armed forces have access to the most sophisticated .weapons systems ever devised. Computer-based missiles that use lasers and satellite positioning systems are highly portable, and soldiers must be kept familiar with their operational procedures.

Thomson-CSF manufacture simulators for training crews of tanks and armoured vehicles. Simulators such as the Turret Team Trainer allow the training of the commander and gunner. The device includes the commander and gunner stations that reproduce the operational environment, as well as an instructor station and a processing and computation system. It can be used for technical training in the operation of the turret and in gunnery procedures, or to train several crews working together. In this configuration, up to six trainers can be networked and, under the supervision of a single instructor, the turret crews are able to train in team working, as they would in a platoon or a squadron.

The Turret Team Trainer is fitted with a display system that generates colour images of a VE in the periscopes and sights of the gunner and commander stations. The display system can present up to five simultaneous targets of two different types, and includes special effects such as gun shot, target damage and grass under target and sight symbology. It also simulates optronic imagery (thermal and light intensification).

The Leclerc Tank Driver Trainer, also manufactured by Thomson-CSF, incorporates two compartments mounted on correlated motion systems, one for the driver and one for the turret crew. A VE provides the simulator with access to 400 square kilometres of terrain decorated with authentic photographic textures. Views of the VE, which incorporates 30 animated targets, are provided by the SPACE image generator. A supervision and animation station allows the instructor to monitor the trainees' work. The instructor also commands the sequencing of strategic manoeuvres where friendly and hostile forces interact with the simulator. Four simulators can be networked at the same site to provide 'troop mode' operation. Plate 20 shows the Leclerc Tank Crew Training Simulator and Driver Simulator.

Stinger missile training

A Stinger missile training simulator has been developed at the TNO Physics and Electronics Laboratory in the Netherlands. The Stinger missile is portable and can be operated by a single soldier. By using an immersive VR system, trainees can practise operating procedures, target identification and acquisition and missile firing. The immersive approach also avoids the use of large dome display systems, which have been the traditional approach of integrating the trainee into an environment.

Team Tactical Engagement Simulator

The Jack system is being assessed in a Team Tactical Engagement Simulator (TTES) designed and built at NAWCTSD in Orlando, Florida. The simulator is being developed to train soldiers how to react when they engage with hostile forces. A Jack figure takes on the role of a hostile person by throwing stones and firing weapons at the soldier, who stands in front of a large video projection screen interacting with the virtual figure.

The VE is shared by the real soldier and the virtual aggressor. The soldier's movement through the environment is effected by head direction and feet movements on a resistive mat, while the aggressor is controlled by Distributed Interactive Simulation (DIS) commands coming from a computer-generated forces (CGF) simulator. The TTES translates the DIS commands into Jack instructions, which in turn animate the virtual figure by interpolating between a pair of postures. In all, there are four postures – standing, kneeling, prone and dead – with several modifiers such as weapons stowed or weapons firing. When this data is combined with a velocity vector, it is possible to simulate jogging, running and crawling behaviours. Future behaviours will include jumping and swimming.

12.4.5 Nuclear industry

Although the idea of heating water from a controlled nuclear chain reaction is an elegant form of energy conversion, it does introduce the controversial issues of radiation and catastrophic accidents such as occurred at Chernobyl. Nevertheless, nuclear power stations feed a significant quantity of electricity into national grids around the world, and it appears that they will become a major source of energy in the future.

There is no doubt that an oil-fired furnace is a much simpler process than moderating a uranium-based chain reaction, but we do possess the technology to control such complex systems. What is difficult is designing systems that can cope with the unpredictable behaviour of human operators. One simple and practical solution is the use of power plant simulators for training personnel. For example, the Kraftwerks-Simulator-Gesellschaft GmbH, in Essen, will have 14 such simulators by the year 2000.

Operators are placed in a 'real' control room, but the power plant is replaced by a real-time simulation program that models the physical dynamics of the plant. The training is completely safe and enables personnel to rehearse emergency situations and also acquire valuable operational skills. These training simulators consist of a computer and a large replica control room, but can be used only for training the control room staff.

Recently, the R&D division of Electricitié de France (EDF) installed a VR system to investigate a range of applications for designing and testing the operating procedures of a nuclear power plant. The system consists of an SGI Crimson RealityEngine and Division's VR software, dVS and dVISE.

EDF has built a VE to model the interior of the reactor building that includes all the major reactor components, piping and ductwork, multi-level scaffolding, control points and even the lifts that transport engineers between levels around the reactor. Plate 18 shows a view of this environment. A radiation plan complements the reactor model to simulate the radiation dosage received per second in any particular part of the building.

Using this complex model, the maintenance engineer dons an HMD and enters the virtual reactor building. Using the controls on a 3D mouse, along with natural human movements, the engineer moves around the virtual building, following the paths and actions proposed for the maintenance activity. While this happens in the virtual world, the system continuously computes the theoretical radiation which would have been received had the engineer performed the actual operation. With this 'virtual radiation dosage' information, operators can plan safer and more efficient procedures.

12.4.6 Accident simulator

Volvo (UK) Ltd identified an unusual application for VR when they used it for an accident simulator for one of their cars. Volvo's Side Impact Protection System is an important safety feature on their 850 GLT saloon, and they decided that immersive VR could be used to visualize a virtual accident.

Plate 19 shows the demonstrator, which is based around the cockpit of a Volvo 850 GLT saloon. A five-minute demonstration sequence begins with the customer sitting inside the cockpit, putting on a seat-belt, donning an HMD and taking hold of the steering wheel. The customer then drives along a virtual road, while a guide explains the car's safety features. A minute and a half into the experience, the guide suggests that the driver looks to the right. At this point an accident happens – a truck travelling at 40 kph drives through a stop sign and collides with the Volvo. In a brief, but realistic, 1.5 seconds, the entire accident is accurately simulated, from the realistic noises of the crash, to the displacement of the driver's seat and the shattering of glass.

12.5 Summary

It would be impossible to address all the applications for VR currently under investigation. Those that have been described have been chosen to illustrate the breadth of applications, and the benefits arising from these projects. There are many more exciting application areas to explore, such as plastic surgery, psychiatry, teaching, drama, artificial intelligence, robotics, simulation, art and design, fashion, information retrieval, museums and retailing. It is left to the reader to pursue these topics through the wealth of papers, journals and books associated with VR.

Within a very short period of time VR has lost its image of a technology looking for a problem, and is now being applied to almost every area of human endeavour. This author does not believe, however, that engineers, scientists and surgeons will have to become accustomed to wearing HMDs every minute of the day. What will happen is that computer systems will acquire interfaces where the benefits of the virtual domain can be utilized whenever it is necessary. VR is now poised to expand in many directions, and will be greatly influenced by technological developments in the next few years.

VR technology is no different to any other technology when it comes to success in the marketplace, and very simple issues will determine how it will be embraced by different communities. System reliability, ease of use, cost, physical side-effects and efficiency are just as important to industry as presence, immersion and spatial awareness. In time, though, such problems will be resolved and we can look forward to a new generation of tools, to which we will quickly become accustomed.

13

The Future

13.0 Introduction

If we look at the relationship between computers and humans over the past 25 years, we detect a subtle plan that appears to be bringing us closer and closer together. Early machines were hidden away in air-conditioned rooms and programmed at a distance using decks of punched cards. Only computer operators were given intimate access to the machine's hardware. With the advent of integrated circuits, processor performance increased and interactive multi-user computers appeared. As users, we were given access to VDUs, but still we could not gain access to the processing cabinet. More advances in technology made computers even smaller, until we reached the point of having them on our desks. Today, they are portable and fit in a briefcase. They even come fitted with a modem and a fax facility. Soon, speech recognition will become a standard feature.

Computer systems come in all shapes and sizes; they can process instructions from 1 to 100 000 MIPs; and their cost can vary from a few hundred to a few hundred million pounds. In general, it is relatively easy to match a computer system to an application, and although we would always desire a machine fitted with every possible peripheral and system enhancement, cost is a powerful constraint. Therefore, it is impossible to generalize about all computers with any accuracy, especially when discussing issues of cost, effectiveness, markets and future trends.

Similarly, in the very short period VR has been commercially available, a spectrum of systems has grown. At one end, we have desktop PC systems based upon 486/Pentium processors, while at the other, we have high-resolution, immersive systems running on high-performance, multiprocessor workstations. These systems also are characterized by different performance specifications and costs, and are designed to meet the needs of a wide range of users. Like computers, it is impossible to generalize about all VR systems, and any predictions about the future must bear this in mind.

In the case of VR, we know that current systems are evolving very rapidly. Today's computers, IGs, HMDs and software were not around five years ago, and the same will be true five years hence. Just what these future VR systems will look like depends upon many factors. To begin with, if VR had been shunned by the marketplace, it would have disappeared without trace. However, this has not happened. There are real markets for VR, but because so many promises were made about its potential, there were unrealistic expectations that it would become a universal mode of interaction in a short period of time.

VR will be embraced by industry if it can be demonstrated that there are real advantages over existing techniques. However, industry cannot afford to invest heavily in any technology that evolves too fast in front of its eyes. Therefore, technological stability will be very important to VR's success. This argument, though, assumes that a VR system remains as a separate 'black box' – which might not be the case in the future.

We know from experience that artefacts used at home and at work are subject to a continuous process of evolution. Changes may be in the form of new materials, or a totally new mode of operation. New technologies also play an important role in the way a design is continuously embellished to improve its functionality. So when it comes to long-term predictions about technology, it is very easy to fall into the trap of extrapolating today's ideas too far into the future. So, rather than make some bland statement about the general future of VR, perhaps it will be useful to divide this speculation into two components: virtual environments and modes of interaction.

13.1 Virtual environments

As mentioned at the beginning of this book, 3D VEs have been around for many years. The majority have been used to represent industrial components, architectural projects and civil engineering structures that could only be interacted with on a frame-by-frame basis. Some early CAD workstations possessed the technical performance that promised real-time working, but never quite achieved it. Today, we take for granted workstations that display complex engineering databases in a few seconds. Many such databases consume hundreds of gigabytes of disk space, and it is normal to be working with models containing one million polygons, or more. The ability to design and manufacture anything from a car engine manifold to an entire aircraft from an electronic virtual description is a real triumph for computer technology.

The simulation industry is also very familiar with modelling, displaying and updating VEs in real time. Training simulators for tanks, ships, aircraft and military vehicles use a VE as a substitute for a real working environment.

This has been very successful and will continue to be developed for many years to come.

The life of a full-flight simulator can extend to 20 years, therefore a Boeing 777 flight simulator built in 1995 could still be operational in 2015! Whether simulators will be around 50 years from now is probably irrelevant. A simulator, whether it be for a plane, ship or tank, is normally built around a specific model. Therefore, if planes, ships and tanks of the future are to be self-piloting, the demand for today's simulators will disappear with the pilots and captains.

The previous chapter showed that VEs were being considered for many other applications, such as medicine, molecular modelling, engineering, architecture, scientific visualization, entertainment and television. These are real applications and are an important pointer to the future. For example, 20 years ago, title sequences and credit lists for TV programmes were prepared on paper and cardboard and held in front of a TV camera. Today, all such imagery is prepared within the virtual domain of video systems. TV images are integrated with synthetic images and composited digitally with typographic information. Animated title sequences are prepared using computer graphics, and real-time animations are everyday features of a news programme. Both computers and digital technology have transformed the TV industry, and any moves to extend this technology into training and virtual 3D studios is a natural progression.

Twenty years ago the drawing office was a familiar feature for any engineering company. Drawings were prepared painstakingly using pencils, ink pens, erasers and tracing paper. A draughtsman was a skilled person who knew how to make drawings of complex assemblies. The job entailed a knowledge of isometric, parallel and perspective projections, elevations, cross-sections, threads, fillets, tolerances, materials, dimensioning and so on. Today, drawing boards have been replaced by CAD workstations, and the expert skills of draughting have been committed to software. These systems, however, are now operated by skilled designers and engineers.

The introduction of CAD systems was not just to remove paper from the design process, but to introduce a digital medium that offered incredible flexibility and potential. Introducing VR into the engineering design process is not a replacement for traditional CAD, but an extension. A VR system simply augments the way a designer interacts with the VE. If HMDs had not been invented, real-time workstations would have still appeared, so, too, would have stereo displays. The 3D virtual world would still exist, but it would not have been so accessible as it is with VR.

We all know how useful it is to hold an object and learn about its shape and construction by turning it over and exploring it with our eyes and fingers. When buying a car, we sit inside and check for comfort, adjust the seats, flick switches, turn knobs, open doors and lift the bonnet and look underneath until we understand something about the car's character. Likewise, VR provides the same opportunity to explore every facet of a virtual design long before it is manufactured.

Virtual environments will continue to be used in all types of training activities, be they for surgeons, soldiers, policemen, firemen, children or astronauts. Surgeons will be able to practise on virtual limbs and bodies, and develop surgical procedures without spilling a drop of blood or causing pain. They will be able to stand inside a virtual gall bladder or heart and for the first time become completely familiar with their geometry.

Soldiers will train in VEs and test their responses to various types of combat duty. Enemy soldiers, helicopters, tanks and weapon systems will be introduced to create the tension and pressure experienced in the theatre of war. Weather effects and time of day illumination, as well as sound, will all add to create an overwhelming sensation of presence.

Police car drivers will be able to practice high-speed pursuit driving, and develop driving skills that are currently acquired in their daily duties. There is no reason why a car simulator should not be just as realistic as a helicopter or plane simulator, and reflect every feature of a car's dynamics and the road's danger. It is highly likely that all members of the public will eventually be obliged to use car simulators as part of their training programme.

Training, though, is only one application of a VE. The application of VR to engineering is understood and no predictions are needed. So what are the new applications for VEs? This author believes that environments for physical simulation will be valuable to all aspects of design and education. Just imagine an environment where a component could be physically evaluated while being designed: articulated structures could be assessed for dynamic properties; resonant frequencies investigated and damped; stresses identified and minimized; elastic properties could be adjusted until an optimum design is achieved. With a knowledge of wear and fatigue properties, the entire structure could be subjected to a virtual simulation where it undergoes a test of one million cycles at different temperature extremes. Imagine how useful such an environment could be to undergraduate engineers who have to visualize the physical meaning of the differential equations that describe their world of dynamics.

If it is possible to build a VE for simulating dynamic engineering systems, then it must be possible to design similar environments for astrophysics and atomic physics, where any set of rules can be plugged in and these imaginary macro and micro worlds simulated and visualized. This vision of the future is not new. This extrapolation of today's world where processes that currently take minutes or hours to compute, into a future world where everything happens in real time is easy to predict, but difficult to substantiate with facts and dates. For none of this will happen on a commercial scale before we possess computers that can provide the necessary processing performance.

13.2 Modes of interaction

To immerse, or not to immerse? That is the question!
There has been some debate as to whether a VR system must be immersive. Personally, I do not believe that it is an important issue. The VE is the central

concept to all the systems discussed throughout this book. The mode of interaction is obviously very important, and can make or break the operational effectiveness of a specific system. However, it cannot be the one feature that determines whether a computer system suddenly becomes a VR system, or not. And after all, it's only a name!

The key quality of VR systems is flexibility. Flexibility in building virtual representations of anything from an atom to an airport, and flexibility to interact with this model via computer screens, stereo displays, gloves, mice and HMDs. That is what makes VR so exciting and promises an open-ended future.

This flexibility is useful for industry, as it means that it can begin to explore the benefits of VR using existing workstations or PCs, simply by buying a VR toolkit. They can learn how to build their environments and how to make them interactive, and possibly incorporate real-world physical attributes. Where required, they can introduce other display systems such as a boom, HMD, stereo glasses or stereo projectors. There are application areas where immersion is the only way forward. In this case, a dedicated VR system is the only choice.

Even as these words are being written, new HMDs are appearing that are lighter, cheaper and possess a higher resolution than anything currently available. Therefore, the next five years are going to be very interesting as new technologies and manufacturing processes influence future designs. One thing we must all be prepared for are new display technologies that provide totally new ways of viewing VEs. There are no hard and fast rules about VR – technology is moving along at such a pace that rules would serve no purpose.

VR systems

The 3D virtual domain is only just being discovered, and we are passing through a phase where different industries are seriously asking themselves 'What can VR do for me today?' In some cases, such as the visualizing of small geometric databases, desktop VR systems can provide an effective solution to many problems. As the applications become larger and more complex, the answer becomes less defined. At the cutting edge of industry, where the visualization of databases containing millions of surface elements is required, there is no immediate VR solution. This is not surprising, as it has taken the CAD industry 20 years or more to develop into a mature technology that can support such complex design methodologies.

What is important for all industries to recognize is that VR proposes new modes of interaction with computers. Like CAD, this will involve new working practices; it will introduce revolutionary methodologies for supporting concurrent engineering; and it will transform the entire design/simulation environment. However, these promises will not be realized unless industry becomes actively involved in the design of these systems today.

It cannot be left to the VR industry to design every type of system required by their future customers. Their customer base is so wide, and demands such a disparate range of configurations, that this has to be a joint venture. Fortunately, this collaboration is happening. There are now many research centres based throughout the universities of the world which, with the cooperation and funding of industry, are undertaking this vital work.

13.3 Conclusion

Twenty-five years have already passed since Ivan Sutherland undertook his pioneering work at the University of Utah. This delay in translating an idea into a useful product that can be enjoyed by industry is nothing new, and many of the inventions surfacing today may not become usable for many years to come. VR is not a totally new technology – it is riding on the back of computer technology, and relies upon an unusual integration of mature system elements.

Its time has arrived, and during the last five years of this millenium we will see a rapid move towards virtual representations of objects and environments. No matter how much we would like to work with some of the more futuristic systems predicted by VR enthusiasts around the world, these will not be with us until the next century. This does not mean that nothing exciting will happen between now and then. Far from it – the next five years will be a period of development and discovery. A period when we learn what we really want to do with VR and how to introduce these systems to an eager and enthusiastic marketplace.

Glossary

Accommodation The eye's ability to alter the refractive power of its lens to focus on near and far objects.

Achromatic light Light without colour.

Active environment A VE that contains processes that are independent of events caused by the user.

Actor Division uses an actor to represent a server.

Acuity A measure of an optical system's ability to resolve fine detail.

Acute angle An angle less than $90°$.

Active matrix LCD An LCD display where the LCD pixel is controlled by one or more transistors to modulate its transmission state.

Adaptive progressive refinement A radiosity technique that progressively refines an image.

Additive colour mixing The technique of creating colours by superimposing two or three light sources from the red, green and blue portions of the visible spectrum.

Additive primary colours The colours are red, green and blue.

Aliasing *Spatial*: In pixel-based display systems, visual artefacts, such as jagged edges and moiré patterns, are caused by insufficient spatial sampling and are referred to as spatial aliasing. *Temporal*: Animation artefacts, such as 'wagon wheels' apparently rotating backwards, are caused by insufficient temporal sampling of moving objects and are referred to as temporal aliasing.

Ambient light A constant term used in illumination models to represent the background light level assumed to arise from multiple reflections.

Ambisonics A technique for recording sound using a Soundfield microphone, and decoding the signal such that it can be replayed using a number of loudspeakers.

Anechoic Without echoes.

Angle of incidence The acute angle formed by the surface normal and the incident light ray illuminating the surface.

Angle of reflection   The acute angle formed by the surface normal and the light ray reflected away from the surface.

Angle of view   The solid angle of incident light transmitted by a lens.

Angular velocity   The rotational velocity of an object about an axis measured in degrees per second or radians per second.

Anti-aliasing   Encompasses strategies concerned with the removal or reduction of aliasing artefacts arising from insufficient spatial or temporal sampling.

Anticlockwise polygon   A polygon that has its interior to the left when its boundary is traversed in the direction of its edges.

Aperture   A measure of the physical area of a lens through which light can pass.

Approximating spline   A parametric curve that approaches its control points without normally intersecting them.

Aqueous humor   The transparent liquid between the cornea and the lens.

Artefacts   Unwanted features introduced by a technology or algorithm.

ASIC   Application Specific Integrated Circuit. ASICs are available to undertake specific tasks in image analysis and image generation.

Aspect ratio   Relates the vertical to the horizontal dimensions of an image or shape.

Asynchronous   Asynchronous processes are independent of one another and run at different speeds.

Attributes   Properties associated with virtual objects such as colour, surface detail and mass.

Augmented reality   Augmented reality systems superimpose computer-generated images over a view of the real world.

Average normal   A single vector representing a collection of surface normals at a common vertex.

Axis   (a) An arbitrary 2D or 3D line about which operations such as reflections and rotations are performed. (b) A line used to construct a system of axes as in Cartesian notation.

Back face   The back face of a polygon is the opposite side to the front face which contains the surface normal.

Back plane   The back plane (yon plane, or far plane) in the viewing pyramid controls the distance up to which objects are visible.

Back face culling   *See* **back face removal**.

Back face removal   Back face removal, or back face culling, refers to the removal of all back-facing polygons in a scene before it is rendered.

Back-projection screen   A translucent screen where the image is projected from behind.

Basilar membrane   A membrane used by the inner ear to distinguish between sounds of different frequencies.

Bézier space curve   A parametric curve generated by computing the curve's coordinates from control points weighted by terms from the Bernstein basis function.

Bézier surface patch   A parametric surface patch description that employs a matrix of control points weighted by terms from the Bernstein basis function.

Bicubic patch   A surface patch definition employing cubic equations of two parameters to generate the coordinates of any point on the patch.

Bilinear surface patch   A patch definition employing linear equations of two parameters to generate the coordinates of any point on the patch.

Binaural   Binaural sound implies the use of two separate audio channels.

Binocular depth cues   Mechanisms such as eye convergence for estimating object distance.

Binocular disparity   Differences in the images seen by the left and right eyes.

Binocular vision   The ability to see two independent views of a scene.

Boom display   A binocular display system mounted on a balanced articulated arm. 3D tracking is achieved by measuring the boom's joint angles.

Boundary representation   A modelling strategy where objects are modelled using their boundary description.

Bounding box   A minimum bounding volume in the form of a rectangular box such that it completely contains an object.

Bounding sphere   A minimum bounding volume in the form of a sphere such that it completely contains an object.

Bradykinin   A chemical messenger used for communicating pain signals.

Brodmann's mapping   A topographical mapping of the somatic cortex in the brain.

B-spline space curve   B-spline curves, especially their rational form (NURBS), are parametric curves whose shape is determined by a series of control points, whose influence is determined by basis functions.

B-spline surface patch   A parametric surface patch controlled by a matrix of control points, whose influence is determined by the product of two B-spline basis functions.

Bump map   A 2D look-up table holding intensity levels used to modulate a surface normal during rendering.

C   A high-level computer programming language often used in computer graphics and VR.

C++   An entended version of C, supporting object-oriented programming concepts.

CAD   Computer Aided Design.

CAM   Computer Aided Manufacture.

Cartesian coordinates   These coordinates enable a point in 2D space to be represented by two measurements, and a point in 3D space by three measurements, relative to some defined origin and system of orthogonal axes.

Catmull–Rom spline   Belongs to the family of interpolating splines, and is also known as the cardinal spline or the Overhauser spline.

Centre of mass   The effective position in an object where its mass can be imagined to be concentrated.

Centre of projection   In a perspective projection, it is the point through which all projection lines pass.

CFD   *See* **computational fluid dynamics**.

CFF   *See* **critical fusion frequency**.

Chemoreceptor trigger zone   An area in the brain for triggering a vomit response.

Cholesteric LCD   Has a layered structure like a smectic liquid crystal, but the axis of the molecules is in the plane of each layer, with a parallel orientation similar to that of a nematic liquid crystal.

Chromakey   A video technique of shooting an object against a blue background, which is then replaced by another image.

Ciliary muscles   Muscles used to adjust the focal length of the eye's lens.

Clipping   The process of removing from a scene 2D or 3D detail that is not required, or is invisible to the viewer.

Clipping planes   Planes that bound the 3D viewing frustum.

Clockwise polygon   A polygon that has its interior to the right when its boundary is traversed in the direction of its edges.

Cochlea   Three coiled tubes in the inner ear.

Collimated   A collimated optical system has light rays appear to come from some origin. This may be set at infinity or some specific distance.

Collision avoidance   The procedures used to prevent two objects from colliding.

Collision detection   The process of detecting collisions between virtual objects.

Colour attributes   The colour codes assigned to an object to enable it to be rendered.

Colour bleeding   When one coloured surface is placed against another, each surface reflects the other's colour, which is called colour bleeding.

Colour gamut   The total range of colours that can be displayed by a system.

Colour model   A convenient system for organizing and specifying colours.

Colour space   A 2D or 3D method of organizing colour attributes.

Compound rotation   A rotation equivalent to two or more single rotations.

Computational fluid dynamics (CFD)   A mathematical technique for modelling the dynamic flow of gas and fluid about an object.

Concatenate   Two matrices can be concatenated (combined) to produce an equivalent single matrix.

Concave polygon   A polygon that has one or more of its internal angles greater than 180°.

Cones   Receptors in the human retina responsible for colour vision.

Constraint-based manipulation   The manipulation of virtual objects that are constrained to move in controlled ways.

Constraints   The limits applied to an object's behaviour.

Constructive solid geometry (CSG)   A modelling methodology where an object is built using the Boolean operators: union, subtraction and difference. It is also known as set-theoretic modelling.

Convergence angle   The angle subtended by the optical axes of the eyes or an optical system.

Converging optics   An optical system is said to be converging when the viewer's eyes are forced to diverge to accommodate the image.

Convex polygon   A polygon that has all of its interior angles less than 180°.

Coons surface patch   A surface patch defined by four boundary parametric curves and four corner vertices.

Cornea   The transparent surface at the front of the eye.

CPU   Central Processing Unit.

Critical fusion frequency   The frequency at which a flashing light appears constant to the eye.

Cross product   *See* **vector product**.

CSG   *See* **constructive solid geometry**.

Cubic interpolation   An interpolation procedure that employs a third-order basis.

Cyberspace   (a) A popular name given to the virtual 3D domain. (b) A software product marketed by Autodesk.

Dark adaption   The process where the eye adjusts to a dark environment, having been adapted to bright levels of light.

Database   A collection of related records organized such that particular classes of records are easily accessed.

Dead reckoning   The accurate determination of an object's linear/angular position, velocity and acceleration.

Deep sensations   Come from receptors deep within body tissue and measure pressure and pain.

Depth buffer   *See* **z-buffer**.

Depth cues   Features in a scene that aid the estimation of depth.

Depth of field   Defines the distance range in the object space of a lens, over which an in-focus image is created; outside these limits, the image appears blurred.

Diffuse reflection   This occurs when any incident light is randomly reflected back into the illumination space.

Diffuse surface   Reflects light equally in all directions and obeys Lambert's cosine law.

Digitizer   A system for capturing 2D or 3D Cartesian coordinates.

Dioptre   A unit of measure for the refractive power of a lens.

Directional light source   Assumed to be located at infinity and emits light in only one direction.

Direction cosines   The components of a unit vector are also known as its direction cosines, as they are equal to the cosine of the angles between the vector and the axes of the coordinate system.

Distributed light source   A light source that radiates energy over an area, rather than from a single point.

Diverging optics   An optical system is said to be diverging when the viewer's eyes have to converge to accommodate the image.

Dot product   *See* **scalar product**.

Driving velocity   The velocity assigned to a virtual object to make it move.

dVISE   Division's virtual world simulation and authoring software tool.

dVS   Division's VR run-time environment.

Dynamic constraints   The physical constraints associated with moving objects, such as mass, stiffness and inertia.

Dynamic vertices   Object vertices that can change their position in a VE.

Eardrum A thin membrane in the middle ear that oscillates in sympathy with incoming sound pressure waves, and connects to the ossicular system.

Edge Part of the border of a shape, or a line formed where two surfaces meet.

Edge table A data structure for storing edge information about an object, in terms of vertices stored in a vertex table.

Elastic collisions Collisions associated with colliding rigid objects.

Environment mapping A rendering technique employing texture maps to create the impression of polished metallic surfaces.

Equation of motion Synonymous with Newton's second law of motion.

Ergonomics Concerning the design of systems that take into account the physical shape of the human body.

Euler's rule States that, for a polyhedron without holes, the number of edges is always two less than the sum of the number of faces and vertices.

Exoskeleton An articulated structure surrounding part of our body, as used in exoskeletal hand and finger trackers.

Exteroceptive sensations The touch sensations we experience over our body surface.

External sound stage The effect when we localize sound sources outside our head.

Extruding A modelling technique where a 3D volume can be created by using a 2D cross-section contour and a path through which it is to be extruded.

Eye convergence The action of rotating both eyes inwards.

Eye dipvergence The action when one eye is forced to 'dip' further than the other.

Eye divergence The action of moving both eyes outwards.

Eye relief The distance between the optics of an HMD and the user's eyes.

Eye tracking The technique of monitoring the gaze direction of the eye.

Far plane *See* **back plane**.

FEA *See* **finite element analysis**.

FFD *See* **free-form deformation**.

Field An interlaced video frame comprises two fields: one contains the odd-numbered raster lines, the other contains the even-numbered raster lines.

Field of view (FOV) The field of view of a lens is the largest solid angle where incident light appears on the image. In an HMD the FOV is often quoted as horizontal and vertical angles.

Finite element analysis (FEA) A mathematical technique for modelling dynamic stresses in an object.

Fixating The deliberate action of looking at a specific point in space.

Flat shading A simple rendering process where a polygon is shaded with a consistent colour intensity.

Flicker The visual sensation caused when an image is not refreshed fast enough.

Flight simulator A system consisting of a cockpit environment for training pilots.

Flying The action of moving from part of the VE to another.

F-number The f-number of a lens is its focal length divided by its 'stopped' aperture.

Focal length The distance of the focal plane to the lens when the incident light is from a distant source.

Focal plane A lens creates a real image in sharp focus on a surface positioned at its focal plane.

Force feedback Force feedback devices exert forces back through the user's fingers, arm or shoulder.

Form-factor In radiosity, a form-factor represents the fractional radiant energy leaving one patch, and arriving at another.

Forward dynamics Concerning the calculation of a body's acceleration when an applied force is known.

Forward kinematics The use of transformations in controlling the future position and motion of objects.

FOV *See* **field of view**.

Fovea The high-resolution, central zone of the eye's retina.

Fractal A data set that exhibits similar properties at different scales.

Fractal surface A surface exhibiting self-similar properties.

Frame An interlaced video frame contains two fields, while a non-interlaced frame consists of the odd and even-numbered raster lines.

Frame of reference A coordinate system and origin to which other points are related.

Frame store A memory device capable of storing one video frame.

Free-form deformation (FFD) A computer animation technique for distorting 2D and 3D objects.

Free-form shape A class of surface that has no implicit geometric description.

Front face The side of a polygon containing the surface normal.

Front plane The front (near or hither) plane delineates the minimum distance where points are visible in the 3D viewing frustum.

Frustum A truncated pyramid.

Fusion frequency The minimum frequency for an alternating source of light to appear constant to the human visual system.

g The acceleration due to gravity ($9.81\,\mathrm{m\,s^{-2}}$).

Ganglion cells Cells that connect to the rods and cones in the retina.

Gaze direction The viewer's eye direction.

Gesture recognition The recognition of hand gestures made by the VR user.

GFLOPS Giga Floating-point Operations per Second.

Gloss coefficient The degree of gloss exhibited by a surface, and the specular coefficient in Phong shading.

Goal-directed animation Techniques used for animating articulated structures that can be given a goal in terms of a final position of one of its elements. The orientation of the entire structure can then be computed.

Gouraud shading Colour interpolation used to shade a surface.

Graceful degradation A system that suddenly degrades to a lower performance profile is said to 'degrade gracefully' if it adjusts to the new state smoothly.

Graphical user interface (GUI)   A graphics-based computer interface.

Graph plotter   An output display device for creating line-based drawings.

Graphic primitive   A simple shape or object used by a graphics system to construct more complex scenes.

Graphics package   A software system that undertakes a task for the user such as animation, modelling or rendering.

GUI   *See* **graphical user interface**.

Half-space   Two half-spaces are created on either side of a planar surface.

Hand tracker   A device for monitoring the 3D position and orientation of the user's hand.

Head-mounted display (HMD)   A display system – normally binocular – attached to the user's head.

Head-related transfer functions (HRTFs)   Encode the physical influence the head and ear have on the incoming sound pressure waves.

Head tracking   The action of monitoring the position and orientation of a person's head in real time.

Heave   Synonymous with the vertical translation of a motion platform.

Hermite curve   A parametric cubic curve sensitive to the end point tangents.

Hermite interpolation   Uses parametric polynomials to interpolate between two points and their associated curve slopes.

Hermite surface patch   A Cartesian product patch employing a Hermite interpolation between the corner points, corner slopes and corner twist vectors.

Hexcone   A cone with a hexagonal base.

Hidden-line removal   A process for identifying edges that are invisible or partially occulted by surfaces, and removing them before they are displayed.

Hidden-surface removal   A process for ensuring that surfaces in a rendered image are ordered correctly.

Hierarchy   An organization of things connected in such a way that a unique path exists between any two.

Hither plane   *See* **front plane**.

HMD   *See* **head-mounted display**.

Homogeneous coordinates   These extend Cartesian coordinates with an extra value such that if (x,y,z) are the existing Cartesian coordinates, the homogeneous form is specified as (x',y',z',h), where $x = x'/h$, $y = y'/h$ and $z = z'/h$.

Homogeneous matrix   This extends standard matrix transformations to include the homogeneous scaling term.

Hooke's law   The tension in a spring is proportional to its extension, and inversely proportional to its length.

HRTF   *See* **head-related transfer functions**.

HSV   Hue, Saturation and Value.

HSV colour space   Uses the attributes of hue, saturation and value to define a colour.

Hue   The attribute given to a colour to describe its relative position within the visible spectrum.

Hue circle Organizes colours in a circle so that any hue can be specified either by an angle between 0° and 360°, or a fractional value.

Human factors Concerning issues pertaining to human behaviour such as sight, sound, haptics and equilibrium.

Hz The unit of measurement to represent cycles per second. It is derived from the scientist Hertz.

Icon A graphic design symbolizing an action or thing.

IG *See* **image generator**.

Iggo dome receptor A touch receptor with a slow rate of adaption.

Illumination model Describes how light is emitted, reflected, transmitted and absorbed within a virtual world.

Image generator (IG) A computer-based system for rendering real-time images.

Image plane Synonymous with the picture plane.

Image space The plane where a projection of a 3D scene has been captured.

Immersion The sensation of being part of an environment, be it real or virtual.

Immersive VR A VR system where the user is 'immersed' in the VE through the use of an HMD.

Implicit patch An algebraic surface is an implicit patch as it describes implicitly the relationship between three variables.

Inbetweening The process of obtaining intermediate images between two key images.

Incident light The light arriving at a surface; the basis for computing the reflected light seen by the viewer.

Instance A reference to the original object plus the matrix operations that position it in space.

Instance transform A matrix representing a scaling, rotation and translation operation to create an instance of an object.

Interactive computer graphics A generic term for computer systems that provide real-time, two-way, graphical communication.

Interactive glove A glove worn by the VR user to monitor finger and hand movements.

Internal sound stage The effect when we localize sound sources inside our head.

Interocular distance The distance between the optical centres of the left and right eyes.

Interpenetrating objects When one virtual object intersects another.

Interpolating spline A parametric spline curve that intersects its control points.

Interpolation The process of computing intermediate values between known values.

Inverse dynamics The technique for determining the forces required to compute the movement of an articulated system.

Inverse kinematics The technique for determining the velocities of an articulated system, such as animating a person running.

I/O Input/Output.

Iris A pigmented, opaque structure positioned in front of the eye's lens. The hole in its centre is the pupil.

Jaggies A popular name for the staircase stepping associated with pixel-based displays.

Joystick An input device used for measuring angles forwards, backwards and sideways.

Key-frame animation The automatic process of generating images between selected key frames.

Lag *See* **latency**.

Lambert's cosine law The light reflected from a dull matte surface is proportional to the incident light and the cosine of the angle between the incident light vector and the surface normal.

Laparoscopic simulator A training simulator based on physical or virtual models for training surgeons in 'key-hole' surgery.

Laparoscopy A form of internal surgery undertaken through small incisions in the patient's body.

Latency The time delay (or lag) between activating a process and its termination.

LCD *See* **liquid crystal display**.

LED *See* **light emitting diode**.

Left-handed axes A set of 3D Cartesian axes where the left-hand thumb is aligned with the x-axis, the first finger with the y-axis, and the middle finger with the z-axis.

Light adaption The process where the eye adjusts to a bright environment, having been adapted to low light levels.

Light emitting diode (LED) A semiconductor device that emits light on the application of a voltage.

Light source A virtual source of illumination upon which a renderer can make intensity calculations for surfaces.

Light source direction Specifies the orientation of the radiant light in the form of a vector for a directional or spot light.

Linear interpolation A means of computing a value between two other values using a parameter, such that linear changes in the parameter produce linear changes in the interpolated values.

Linear transformation Linear transformations, such as shearing, scaling, rotation and reflection, ensure that when they operate upon a linear combination of vectors, linearity is preserved.

Liquid crystal cell A layer of liquid crystal about 10 microns thick sandwiched between two glass substrates on which are formed transparent electrodes.

Liquid crystal display (LCD) Employs liquid crystals whose molecules can be oriented to different positions by the application of an electric field.

Mach band This is created by the human visual system by emphasizing intensity changes in an image.

Macula Hair cells in the utricle within the vestibular system for sensing gravity.

Maths co-processor A separate processor for speeding up the execution of basic mathematical operations.

Matrix An $n \times m$ arrangement of numbers that can encode a geometric transformation.

MAZ Division's file format for dVISE.

Meissner's corpuscles Receptors for measuring touch sensations in the fingertips.

Mini-max testing Involves the comparison of an object's spatial extents.

MIPS Millions of Instructions Per Second.

Mip maps A hierarchical set of filtered texture maps developed to reduce the time spent in anti-aliasing during texture mapping operations.

Model board A physical scale model of an airport, used before the introduction of VEs.

Model library A collection of pre-built 2D shapes and 3D models.

Modelling The process of constructing a VE.

Modelling transformations Used to position objects in the WCS, such as scale, rotate and translate.

Molecular modelling The process of investigating molecular structures. Sometimes performed with computer graphics and VR.

Momentum The product of an object's mass and velocity.

Monochrome Use of only one colour, as in black and white photography.

Monocular The use of one eye.

Monocular depth cues Mechanisms such as motion parallax and perspective for estimating depth with one eye.

Motion parallax The visual cues in a moving scene for estimating depth.

Motion platform A platform that can be moved in real time to take up specific orientations.

Motion sickness A group of unpleasant symptoms experienced when the brain receives conflicting visual and motion cues.

Mouse A pointing device used in interactive computer graphics systems to control a screen's cursor.

Near plane The clipping plane nearest to the observer.

Negative light Arises when a virtual light intensity is set negative. Instead of adding to other light sources, negative light is subtracted.

Nematic A nematic liquid crystal has rod-shaped molecules aligned parallel with each other, like smectic liquid crystals, but the individual molecules move relatively easily in the direction along their axis, so that there is no layering structure.

Newton's first law of motion The momentum of a particle is constant when there are no external forces.

Newton's second law of motion A particle of mass m, subjected to a force F, moves with acceleration F/m.

Newton's third law of motion If a particle exerts a force on a second particle, the second particle exerts an equal reactive force in the opposite direction.

Noncommutative Implies that a mathematical operation such as $a \times b$ is not the same as $b \times a$.

NTSC National Television Systems Committee, who defined the American television standard.

Object coordinate system (OCS) The frame of reference used for building objects.

Object constancy Relates to the way stationary objects in the real world still appear stationary when we move our heads. Through head-tracking, such object constancy also occurs when we observe objects in a virtual world.

Object inbetweening The process of creating inbetween object descriptions from two reference objects.

Object picking The action of selecting an object in a VE.

Object sorting The process of identifying the depth sequence of objects from the observer.

Object space The VE.

Obtuse angle An angle between 90° and 180°.

OCS *See* **object coordinate system**.

Opacity An attribute associated with a surface describing its efficacy at absorbing light; the opposite to transparency.

Opaque surface A surface that does not transmit light.

Optical mapping functions Relate to the non-linear mapping functions used to correct an image.

Optic nerve Communicates visual data from the eye to the brain.

Orthogonal At right angles to some datum.

Ossicular system A system of small bones in the inner ear.

Pacinian corpuscles Touch receptors used for detecting vibrations.

Painter's algorithm A technique that renders an image by rendering distant objects before close objects. It is also known as the depth sort algorithm.

PAL Phase Alternation Line, the UK television broadcast standard.

Palette A collection of colours.

Paradigm A pattern or model.

Parallax The apparent change in the position of an object arising from a change in the position of the observer.

Parameter A variable used for controlling the value of a mathematical function.

Parameter space The spatial domain where parameters belonging to some parametric process can be organized and manipulated.

Parametric curve Defined by coordinates derived from functions sharing some common parameter.

Parametric surface patch A surface patch model employing two parameters, for example, Bézier, B-spline, Coons and Ferguson patches.

Parabolic Implies a second-order equation.

Particle system A collection of discrete particles controlled by numerical values representing their position, size, velocity, colour, lifetime, birth, time and so on.

Passive environment A VE that reacts only to events caused by the user.

Patch A portion of a surface whose geometry is defined parametrically such that slope continuity across patches is preserved at the boundaries.

Penumbra The blurred border of a shadow caused by multiple diffuse reflections or a distributed light source.

Percentile One of 99 actual or notional values of a variable dividing its distribution into 100 groups with equal frequencies.

Peripheral vision The awareness of visual information at the periphery of our field of view.

Persistence of vision The eye's ability to record a visual signal after the stimulus has been removed.

Perspective depth cues The size changes that enable us to estimate an object's depth.

Perspective foreshortening The size reduction as an object recedes from the observer.

Perspective transformation Used to create a perspective projection by projecting points in object space onto a picture plane.

Phong shading A shading technique that employs average normal interpolation to compute the colour intensities across a surface.

Phonon A unit of sound energy.

Photon A unit of light energy.

Photopic vision Vision through the use of cone receptors.

Photopsin A protein found in cone receptors.

Photorealism Very realistic computer-generated scenes.

Photoreceptors The rods and cones that convert light photons into electrical signals.

Physical simulation Concerning the algorithmic basis for physical behaviour.

Picking *See* **object picking**.

Picture plane The projection plane used to capture an image, especially for perspective projections.

Piecewise curves Curve segments that can be used to construct more complex curves.

Pinna The outer part of the human ear.

Pinhole camera A light-tight box containing a small hole which allows light rays to impinge upon an enclosed photographic film.

Pitch angle A rotational angle about a horizontal x-axis, orthogonal to the forward-facing z-axis.

Pitch matrix Encodes the transformation to rotate a point about the horizontal axis, orthogonal to the forward-facing axis.

Pixel The smallest addressable picture element on a display screen.

Pixel footprint A pixel's shape when projected back onto some surface in object space.

Planar polygon Has its vertices contained in one plane.

Plasma display A display device that utilizes the light produced at an intersection point of a matrix of electrodes by a plasma discharge in an inert gas.

Point-and-fly A gesture/action combination equivalent to a pointing gesture, followed by a flying action.

Point light source Radiates light equally in all directions.

Polar coordinates Fix a point in space using radial measurements and angles.

Polygon A shape bounded by straight edges, such as a hexagon.

Polygonal mesh A structure formed from a system of abutting polygons.

Polygon table   A data structure for storing the boundary polygons of an object in terms of its edges.

Polyhedron   An object having a polygonal boundary.

Polynomial   A mathematical construct consisting of one or more variables raised to different powers.

Pop-up menu   A menu that 'pops up' on the screen when a specific task is requested, and disappears after a menu item has been selected.

Portal   A 'doorway' in space connecting two virtual worlds.

Position vector   Connects a point in space to the origin, and creates a vector.

Post-production   Encompasses all the procedures needed to integrate the many individual sequences that make up the final piece of video graphics.

Presbyopia   A medical condition when the eye's lens is unable to alter its refractive power.

Presence   The sense of realism created by a virtual experience.

Primary colours   Pure colours, not the product of a mixing process.

Primitive   A graphical entity, such as a line, circle, cube or sphere, that can be used for constructing more complex objects.

Procedural animation   Involves algorithmic procedures to describe an animation sequence.

Procedural modelling   Uses algorithmic procedures to build a 3D object.

Procedural texture   Generated by functions rather than from real-world photographs.

Projection   A mathematical technique for converting a system of n-dimensional points into an $(n - 1)$-dimensional space.

Projection plane   A planar surface, generally orthogonal to a principal 3D axis, which enables points of intersection to be calculated where lines connect object vertices to a centre of projection.

Proprioceptive sensations   Used to monitor the status of the body, such as position, equilibrium and muscles.

Pseudo-colouring   The substitution of values stored in a frame store by colours held in a look-up table.

Quadratic interpolation   An interpolation procedure that employs a second-order basis.

Quadratic surface patch   A surface patch description which relies upon second-order equations to identify points upon the surface.

Quaternion   An extension of the notion of complex numbers; used in computer graphics to rotate objects about an arbitrary axis.

Radiosity   A global illumination model used for computing light intensities resulting from multiple diffuse reflections.

RAM   Random Access Memory.

Raster   One line of a frame or field displayed on a CRT.

Raster computer graphics   Encompasses those techniques associated with the display of images upon raster-based displays.

Raster display   A display device that creates an image on a raster-by-raster basis, such as a television.

Rational number   Can be represented by the ratio of two whole numbers.

Rational polynomial   Can be expressed as the ratio of two polynomials.

Ray casting   A hidden-surface detection algorithm generally associated with the rendering of CSG objects.

Ray tracing   Renders an image by tracing the origins of the single light ray that arrives at the centre of every pixel.

Real time   Implies reacting instantaneously to any changes in the signals processed.

Recursive algorithm   References itself as part of its strategy in solving a problem.

Reflection coefficient   A surface attribute controlling the quantity of light reflected back from some incident light source.

Reflection model   A basis upon which reflection calculations are made.

Reflection vector   Identifies the direction of a reflected light ray away from a surface.

Refraction of light   The change of direction of light when it moves from one medium to another and undergoes a speed change.

Refresh rate   The frequency with which a raster display is refreshed in Hz.

Renderer   **Image**: A program for creating a shaded synthetic image based upon 3D geometric descriptions, surface attributes and an illumination model. **Acoustic**: The process of simulating the propagation of sound within a VE.

Rendering pipeline   Computer graphics workstations normally have a pipeline architecture where the rendering process is divided into three stages: selecting the visible part of the database; performing a perspective projection; and rendering the image. Some pipelines may only involve two stages.

Resolution   A measure of a system's ability to record fine detail.

Restitution   The energy loss associated with a collision, expressed as a fraction.

RGB   The additive primary colours: Red, Green and Blue.

RGB colour space   A 3D set of Cartesian axes labelled red, green and blue.

Rhodopsin   A light-sensitive pigment found in the rod receptors.

Right-handed axes   Cartesian axes can be formed with a left- or right-handed configuration: the latter would have one's right-hand thumb aligned with the x-axis, the first finger with the y-axis and the middle finger with the z-axis.

Rigid body   An object whose geometry is fixed.

Rigid-body animation   Concerning the modelling and animation of rigid bodies physically interacting with one another.

Rods   Light receptors in the retina that are active in dim lighting conditions.

Roll angle   The angle of rotation about the forward-facing heading vector.

Roll matrix   Encodes the transformation to rotate a point about the forward-facing heading vector.

Rotation matrix   Used for rotating an object about an axis or a specified point.

Ruffini's end-organs   Touch receptors in deep tissue that do not adapt to any extent.

Rule-based animation   *See* **procedural animation**.

Saturation   The purity of coloured light in terms of the white light component and the remaining colour component.

Scalar   A quantity that has only magnitude, such as a pure number.

Scalar product   The scalar product, or dot product, of two vectors is a scalar quantity equal to the cosine of the enclosed angle, multiplied by the modulus of each vector.

Scaling matrix   Used for changing the size of a shape.

Scan-line algorithm   Proceeds on a raster-by-raster basis, such as a scan-line renderer.

Scanner   A device for converting a colour photograph into a digital format.

Scientific visualization   Concerning the use of computer graphics to visualize multi-dimensional data associated with scientific projects, as an aid to its understanding and interpretation.

SCL   Superscape's Control Language.

Scotopic vision   Relating to rod vision or night vision.

Scotopsin   A protein found in rhodopsin; aids the conversion of light into electricity.

Screen coordinates   Used for addressing points on the picture plane.

Semicircular canals   The anterior, posterior and horizontal ducts in the vestibular system for sensing equilibrium.

Set-theoretic modelling   *See* **constructive solid geometry**.

Shading   The process of colouring the surfaces of an object.

Shadow volume   A volume of space behind an object that is in shadow.

Shape inbetweening   A procedure for creating inbetween shapes from two reference shape descriptions.

Shear matrix   Used for shearing an object about an axis.

Silhouette edge   The boundary shape of an object.

Slow-in/slow-out   The temporal spacing of drawings in an animated sequence that ultimately influences the degree of attack or decay incorporated in a movement.

Smectic   A smectic liquid crystal has its rod-shaped molecules arranged parallel with each other, and aligned typically perpendicular to the layers.

Soft objects   A class of non-rigid structures modelled from surfaces of constant value from a scalar field.

Solid angle   The 3D angle subtended by a point to some arbitrary boundary.

Solid modelling   A modelling scheme for describing 3D objects containing sufficient geometric detail that a numerically controlled machine can be used for their creation.

Solid texture   Generated by procedures for assigning texture attributes to a volume of space.

Somatic senses   Encompasses the senses of touch, pain, position and temperature.

Spaceball   A six DOF pointing device manufactured by Spaceball Technologies, Inc.

Specular reflection   The reflection of a light source seen by an observer on a reflective surface.

Specular reflection coefficient   A fractional value used to modulate the intensity of the specular reflection.

Spline curve   A polynomial curve formed by a sequence of control points.

Spot light source   Illuminates a scene within a restricted angular cone.

Stochastic   Synonymous with random processes.

Stereocilla   Small hairs in the vestibular system for monitoring head position.

Stereogram   A 2D image that contains parallax information, such as random dot stereograms.

Stereopsis   The process of obtaining two distinct views of an object with two eyes.

Stereoscope   A device for creating a stereoscopic image from a pair of images containing parallax infomation.

Stereoscopic   A stereoscopic system provides two images with parallax information, giving the illusion of depth and relief.

Surface attributes   Qualities such as colour and texture assigned to an object.

Surface normal   A unit vector orthogonal to its associated surface.

Surface of revolution   *See* **swept surface**.

Surface patch   A surface description that can be used with other patches to form a complex surface.

Surge   Synonymous with a forward movement of a motion platform.

Sway   Synonymous with the horizontal movement of a motion platform.

Swept surface   A 3D surface formed by rotating a contour about an axis.

Tablet   A small active surface used as a digitzer in conjunction with a stylus.

Tactile feedback   Sensory information that can be detected through the sense of touch.

Tactile receptors   Used to measure sensations of touch.

Teleporting   The action of moving directly from one position in a VE to another.

Telepresence   Relays a view of a scene back to some distant viewer. Very often the view is binocular.

Texel   The smallest addressable element of a texture map.

Texture map   A 2D pattern of pixel intensities derived synthetically or procedurally, or input from an external image, for use as surface decoration.

Texture mapping   The process of substituting detail stored within a texture map onto an arbitrary surface.

Toolkit   A software system for building, visualizing and interacting with VEs.

Torque   A rotational force.

Tracking   The action of locating an object's 3D position and orientation.

Transfer functions   Used to shape various types of signals.

Transformation   A mathematical operation performed upon a set of coordinates.

Translation matrix   Displaces an object in space.

Translucency   An attribute associated with materials that, while transmitting light, destroy any coherence associated with the incident light.

Transparency   An attribute assigned to objects to mimic the light transmissive qualities of materials such as glass.

Transparency coefficient   A fractional value associated with an object controlling the amount of incident light transmitted by the surface.

Transpose matrix   Changes every element of a matrix $M_{row,\,col}$ into $M_{col,\,row}$.

Triad   A group of three colour display pixels used to encode one image pixel.

Triangular mesh   A system of abutting triangles.

Triangulation   The process of reducing a shape into a triangular mesh.

Twisted facet   A facet that is not flat and has no unique surface normal.

Twisted nematic LCD   A popular type of LCD where the liquid crystal molecular orientation is twisted through 90° between the electrodes.

Twist vectors   Vectors are associated with the definition of a Hermite surface patch, where four twist vectors are used to control the degree of 'twist' applied to the corners.

Unit vector   A vector with a magnitude of one.

Update rate   The rate at which a process is modified. In VR this applies to the speed of head tracking, image generation and physical simulation processes.

***uv*-coordinates**   A parameter space for texture mapping and surface patches.

Value   Equivalent to the term 'lightness' in HSV notation.

VE   *See* **virtual environment**.

Vector display   A display device that forms an image from lines.

Vector product   The vector product, or cross product, of two vectors creates a third vector orthogonal to the plane containing two reference vectors.

Vertex   The end of an edge.

Vertex colour   The colour assigned to a vertex for achieving a blended colour effect across a surface.

Vertex normal   An orthogonal vector associated with a vertex.

Vertex table   A data structure for storing the vertices of an object using its coordinates.

Vestibular system   This system is located within the inner ear and monitors the body's acceleration, equilibrium and relationship with the earth's gravitational field.

Viewing frustum   A truncated pyramid associated with the viewing volume for one eye.

View vector   A vector that defines the orientation of the observer, and is established by the 3D tracking system.

Virtual domain   The imaginary space inside a computer for organizing data.

Virtual environment (VE)   A 3D data set describing an environment based upon real-world or abstract objects and data.

Virtual hand   A simple model of a hand built into the VE to represent the user.

Virtual lens   An imaginary lens that is equivalent to the compound refractive elements in the human eye.

Virtual observer (VO)   In this book, the imaginary observer in the VE.

Virtual reality (VR)   A generic term associated with computer systems that create a real-time visual/audio/haptic experience.

Virtual therapy   The use of VR to treat medical disorders.

Visceral sensations   Sensations that come from the viscera organs in the chest, and record discomfort or pain.

Visual acuity   A measure of the eye's ability to distinguish between two distant points of light.

Visual cortex That part of the brain used for processing visual information.

Visual cues Signals or prompts derived from a scene.

Vitreous humor The transparent liquid between the lens and the retina.

VO *See* **virtual observer**.

Vomit centre An area of the brain responsible for initiating vomiting.

Voxel A volume of space representing the 3D equivalent of a pixel.

VR Virtual Reality.

VRT Superscape's Virtual Reality Toolkit.

Walk-through The activity of moving through a VE.

WCS *See* **world coordinate system**.

Weight The weight of an object is equal to mg, where m is the object's mass and g is the acceleration due to gravity.

Wire frame A view of a 3D object where all edges are drawn, producing a 'see through' wire-like image.

World coordinate system (WCS) A reference space for constructing a virtual world.

WTK Sense8's WorldToolKit.

XYZ **Euler angles** Three angles of rotation relative to a rotating frame of reference.

XYZ **fixed angles** Three angles of rotation relative to a stationary frame of reference.

Yaw angle A 3D angle of rotation about a vertical axis.

Yaw matrix Encodes the transformation to rotate a point about a vertical axis.

Yon plane *See* **back plane**.

z-buffer A memory device for storing z-depth values in eye coordinate space of the nearest surface, for every pixel.

z-buffer algorithm A hidden-surface removal algorithm that uses a z-buffer.

References

Appel A. (1968). Some techniques for machine rendering of solids. *AFIPS Conf. Proc.*, **32**, 37–45.

Arbab F. (1990). Set models and boolean operations for solids and assemblies. *IEEE CG&A*, **10**(6), 76–86.

Badler N., Phillips C. B. and Webber B. L. (1993). *Simulating Humans: Computer Graphics, Animation, and Control*. Oxford: Oxford University Press.

Badler N., Bindiganavale R., Granieri J. *et al*. (1994). Posture interpolation with collision avoidance. In *Proc. Computer Animation '94*, Geneva, Switzerland.

Bajura M., Fuchs H. and Ohbuchi R. (1992). Merging virtual objects with the real world. In *Proc. SIGGRAPH 1992: Computer Graphics*, **26**(2), 203–10.

Berlin E. P., Jr. (1985). Efficiency considerations in image synthesis. *SIGGRAPH Course Notes*, **11**.

Blinn J. F. (1978). Simulation of wrinkled surfaces. *Proc. SIGGRAPH 1978: Computer Graphics*, **12**(3), 286–92.

Bryson S. (1994). Tutorial notes: Introduction to VR. In *Proc. Virtual Reality and its Applications*. CGS, Leeds, UK.

Cohen M. F., Chen S. E., Wallace J. R. *et al*. (1988). A progressive refinement approach to fast radiosity image generation. *Proc. SIGGRAPH 1988: Computer Graphics*, **22**(4), 75–84.

Cook R. L. and Torrance K. E. (1982). A reflectance model for computer graphics. *ACM Trans. on Graphics*, 1, 7–24.

Coons S. A. and Herzog B. (1967). Surfaces for computer-aided aircraft design. In *Proc. AIAA 4th Annual Meeting and Technical Display Conference*, (Paper 67–895), Anaheim.

Crow F. C. (1977). Shadow algorithms for computer graphics. *Proc. SIGGRAPH 1977*, **11**(3), 242–8.

De Schutter E. (1992). A consumer guide to neuronal modeling software. *Trends Neuroscience*, **15**, 462–4.

Farin G. (1988). *Curves and Surfaces for Computer Aided Geometric Design*. London: Academic Press.

Fellgett P. B. (1974). Ambisonic reproduction of directionality in surround sound systems. *Nature*, **252**, 534–8.

Foley J., Van Dam A., Feiner S. *et al.* (1990). *Computer Graphics: Principles and Practice* 2nd edn. Reading, Mass: Addison-Wesley.

Galyean T. (1991). Sculpting: an interactive volumetric modelling technique. *Proc. SIGGRAPH 1991: Computer Graphics*, **25**(4), 267–74.

Gerzon M. A. (1970). The principles of quadrophonic recording. Part I. *Studio Sound*, 338–42.

Gillies D. and Williams C. (1987). An interactive graphic simulator for the teaching of fibre endoscopic techniques. In *Proc. Eurographics '87* Marechal G. (ed.) North Holland/Elsevier.

Girard M. and Maciejewski A. A. (1985). Computational modelling for the computer animation of legged figures. *Proc. SIGGRAPH 1985: Computer Graphics*, **19**(3), 263–70.

Glassner A. S., ed. (1990). *Graphics Gems*. San Diego: Academic Press.

Goral C. M. *et al.* (1984). Modelling the interaction of light between diffuse surfaces. *Proc. SIGGRAPH 1984: Computer Graphics*, **18**(3), 213–22.

Gouraud H. (1971). Computer display of curved surfaces. PhD Thesis, University of Utah.

Gregory R. L. (1979). *Eye and Brain: the Psychology of Seeing* 3rd edn. London: Weidenfeld and Nicolson.

Hamilton Sir W. R. (1969). *Elements of Quaternions* 3rd edn. New York: Chelsea Publishing.

Jennings R. T., Davis R. J. and Santy P. A. (1988). Comparison of aerobic fitness and space motion sickness during the shuttle program. *Aviation, Space and Environmental Medicine*, **59**, 448–51.

Julesz B. (1971). *Foundations of Cyclopean Perception*. Chicago: University of Chicago Press.

Kalawsky R. (1993). *The Science of Virtual Reality and Virtual Environments*. Wokingham: Addison-Wesley.

Laidlaw D. H., Trumbore B. W. and Hughes J. F. (1986). Constructive solid geometry for polyhedral objects. *Proc. SIGGRAPH 1986: Computer Graphics*, **20**(4), 161–70.

Longhurst C. (1994). Event-driven visual effects in flight simulation VEs. In *Proc. British Computer Society: Virtual Reality Applications*, pp. 257–71. Leeds.

Loop C. and De Rose T. (1990). Generalized B-spline surfaces of arbitrary topology. *Proc. SIGGRAPH 1990: Computer Graphics*, **24**(4), 347–56.

Malham D. G. (1993). 3D sound for virtual reality systems using ambisonic techniques. In *Proc. Virtual Reality '93*, London.

Mandlebrot B. and van Ness J. (1968). Fractional Brownian motions, fractional noises and applications. *SIAM Review*, **10**(4), 422–37.

Max N. (1986). Atmospheric illumination and shadows. *Proc. SIGGRAPH 1986: Computer Graphics*, **20**(4), 117–24.

Miller L. (1984). Computer graphics and the woven fabric designer. In *Proc. Computers in the World of Textiles*, pp. 634–44. Hong Kong.

Mon-Williams M., Wann J. P. and Rushton S. (1993). Binocular vision in a virtual world: visual deficits following the wearing of head-mounted displays. *Opthalmic and Physiological Optics*, **13**, 387–91.

Nelson T. R. and Elvins T. T. (1993). Visualization of 3D ultrasound data. *IEEE CG&A*, **13**(6), 50–7.

Penfield J. and Rasmussen P. (1968). *Cerebal Cortex of Man: A Clinical Study of Localization of Function*. New York: Macmillan.

Phong B. (1973). Illumination for computer generated images. *PhD Thesis*, University of Utah, also in *Comm. ACM*, **18**, 311–17.

Piegl L. (1991). On NURBS: a survey. *IEEE CG&A*, **11**(1), 55–71.

Plenge G. (1974). On the difference between localization and lateralization. *J. of the Acoustics Society of America*, **56**, 944–51.

Poon A., Gillies D. and Williams C. (1988). The use of three-dimensional dynamic and kinematics modelling in the design of a colonoscopy simulator. *New Trends in Computer Graphics, Proc. CG International '88*, pp. 565–74. London.

Poon A. (1991). Real time simulation of colonoscopy using dynamic models. *PhD Thesis*, University of London.

Rayleigh Lord J. W. S. (1907). On our perception of sound direction. *Phil. Mag.*, **13**, 214–32.

Reason J. (1974). *Man in Motion: The Psychology of Travel*. Cox and Wyman Ltd.

Reeves W. T. (1983). Particle systems – a technique for modelling a class of fuzzy objects. *Proc. SIGGRAPH 1983: Computer Graphics*, **17**(3), 359–76.

Regan C. (1994). Some human factors research and issues in immersive virtual reality. In *Proc. Virtual Reality and its Applications*, CGS, Leeds, UK.

Robinett W. and Holloway R. (1992). Implementation of flying, scaling, and grabbing in virtual worlds. *SIGGRAPH Course Notes: Interactive 3D Graphics*, 1–4.

Rogers D. F. (1985). *Procedural Elements for Computer Graphics*. Maidenhead: McGraw-Hill.

Rolfe J. M. and Staples K. J. (1991). *Flight Simulation* 2nd edn. Cambridge: Cambridge University Press.

Saulnier A., Viaud M. and Geldreich D. (1994). Real-time facial analysis and synthesis for televirtuality. In *Proc. Imagina '94*, pp. 174–82. Monte Carlo.

Scanlon W. (1990). Animating the drape of cloth. In *Proc. CG-90: Computer Graphics*, pp. 263–74. London.

Shaw E. A. G. (1974). The external ear. In *Handbook of Sensory Physiology*. (Keidel W. D. and Neff W. D., eds.). New York: Springer-Verlag.

Stanger V. J. (1994). Networked Virtual Reality for Medical and Surgical Applications. In *Proc. VR in Surgery and Medicine*. CGS, Leeds, UK.

Terzopoulos D. and Witkin A. (1988). Physically based models with rigid and deformable components. *IEEE CG&A*, **8**(6), 41–51.

Thibault W. C. and Naylor B. F. (1987). Set operations on polyhedra using binary space partitioning trees. *Proc. SIGGRAPH 1987: Computer Graphics*, **21**(4), 153–62.

Torrance K. E. and Sparrow E. M. (1967). Theory for off-specular reflection from roughened surfaces. *J. of the Optical Society of America*, **57**, 1105–14.

Ungs T. J. (1989). Simulator induced syndrome: evidence for long-term after effects. *Aviation, Space and Environmental Medicine*, **60**, 252–5.

Vince J. A. (1992). *3-D Computer Animation*. Wokingham: Addison-Wesley.

Von Ramm O. T., Smith S. W. and Pavy H. G. Jr (1991). High-speed ultrasound volumetric imagine system – part II: parallel processing and image display. *IEEE Trans. on Ultrasonics, Ferroelectrics, and Frequency Control*, **38**(2), 109–15.

Waters K. (1987). A muscle model for animating three-dimensional facial expression. *Proc. SIGGRAPH 1987: Computer Graphics*, **21**(4), 17–24.

Watt A. (1993). *3D Computer Graphics* 2nd edn. Wokingham: Addison-Wesley.

Watt A. and Watt M. (1992). *Advanced Animation and Rendering Techniques*. Wokingham: Addison-Wesley.

Weil J. (1986). The synthesis of cloth objects. *Proc. SIGGRAPH 1986: Computer Graphics*, **20**(4), 49–54.

Whitted T. (1980). An improved illumination model for shaded display. *Comm. ACM*, **26**(6), 342–9.

Williams L. (1978). Casting curved shadows on curved surfaces. *Proc. SIGGRAPH 1978: Computer Graphics*, **12**(3), 270–4.

Williams L. (1983). Pyramidal parametrics. *Proc. SIGGRAPH 1983: Computer Graphics*, **17**(3), 1–11.

Zhao J. and Badler N. (1989). *Real-time Inverse Kinematics with Joint Limits and Spatial Constraints*. Technical Report MS-CIS-89–09, Computer and Information Science, University of Pennsylvania, Philadelphia, PA.

Index

Plate 23

Historical events remind us that tactics and strategic planning play an important role in deciding the outcome of wars. With today's hi-tech military systems playing an increasing role in the theatre of war, it is inevitable that equally sophisticated systems are employed to assist in the role of command. This image depicts an imaginary military scenario where an immersive VR system is employed as a tactical management tool. (Courtesy Division Ltd)